Orestes Brownson

THE MACMILLAN COMPANY
NEW YORK · BOSTON · CHICAGO · DALLAS
ATLANTA · SAN FRANCISCO

MACMILLAN AND CO., Limited
LONDON · BOMBAY · CALCUTTA · MADRAS
MELBOURNE

THE MACMILLAN COMPANY
OF CANADA, Limited
TORONTO

ORESTES AUGUSTUS BROWNSON

"The most perfect [likeness] is a mere photograph, taken in haste
and accident by Mr. Wallace, an artist of great promise, who died at
a very early age, leaving unfinished a marble bust of Dr. Brownson
which he had commenced . . . Asking him to sit down, he placed him
in position for a profile and took the photograph, one of the most
successful specimens of this kind of art we have ever seen."

—FRANCIS AUGUSTINE HEWIT in the *Catholic World* for
June, 1876, p. 366.

ORESTES BROWNSON

Yankee, Radical, Catholic

by

Theodore Maynard

Author of "The Story of American Catholicism"

1943

THE MACMILLAN COMPANY

New York

To VAN WYCK BROOKS

When there is work to be done, a cause to be advanced, the unsafest men in the world to confide it to are those who are usually termed safe men.

— ORESTES BROWNSON in 1856: Vol. XI, p. 578 of *Brownson's Works*.

This was all his glory and all his trouble; all his quarrels, friendships, aversions, perplexities, triumphs, labors—all to be traced to love of truth.

— ISAAC HECKER in the *Catholic World*, Vol. XLVI (1887), p. 234.

Contents

Introduction

THE thing ordinarily said about Orestes Brownson is, "Ah, yes—
a very brilliant man! But he disappeared; the last I saw of the poor
fellow, he was wandering off in the direction of the Catholic
Church." Even those who seem to have some faint inkling of his
importance, such as Henry Seidel Canby, in his biography of
Thoreau, write about "the raging discontent [which] took him
from camp to camp until he sought the safety of the Roman
Catholic Church, where historians have left him, forgetting his
prophetic activities in the cause of labor and a socialized democracy." In other words, his life's work—as manifested in the twenty
bulky volumes of his collected writings—is to be regarded as negligible, and himself interesting only for a false start. That his "raging
discontent" ended in complete contentment indicates (according to
this view) no more than intellectual suicide—a "suicide" that resulted in thirty years of the most vigorous American writing of his
time, dealing with all the most vital issues confronting society.
Leaving Brownson unread, the critics fall back upon the facile supposition that he was looking for a refuge, ignorant that, for him,
the refuge was about as stormy a one as can be imagined.

The main reason for his neglect is of course that no writer can
become a Catholic without having his standing adversely affected
in the eyes of a reading public still so badly informed as to believe
Catholicism moribund. There are, however, other minor reasons:
all of Brownson's writings have long been out of print and, when
obtainable, are in such a format as to be unenticing; he was primarily a journalist—that is, a writer who, the fresher he is for his
day, is all the less likely to survive beyond it; and, finally, he was
a thinker, certain features of whose metaphysics got him a bad

name in Catholic circles. He had antagonized so many people that they used this as a handle against him. Catholics have therefore conspired with everybody else to bury him quietly.

In spite of this, it is not altogether easy to bury Brownson. Several biographies during the last few years point to a revival of interest. Of these by far the best is that by Mr. Schlesinger. If I write at all, it is only because his book, though eminently satisfactory up to the year 1844, when Brownson was received into the Catholic Church, deals in a hurried, huddled fashion with his Catholic career. Even the nun who writes under the name of Doran Whalen gives two-thirds of her book to his early life. The true proportions are preserved in the three-volume life by his son; its main defects are that Henry Brownson got entangled in the abundance of his documentation and that there were a number of documents not at his disposal and others which he decided not to use. While he was, upon the whole, admirably objective, it was natural enough that he should have been his father's partisan.

Yet he was much less of a partisan than some of those who have been so indiscriminate in praise as to do Brownson little service. The very title of Father Raemer's monograph, *America's Foremost Philosopher,* is a case in point. Nor does it help very much to be told by Doran Whalen that "had [Brownson] ventured upon poetry it must have been an epic." That sort of thing tends to put a reader's back up. So I might as well announce at the outset that I have no thesis. What I am about to attempt is the portrait of a very remarkable man, but one with faults and eccentricities. To lively portraiture everything else must be subdued.

This does not mean that no critical evaluation of Brownson as a writer or as a philosopher will be allowed to appear; it is rather that I shall try to keep this secondary to the story of his life, and introduce it only in so far as it was part of his life. But perhaps I can say at once that I believe him to be—if not precisely a great man of letters, in the ordinary sense—at least a great pamphleteer and controversialist with a style which in its force and lucidity reminds one of Swift, and even more of Cobbett and Paine, two men whom he heartily disliked. As for his philosophy, it seems to me that the common charge of ontologism—which is still frequently brought against him to his damage—cannot be substantiated. That it was brought at all was largely due to his marvellous gift for making enemies.

Yet it must not be imagined that I consider all of Brownson's philosophical ideas sound, still less that I think he had in his possession the master-key to philosophy. Indeed, my main difficulty will be that of avoiding getting into arguments with him as I go along. I shall do my best to steer clear of this, but it is likely enough that I shall not always succeed. He strikes me as being often a wrong-headed man, and one very positive in his opinions. As I also am somewhat positive in my opinions—though it is hardly necessary to add, not wrong-headed—my disagreements with him are many. It is, however, no more than fair to say that, even when I think him most wrong, I think him worth listening to. There is always pleasure in observing a perfectly logical mind at work; and when that logic is—as in this instance—fiery and entwined with odd quirks of character, there is a good deal of amusement as well.

In many ways Brownson must be admitted to seem unaccountable. Because he had often changed his opinion, he came to be regarded as unstable. He is even thought to have been actuated by pride of opinion. Mr. Schlesinger expressed this view when he said, "humility was the one Catholic virtue he never possessed." That he was vain of his logical powers is not to be doubted, or that he trusted in them too much. But a man who changes his opinion cannot be justly accused of pride of opinion. Brownson's very instability (if it is to be called that) was due to his instantly announcing whatever it was that his inordinately swift and ingenious mind had just hit upon. What he lacked was the patience to test his discoveries before proclaiming them. But he should be given credit for guilelessness. Having reached truth—at any rate truth as he saw it—he never wavered, though he continued to develop, not as do most men, slowly and cautiously, but with the impulsive explosive-ness of a boy. These apparent caprices, though they never affected the core of his faith, were exhibited to the end. The fact that the vagaries of his early life had an underlying consistency which was all the time bringing him nearer to his Catholic goal still puzzles many people. Father Hecker, the earliest of his disciples and the man who knew him best, touched the heart of the psychological problem which was Brownson when he wrote, "Without seeing clearly this passionate love of truth in him, it is, I think, hardly possible to understand him." (*Catholic World,* Vol. XLVI (1887), p. 3).

Not very confidently do I hope to avoid giving some offence. The Brownson enthusiasts are unlikely to consider that I have done him justice; nothing short of his being made a Doctor of the Church will ever content them. On the other hand, my references to some of the highly placed ecclesiastics with whom he had to deal may be equally offensive. But I trust that nobody will be so undiscerning as to suppose that, when I discuss Brownson's embroilments with the Irish and the Jesuits, his views are necessarily my own. Doran Whalen incensed the Paulists by her inability to understand that a roaring masculine debate, even though the table was thumped, made no difference to friendship. Her partisan spirit led her to cast unwarrantable aspersions on Fathers Hecker and Hewit. As it is now and then an advantage to be a man, even in the modern world, perhaps I can escape this particular blunder. Being the kind of man I am, I shall probably fall into others. If so, it will be unintentionally. Whatever may be my reputation, I am really a very peaceable sort of fellow.

To permit myself one more personal word: my own religious experience follows Brownson's rather closely. Like him, I began in what might be called the extreme of Protestant fundamentalism; like him, I passed, via Unitarianism, into the Catholic Church. This should give me a special advantage in explaining him. The differ-ence between his case and my own should itself be an advantage:

I became a Catholic when I was just over twenty; Brownson became a Catholic when he was over forty; whereas I was young enough to get rid of my Protestantism as though it had never been, he was too old to get completely rid of his. This most belligerently orthodox of men carried with him into the Church a good deal of the rigid Puritan spirit. At the very moment when he was most strongly repudiating the Calvinist assertion of man's total depravity, he was being unconsciously affected by it, to the extent of having too little confidence in human nature.

For this reason his apologetic methods were to a large extent ineffective: he pulverized opponents by his formidable logic, without persuading them. It is not a question of his being "intolerant"; any man with firm convictions is obliged to be intolerant of what he believes to be disastrous error. Nor is the question altogether one of "tactics," though conciliation is commonly better than the most cast-iron syllogism. It is rather that Brownson looked for an error to confute instead of trying to find whether there might not be an imperfectly apprehended truth which, once explained, would lead men of good will to complete truth. The rigor with which he stated Catholicism was often unCatholic in tone. He had a power which, in its own way, has never been paralleled; but he was deficient in the kind of strength that can be subtle and make due discriminations.

This is what I mean by saying that he retained a Calvinist tinge. He had had it while he was a free-lance Unitarian minister. And when he became a Catholic, he showed now and then that he was still tinged with the fantasies of "liberal" Christianity, despite his violent denunciations of them. This, however, is itself a remarkable proof of Catholic freedom of discussion, used to the limit. He was constantly under attack, and at least twice his enemies did their best to get him condemned by the Holy See. He was not condemned.

For the times in which he lived—when Catholics were a timid and despised people in America—perhaps only a truculent man could have performed his special function. Certainly for all times his forthrightness and honesty and courage are bracing. As they were united to a power of exposition that has rarely, if ever, been equalled, his work has permanent value. There can be no doubt that his was the greatest and most luminous mind that has so far appeared among Catholics in this country. If he had the defects of his virtues, he also had the virtues of his defects.

Brownson's own writings and his son's biography are the basis of this study. For this reason I have been careful to give chapter and verse for everything, including the secondary sources and the archival material not drawn upon by Henry Brownson or his other biographers. But I am not prepared to vouch for the objective accuracy of everything said by either father or son. While I fully credit them with being invariably subjectively truthful, there are many passages in Orestes Brownson (who brought personal matters freely into his most abstract discussions) when I suspect that his version of what he has to relate is highly colored, and some other passages in which—writing as he did long after the event—I can see how a faulty memory has betrayed a hasty writer. Whenever possible I have cited from Brownson's separately published books, because these are less hard on my eyes than the small print which embalms them in his collected *Works*. What would be very useful to the student is a list of his articles in their chronological order. Henry Brownson, who was his editor, instead classifies his writings under subject headings—"Philosophy," "Religion and Society," "Controversy," "Civilization," "Politics," "Scientific Theories," "Literary Criticism," and so forth—a method which has its advantages but which frequently makes the reader lose the historical thread. And he excluded several of the most important of the essays—especially the early ones—when compiling his edition. Now and then, therefore, I have had to fall back upon the bound volumes of the many magazines to which Brownson contributed, or which he edited.

It has been decided to put the notes at the end of the chapters to which they refer. I wish, however, that there were some way of inserting the explanatory notes at the foot of the page, for these often contain important additional documentation. As this cannot be, at least I should point out that they are intended to be read; so I draw the reader's attention to them.

The main collection of documents is at the University of Notre Dame. When they are to be found in Henry Brownson's *Life,* I have quoted them from that source, for the sake of convenience all round. That I was able to examine the *Brownson Papers* I must thank the Very Rev. J. Hugh O'Donnell, C.S.C., the President of the University, for his hospitality, and its Archivist, the Rev. Thomas T. McAvoy, C.S.C., for his invaluable assistance. The Rev. Joseph I. Malloy, C.S.P., was equally gracious with regard to the Paulist Archives in New York. The Library of Congress, the Colleges of Woodstock and Mount St. Mary's and St. Mary's Seminary at Baltimore have been generous in the loan of books. Otherwise I could not have written this book.

During the course of its composition I have often consulted the Rev. Joseph P. Donovan, C.M., of the Kenrick Seminary, St. Louis, and the Rev. Thomas Ryan, C.PP.S., of Charlottesville, Virginia. Father Donovan also read my manuscript, as did Father Malloy and Fathers Edward A. Ryan and John F. Sweeney, S. J. and Mr. Joseph R. Frese, a scholastic of the same order. From them came many criticisms and suggestions from which I have benefitted. Mrs. Thomas H. Odiorne, of New York, one of Brownson's granddaughters, and her daughter, Miss Helena Odiorne, not only read what I had written but supplied me with transcripts of a number of family letters in their possession. The photograph used as the frontispiece also comes from them. The Very Rev. Bonaventure Schwinn, O.S.B. and Mr. Van Wyck Brooks helped me with the proofs. Mr. Cornelius J. Carr, S. J., has been so kind as to prepare the index. I should add that none of those to whom I have referred agrees with all my views—nor do I expect anybody else to do so—and that I am sorry to record that I do not agree with all the views of Mr. Schlesinger, still less those of Sister Rose Gertrude (Doran Whalen). I am the more sorry because I have had correspondence with them and have talked to them about the work I had in preparation. My hope is that they will be Brownsonian enough to recognize that I have proceeded on the Brownsonian principle of trying to be perfectly honest.

CHAPTER I

A Boy Gets into an Argument

ONE AUTUMN AFTERNOON of 1812 a boy of nine was told that he might go to the "square" of the little Vermont town of Royalton to see the muster of the militia. The two elderly people with whom he had lived since the death of his father, some three years before, gave him a card of gingerbread to eat on the way and put him in the charge of an older boy. Eager to see the soldiers, the two lads set out.

The younger boy, Orestes, tall and thoughtful-looking for his age, was indeed interested in the drilling and the rifle practice. But he soon found something that interested him much more, and that though he took pride in having come from a military family. He even forgot—or almost forgot—to eat his gingerbread when he encountered two old men on the outskirts of the crowd who were discussing religion. After listening to them for some time, he at last managed to edge himself into their argument, as it was on the fascinating subject of predestination. All his life long he had little hesitation about getting into an argument with strangers on stage-coaches, ferries or railway trains. Here were two old men wrangling over something that he had already read and thought about. It was too good an opportunity to miss.

Lying in front of the fire in his foster-parents' farm-house, he had studied Jonathan Edwards' *A History of the Work of Redemption*.[1] This, though he had never gone to school as yet, he devoured along with the Bible and Dr. Watts's poems, an odd volume of sermons and a novel called *Philip Quarle,* written in imitation of *Robinson Crusoe, The Franklin Primer* and a weekly newspaper published at

1

Windsor.[2] Of all these the Bible and Jonathan Edwards, of the
tender precision and delicate ruthlessness, interested him most.
Armed with them and a precocious sense of logic, he defended free-
will, telling the astounded but good-humored old men that Edwards
had confounded volition with judgment. Very pleased with himself,
except for having forgotten a few things he might have said, he
returned home.

It was not really home, though the couple with whom he lived
treated him with kindness. His home was at Stockbridge. There
were his mother and his elder brothers, Oran and Daniel, and an
elder sister, Thorina. His twin, Daphne—he had very nearly been
called Daphnis—had also been put in the care of friends, as their
widowed mother had been left too poor to support so many children.
Only very rarely did he see any of his own family.[3] Being alone with
what few books he could find, and a sedate elderly couple, Orestes
had no playmates and had already acquired the manners and tastes
of an old man.[4]

If much was lost by this, something was also gained. He was able
to live all the more in his imagination, and that was the vivid imagination of a child. Never did he feel less alone than when he was
alone.[5] Sometimes he thought himself to be holding long intimate
conversations with Christ and—what is surprising, when his Puritan
upbringing is remembered—with the Virgin Mary and the archangel Gabriel. By merely reading the Bible the mind of little Orestes
had been filled with the love of God. He had already decided that
he was going to be a minister when he grew up.

Yet he had been taught hardly anything definite about religion.
He had been made to memorize the Shorter Catechism and the
Apostles' Creed, without being required to believe what they contained. Though he did in fact believe most of it, he attached no
meaning whatever to the articles about the Holy Catholic Church
and the Communion of Saints, nor did it even occur to him to
ask whether they meant anything at all. He said the verse, "Now
I lay me down to sleep" as his night prayers, by rote. What really

nourished him was the Bible, especially the accounts of the Passion.

The people with whom he lived were nominally Congregationalists, but as their church was on the square, four miles away, they rarely bothered to attend, or to send Orestes there. Puritan morals had to suffice. He was not to play on Sunday—as if he played much on any day!—and was not to tell lies or to take what did not belong to him, even if it were only a pin. But he was absorbed by religion and looked upon himself as one set apart to its service. As he was to be a minister, he tried hard to control a temper he had already discovered to be irritable. And as he was to be a minister, he hoped the time would come when he would be able to go to school.

That time did not come till he was fourteen. Until then he lived with the old man and his wife at Royalton, doing his little chores, and later—having immense physical strength—a man's work. For this he got some wages, all of which he saved towards his education. He did, however, get one lesson at Royalton which he never forgot. About the time he was twelve he became very exercised over the fact that he did not belong to any church. He was continually hearing that he had to "get religion," to have a "change of heart" and "be born again." It was not very clear to him what was meant. and he did not have the faintest idea how this was to be brought about.[6] He was not even baptized, and nobody seemed to be thinking of that. He did not understand that the psychological experience of "Evangelical" conversion was regarded as being virtually the only sacrament, one not conferred by any priesthood but given directly by God. There was an old-fashioned church of Congregationalists— that of the "Standing Order"—in the little town, but he was drawn instead to a choice between the Methodists and the Christians, or the "Christ-yans" as they insisted on calling themselves, a sect founded in 1800. He could not discover that there was any difference in their doctrines. All that he noticed was that the Methodist preachers appeared to have the stronger lungs and painted the tortures of hell more vividly than their rivals. The more he listened, the more he feared damnation and the less he loved God. At times he thought, in his terror, that the devil was about to carry him off bodily. And yet he was trying desperately hard to be "saved." It was all the harder for him to find out how this was to be managed because of the roaring of the preachers and the shouting of the people.[7]

In his perplexity he consulted an old woman—one better educated than most people there—who lived in a wretched cabin on a corner of the farm. To his surprise, she did not urge him to join the Congregationalists, though she belonged to them, but told him instead: "My poor boy, God has been good to you. But do not join the Methodists or any of the sects. You yourself know the founder of the Christians, and I personally knew both Wesley and Whitfield. When you join any church, find out the one that began with Christ and His Apostles." She took it for granted that he would see that this was the Congregationalist. He thanked her and went away in thought. Years later, he said that he believed it was this conversation that prevented him from ever being a thorough-going Protestant.[8]

Except for his religious perplexities, his years at Royalton were among the happiest of his life. Looking back upon it in middle-age he saw that he had missed much by not having had any childish companions; but he did not miss them at the time. He was unable to imagine greater enjoyment than he had had as a boy when lying on the hearth reading by the light of pine-knots. The shelf of books in the little farm-house was now being supplemented by borrowing here and there among the neighbors. It was astonishing how many books the lad contrived to find in that up-state town—or would be astonishing did we not know that many an educated man was to be found even on the edge of the Frontier. In one house he came across many of the classics of Queen Anne's reign; in another, a fifty-volume set of the English poets; in still another, a work on universal history and Pope's translation of Homer and Locke's *Essay Concerning Human Understanding*. All these he eagerly read.

Never did a leisure moment find him without a book in his hand. The fact that he did not always understand what he read, or gave to it only a child's meaning, did not lessen his enjoyment. It fastened in him the conviction that children's books, by removing all necessity for hard thought, softened children's minds.[9] His own mind was assuredly toughened by his tough reading.

He was somewhat awkward and bashful among people, except among the really well-bred. Those who lent him books discovered that the tall, lanky, grave boy was out of the ordinary, and their simple and unaffected manners put him at an ease he never felt in other society. His aloofness developed in him a certain prickliness and asperity that were to remain throughout life. But again he may have been more fortunate than he knew: a "polished" Brownson might have had all his character rubbed off. What he was getting was the training of an independent, an individualist.

His shyness, however, did not prevent him from keenly observing his fellows. Sixty years later, when reviewing a novel by Henry Ward Beecher, he denied that, so far from the New England Puritans being "a set of gloomy fanatics, austere, unbending, harsh and cruel, minding everybody's business but their own," they were actually sociable, kind-hearted and hospitable. Even more surprisingly, in view of what he had previously written, he said that "Puritanism keeps alive in the community a certain Christian habit of thought, a belief in the necessity of grace, and a more or less Christian conscience." As for the Vermonter, he was "the Kentuckian of the East." He further characterized him as one who "has no conservative tendency by nature; he cares not the snap of his finger what his father believed or did; is personally independent, generally free from snobbishness, no slave to public opinion, and for the most part has the courage of his convictions; but he loves his state, loves her green hills and fertile valleys, and when abroad holds a fellow-Vermonter dear as his brother."[10] The generalized description of the Vermont scenery leaves one with the impression that it left little impression on him. The truth would seem to be that, though he was anything but lacking in imagination, as his record of his spiritual visitations shows, he paid little attention to physical beauty. Perhaps this is why this man whose pen was never idle, and who as a boy read a great deal of poetry, never attempted any verse.

In 1817 his mother moved to Ballston Spa, to the north of Albany. It was then a fashionable resort, but the reason for the move probably was that there was an academy there which Orestes could attend. All the children were now together under one roof, and the youngest son was able to use his savings to obtain his long dreamed-of education.[11]

How long he attended this school is uncertain. About such matters he is vague in his autobiography, which is almost entirely concerned with his spiritual development and ignores ordinary biographical details. Henry Brownson writes about his father learning Latin and Greek,[12] the Greek being very improbable, and the Latin itself so sketchy that he had to learn it over again fifteen years later. Moreover, Orestes Brownson seems to indicate that he was still pursuing his academic studies when he was nineteen, whereas his son tells us that he had left the academy and was working in James Comstock's printing office at that time.[13] It was the only formal education he was ever to receive, but in a case like his its inadequacy did not greatly matter. He had already educated himself much in advance of most boys of his own age, so far as literature and history were concerned; and no education is ever of any use unless it is implemented by self-education. At all events, he obtained what was a little later considered sufficient for a school-teacher, in days when standards were not exacting. The immediate result of his schooling was that he got a job in the local printing office. Whether or not he afterwards attended the academy again, we may be sure that he did not cease studying. We may also suppose that what he earned was useful to eke out the meagre means of his mother.

During this period of adolescence his mind passed from perplexity on the subject of religion to complete confusion. He was now suddenly thrown among people, some of whom were professed atheists and more who were totally indifferent; and he began to wonder whether all religion were not a delusion. It seemed to him at times that his life was "a stream that flows out of darkness into darkness." [14] He felt without faith, or hope, or love, hungering for religion, and in despair.

Yet in spite of everything he somehow managed to hold on to his early conviction as to man's need of God, and there were moments when the feelings of his childhood revived and he seemed close to heaven again. His more normal mood was one of doubt: he was wandering in a labyrinth, finding that his reason was unable to guide him. Often he thought he would have to resign himself to support uncertainty. "If doubt is all there is for me," he asked himself, "why cannot I discipline my feelings into submission to it?" [15] Then came the other question: "Why this craving to believe, when there is nothing to be believed?"

He was ready to snatch at any straw that would save him from being engulfed in total unbelief. One beautiful September morning he happened to be passing the Presbyterian church at Malta, just when the people were entering for the service. The serene sky and the soft air induced a Sabbath mood in him, so he entered the church, though it was a long time since he had been in any place of worship. If the singing was not particularly good, at least it soothed him, and even brought tears to his eyes. And though the sermon was commonplace, he left asking himself what he had gained by his speculations and why he should not seek a religion to sustain him. Had he not mistaken his way? [16]

A day or two later he went to see Mr. Reuben Smith, the Presbyterian minister at Ballston, whom he found a kindly man. As a result of the interview, he was baptized the following Sunday and received into the Presbyterian communion. [17] That he was accepted at all shows that Mr. Smith and the session of the church must have been satisfied that he had gone through the experience known as "conversion." Orestes Brownson would not have been received on any other terms. About this he says nothing in his autobiography. What he does say is that his becoming a Presbyterian was ."the act of an intellectual desperado." [18] His motives, however, were not essentially different from those of any "Evangelical" Protestant joining a church. He was just nineteen.

Brownson's stay among the Presbyterians was brief. They were the only Evangelical sect with which he was ever associated, and also the sect which he came to detest most. It is easy enough to believe that Presbyterianism at that time, especially in up-state New York, was narrow, illiberal and intolerant. At the same time it is a little difficult to believe all that Brownson says of these Presbyterians. Here would seem to be an instance of his too forceful writing. As always he is perfectly honest, but simply because he could write in no other way than strongly, he conveyed an impression that is unconvincing. There may well have been a good deal of the espionage he tells about; that sort of thing is liable to be found among the "unco guid" of all denominations. But when he says that the Ballston Presbyterians would associate with nobody—not even in business— who was not a Presbyterian and that they forbade the reading of all except Presbyterian books, one cannot help feeling that he was exaggerating.[19] Belief snaps altogether when he adds that the minister of the ferocious pharisees he describes told him—when he mentioned his difficulties about believing the Calvinist doctrine that God foreordains the wicked to sin necessarily, so that He might damn them justly—that he had tried to get it modified at the General Assembly in 1821 and had failed only by one or two votes.[20]

It may well be that the Ballston Presbyterians were more obnoxious people than other Presbyterians, though if they took their tone from their amiable minister, this could hardly have been the case. What cannot be doubted is that Brownson was very unhappy among them. The root of his objection, after all, was not to the personal qualities of a particular group of human beings in a small New

York town but to the Presbyterian (or Calvinist) theology. But he was clearly in a very over-wrought condition at this time, a condition which may not have been induced by the Presbyterians but which his contact with them certainly accentuated. The diary he was keeping indicates that he was oscillating between morbid self-reproach and hysterical exaltation. "Yes, I have sinned every day, every hour, yea, and every breath has been drawn in iniquity," the neophyte wrote: "every thought, and every imagination of my heart has been evil, only evil, and that continually." Then the mood changes. "Attended church.—A most precious day. There was exhibited that love, that self-moved love that gave a saviour to a lost and perishing world . . . O hide thy face in shame and confusion, for thou hast murdered the King of Heaven and he forgives thee, grants thee pardon, and bids thee live!" [21]

He now dreamed again of becoming a minister, and even of going as a missionary to the heathen. But here, too, the uncertainty of his purpose appears. On May 30, 1823, he is, if not precisely decided upon this idea, at least inclining in its favor; on June 6, his tune has changed: he is still for missionary work in theory—but he wonders whether it actually does much good. A week later his ardor has dampened further. Before the year was out he was ranting: "Call you this God's World? To me it seems more like the devil's world, in which Ahriman, the prince of darkness, is supreme . . . If [God] is good, the good in itself, and the maker of heaven and earth and all things therein, visible and invisible, whence comes evil? . . . I am nobody, and if I venture to say anything, the only answer is, he is a poor devil, has not a red cent in his pocket,—heed not his sayings." [22]

If Brownson's account of the Presbyterians is not very satisfactory, his criticism of their creed is acute, and explains his subsequent career. He soon realized that he had joined Presbyterianism because, despairing of reason, he had thrown himself on authority. The difficulty was that he could not trust the authority to which he had fled for refuge. A creed was indeed given him, but only as a general summary, he was told, of the doctrines the Presbyterians believed the Scriptures to teach. "While the church refused to take the responsibility of telling me what doctrines I must believe, while she sent me to the Bible and private judgment, she yet claimed authority to condemn and excommunicate me as a heretic, if I departed from the standard of doctrine contained in her Confession. This I considered unfair treatment. It subjected me to all the disadvantages of authority without any of its advantages." He had surrendered the exercise of his reason in the expectation of getting an authoritative teacher, and had found no such teacher. When he enquired what commission the Presbyterian church had, he was told that Christianity, having become papistical and prelatical, had to be reformed to its pristine purity.

At this point he demanded to know: "Had they a warrant from Christ to do that? Or did they act on their own responsibility, without warrant? If you say the former, where is the proof? If the latter, how can their acts bind me? . . . If they had a right to break from [the Catholic Church] and set up their private understanding of Scripture, why have I not the right to break from them, and from the Presbyterian Church, follow my private understanding, and set up a church of my own? . . . The question with me was not what but whom I was to believe; not what doctrines I must embrace, but on what authority I was to obey, on what authority I was to take my belief." [23]

Naturally he got no convincing answers to such questions. Already he saw that if Christ had founded a Church, with authority to teach in His name, it must be the Roman Catholic Church. "But that Church," he quickly added, "of course was out of the question. It was everything that was vile, base, odious, and demoralizing." The idea of becoming a Catholic was refused entrance into his mind. It took him nearly twenty years to reach clarification. Yet even at this stage he was confronted with the choice: "It was the Catholic Church or no Church." [24]

Other doubts, equally devastating, but ones that were to bring him eventual release, came to him. Any revelation must be made to a rational being. Only reason could receive revelation. If his reason was totally depraved, how could it know whether the Bible was God's word, or whether there was any God at all? "No, no," he concluded, "it will not do . . . Just in proportion as we discredit reason, we must discredit revelation. Reason must at least be the preamble to faith, and nature must precede and be presupposed by grace." [25] In all likelihood his difficulties were not framed quite so clearly as this in his mind at the time, but at all events he saw with sufficient distinctness to be thoroughly disillusioned with Presbyterianism. The only alternative was to claim the right to think freely on any subject. Perhaps the Scriptures were infallible in themselves, but how was he to have an infallible means of determining that, even apart from the question as to what was their infallible meaning? All he could do was to accept them in the sense in which they presented themselves to his reason and then abide the result.[26] He felt the decision to be the beginning of his intellectual life. He was just twenty-one.

[1] In his autobiography he gives the title of this work as *The History of Redemption*. (*The Convert*, p. 3). It was a book never completed by its author but rounded out from some of his sermons by his son and published at Edinburgh in 1774 as the second volume of his collected works. The edition that Brownson read probably was the one published in 1808 at Worcester, Mass.

[2] *The Convert*, p. 3.

[3] All of them lived to a ripe old age. Daphne was apparently living in 1898 when Henry Brownson wrote the first volume of the life of his father. Her mother lived to be ninety. We hear of Thorina and Oran as alive in the 'seventies. Of all this hardy stock—except for the six-foot-four father who was carried off by pneumonia in his early thirties—Orestes Brownson died youngest; and he lived to be seventy-three.

[4] *The Convert*, p. 2. He added, writing in 1857, that he had more of the feeling of a child than he had had at eight.

[5] *Ibid.*, p. 5.

[6] *Ibid.*, pp. 8–9.

[7] *Ibid.*, pp. 9, 10.

[8] *Ibid.*, pp. 11, 12. Doran Whalen—*Granite for God's House*, p. 15—unable to make any sense of this, surmised that the old woman must have been a Catholic at one time. This is because she knows nothing about old-fashioned Congregationalism. Brownson understood the situation perfectly and wrote, "However erroneous were the views of the New England Puritans, they retained a conception of the Church of

Christ, held that Christ had himself founded a Church, established its order, and given it its ordinances, and taught that it was necessary to belong to it in order to be saved."

9 H. F. Brownson, *Brownson's Early Life* (hereafter referred to as *Early Life*), pp. 6, 7.

10 *Brownson's Works* (hereafter referred to as *Works*), Vol. XIX, pp. 536–537, 541, 543.

11 [A. F. Hewit], "Dr. Brownson," *Catholic World*, Vol. XXIII (1876) p. 368.

12 *Early Life*, p. 9.

13 The passages may be compared in *The Convert* (p. 16) and *Early Life* (p. 10). The discrepancy may perhaps disappear if we suppose that, after Orestes had exhausted his savings, he worked as a printer, and then, having earned enough, resumed his studies. Writing hastily, Brownson was frequently hazy about details of this sort, impatiently disposing of them in order to reach what he was really interested in— the argumentative portions of his book.

14 *The Convert*, p. 15. The image is fine, but it may be a memory of the more famous one in the Venerable Bede about the sparrow flying into a lighted room from the wintry darkness, and then out into the darkness again. (*Ecclesiastical History*, Chapter XIII).

15 *The Convert*, p. 15.

16 *Ibid.*, p. 14.

17 *The Convert*, p. 17.

18 *Ibid.*, p. 34. When Brownson published his novel, *Charles Elwood*, in 1840 he introduced as one of the characters a Presbyterian minister named Smith. Some correspondence followed with his old acquaintance, who naturally supposed himself pilloried. Brownson explained that he had not intended any personal reference but had used the name merely because it was so common, and with this Reuben Smith was content. (*Early Life*, pp. 416–420.) Smith was, however, afterwards greatly incensed at the account given of his church at Ballston and of the Presbyterians generally in *The Convert*. To all of Brownson's charges he gave a categorical denial in the *Princeton Review*—Vol. XXX (1858), pp. 390–392—a denial that sounds convincing. It is nevertheless amusing to notice that he could be tolerant towards Brownson, when Brownson was merely a Unitarian, but grew bitter towards him, when Brownson had become a Catholic. Though he had written to Brownson in 1841, saying that he found his relation of "experience" to the session of the church recorded as "being very satisfactory," in 1858 he explained that the church at Ballston had failed to do its duty with regard to "this man's" piety.

19 "We were by our manner to show all not members of the Presbyterian church that we regarded them as the enemies of God, and therefore as our enemies, as persons hated by God, and therefore hated by us." (*The Convert*, p. 19.)

20 *The Convert*, pp. 35–36. It was this that the Presbyterian reviewer seized on when reviewing *The Convert* in the *Princeton Review*. He also makes the point that Brownson could never have been "converted." I have already anticipated that objection. And it may be that the passage in *Charles Elwood*, describing the "inquiry meeting" is autobiographical; it assuredly must have been drawn from direct observation. (*Works*, Vol. IV, pp. 191 *et seq.*) In his rejoinder to the *Princeton Review*, Brownson reaches beyond Presbyterianism to attack all kindred sects. He declares that when Protestantism pretends to rise above bald rationalism or dry formalism, it cannot avoid illuminism. The naked position of Protestants being untenable, they have to

assert, not the authority of the Scriptures, but the Scriptures illuminated by the Holy Ghost, while in practice being obliged to insist on uniformity of doctrine, at least in what they consider essentials—and this though they disclaim infallibility. Theoretically they have virtually to maintain that every Christian, under the guidance of the Holy Spirit, is infallible. As for the accuracy of what he had said about the Ballston Presbyterians, he says again that he had found Presbyterianism the form of Protestantism most unfavorable to the finer and more genial qualities of human nature. But even Presbyterians are pleasant enough people, aside from their religion. "It is only when the piety fit is on them, and they think they must be saintly, that we find them disagreeable." (*Works*, Vol. V, pp. 206–247).

As for the charge of the *Princeton Review* that his conversion could not have been genuine, Brownson said that he could not answer on that point, except that the Presbyterians at the time had decided that he had been genuinely converted. This he follows up with the thrust that "as on Presbyterian principles grace is inamissible, the reviewer must suppose he continued in grace during all his subsequent aberrations, and so continues even now, and consequently is sure of salvation." That, however, though very neat logic, is not a final answer. Brownson knew very well that all the Evangelical sects that insist on the experience of conversion as a *sine qua non*, freely admit that they often make mistakes in judging the genuineness of particular conversions. According to their convenient theory, he would never have lapsed—in fact, he *could* not have lapsed—had he really been converted. On neither side could such logic-chopping lead anywhere.

21 From passages quoted in *Early Life*, pp. 11, 13, 14.
22 *Ibid.*, p. 19.
23 *The Convert*, pp. 23, 24, 26, 27, 29.
24 *Ibid.*, p. 28.
25 *Ibid.*, pp. 33, 34.
26 *Ibid.*, p. 36.

CHAPTER II

Escape from John Calvin

HAD ORESTES BROWNSON been a mere logician without any spirituality in his make-up—as was frequently charged—he would probably at this point have declared himself an atheist. But atheism was utterly impossible to him: he could not forget his spiritual experiences while a child. He still felt a hunger and thirst for God; he had to find some sort of religion. The only one of the "liberal" variety at hand was Universalism; that at least had the merit of being a protest against Calvinism.

He had been teaching school for a year at near-by Stillwater, possibly obtaining the position largely on the strength of his church membership, as he may have lost it on account of his rebellion against the Presbyterian system. Now he was not sorry to get away. At Springwells on the River Rouge, eleven miles from Detroit, another teaching job offered itself, and he accepted it.

In 1824 Detroit was a town of eleven or twelve hundred inhabitants, and the whole territory of Michigan contained only seventeen thousand people. Writing to his son Henry in 1867, Brownson told how Jefferson Avenue was just being laid out, to run from Lake St. Clair to the Fort.[1] It was in Detroit that he saw, for the first time in his life, a Catholic church. It was the one dedicated to St. Anne and built by the famous Père Richard. From the rebuilt St. Anne's Brownson was to be buried fifty-two years later.

He nearly died during his year near Detroit. The River Rouge was a cess-pool of malaria during August and September, and the new teacher said that he could see the fever and ague spawn on that stream thick enough to cut with a jackknife.[2] For several

14

months he lay ill, but put his illness to good use. During that time
he thought things through.

From the Presbyterians he had already definitely separated. Yet
even before he joined them he had read some books by Dr. Elhanan
Winchester, the founder of Universalism in America. This was
shortly after he had joined his mother at Ballston Spa, and the books
had belonged to her sister, who in her youth had heard Dr. Winchester preach. If they had affected the fifteen-year-old Orestes at
the time, it was only to add further to his confusion about religion.

Now lying in bed in Springwells, he took Dr. Winchester up again
for close study. Universalism had come to seem a way of getting
rid of Calvinism; the earnest young man did not want merely to
slough off religion: he felt it necessary to replace Presbyterianism
with something else, and Dr. Winchester served this purpose. The
judgment passed on him in *The Convert* was that he was a good
scholar but a poor theologian.[3] At the time the young Brownson
read him, he was hardly capable of judging on these points. Winchester's arguments struck him as sufficiently plausible for acceptance. Even the good Doctor's epic poem on the Triumph of the
Empire of Christ—versified Universalism—was examined. Of this
the author had boasted that he had written it all during the leisure
moments of three months, and that if he had been able to devote
all his time to it, he would have composed it much more quickly. On
which Brownson drily commented, "I recollect nothing in the poem
to cast any doubt on this statement."[4]

Judging from the number of Universalist works he lists, he was
well supplied with that commodity; we must suppose that he had
borrowed his aunt's library when he left Ballston. The work that
made the deepest impression upon him was by a man whom he
was afterwards to know well, Hosea Ballou. Here was the prophet
of the new school of Universalism, for Ballou did not merely reject
the doctrine of the eternity of punishment for the lost but attacked
the whole fabric of "orthodox" Christianity as understood by Protestantism. In later years Ballou was to tell Brownson that his only

aids in writing his treatise on the Atonement had been the Bible, Ethan Allen's *Oracles of Reason,* and his own reflections. Here, Brownson came to decide, were all the possible heresies; but though none of them was new, all were at least original to the author— spun out of his inner consciousness.[5] Even at Springwells Brownson suspected that these works contained a good many sophistries, but he thought Winchester and Ballou were better than nothing. He wanted to find something to believe. Tentatively, without any hard core of conviction created in himself, he accepted Universalism, which after all committed him to nothing very definite, except the rejection of the already rejected Calvinism.

He had still a long way to go, but he had already started on the way, for he had by now convinced himself that religious belief is nothing if it is not a rational act. From that certain fact he was never to recede, and it is the key to everything in his career. Could he have accepted the Presbyterian creed on the basis of belief in Presbyterian authority, that would have been a rational act. While taking the details of the creed on trust, the acceptance of authority would have been a judgment of the mind. This, however, he had found it impossible to do. Now, in despair of authority, he had decided to follow his judgment wherever it might lead him. From that point on, he was to make steady progress—not progress in a straight line, but in a spiral, sometimes losing sight of his goal, but swinging upon it again from behind. Always from now he had reason as his guide.

Nor did his confidence in reason ever diminish. He came, quite reasonably, to recognize that reason is not self-sufficient. But to see that more clearly was but to see reason in greater grandeur. It was by reason that men came to God, the Infinite Reason. By renouncing John Calvin, Brownson had struck off his intellectual shackles. Universalism was, for him, the first step towards the Universal Church.

By the Fall of 1825 his mind was sufficiently made up for him to apply to the Universalist Association at the General Convention at

Hartland, Vermont, for a license as a preacher.[6] On being accepted, he studied under the direction of a minister for a year, preaching as occasion served. On June 15, 1826, he was duly ordained a minister at Jaffrey, New Hampshire. For the next three years he worked with the Universalist denomination.

While preparing for the ministry, Brownson had another brief spell of school teaching at Elbridge, New York. It is important only because of one thing: while there he met the girl whom he was to marry. She was Sally Healy, the daughter of a fairly prosperous farmer, in whose house he had boarded while teaching. In the account Henry Brownson left of his father she appears as a rather shadowy figure; in fact, her son forgets to mention her at all until he is on page 481 of the *Early Life*.[7] There he describes her as "a tall, slim girl with regular and refined features, and the most beautiful dark eyes such as are seen so frequently amongst the Spanish women." According to a family tradition she may have been partly of Indian blood.[8] She was married to her tall, somewhat stern-looking husband, on June 19, 1827.

Having introduced his mother, Henry Brownson expatiates on her superior education and her intelligence. Of formal schooling she could have had but little, but it is clear that her husband relied a good deal on her judgment, even if he usually followed his own. He must have been a good deal of a trial to her during the early years of their married life, because of his growing radicalism; for this not only wounded her piety but seemed to be leading the family to economic disaster. But in order to dissipate the notion that Orestes was a mere "logic-grinder" Henry assures us that "feeling in him was stronger than intellect. . . . There is, perhaps, nothing in a man's disposition about which more erroneous opinions are almost universally formed than this of the strength of the affections. A self-seeking, cold-hearted, calculating man, who looks at every thing with a view solely to his own satisfaction or emolument, naturally cultivates the attractive, pleasant exterior or manners, which will contribute to the gaining of his purpose, and wins the reputation of amiability and good nature; whilst the warm-hearted, generous one is quick to every emotion, whether of anger or sympathy." Having followed this with a long disquisition on the character of his father, he returns to the domestic relationship by saying, "In his home, Brownson was an affectionate husband and father, in spite of the quickness and irritability of his temper. A pastor of a congregation is very apt to grow arbitrary and somewhat despotic, when much deference is paid him by his people,—which fact might furnish an argument for clerical celibacy,—for such pastor naturally carries that arbitrariness into his domestic life, and if the truth were known, it would very likely appear that in most clergymen's families it is a burden that wives and children have to bear." [9]

Whether or not this is true of clergymen's families it is often true of the families of writers, most of whom are temperamental and explosive. When, on top of that, we remember that Brownson was a man closely absorbed in his studies, usually reading until the small hours, it is easy to believe that Sally and the children had much to put up with. Henry indicates as much by saying, "Brownson's wife was so patiently constituted that whatever she may have suffered from marital harshness, she was always affectionate and loving to husband and children, ever cheerful and devoted to their comfort and happiness." The word "harshness," however, is itself a bit too harsh or was not sufficiently weighed. That Brownson was not a very uxorious man, in the sense of rhapsodizing about love, is no doubt true. It is also true that he had what were, even for those times, somewhat old-fashioned ideas as to woman's function in the scheme of things. But it is certain from the letters we have—and which will be drawn upon later—that the marriage was happy and that Brownson depended more upon his wife than perhaps even he realized. During their separations he always felt lost and he gave her an undeviating loyalty that is, after all, a more solid thing than poetic gush. Mrs. Brownson may sometimes have wistfully wished that her husband were more "romantic," and had more time to spare for her, or even that he were less eccentric and irritable. As a woman of good sense she recognized her good fortune. There is not the slightest need to pity her or to read into her story more than is really there. If Sally willingly remained in the background, the background would have been incomplete without her.

The details of Brownson's Universalist ministry are of slight importance. It is enough to say that he served for short periods at several churches in the states of Vermont, New Hampshire and New York, his chief charge being at Auburn, where he edited the denominational magazine, the *Gospel Advocate,* up to the time he left Universalism late in 1829. That he remained as long as he did was due simply to the fact that doctrinal obligations were light. In his autobiography he dismisses what he wrote for his paper with, "In it is a confused medley of thoughts, and the germs of nearly all I subsequently held or published till my conversion to the Catholic Church." [10]

What is clear is that he was by no means free from intellectual difficulties. He soon perceived that the distinctive Universalist doctrine could be defended only on the ground that eternal punishment was repugnant to reason. As it could not be denied that Universalism was not taught in the Bible, he was obliged to take the ground that the general tendency of the Scriptures rather than their strict letter was to be followed—which meant as wide a latitude of interpretation as anyone chose to accord himself. And this itself induced further doubts as to the infallibility of a book which had to be handled in so free and easy a fashion to make it acceptable at all.[11] He became so very liberal that he was looked upon with suspicion by the Universalists themselves.

There is little wonder for this. In his paper for June, 1829, he offered his readers a creed of five points: a man should be honest, kind, provide for himself and his family, cultivate his mental powers, and believe that, if the other four points are observed, God will be well enough served. He probably intended it as a kind of joke; if so, it missed fire. What people got out of it—not unnaturally —was that he attached no importance to anything recognizably Christian. When, by way of undoing the damage, he offered them another creed, they found it only slightly less objectionable; for while affirming what was usually held by Universalists, he put this in such an off-hand style that he struck them as flippant. His conclusion was "Though my heaven has not as much immediate felicity as the Universalist supposes, neither has it the misery of the orthodox hell." What it amounted to was a kind of mild and perpetual purgatory, a dim and dull eternal existence—hardly more.[12]

Brownson was, in truth, by now little interested in the supernatural. Whatever after-life there was could be only a continuation of earthly existence in which the positive ills of earth were removed. But perhaps he turned away from the supernatural because Universalism, in the very act of abolishing hell, degraded heaven to a place insufficient for the hunger of the human soul. He brought much the same charge afterwards against the Unitarians. The best he could do at the moment was to use his ministry as a means of helping to make earth more tolerable. Revelation no longer meant a great deal; he admitted that it might have been supernaturally imparted, but he could not admit that it was able to convey any truth transcending the natural order. Any matters that could not be subjected to the judgment of human reason, it was clear, would demand a supernaturally endowed and assisted teacher to bring it within the reach of man's understanding. "Natural reason," he said, "thus became the measure of revealed truth." [13]

Without being satisfied with such a conclusion, he pushed it to see how far it would reach, and was appalled by the speculative and moral dilemmas he encountered. He could not escape the fact that the doctrine of unending punishment—however repugnant his reason might consider it—was taught in the Bible. Therefore he must either give up reason or the Bible, or at least make reason the judge of the Bible, though this obviously purported to be revelation. "I chose," he was to write, "as was reasonable in my position, the latter alternative, and rejected the authority of the Scriptures." [14]

There was one way, and only one way, that he could accept the authority of the Bible: it was by accepting the authority of the Catholic Church—something quite out of the question.[15] "As without reason I can neither determine that the Bible is inspired or [sic] what is its sense, I cannot surrender my reason to it in cases where it appears to me unreasonable. I may believe on competent authority that a doctrine is reasonable although I do not perceive its reasonableness, but I cannot, if I try, believe what appears to me unreasonable, on the authority of reason alone. . . . Belief always is and must be a reasonable act. . . . The Bible, then, without an infallible authority to assert it and deduce its sense, can never be authority sufficient for believing a doctrine to be reasonable, when that reasonableness is not apparent to the understanding." The logical deduction was inescapable. He decided that, to one unable to accept external authority, "Revelation . . . is superfluous. I can know without it all I can know with it." In fact, it appeared that he not only ought to reject the Bible but do all in his power to destroy belief in it as the word of God.[16]

Nor was that the last of his speculative difficulties. What was the use of talking about a Saviour? In the mouth of a Universalist this struck him as sheer cant. From what did the Saviour save men? He could not save them from their sins, when sinners, by being assured that they would incur no punishment—except that which nature sometimes imposes on excess—had no inducement to be other than sinners. "As God never . . . punishes sin or rewards virtue, all idea of moral accountability must be abandoned. God will never bring us into judgment for our conduct. Then there is no power above us to defend oppressed innocence, and to vindicate the majesty of right. Then what is the criterion of right and wrong? . . . Here, said I, is the very foundation of morality undermined." [17]

Worse still, this destroyed the idea of the goodness of God. It was useless to attempt to prove the divine goodness from nature, as the evil in nature seemed to surpass the good. Nor was it any use to say that nature herself punished—for it was open to observation that this was not invariably the case. Many a hardened sinner escaped the consequences of his misdeeds; many a good man suffered from what should have fallen upon the wicked, and that did not so fall. There was no sense in worshipping a God who had created a world governed merely by general laws—laws which permitted the existence of evil and which gave no assurance as to the ultimate triumph of good.[18]

Brownson did not accept all the conclusions of his remorseless logic, even though they followed from his premises. His good sense forbade his doing so. But he hung suspended between irreconcilables, and therefore determined to dismiss all metaphysical and speculative considerations from his mind. This, however, made it impossible for him to stand honestly before the public as any sort of Christian minister. To use his pulpit as a rostrum for advocating social reform probably did some service to those who heard him; yet he was inflicting a wound upon his own mind with every word he spoke. More and more he felt his situation to be intolerable.

When he spoke of his doubts to his brother-ministers, he found that they had similar doubts. Indeed, he came to suspect that some of them remained in the ministry "only because they could combat all religion more successfully under a nominally Christian banner." [19] In this, he immediately adds, he felt inclined to believe that he did them injustice, for he was crediting them with being better logicians than they really were. In moods that were less black he conceded that they probably entertained only fleeting doubts and therefore were able to profess themselves Christians with a fairly good conscience. But what merely flitted across their minds obsessed and tormented his own; it was impossible for him to tuck himself up comfortably in intellectual slumber. Something had to be done about it. He recognized that for two years he had been positively anti-

Christian. He now openly declared himself an unbeliever. In his
case it was another step towards genuine belief.

[1] *The Brownson Papers* at Notre Dame University, January 1, 1867.
[2] *Early Life*, p. 20.
[3] *The Convert*, p. 40.
[4] *Ibid.*, p. 41.
[5] *Ibid.*, p. 51.
[6] *Ibid.*, p. 60.
[7] But he says hardly anything about Brownson's domestic affairs, and definite
details about the birth of the eight children (and the early death of some of them)
are also not given.
[8] I get this information from her grand-daughter, Mrs. Thomas H. Odiorne,
who showed me her portrait in oils. It was made in later life, when she was still
slim but rather faded and sad in appearance. It may have been Sally's putative Indian
origin that was in Elizabeth Peabody's mind when in her *Reminiscences of Rev. Wm.
Ellery Channing* (p. 353) she said that Orestes Brownson was of mixed French
and Indian ancestry. She was writing in old age, when her memory was not of the
best; and there are many instances of her unreliability on small points. She seems
to have thought that Brownson's knowledge of French indicated his French extraction; as a matter of fact, his was only a reading knowledge. He never learned
to speak it or even to write it. Perhaps Miss Peabody was not the safest of authorities
on genealogy. She believed herself to be descended from Boadicea!
   Now for the true genealogy of the Brownson and Healy families. It was prepared
for me by Mrs. Odiorne, who cites as her authorities *Media Research* (Washington,
D. C.), *Early Puritan Settlers of the Colony of Connecticut*, by Royal Hinman
(pp. 341–343), Camp's *History of New Britain* (pp. 184–185), *Farmington Vital
Records* (Vol. 1r17, p. 432), *History of Waterbury, Connecticut*, by Henry Bronson,
Brownson Lineage, by Harriet Sibley, William W. Wight's *The Wights, Dedham
Town Records, Abridged Compendium of American Genealogy*, Vols. I & II, and
The History of Washington, New Hampshire (p. 471). The name of Brownson is
believed to be derived from Bransston. In the fifteenth century we hear of a
William Brownson in the county of Suffolk, whose descendants, John and Richard,
came to America in 1636 and first settled in Hartford, Conn., and then in
Farmington and Waterbury, Conn. John Brownson fought in the Pequot War in
1637 and was in 1651, and at several subsequent sessions, deputy to the General
Court. He died in 1680, leaving several children. From him the line is Isaac Brownson (born ?, died 1719, married to Mary Root about 1664), Samuel Brownson (born
1676, died ?, married Ruth Smith), Elijah Brownson (dates of birth and death
unknown, married Abigail Winchel 1739), Nodiah Brownson (born 1740, died 1803,
married Sybble Horsington 1766), Sylvester Augustus Brownson (born New Britain,
June 7, 1772, died 1805, married Relief Metcalfe of Keene, N. H.). These last are
the father and mother of Orestes Brownson. The other branch of the family began
to spell its name Bronson about the end of the eighteenth century. Bronson Alcott
and Orestes Brownson had reason to believe themselves distantly related. The Healys
came from England and settled in Roxbury, Mass., between 1630 and 1635. Their
American progenitor was William. From him the line runs: Nathaniel (born 1659,
died 1734, married ?), John (born 1698, died 1783, married Hannah ?), John

(born 1732, died 1810, married Mary Wight 1762), John (born 1773, died 1826, married Dolly Rude). These are the parents of Mrs. Orestes Brownson. Mrs. Odiorne suggests that "this name Dolly Rude is suspiciously Indian." As for the Wights, a Thomas of that name came from the Isle of Wight and settled at Watertown, Mass., in 1635. He died in 1673. From him the line descends: Henry Wight (born about 1629, died 1680, married Jane Goodenow about 1652), Joseph Wight (born 1654, died 1729, married Mary Stearns 1685), Ebenezer Wight (born 1696, died ?, married Subiah Hall 1743), Mary Wight (born 1745, died 1827, married John Healy 1762). This Mary Wight was the grandmother of Mrs. Orestes Brownson. It will be seen from all this that, except for a possible strain of mixed French and Indian blood, the family on both sides was purely English, though of course the Healys must have been of Irish extraction far back.

9 *Early Life*, pp. 481–482, 484–485.

10 *The Convert*, pp. 66–67.

11 *Ibid.*, pp. 56, 57, 58.

12 *Early Life*, pp. 25–32. George Parsons Lathrop, writing in the *Atlantic Monthly* (Vol. LXXVII, 1896) twenty years after Brownson's death, calls the first of these creeds "one of the rawest and most jejune we have known." He adds, however, "It had its value at the time." (P. 772.) What value, is not very clear—unless Brownson wished to irritate people.

13 *The Convert*, p. 58.

14 *Ibid.*, p. 68.

15 *Ibid.*, p. 69. He therefore preached that none of the existing denominations was the Church founded by Christ—for he saw (and said) that if it were once so much as admitted that that Church actually existed, there could be no stopping short of Rome. (*Middle Life*, pp. 29–30.)

16 *Ibid.*, pp. 69–70, 71.

17 *Ibid.*, pp. 77, 78.

18 *Ibid.*, pp. 78, 79.

19 *Ibid.*, p. 80.

CHAPTER III

Jezebel to the Rescue

"MY HONEST AVOWAL of unbelief," Brownson wrote afterwards, "was, under the circumstances, a step that brought me nearer the kingdom of God." [1] Though he longed to be able to believe, he longed still more for the truth. As religious certitude seemed to be unattainable, he gave himself to moral and practical considerations. The other world having grown more and more faint, he looked for a work to do in this world, and he found it in socialism. "Not in seeking to save my soul, to please God, or to have the true religion [was] I led to the Catholic Church, but to obtain the means of gaining the earthly happiness of mankind." [2]

It was socialism rather than Christianity that he had been preaching during his last two years as a Universalist. And it is evident from the letters published by Henry Brownson that his father's mind was divided until an unexpected event occurred to heal it. Moreover, it is also evident that, within a month or two of his severing his connection with Universalism, Orestes Brownson sometimes wrote with almost smug satisfaction about the progress the denomination was making. The suggestion made here must not be taken as in any degree impugning his honesty; it is merely one more instance of a man not being able to trace with perfect accuracy the intellectual processes he had followed twenty-five years previously. So much happened to Brownson between 1829 and the time he wrote the story of his conversion, that he could hardly help coloring his previous ideas or seeing them as much more sharply defined than they had appeared to him at the time. No one need doubt that the arguments he gives in the third and fourth chapters of *The Convert*

25

occurred to him while he was still a Universalist; what may be doubted is whether they were nearly so crystal clear as he describes them as being. At all events, writing to Ulysses F. Doubleday, the publisher of the *Gospel Advocate* and later a member of Congress, Brownson almost smacks his lips and hugs himself over what he had witnessed of the decline of "orthodoxy" and the hopeful condition of Universalism in Hartford and Boston. Of Charlestown he says, "There is a fine society of Universalists in this place. One day's residence among them is sufficient to refute the slanderous assertion that Universalism is a licentious doctrine." Later in the same letter he adds, "Orthodoxy has seen her best days here. . . . My visit has been so far attended with high satisfaction to myself." The only word of criticism is mild: "They observe the Lord's Supper, an institution which I have generally considered of no great practical benefit. It is doubtless attended, as I have before remarked, with some advantages. Mankind must have some outward ordinance." [3] What one draws from all this is that Brownson, like the rest of us, had his ups and downs of feeling. In retrospect his attitude towards Universalism seemed to have a greater consistency than it really possessed.

Two things—both said by him very candidly—may be set side by side. The one is: "My end was man's earthly happiness, and my creed was progress. In regard to neither did I change or swerve in the least, till the truth of the Catholic Church was forced on my mind and my heart. During the period of fourteen years [1829–1843], the greater part of which I was accused of changing at least once every three months, I never changed once in my principles or my purposes." The other—equally important to remember—is: "I trust I shall always have the honor of being regarded by my friends and associates as impolitic, as rash, imprudent, and impracticable." [4] He had every right to claim an essential intellectual consistency, from the time he shook off Calvinism till the day he died, over fifty years later, as a Catholic. Nobody would refuse him the honor of being to the end impulsive and unpredictable.

It was as such that he now showed himself. Little wonder that his Universalist associates—especially those who, like Brother Doubleday, had been receiving glowing letters concerning the decay of orthodoxy and the spread of the glorious light of Universalism—did not know what to make of it. They knew of course that Brownson had gloomy moods and that he talked indiscreetly. But they took the talk as a letting off of steam. They were not prepared for what came upon them without warning—a sudden break.

The preaching of social reform is less of a novelty among Protestant ministers today than it was a hundred years ago. But it was not unknown even then. Probably the shrewder of his friends hoped that Brownson's new enthusiasm would enable him to forget his metaphysical problems. That social reform may be an anodyne for a troubled mind was clear to Brownson himself, when speaking of what he had gone through, he declared, "Our philanthropists and world-reformers may become so engrossed in their plans that they do not experience that aching void within, that emptiness of all created things, which we sometimes imagine. Their philanthropy is a religion unto them." [5]

So far he had not done much more than read and talk about social reform, though by doing so he had got himself in line with what was to follow. As is often true of people with a general desire for "progress," he was by no means sure as to the direction he should take. His mind was very nearly balanced between the two extremes of communism and individualism. He was simultaneously studying Robert Owen and William Godwin.

The very title of Owen's book, *A New View of Society,* was taken over when Brownson published in 1836 the first of his own volumes, *New Views of Christianity, Society, and the Church,* though there is not much of Owenism there. But he read with interest about the experiments carried out at New Lanark, and had accepted the doctrine that, as man is formed by his environment, all that is necessary for the obtaining of a perfect human society is to form character by the right sort of education. And it must be acknowledged that, whatever theoretical fallacies underlay Owen's schemes, their practical utility was considerable. Largely because of his efforts, factory reform was achieved, and his mills were models of their kind. Though his coöperative community at New Harmony in Indiana had failed only a year previously, philanthropists were still full of sanguine Owenite dreams. To all this Brownson was at least sympathetic, while making some reservations as to the feasibility or the desirability of everything Owen proposed.[6]

Owen's ideas, though apparently poles apart from those of William Godwin, largely stemmed from the former Sandemanian minister's *Political Justice,* which had been published twenty years before his own *New Views*.[7] The two men at least agreed that the ills of society were caused by the institutions of property, marriage and religion. The gist of their perfectionism was stated in a single sentence by the dramatist, Thomas Holcroft: "Men do not become what by nature they are meant to be but what society makes them."

Godwin, however, was a pure theorist, an idealist who was content that men should have the right ideas. In his anarchic system men became free as soon as they knew themselves to be free. As his disciple and son-in-law, Shelley, who versified so much of his prose, was to sing:

> But Greece and her foundations are
> Built below the tide of war,
> Based on the crystalline sea
> Of thought and its eternity.

The equally idealistic but more mystical Blake put the same notion with:

> I will not cease from Mental Fight,
> Nor shall my Sword sleep in my hand,
> Till we have built Jerusalem
> In England's green and pleasant land.

The symbols of perfection of the two poets were dissimilar—though less dissimilar than the poets themselves—but each agreed with

Godwin that once a thing was in the mind it really existed. It only remained for the practical man to remove what brought about man's deformation—and immediately man would restore himself to his inherent perfection. As the author of *Political Justice* was obviously not a practical man, the government thought there was no need to prosecute him. Besides, was not a book published at four guineas too expensive to do much harm? The young Wordsworth might tell a friend in the Inner Temple to burn his law-books and read Godwin on necessity. But the ruling classes did not care how many people read him; in one sense, the more the better; once they got it into their heads that ideas were realities, they could be relied on to do nothing calculated to disturb the existing order of society. It was Godwin's famous book that Brownson was most closely studying at this time. Of it he was able to say, "I think it has had more influence on my mind than any other book, except the Scriptures, I have ever read." [8]

He was also to write of it: "There is scarcely a modern error that it does not contain;" but he added a few pages later, "even the absurdest and most mischievous of Godwin's principles have a certain reflection of Christian truth." [9] As for Godwin's style, upon which he had largely formed his own—though his was at once lighter and more vigorous than Godwin's—he pronounced: "He is almost the only English writer, since Burke's unhappy influence on the language, who has written truly classical English, or our language according to its true genius." [10]

Suddenly Brownson encountered one who appeared to him to combine the best features of the thought of Godwin and Owen, though surely not one whose literary style merits much praise. He was returning from Boston and Hartford, from where he had written his letters to Doubleday about the progress of Universalism, when he heard that Miss Frances Wright was to lecture at Utica. Instead of completing his journey, he went to hear her. He believed her to "have hit upon a just medium between the individualism of Godwin, and the communism of Owen." [11]

Brownson had already reprinted some of Miss Wright's articles in his *Gospel Advocate,* but knowing that the respectable and the godly might gasp to see that scarlet name there, he had explained why he had done so: "We would have our readers understand that we are not afraid to copy from a paper [the *Free Enquirer*] which many think it would be a crime even to name without reproach." It was because "the article in question is really meritorious and deserves to be read by every one who does not choose to be a bigot"; also "because it states in a clear and impressive manner sentiments which we have ever laboured to defend . . . Abating her views on matrimony, which probably are more censured than understood, and censured by more than believe them ill-founded, we have seen nothing in her *ethicks* that should be discarded." [12]

But her views on matrimony were the trouble, or the main part of it. She had established at Nashoba, Tennessee, a coöperative colony for Negroes in which the slaves were to work out their own value during a term of years, after which they were to be regarded as having purchased themselves. It was a scheme that had been approved by Lafayette (whose adopted daughter Fanny Wright was) and by Jefferson, Madison, and Chief Justice Marshall. [13] So far, so good—even though most slave-holders did not like the idea at all. When it came out that Miss Wright held that marriage should be dissolved at the will of those who had entered into the "free union," she was charged with being an advocate of free-love. And so she was, in an airy and speculative fashion, though without intending to practice it herself and merely believing that it was the form of the union of the sexes that would prevail in the perfect society of which she dreamed. Unfortunately, the overseer of Nashoba, Richardson, was disinclined to wait for the Utopia. He openly took a Negro mistress and announced that all in the colony —whether white or black—were to have the same rights and privileges. Further, as the whole idea of Nashoba was to obtain— by gradual means—racial equality, the logical conclusion was not flinched from: the Negro problem would be solved by miscegenation.

In all this Richardson rather than Fanny Wright was at fault. She and her sister (who was with her in America) were strictly moral people who made ordinary marriages and kept their vows. But her theoretical notions received publicity and obtained for her a lurid notoriety.

Many of those who took the lead in denouncing her were of the slave-owning class who forbade real marriages among their slaves and freely begot children from their Negro women—often selling their own offspring down the river. Their holy horror at miscegenation was a trifle comical. There were, however, many other people—most of them very imperfectly informed as to what it was that Fanny Wright really proposed—who were sincerely shocked. They imagined the wildest orgies at Nashoba.

The colony failed for a number of reasons. The site was badly chosen; the management was incompetent; and it was all but impossible to get the Negroes to do any work—except under the lash, which was on principle foregone. Moreover Fanny and her sister both got ill and had to leave everything to Richardson. Mrs. Trollope, the mother of the novelist, arrived to settle there, but, having taken one look at the slatternly place, hurried on to Cincinnati, to open her emporium and to write her famous book, *The Domestic Manners of the Americans*. In the end Fanny had to give up, after having lost a large part of her fortune in the venture. It is to her credit that she took her slaves to Hayti, where she set them free—a further dead loss to herself. Then she turned to the lecture platform.

By now she realized that black slavery was only one—and a minor branch—of the huge trunk of human servitude. Her mission in life henceforth was to work for the liberation of the white working-classes who, whether they knew it or not, were quite as much slaves as their colored brethren. In all of which she had noble motives, however faulty her judgment may have been.

A woman on the lecture platform was, in those days, almost as scandalous as a woman advocating free-love. But she was also an attraction. People went expecting to hear horrible doctrines and to gaze gloatingly at a Jezebel. They continued to go because Fanny turned out to be a remarkably good public speaker. Brownson who, when he wrote in 1857, was a connoisseur of oratory, gave this description of his friend: "Her free, flowing, and ornate style—French rather than English—her fine, rich, musical voice, highly cultivated and possessing great power, her graceful manner, her tall, commanding figure, her wit and sarcasm, her apparent honesty of purpose, and deep and glowing enthusiasm, made her one of the most pleasing and effective orators, man or woman, that I have ever heard." [14] He tells how she opened her first lecture at Auburn by remarking, "in the sweetest manner imaginable" that she had seen in that town of four thousand inhabitants no less than six churches, from which she gathered that religion must be well discussed there. Then she gave her thrust: "I have travelled much and visited many countries, and in no place have I been so uncourteously received, or have been the subject of so much personal insult, as in your most religious village. Perhaps it will not be inappropriate for us to spend one evening in discussing the subject of Morals." [15]

Brownson and Fanny Wright took to one another at once, this six foot woman of thirty with her rather masculine good looks—whom her friend, Shelley's widow, used to call "Minerva"—and the even taller young Vermonter, who in those days was so gaunt and grim. Each perceived the other's sincerity and courage and ability; neither objected to the other's supreme self-confidence. When Fanny visited Auburn in November for her lectures it was arranged that Orestes should act as corresponding editor for the *Free Enquirer*. It is evident from the announcement made by that paper in its issue for December 7th that, just as Brownson had reprinted some of Miss Wright's articles in the *Gospel Advocate,* so the *Free Enquirer* had been quoting freely from him. "We recognized him by his writings," Fanny editorialized, "for an honest labourer in the same vineyard with ourselves; we saw that if nominally attached to a sect, he was neither in thought nor feeling sectarian, we saw that he had dropped from the clouds upon the solid earth, and that he had renounced the chair of dogmatism to pursue enquiry in the field of nature and human life." [16]

✓ That is putting it mildly; Brownson had had no dogmatic position since leaving the Presbyterians, and for two years even the pallid notions of Universalism had been fading from his mind. But it needed the catalysis of this meeting with Fanny Wright to bring him to the decision of cutting loose from the ministry. Sooner or later the thing would have happened, even had he not encountered her; her influence over his vastly superior mind could not have been great; but the decision nevertheless was reached as a result of that encounter. It is therefore important in his story.

The Universalists can hardly be blamed for feeling bitter about this apparently unaccountable defection. At the same time it must be added that had Brownson not left the ministry, he would probably have been ejected from it. Not even the Universalists were so liberal as to put up with an associate of Fanny Wright. But we may dismiss Doran Whalen's imaginary account of Sally Brownson's jealousy of Fanny, for which there is not a particle of evidence. [17] That Sally did not like her husband's being mixed up with a notorious woman is, of course, likely enough; for that matter she was deeply distressed by his heretical and radical tendencies. But we may credit Sally with enough sense to understand that the relationship was solely on the plane of ideas. To the end Brownson always spoke in the friendliest way of "poor Fanny," and it is from him that we learn that when she died—estranged from her unpleasant husband Phiquepal D'Arusmont, impoverished and forgotten— the only person who did not desert her was a lady who was a convert from Quakerism to Catholicism. [18]

At this point we must go back a little way. In 1827 there occurred a strike at Philadelphia in the building trades which resulted in the first really effective labor union, and this soon led to the formation of the Workingmen's Party. [19] Simultaneously, and perhaps by way of reaction against a movement which the respectable and the

prosperous considered subversive—though all that was being demanded was a ten-hour working day—there came into being in the
same city the Christian Party in Politics. Its actual program was
rather vague, if one is to take it as contained in Dr. Ezra Stiles
Ely's Fourth of July Sermon at Philadelphia, and amounted to little
more than a demand by blue-noses for more stringent blue-laws.[20]
But some speech-making followed of the kind that made both the
Workingmen and the Political Evangelicals seem more important
than they actually were. This gave Fanny Wright a further reason
for attacking religion as an impediment to reform.[21] The delightful
phrase about pie in the sky when you die had not yet been thought
of; the idea it expressed was even more prevalent then than now.

Yet the Workingmen's Party, to whom Miss Wright and her
friends began to address themselves, actually made very moderate
demands: they asked for a modification of the laws that imprisoned
men for trifling debts, for the abolition of capital punishment, and
for a ten-hour day. They also asked, among other things, for the
suppression of lotteries and for the promotion of temperance in the
interests of the working-classes. So far from countenancing irreligion,
they pointed to "the fact of the workingmen's existence as a body,
on the same principles they now profess, for nearly a year previous
to [Miss Wright's] appearance amongst us." [22] Though they later
accepted Thomas Skidmore's agrarianism, which advocated an equal
distribution of property—to be brought about by the abolition of
the right of bequest—this was only for a short time. And it was
advocated only by a section among them. Even Fanny Wright
soon withdrew that item from the list of aims she printed in each
issue of the *Free Enquirer*.[23]

Miss Wright's assistance, however, was too powerful for the
Workingmen to refuse. She had a paper at her disposal and some
funds for an otherwise empty war-chest. Besides, she was by far the
most popular public speaker they had. Through her paper and her
lectures she attracted wide, if not always favorable, attention. But
while she was excellent as a speaker, and by no means feeble as a

journalist, she was a failure as a writer when she attempted more than journalism. Her free-thought odes that were sung in the Hall of Science on the Bowery were a diluted mixture of Shelley and Byron, and her parody of the Bible—which some may have considered exquisitely funny—was feeble and flatulent.

Though as a thinker she was negligible, she had a wonderful faculty for stirring things up. But feminism, free-love and atheism became, because of her, equated in the popular mind. One New York paper declared roundly that she was a female "impervious to the voice of virtue and case-hardened against shame, a voluptuous preacher of licentiousness." [24] And William Cullen Bryant's New York *Evening Post* wrote in the same vein about "the singular spectacle of a female, publicly and ostentatiously proclaiming doctrines of an atheistical fanaticism, and even the most abandoned lewdness." [25] Bryant even composed an ode on the

> Wonder of the age, from whom
> Religion waits her final doom,
> Her quiet death, her euthanasia,
> Thou in whose eloquence and bloom
> The age beholds a new Aspasia! [26]

Fanny took it all with careless good-humor; after all, Bryant's attack admitted her personal charms. She was not to be turned aside from her purpose by a few stupid men. Among the things she stood for were women's rights—a grand theme for ridicule, had it been easy to ridicule her! This particular doctrine Brownson gulped down rather unwillingly but without violent protest, so long as it came from the fascinating Fanny. It was only when he heard it advanced later by the far less attractive Margaret Fuller and Harriet Martineau —who seemed to him to be scorning equality and claiming superiority —that, as he put it, he became aroused, and ventured to assert his masculine dignity.[27] While associated with the feminist Fanny Wright, he was content to let that part of her program pass without special comment.

Brownson's interest in Fanny Wright was due solely to his seeing in her a courageous advocate of better social conditions—especially shorter hours for artisans. The ten-hour day was asked for mainly because it would give the laboring classes more leisure for self-improvement, which was then considered the golden key to prosperity. So long as they remained illiterate they would not be able, as a group, to use their political power; nor would they be able, as individuals, to raise their economic position. It was here that Miss Wright promised to be of most help. She had worked out a complete educational scheme in conjunction with Robert Dale Owen, Robert Owen's son, a man six years younger than herself, an ugly little fellow with a nose almost as large as his father's and a loose-lipped mouth, but with plenty of intelligence and charm. She and Owen believed that they could not expect to achieve their goal of world reform unless they first moulded the minds of the next generation to the acceptance of their ideas, and that this could be done only by obtaining complete control of their education. What is not clear is how they expected to get those who were admittedly corruptly educated or illiterate parents to agree to hand over their children to be brought up according to "Wright reason." Only those who were so fanatically enthusiastic as to have lost all ordinary human traits could be brought to listen to what Fanny had to say. But some did listen, among them Brownson—though he, much against his better judgment.

Her scheme can be best described in the capitals used to advertise it as: "National, Rational, Republican Education; Free For All At The Expense Of All; Conducted Under The Guardianship Of The State, And For The Honor, The Happiness, The Virtue, The Salvation Of The State." [28] Explicitly, the children were to be taken from their parents at the age of two and kept in state-supported boarding-schools until they were sixteen. During those fourteen years they might be visited by their parents at regular intervals but they were to be the wards of the state. There was to be no distinction between the children of the rich and those of the poor; all were to have the same accommodation and the same food; and all were to wear a uniform.[29]

Obviously so preposterous a plan had no chance of being accepted by Americans as a whole, and even the Workingmen's Party gave it very lukewarm backing. Brownson describes it unfairly, however, when he writes that the aim was, "on the one hand, to relieve marriage of its burdens, and to remove the principal reasons for making it indissoluble; and on the other, to provide for bringing up all children in a rational manner"—as rationality was understood by his associates.[30] There is no indication, however—at any rate in the writings of these people—that they had any other object than the one Brownson indicates as secondary. Deluded as she was, Fanny Wright should be credited with good intentions.

Still less to be believed is Brownson's account of the secret plans laid for getting the schools established. There is no need to argue that plans of that sort could not be kept secret, for it is a matter of historical fact that no secret was made of what Fanny and Owen and D'Arusmont intended. Nevertheless Brownson says they tried to establish something like Carbonari cells and to organize the whole Union in this way. "The members of this secret society were to avail themselves of all the means in their power, each in his own locality, to form public opinion in favor of education by the State at the public expense, and to get such men elected to the legislatures as would be likely to favor our purposes. How far the secret organization extended I do not know; but I do know that a considerable part of the State of New York was organized, for I was myself one of the agents for organizing it. I, however, became tired of the work, and abandoned it after a few months. Whether the organization still exists, or whether it has ever exerted any influence or not, is more than I am able to say, or have taken the pains to ascertain." [31]

This is all very vague and unsatisfactory. Brownson no doubt made the suggestion of secrecy in good faith, and it is not impossible that at the outset secrecy may have been attempted. If so, it was soon given up and the plan openly advocated.[32] Brownson could hardly have taken his own statement very seriously, as he admits lack of further knowledge or interest—which would hardly be the case if he really believed his "Carbonari" story. The casual explanation of lack of interest rings true; he was not by temperament an organizer, and the plan for taking away children from their parents had never commended itself to his judgment. He had merely acquiesced without approving.[33] Owen's explanation of Brownson's defection was that he had a family to support.[34] Sally had already borne him two sons. Under the circumstances he did not feel inclined to wander about New York state organizing "Carbonari" cells.

But if Brownson, simply by writing in a hurried off-hand style, gives a hint of melodrama, his biographer, Doran Whalen, has a sensational story, which had best be given in her own words: "When Frances Wright discovered that the native American, Brownson, was drawing more adherents to the cause than all of the others put together, she advised that the giant orator from Auburn be offered some share in the contributions towards the Party's success . . . She meant to seal Brownson to the Working Man's Party. This gesture would have bound a hireling; but it only awakened a shepherd. Brownson was summoned. After compliments upon his success, Miss Wright and Owen laid before his astonished gaze their entire brilliant design. They caught the shocked awakening in the face of the zealous apostle of justice; but they interpreted it as admiration. It encouraged them. They offered him shares in such booty as would make them all millionaires within a year after the election. . . . His reply was only: 'You, more than my former friends, have misunderstood me.' He reached for his hat and was out of the door in two strides." [35]

That whole scene is, I am afraid, sheer invention. Not a single particle of evidence supports it. Brownson was not notably successful as an orator at any time in his life; he did not bring many adherents to the cause; he was not even very enthusiastic in the cause, or he soon tired of it. And for Fanny he retained a respect and affection that would have been impossible had he been offered this bribe. But it is waste of time to argue the point: Fanny and Owen had no bribe to offer, and they must have known that they had no chance of getting their candidates elected. About the only definite information we have concerning Brownson's brief association with Fanny Wright is what he has himself told us—and that is not always to be taken at its face value. He left Fanny Wright partly because he was weary of uncongenial work, and partly because he had come to see that little good was to be achieved by working with her.

Here occurs another curious mistake. It is one made by Henry Brownson, who is incautiously followed by Mr. Schlesinger, both of whom say that Brownson supported William H. Seward's anti-Masonic Party in 1830.[36] The exact opposite is the case. Brownson was himself a Mason at this time, and he tells how, when he had "tired" of the work he was doing for Miss Wright, he gave his support to E. T. Throop, the Jacksonian candidate for the governorship of New York, against Francis Granger, the candidate of the anti-Masons, by founding a paper and assisting in the conduct of the *Daily Sentinel*.[37] The curious thing is that his son, after quoting what his father had said in his autobiography, apparently forgot all about it and wrote in *Middle Life* that "as Seward was the leader of the anti-Masonic Party, in western New York, Brownson did all in his power to push him forward." [38]

The explanation is probably that the whole anti-Masonic episode is so confused that it is hard to make head or tail of it. Dr. Charles McCarthy, its historian, in his careful study points out that the incident of the alleged Morgan abduction and murder [39] was used by wily politicians to fuse all the elements opposed to Jackson's administration into what eventuated as the Whig Party. Thurlow Weed skilfully played both ends against the middle, so that before long the anti-Masonic issue was lost sight of—with such completeness that, in some instances, Masons were themselves voting the anti-Masonic ticket.[40] Moreover, abolitionism was played up by the anti-Masons—in those sections where it appealed—and their party tended also to be that of "orthodox" Protestants as against the Unitarians and Universalists.[41] It is understandable that Henry Brownson could make nothing of such a tangle of cross-purposes.

There is another possible explanation of Henry Brownson's slip. His father in later life looked upon Masonry, as do most of the uninitiated, as a compound in equal parts of benevolence, bonhomie and buffoonery. Hearing him talk, Henry may have jumped to the conclusion that he had been a member of the anti-Masonic Party. But so far from Brownson having at any time been a friend of W. H. Seward's, they never liked one another, though there was not the degree of animosity imagined by Doran Whalen. As for Weed, Brownson brought against him in 1864 the familiar charge—constantly denied by Weed—of "making the body of Timothy Monroe look that of Morgan. 'But it is not the body of Morgan.' 'No matter, it is a good enough Morgan till after the election.' "[42]

Brownson's connection with New York state politics was brief—briefer even than his connection with Fanny Wrightism. "The truth is," he said, "I never was and never could be a party man, or work in the traces of a party." This, though said of his Workingmen's period, was even more true of his anti-Masonic Party days, when no principles were involved. In the midst of that political jockeying, Brownson was a babe in arms. Though he retained an interest in the Workingmen's Party for some years, neither in that organization nor any other was he ever able to be anything but a free-lance; and in that capacity he always sooner or later made himself a thorn in the flesh. Only to the Catholic Church did he find he could give an undeviating loyalty—and he had still a long and tortuous road to travel before he reached Rome.

[1] *The Convert*, p. 100.

[2] *Ibid.*, p. 102.

[3] *Early Life*, pp. 34–39. It is interesting to note that Brownson's attitude towards the Lord's Supper antedated by three years Emerson's refusal to administer it to his own congregation. But it was an idea that seems to have been in the air. Bronson Alcott expressed it in 1829. (See his *Journals*, p. 20.)

[4] *The Convert*, pp. 96, 102.

[5] *Ibid.,* p. 104.

[6] *Ibid.,* pp. 89–91.

[7] Max Beer puts the matter well when he says (*A History of British Socialism,* Vol. I, p. 115): "In order to understand Godwin it must always be borne in mind that he was essentially a Calvinist preacher. God is reason; predestination necessity or determinism, Providence causation, the Kingdom of God, ethical communism. His criticism is one long Nonconformist sermon." H. N. Brailsford pleasantly explains the difference between a Sandemanian and an ordinary Calvinist: "A Calvinist held that of ten souls nine will be damned. A Sandemanian hoped that of ten Calvinists one may with difficulty be saved." (*Shelley, Godwin and Their Circle,* p. 79). It is easily discernible how the wreckage of Calvinism remained fast in Godwin's mind; rejecting all else, he retained its determinism and its idealism.

[8] *The Convert,* p. 110. And by that date (1857) all the formative influences he was ever to receive, including that of Gioberti, had done their work.

[9] *Ibid.,* pp. 110, 117.

[10] *Ibid.,* p. 109.

[11] *Ibid.,* p. 120. This is a juster distinction between Godwin and Owen than is sometimes made. For example, Marx and Engels grouped Godwin among those whom they called "Utopian Socialists." The fact is, however, that though Godwin made his contribution to socialist thought, and was "Utopian" in the sense Dr. Anton Menger indicates—that of being unscientific and of expecting men to be moved by another sequence of cause and effect than that of actual conditions (*The Right to the Whole Produce of Labour,* p. 111)—he was essentially anarchistic and not socialistic at all. Brownson's word "individualism" covers the point sufficiently well, if it be understood that Godwin's individualism was of the most extreme sort and was almost wholly intellectual.

[12] *The Gospel Advocate,* Vol. VII (1829), p. 253.

[13] Fanny Wright had rather a weakness for distinguished old men. The first of her patrons was Jeremy Bentham, who called her his "favourite pupil" and (in a letter which she kept to her dying day), "the strongest sweetest mind that ever cased in a human body." (Perkins and Wolfson, *Frances Wright: Free Enquirer,* p. 60.)

[14] *The Convert,* p. 124.

[15] *Ibid.,* p. 125.

[16] Quoted from *Early Life,* pp. 41–42.

[17] *Granite for God's House,* pp. 58, 64. It is insinuated rather than definitely stated, but insinuated several times.

[18] *The Convert,* p. 127.

[19] Helen L. Sumner in J. R. Commons's *History of Labor in the United States,* Vol. I, p. 169.

[20] An account of the matter is given in Waterson's *Frances Wright,* pp. 139–143.

[21] She was not, strictly speaking, an atheist. She merely complained—and with some justice—that the bulk of the clergy supported the social iniquities she was attacking. Her solution was to have all children brought up by the state, and have no religion taught them. Brownson in 1840 put far more fiercely than she ever did the charge of clerical social obscurantism.

[22] Quoted by Miss Sumner, *op. cit.,* p. 212.

[23] *Ibid.,* pp. 242–245.

[24] Quoted in Perkins's and Wolfson's *Frances Wright: Free Enquirer,* p. 233.

²⁵ *Ibid.*, p. 232.

²⁶ New York *Evening Post*, January, 1829.

²⁷ *The Convert*, p. 215. He had, however, nothing of special importance to say on this subject in his autobiography; there he dismisses it rather loftily and perfunctorily. In later years he came to think that the women's rights movement was really aiming at free-love and was hostile to marriage. As for the vote, he denied that women—or, for that matter, men—had any natural right to it. (*Works*, Vol. XVIII, pp. 382–417.) He always professed enormous respect for women, yet he accused them of being spiteful, especially towards their own sex, and less modest than men. (*Works*, Vol. XIX, pp. 601, 602 and elsewhere.) It should be added that he was virtually forced to assume this attitude as part of his general conservatism. He was by no means peculiar in his views at that time.

²⁸ Waterman, *Frances Wright*, p. 156.

²⁹ Perkins and Wolfson, *op. cit.*, p. 289, and Waterman, *op. cit.*, p. 194. Some of the details were proposed by the Frenchman, William Phiquepal D'Arusmont, who was a Pestalozzian and who had studied under the celebrated alienist, Pinel, whose position as superintendent of the Sâlpetrière he was offered but refused. (Waterman, *op. cit.*, p. 232.) Not much is known about him, but Brownson heartily disliked him, with some justice. Not long afterwards he married Frances Wright and, after the marriage proved unhappy, he asserted under French law his right to her whole estate.

³⁰ *The Convert*, p. 129.

³¹ *Ibid.*, p. 134. The first time he mentioned this plan publicly—and there too he used the word "Carbonari"—was in an address at Mount St. Mary's College, Emmitsburg, in 1853. (*Works*, Vol. XIX, p. 442.)

³² Waterman, *op. cit.*, pp. 196–198. Here Fanny Wright's and Owen's own explicit statements are given.

³³ *The Convert*, p. 139.

³⁴ This was what Owen wrote to N. P. Trist on February 23, 1831. I take the reference from Schlesinger's *Orestes A. Brownson*, fn. p. 21.

³⁵ *Granite for God's House*, pp. 68–69.

³⁶ Yet he contradicts this in *Early Life*, pp. 48–49. See also Schlesinger, *Orestes A. Brownson*, p. 15.

³⁷ *The Convert*, p. 136.

³⁸ *Middle Life*, pp. 283–284.

³⁹ William Morgan, having left Masonry, wrote a book in which he pretended to expose its secrets. When in 1826 a body was produced, which was supposed to be his, there was a popular revulsion of feeling against the order. It was this feeling that gave the first impulse to the anti-Masonic Party.

⁴⁰ McCarthy, *The Anti-Masonic Party*, pp. 400, 405.

⁴¹ *Ibid.*, pp. 542, 543, 546.

⁴² *Works*, Vol. XVII, p. 545. This is dragged into an article on "Abolition and Negro Equality."

CHAPTER IV

Self-made Scholar

IT WAS ONLY a year since Brownson had left the Universalists in order to work with Fanny Wright. The moment he declared himself an unbeliever, he felt restored to his manhood. He also found that the moment he ceased to profess—or rather, to seem to profess —more than he really believed, he ceased to be irritated against religion.[1] In fact, he saw that he needed "religion of some sort as the agent to induce men to make the sacrifices required in the adoption of my plans for working out the reform of society, and securing to man his earthly felicity." [2] He was still very far from having recovered a sense of his personal need of religion, and he was no clearer than before as to which was the true religion; all that he was sure about was that it was useless to attempt world-reform without faith. Fanny Wright had served a double purpose in his life: she had sharply dragged him out of the haze of Universalism, and she had brought him to the edge of an abyss. From that abyss he had now turned back, one important lesson learned. He did not delude himself into thinking that religion was true merely because it was socially useful; but he had reached the belief that "the conviction that it is necessary for that purpose, if not rudely treated, may, in an ingenuous mind, lead to something more." [3] On this somewhat flimsy basis he set up shop again as a minister.

This time it was as an independent, and in Ithaca, where he had already worked for a short time as a Universalist. But he now made it clear that he was no longer a member of that body; the Universalists disowned him, for good reasons, and he disowned them for better. He had no intention of returning to a situation he had already

43

proved to be impossible. In his first sermon—at the beginning of February, 1831—he announced, "I belong to no party, I disclaim all sectarian names . . . Should I assume the name of any party, it should be Unitarian, as that denomination approximates nearer, in my estimation, to the spirit of Christianity than any other." [4]

As it was apparently very easy in those days to found a magazine, he promptly founded one, which he called the *Philanthropist*. He had to have an organ in which to express himself and to let off his excess energy. He was much more of a journalist than a preacher; in fact his preaching and lecturing were only journalism—of a kind less effective than his written word. His was not the ability, so essential to the public speaker, of getting into immediate contact with his audience. His physical presence and his resonant voice stood him in good stead; and people listened with respect to a man so obviously sincere. But he was always rather aloof in the pulpit or on the platform. Not so when he took his pen in hand; then— only then—was he able to take his audience into his confidence. The editorial "we" never cloaked his individuality. Though this magazine lived only until the middle of its second year—when, many of his subscribers having failed to pay their dues, he discontinued it, as he did not wish to run up printers' bills that he might be unable to pay—it was the first time he had had a magazine in which he could be completely free. In its last issue he told his readers that the Unitarians had all that was good in Universalism, "without its revolting and mischievous errors." [5]

With equal candor he addressed his congregation. "I warned them that I was a fallible man, and that they must believe nothing simply because I believed or asserted it. . . . As yet we were learners and enquirers, and we must enquire earnestly for the truth, and hold ourselves ready to embrace it, let it come in what shape it may, and follow it, let it lead whithersoever it will." [6] His preaching was not very different from the lecturing he had done for Fanny Wright, but it had a different tone and temper—and this made all the difference in the world.

He now wanted to be as much of a Christian as he could, and so encouraged in himself feelings that were at least in accord with natural religion.[7] But he says that his main purpose was still the service of man rather than the service of God; while he looked upon religious sentiments as things to cherish, as they were part of the make-up of human nature, he seldom bothered to ponder them as the expression of anything objective. "I had become a believer in humanity, and put humanity in the place of God. The only God I recognised was the divine in man, the divinity of humanity, one alike with God and with man, which I supposed to be the real meaning of the Christian doctrine of the Incarnation . . . I regarded Jesus Christ as divine in the sense in which all men are divine, and human in the sense in which all are human."[8] Such ideas were very much in the air at the time. Dr. Channing of Boston[9] was talking along much the same lines, and Brownson had already printed several of his sermons in the *Philanthropist*. Vague as all this was, it stood for Brownson as a sign-post pointing in the direction of the Catholic Church.

In Ithaca he had not been formally a Unitarian, but he had preached in such a way as to make it easy for him to pass into open communion with that body. When the *Philanthropist* failed, part of his livelihood was also lost. Therefore he now began to look for a Unitarian pulpit. While Sally went home with her babies to her widowed mother at Elbridge, her husband set out on his travels to find what he could. He wrote tenderly to her on August 24, 1832, from Brattleboro, Vermont: "I think of you often, my little boys come to me in my dreams. I embrace you in my sleep, but I awake alone. A kind Father above will yet smile upon us. The object of my journey I think will be answered. My good friends in Trenton gave me a new hat and coat, so I am decently dressed."[10] He had heard of a possible "call" from Troy, and enthusiastically commented, "Say what they will, New England has not the energy and free views of New York."

New York soon faded as a possible field of labor. On October 15th he wrote again to Sally to tell her how at Walpole, about ninety miles from Boston, "where have preached some of the greatest men of the order, I have been pronounced superior to any of them. Probably, this is exaggeration. My own conviction is, that I am inferior to all I have met in mere useless browsing, but superior in practical knowledge. I do not think that I have met here a clergyman who has so thoroughly sifted the human heart, or who is so capable of taking enlarged and comprehensive views of religion, as myself. I believe it is in my power to impart two ideas where I may receive one." [11] It is touching to see the innocent vanity of this tall gaunt man, grateful for a second-hand suit and pluming himself that his lack of learning was no disadvantage. This last deficiency was soon to be remedied, though a large part of his subsequent reputation for learning was due to his ability to make one idea do the service of two. The result was an invitation from the Unitarian church at Walpole at a salary of five hundred dollars a year. "Not large, but we can live on it," he commented. Supplemented by an occasional Lyceum lecture and his articles, he could manage sufficiently well.[12]

Walpole had a number of advantages. For one thing, it was beautifully situated on the east bank of the Connecticut river, with the town of Bellows Falls on the Vermont side, and the cascades and the rapids to delight the eye. Here, too, there was a more congenial and cultivated society than any he had so far known. Best of all, there was a little money to spare for books. In spite of what he had written to Sally, Orestes realized that he knew very little. Never again was he to call reading "useless browsing." It was with him ever afterwards a furious and relentless search for truth.

Now at the age of twenty-nine he taught himself French, and brushed up the scanty Latin he had acquired at Ballston—which meant learning it all over again. From that he went on in time to German and Italian and Spanish—in each case with nothing but a grammar and a dictionary and a Bible. Though he never learned to speak or even write any of these languages—that was not necessary for his purpose—a reading knowledge unlocked foreign literature for him, which was all he wanted. As soon as he had got enough French for it, he attacked Benjamin Constant's formidable five-volume work, *De la Réligion Considérée dans sa Source, ses Formes et ses Developpements.* He had already done some hard thinking, but without any direction except what he had obtained from Godwin and, to a lesser extent, Owen. And these were sociologists rather than philosophers. He now felt that it was necessary to get to the metaphysical foundations.

Self-taught scholars were typical of his time. There was, for example, Elihu Burritt, the "learned blacksmith" of Worcester, who mastered no less than forty foreign tongues. But Burritt was content with knowledge for its own sake; Brownson—like the self-made mathematician Bowditch—learned for a practical purpose, to use what he obtained. As compared with men who were soon to be his friends—Theodore Parker or even George Ripley—Brownson's reading was not wide. What he had par excellence was the faculty of bringing every particle of what he mastered into play, often before he had fully mastered it. He was before long to state his own concept of the function of the writer. "It will be because a man has felt with the American people, espoused their cause, bound himself to it for life or for death, time or eternity, that he becomes able to adorn American literature; not because he has lived apart, refused 'to serve society,' held lone reveries, and looked on sunsets, and sunrises." [13] What set Brownson in a special class was that, while being as American as Emerson or Thoreau, he had a broader world outlook. Writing exclusively for an American audience, he took a keen interest not only in European speculative thought but in European politics. He was in that sense the least provincial of Americans, and served them all the better because of his wide intellectual range. His catholicism led to Catholicism.

Yet he was never to be a man of many books, though in later life he was obliged to read many in order to review them. His sound belief was that a few solid works, thoroughly digested, were of far more benefit than a discursive skimming. His method then, and for some years to come, was to analyze whatever he read, chapter by chapter, writing out in a notebook what it was the author was trying to explain, illustrate or prove, and his own judgment on each point. The process was one that he was able to discard in time, so far as taking notes was concerned, for the simple reason that it became automatic and the habit of his mind. This was the painful way he attained to precision.[14] It should be added that nearly all the authors who put the deepest impression on his mind were those whom he had to read in a foreign language.

He discovered in Benjamin Constant a confirmation of his own ideas. Paley had only unsettled his mind, so much so that he told his Ithaca congregation that his doubts were first awakened when he read the *Natural Theology*.[15] And the almost officially accepted philosophy of Locke had not satisfied him. But in Constant he found the doctrine (such as it was) that the religious sentiment was a revelation made by the Invisible to the heart of man, and that the particular form of revelation—from the lowest fetishism to the highest monotheism—depended upon the receptiveness of the intelligence receiving it. Therefore one might trace in the history of religion a continuous ascent, with each new religious institution at once an advance upon what had preceded it and the stepping-stone to new and greater progress. Viewed in this light, the critical periods of upheaval in human history, however terrible they might be to those who were obliged to live through them, were essential to man's progress. So far from being hostile to religion, they prepared for its advance. This theory, Brownson remarked, "corresponded with my theory of the progress of mankind, and had for me many charms. I was prepared in advance to accept it, and did not at the time think of enquiring whether it really had any historical basis or not." [16]

It is easy to see how such an hypothesis had its attractiveness for a serious and callow young man. He could apply it to his own personal history. As long ago as the time when he was editing the *Gospel Advocate* he had written, "All faith must arise from intuitive perception, experience, or from testimony. Intuition is undoubtedly the strongest evidence we have." [17] In the *Philanthropist* he was more definite, because more personal. "My own experience must count for something to myself. Theology has been to me something more than mere speculation. It engrossed my infant mind. It is connected with all I remember of my early visions. . . . When reason first awoke, while thought was unfledged, it was to me a subject of deep and cherished feeling. In the early dawn of youth, there was nothing I so much dreaded as that which should divert my thoughts from the Deity, and interrupt my silent but blissful intercourse of soul with the Father of our spirits. . . . I was never alone. I felt the Deity with me. I loved his presence. . . . [Such feelings] were not learned from books; they were not produced by human teachers. They were the simple feelings of nature, the child led by instinct to seek the embrace of its parent. . . . I have thus a witness within, and having this witness, I find its testimony corroborated by the whole of external nature." [18]

Now it was comforting to have the facts he had reached by intuition corroborated and confirmed by a distinguished French philosopher. Nor did Brownson ever deny the value of such intuition. In his later contribution to philosophy he retained this ontologism, making it as Catholic as he could by modifying it and stating it more clearly, and then by fighting for it against many Catholic critics. Without it, he would never have found his way into the Catholic Church. In fact, without it he would have probably remained a life-long infidel.

There was something else he took out of Benjamin Constant, and from some of the other philosophers he was soon to read; that too, he thought, corroborated his own experience and observation. It was that no religious institution could be permanent. With Protestantism he was growing disillusioned. But at least he could still look upon it as being a necessary (though also temporary) stage in the development of religion, one that superseded a Catholicism which, having served its purpose, had to be abandoned. He had longed for an authoritative teacher; now he believed he must give up, once and for all, the hope of finding one. Ever upwards and onwards was to be his motto. Catholicism had failed because it had been too spiritual, by neglecting to take into account—in its asceticism and other-worldliness—the whole nature of man. But Protestantism had also failed: it had been too materialistic. What was necessary was the establishment of a dialectic harmony of spirit and matter, body and soul.[19]

Heine at this time was making the same antithesis—which has also been applied to Hellenism and Hebraism—but it is a question whether Brownson had heard of Heine as yet. He had, however, a great journalistic flair for ideas that were vaguely "in the air." Hardly ever did he read a philosopher without making the claim that he had anticipated his ideas. So now he set out his discovery in an article for the *Christian Examiner* in 1834. Catholicism was something the world had outgrown; on the other hand, Protestantism was merely a destructive force, whose rise proved no more than that there was a need in man which Catholicism could not supply. What then was needed? His answer came pat: "It is to labor directly for a new religious institution, church, or organization, which shall embody the most advanced ideas and sentiments of the Race, and be *The Church of the Future*." [20]

For once Brownson's logic had failed him. What he was virtually proposing was a new synthesis of Protestantism and Catholicism—and this meant (according to his hypothesis) that two corpses had to be combined in order to make a living body. Yet his main error was not philosophical but historical: the only thing he had to learn was that the "dialectic harmony of spirit and matter, body and soul" he postulated, had already been achieved by Catholicism. He could not know that what Constant had in mind was not the official teaching of the Church but the Manicheean extravagance so steadily resisted by the Church, the rigor that Constant found, in his own day, exemplified, though in a much milder form, by Jansenism. To Brownson the categories appeared very neat: all that was necessary was to work for the founding of a new religious institution which should contain in itself "what was wanting in the religion of the past—the principle of its own progress." [21]

The sky was gilded with hope, a hope that was stimulated by the contacts he now had with a Boston that was within fairly easy reach. He met Dr. Channing, to whose sermon, "Likeness to God," he owed so much, and though the Doctor was, as usual when encountering strangers, somewhat distant at their first meeting, Brownson named his third son (born on January 4, 1834) after him. Soon he was exchanging pulpits with Channing as well as with Ripley, who became his closest friend, the one to whom he most fully unbosomed himself. Emerson and Convers Francis were beginning to talk with interest about the new luminary, even if others were still a little uncertain as to how far he could be relied on.

Channing highly approved his concept of social reform as reflecting his own. For at the beginning of 1834, when the *Unitarian* was founded, Brownson contributed an article in which he declared: "To effect any real reform, the individual man must be improved . . . The reformer's concern is with the individual. That which gives the individual a free mind, a pure heart, and full scope for just and beneficent action, is that which will reform the many. When the majority of any community are fitted for better institutions, for a more advanced state of society, that state will be introduced, and those institutions will be secured." [22] It represented a complete recantation of Owen and Fanny Wright. So pleased was Bernard Whitman, the editor of the *Christian Register,* with the letters that Brownson had written for his columns that he suggested that they be gathered into a volume and published. [23] And from George Ripley came a suggestion in a letter dated March 26, 1834, that was two years later to be acted upon when Brownson set up his Society for Christian Union and Progress in Boston.

What Ripley had in mind was not that Brownson should come to one of the Boston Unitarian churches—which he knew only too well were attended by those frosty in respectability—but to do a work addressed to people "who are disgusted with Orthodoxy and insensible to Liberal Christianity in any of the modes, in which it is now presented, but who would gladly hear the Gospel preached in the spirit of Jesus, in a way to meet their intellectual and moral needs." [24] Which meant that Brownson should become a free-lance Unitarian evangelist. In that work Ripley told him that his former connections with scepticism fitted him to deal with "larger and different classes of men from those to whom you now have access." It was a suggestion to which Brownson acknowledged his grateful indebtedness when he wrote *The Convert* and referred to one whom "from motives of delicacy I do not name. . . . He encouraged me, and through him chiefly I was enabled to remove to Boston and commence operations." [25] If it was a couple of years before Brownson was able to act on Ripley's suggestion, it was something that he turned over continually in his mind until the time was ripe.

Meanwhile Brownson had been approached by the church at Fall River, with an offer of a thousand dollars a year as salary. But Brownson, writing to his wife on February 19, 1834, and signing himself "Yours forever and longer," showed himself far from enthusiastic. The salary was "nominally large, but really not better than six hundred in Walpole." The congregation was small and timid, and he felt in his bones that he would not suit them nor they him. "They want me to go to Boston and raise up a New society —also to New York city—But, I shall stay at Walpole if they make me out five hundred dollars, let who will call—I see no place so pleasant, no people I like so well as Walpole and my own congregation. We may look farther and not fare so well. I am anxious to get home, to kiss my wife and children and sit down in peace." [26]

In the same letter he indicates that Canton, Massachusetts, had also made an offer. But he did not think he would accept, as all he would gain would be access to Boston and Cambridge libraries. It was, however, this offer that he closed with in the end. Though he may have known no congregation that he liked better than the one at Walpole, it is clear that some of its members did not like all his opinions. This was indicated in the resolution they passed on March 10th, mentioning differences between them and their minister but also expressing their friendly regard for him and testifying to his ability and high moral character.[27] By the middle of May he was formally installed at Canton, Ripley preaching the sermon with Adin Ballou—as he tells us in his *Autobiography* [28]—gracing the occasion with his presence. It was a sign that at least some of the Universalists had now forgiven Brownson's defection.

At Canton Brownson was immensely busy. Not only did he preach four sermons a week, but he was in increasing demand as a Lyceum lecturer and temperance speaker. He did not stand for prohibition, however; in fact, it is rather remarkable how this supposedly wild man managed to steer clear of all such extremes, including abolitionism. Perhaps the explanation is to be found in his Fourth of July speeches, several of which were published as pamphlets. There his sobriety of judgment is plain. His grasp on philosophical and constitutional principles prevented him from ever being really as radical as he sometimes seemed to be.

He was not what may be called a natural orator, as he himself recognized. During the early years of his public speaking he was always so nervous that at the end of his address or sermon his clothes were wringing wet from perspiration. His gestures, too, were at first a bit awkward. But he gradually schooled himself and learned to adapt his voice and manner to what he was saying. He never attempted overpowering outbursts, and he left the tricks of the orator to Edward Everett, whom he invited to speak for the Lyceum he had founded at Canton. What he had was well thought-out matter, and he never failed to impress people with his deep sincerity. One of his chief complaints about the New England style of public speaking was that it was lacking in life, directness and earnestness, being more studied and polished than powerful.[29] Nobody could bring that charge against him.

Somehow he still found time for study. It was remorseless study, late into the night, varied only by writing and preaching. For stimulation he would visit Boston, and for relaxation he would play chess for hours on end with his eldest son, a boy of six who was later to edit a chess magazine. In 1887 he was to write describing these games to his younger brother Henry. Their father would sometimes send for him at eight in the morning, and they would play until midnight, without respite. "How our dear father loved a game of chess!" he exclaimed. "How he suffered, if he lost a game."[30] The preacher's library was still small, but Ripley lent him books—Jouffroy and Cousin and Saint-Simon, all of whom put a stamp upon his mind. Of the first two he was to say, "[They] served me hardly less by their errors than by their truths,"[31] but he denied that Jouffroy had genius and was less affected by him than by Cousin and Saint-Simon. At this time he was so great a devotee of the French eclectics as to propose to James Walker, who was then minister at Charlestown and subsequently professor of philosophy and finally president at Harvard, that he bring out a volume of selections in English translation. He was deterred only because Walker expressed some doubts as to whether such a book would sell.[32]

One day in December, 1835, there descended upon him a young man with a long nose and a prickly manner who said his name was Henry Thoreau. He was in his junior year at Harvard, and at that time impoverished students were allowed a year's absence in order to teach school and so earn a little money. He applied to Brownson to help him get a job, and Brownson, finding that he knew German, "sat up until midnight talking with him," after which they "struck heartily to studying German, and getting all they could of the time together, like old friends." [33] How long Thoreau taught school at Canton is not quite clear. Mr. Canby says that the class mark-book shows that he kept no record until March 19th, which was the beginning of a new term, and that he was absent again until April 29th.[34] But we hear that he acted as tutor to the Brownson boys, and Henry Brownson quotes a letter Thoreau wrote his father from Concord on December 30, 1837, to say: "I have never ceased to look back with interest, not to say satisfaction, upon the six short weeks I passed with you. They were an era in my life— the morning of a new *Lebenstag*. They are to me a dream that is dreamt, but which returns from time to time in all its original freshness. Such a one I would dream a second and third time, and then tell it before breakfast." [35] He goes on to let Brownson know that he had tried to look him up in Boston and that his purpose was to ask him again for help in obtaining employment, "for say what you will, this frostbitten 'forked carrot' of a body must be fed and clothed after all." He hoped to get another appointment as a school-teacher or a private tutor.

It was something to get such a letter from a man who so hated letter-writing, and the letter was an excellent one, not calling for the post-script: "I add this . . . merely to ask if I wrote this formal epistle. It absolutely freezes my fingers." But perhaps Brownson remembered that Henry's regularity in the class-room left very much to be desired, or Henry decided that he preferred a life of solitude and leisure, for which work now and then as a day-laborer sufficed to provide. Brownson got him no job, nor do we hear of Thoreau again in Brownson's life. The closest he was to come to re-emerging in connection with the man who had given him his intellectual awakening was when Isaac Hecker, Brown-son's first Catholic disciple, stayed with Mrs. Thoreau at Concord and did his best to convert her son.

When Brownson gave up his connection with the Workingmen's Party, he did not cease to be interested in the condition of the workingman. It was merely that his association with Fanny Wright had convinced him that "it was idle to attempt to carry out our plans by means of . . . a proletarian party." [36] His reason for this view was sensible; he argued that, except in the cities, the artisans were only in a minority. The United States was still an agricultural country. But he pushed the matter further: in any contest for political power, capital and credit would always be forces too great for labor. "The movement we commenced could only excite a war of man against money, and all history and all reasoning in the case prove that in such a war money carries it over man." [37] He therefore argued that his policy must be that of trying to induce all classes of society to coöperate in efforts to better the condition of the workingman.

He kept up a correspondence with Samuel C. Allen, the minister of Northfield, who was the Workingmen's candidate for governor of Massachusetts. Allen wrote to him as a Christian Socialist on August 18, 1834: "The gospel was good news to the poor, *as a class,* and the poor were the laborers, whether held in actual slavery, as most of them were, or not. I believe it was intended to have its first effects *in the present world,* and if there is any one cause which has contributed more than any other, to defeat its influence, and to render the mission of Jesus frustrate, it is that its ministers, as well as other priesthoods, have attached themselves to the privileged class . . . The clergy, as a class, have always been ready to come in for a share in the advantages of the privileged classes, and in return for the ease and convenience accorded to them by these classes, to spread their broad mantle over them . . . Their sympathies have always been with the rich and the powerful, and it seems not to have entered into their conception that the gospel was designed, or had any efficacy, to *change the condition of the poor as a class.* . . . That cannot be Christianity which adapts itself to the social order which it was the prime design of Christianity to change." [38] Oh, yes, the clergy would do what they could for the alleviation of the sufferings of individuals, but what was wanted was legislation, to which the science of political economy pointed the way. "What have governments been," Allen asked, "and what are they now, but the combination of the rich and powerful to increase their riches and extend their power?" It was what Brownson himself still believed—and in which there is a great deal of incontestable truth: he was before long to say the same thing with even greater emphasis.

But he was not for the moment to be drawn into active politics, and certainly not into alignment with the Workingmen's Party; in so far as he had any political connections, he was an independent Democrat. All his youthful associations had been with those who belonged to this party.[39] Yet Father Elliott, the first biographer of Father Hecker, writes of Brownson speaking for the Workingmen in New York in the old Stuyvesant Institute on Broadway in 1834.[40] He drew upon an article Hecker wrote when the author's memory was manifestly in error.[41] The Workingmen's Party disappeared in New York in 1831 [42]—factions of it being absorbed by both the Whigs and the Democrats—and the old Stuyvesant Institute was not completed until 1838. The party Hecker had in mind was that of the "loco-focos," but there is no evidence that Brownson ever spoke in New York in their behalf.[43] The first record we have of Brownson in New York—and then he did speak in the hall Hecker mentioned—was in 1841. It must have been that occasion that Hecker had in mind. We can well believe that Brownson's immense energy and his great voice made the windows rattle.[44]

But though Hecker, writing—or more probably dictating [45]— fifty years after the event, may have been vague about some of his details, there is no reason to doubt what he has to relate about his own political activities in 1834. Though he was only fifteen then, he and his two brothers were all aflame with revolutionary ideas. Indeed, Isaac at the age of eleven proposed and put through a number of resolutions on the currency question at ward meetings. He was tall for his years. We hear of the Heckers pasting up posters at three o'clock in the morning and of their printing on the backs

of the bills they took in at their bakery a quotation they believed
to come from Webster: "Of all the contrivances to impoverish the
laboring classes of mankind, paper money is the most effective. It
fertilizes the rich man's field with the poor man's sweat." When
the authorities tried to stop this on the ground that they were
defacing money, they argued—successfully—that they were not defacing it at all, only printing something on it.[46]

As this has been a convenient place to introduce the young
Hecker, it will be also a convenient one to give an account of the
first impression made upon him by Brownson. In 1841 Brownson
stayed with the brothers and their mother at their house on Rutgers
Street—where Margaret Fuller and Alcott also stayed when visiting
New York a couple of years later [47]—and the first Hecker letters to
Brownson were written in this year. Isaac Hecker described him as
looking like Proudhon, the French Socialist, and of really being
the American Proudhon, though he never went so far as to say *La
propriété, c'est le vol.* "As he appeared on the platform and received
our greeting he was indeed a majestic man, displaying in his de-
meanor the power of a mind altogether beyond the ordinary. But
he was a philosopher, and that means that he could never be what
is called popular . . . He never seemed to care much about the
reception his words received, but he exhibited anxiety to get his
thoughts rightly expressed, and to leave no doubt about what his
convictions were . . . He never used manuscript or notes; he was
familiar with his topic, and his thoughts flowed out spontaneously
in good, pure, strong, forcible English . . . But to stir the emotions
was not in his power, though he sometimes attempted it; he never
succeeded in being really pathetic." The thesis was always that
"Christ was the big Democrat and the Gospel was the true Democratic platform!" Hecker adds that none of them had the remotest
idea of the Catholic Church at the time. Christianity was interpreted by them as being altogether a social institution.[48]

It was a strange but lifelong friendship that was begun between the
young German baker and the gaunt Vermont preacher in the rusty

swallow-tail coat he always wore. The youth at once decided that he had met a great man.[49] Soon Isaac was struggling through a volume of Kant propped up in front of him while he mixed the dough in the bakery. Soon he was to be at Brook Farm. At the end it became a kind of race to see which of them—he or Brownson —should get into the Catholic Church first, each man alternately prodding the other or holding the other back. Taken together, they might almost be regarded as the two lobes of the American Catholic mind of their age, operating separately and in very dissimilar fashion for a single purpose. In the case of each the initial steps of approach to the Catholic Church were through social reform.

[1] *The Convert,* pp. 82, 141.

[2] *Ibid.,* p. 142.

[3] *Ibid.,* p. 143.

[4] *Early Life,* pp. 51–52. "The fact is," he concluded, "nearly all churches, as now organized, are unfriendly to the full development of religious or mental excellence . . . To preach righteousness, then, I do not conceive it necessary to urge you to join a church." (*Ibid.,* p. 55.)

[5] Vol. II, p. 255.

[6] *The Convert,* p. 147.

[7] *Ibid.,* p. 150.

[8] *Ibid.,* pp. 148–149.

[9] As there are several Channings to be mentioned in these pages, it might be as well to say at once that, except when the distinction is drawn, the Channing referred to *tout court* is this one, Dr. William Ellery Channing, the most celebrated of his family. The poet, William Ellery Channing, was his nephew; so also was the Unitarian minister, William Henry Channing.

[10] Letter in the possession of Mrs. Thomas H. Odiorne.

[11] *Ibid.*

[12] His writing, however, could have brought him in very little, as it was all done for denominational magazines that paid their contributors poorly, if at all.

[13] *Boston Quarterly Review,* Vol. II (1839), p. 26.

[14] *Early Life,* p. 86.

[15] *Ibid.,* p. 60.

[16] *The Convert,* p. 158.

[17] *Gospel Advocate,* Vol. VII, p. 37.

[18] *Philanthropist,* Vol. II, p. 113, *et seq.*

[19] *Early Life,* p. 87.

[20] *The Convert,* p. 161.

[21] *Ibid.,* pp. 161, 162.

[22] Quoted in *Early Life,* pp. 96–97.

[23] *Ibid.,* p. 101.

[24] *Early Life,* p. 105.

[25] *The Convert*, p. 177. Doran Whalen, after arguing, rather unnecessarily, that the reference could not be to Emerson, as Henry Brownson supposed, says confidently that the unnamed person was Bancroft. (*Granite for God's House*, p. 156). Bancroft did, indeed, obtain a political appointment for Brownson, but was mainly a political friend. Moreover Brownson had been at work in Boston for a couple of years before Bancroft performed this service. There can be no doubt that Ripley was referred to.

[26] Letter in the possession of Mrs. Odiorne.

[27] *Early Life,* pp. 109–110.

[28] P. 254.

[29] *Early Life,* p. 89.

[30] Letter in the Notre Dame Archives dated February 22, 1887. Perhaps it was this remorseless playing that gave Orestes Junior a distaste for anything except the problems of chess. His chess journal, he told Henry, was not for games, "nor for those *professional* chess players who do nothing but play for money. I cultivate and practice the problem part or ars poetica of the game." And he goes on to mention to his brother, who was also interested in chess problems, some of the little novelties he had invented.

[31] *The Convert*, p. 279.

[32] *Early Life,* p. 121.

[33] William Ellery Channing, *Thoreau, the Poet Naturalist*, p. 32.

[34] *Thoreau*, p. 58. Mr. Schlesinger (*op. cit.,* pp. 31–32) is in error about the year. It was not the summer of 1835 but the spring of 1836 that Thoreau was at Canton.

[35] *Early Life,* p. 204. There is no indication, however, that it was Brownson who "roused his enthusiasm for external nature"—or that Brownson had any such enthusiasm himself, to any marked degree.

[36] *The Convert*, p. 138.

[37] *Ibid.,* 138.

[38] *Early Life,* pp. 114–115.

[39] *Early Life,* p. 179.

[40] *Life of Father Hecker*, p. 19.

[41] *Catholic World*, Vol. XLV (1887), p. 203.

[42] Helen L. Sumner in Commons's *History of Labor in the United States*, pp. 268–269.

[43] This question of dates has recently been carefully examined by another Paulist, Father Vincent V. Holden, in his *Early Years of Isaac Thomas Hecker*, pp. 32, 47, 52.

[44] *Catholic World*, Vol. XLV (1887), p. 466.

[45] I surmise the dictation because the name of Bronson Alcott is consistently spelled "Olcott."

[46] Elliott, *Life of Father Hecker*, p. 17.

[47] *Early Life,* p. 341.

[48] *Catholic World*, Vol. XLV (1887), pp. 204, 205, 206.

[49] *Ibid.,* p. 208.

CHAPTER V

The Church of the Future

No RELIGIOUS BODY was at this time quite so respectable as the New England Unitarians, or any Unitarians quite so respectable as those of Boston. The movement, which had begun as a protest on the part of some of the Congregationalist ministers against the rigors of Calvinist "orthodoxy," was in its inception hardly more than a rejection of the doctrine of man's total depravity and an assertion of man's free-will. But it speedily became frozen into an orthodoxy of its own. Those of the old school, led by the wealthy and learned and redoubtable Andrews Norton, still regarded themselves as the official exponents of Unitarianism, and would have no truck with the younger and more liberal men. The result was that one after the other—Emerson and Ripley and Bradford and Dwight, to mention only a few—had resigned their pulpits or were soon to do so. Even Theodore Parker was eventually obliged to organize the Twenty-eighth Congregational Society and to preach in the Old Melodeon on Washington Street. It was an idea he had taken over from Brownson.

Some of these ministers were, of course, men who were temperamentally quite unfitted for the ministry—though hardly less so than others who had become ministers to obtain a life of learned leisure. That was probably true of Emerson. As for Bradford, Andrews Norton told him after hearing him preach that his sermon did not have a single one of the qualities a good sermon should have; and Dwight completely forgot for the whole week following his ordination that he was to preach the coming Sunday and neglected to prepare anything for his congregation, so engrossed was he in

61

his music. But all these men were at least recognized as "belonging" to Boston respectability. Brownson was an uncouth outsider, and a dangerous man—as all his antecedents showed.

Yet Brownson, perhaps just because he did not "belong," was all the more able to diagnose the ills of the denomination with which he was now affiliated. "It is negative, cold, lifeless, and all the advanced minds among Unitarians are dissatisfied with it," he wrote. The "advanced" minds—and he came into contact with no others —were, like himself, "sick at heart with what they had, and were demanding in their interior souls a religious institution of some sort, in which they could find shelter from the storms of this wintry world." [1] Of them all he was the man most hopeful of the future and the most disposed to act.

There had been a time when he had looked to Dr. Channing, whose printed sermons had reclaimed him from the infidelity of his Fanny Wright period, as "the one who was to take the lead in this work of reorganization." The fervent little saint with his frail body did, indeed, radiate a spiritual light. But though Brownson retained his affection for Channing, and even some admiration, he came to the conclusion that he was not, after all, a great man. What he noticed very shrewdly was that Channing was "felicitous, when the matter did not lie beyond his depth, in summing up and clearly stating the various points in a question after it had been thoroughly discussed by more vigorous and original, but less polished and graceful minds than his own. . . . [But] as he usually chose his time for intervening with adroitness, he not infrequently received the credit due to those who had gone before and enlightened him" [2]—among whom of course Brownson grouped himself.

This was a disappointment to Brownson, for he had picked Dr. Channing out as the new Messiah. With candor and some humor Brownson admitted that he had fleeting thoughts that he himself was to be the "providential man," but he added that he put this idea from him. "I could not be more than John the Baptist, or the Voice of one crying in the wilderness. . . . My business was not to found the new church, but to proclaim its necessity, and to prepare men's minds and hearts to welcome it." [3] If even that notion strikes some people as slightly comical, it might be remembered that history proves amply enough that one of the best means of getting a prophecy fulfilled is to keep on reiterating the prophecy. By assuring everybody that the Church of the Future was about to come, Brownson felt that its founder would be drawn forth. He adds, however, "The truth is, I was quite modest in claiming for myself only the part of the Precursor, and many came to ask me, if I was not myself a second Messias." [4] Such a suggestion he always pushed aside. He knew what his own function was: "Not finding among my friends and acquaintances the 'representative man,' and waiting till he should reveal himself, I concluded to commence a direct preparation for his coming." [5] To effect this he did two things: he founded a society and he published a book.

At the beginning of 1836 he had moved to Chelsea, separated from Boston only by the Mystic river, and there he found a pleasant house on the Common, from which he had a view of the harbor and of the blue hills of Canton, and where he could indulge his love of gardening. He had no definite pastoral duties, except that of preaching, and Charlestown was only a few minutes away on the ferry. It was Boston that he had wisely chosen for his experiment of bringing the gospel of the Church of the Future to the unchurched— those who had broken away from "orthodoxy," even to the extent of inclining to infidelity, and who could not find a home in the icy and aristocratic Unitarian churches.

In starting his Society for Christian Union and Progress—with meetings first held in the Lyceum Hall and then in the Masonic Temple—he made one serious mistake from which he never wholly recovered. Instead of addressing his gospel to everybody, he confined it to the working classes. Not yet was he completely free from Fanny Wright's apron strings. Nor was he altogether clear of his Godwinism: he made a special point of giving his children no religious instruction; they were on principle to be left free to choose their religion for themselves.[6] He did not doubt what their choice would be.

Obviously, if he was the prophet of the Church of the Future, he should have preached it to all kinds and conditions of men. His original intention was just that—to get hold of people of any social class who were resentful of religion or suspicious of it. It was on the advice of others—and against his better judgment—that he was led to narrow his appeal. He had to admit the force of their argument: "The poor have the gospel preached unto them"; it was the working classes who had in the main drifted away from church attendance—the well-to-do still regarded it as being at least socially advantageous. Moreover, the working classes would be attracted only by preaching of a kind that was specially directed towards them and they would stay away from services attended by well-dressed people. Yet he had declared that the chance of social betterment lay, not in a class-war, or even in the efforts of organized labor, but in enlisting the sympathies of all classes for the working man. Rather unfortunately he was persuaded to capitalize his reputation for radicalism in the belief that it would enable him to reach those who could not otherwise be reached.

He was, however, not much of a radical by now, if he had ever been really very red. Nor did he conceive his to be solely a social mission. At first he thought of calling his association the Society for Social Reform, but he soon decided that the name did not correctly convey his purpose: Christian Union and Progress —that was what he had in mind. All the words were carefully chosen: the Union of all men, the concept of a progress to which no bounds were to be set, and all on a Christian basis. The result was that he was accused by many of the prosperous of being a social fire-brand, while genuine fire-brands were often disappointed in him, as they wanted him to go further than it had ever been his intention to go. When he urged social reform, the opponents of the Trade Unionists read more into his words than he meant; when he tried to redress the balance by bringing out another side of his doctrine, the working men called him a betrayer.[7] As so often happened with him, Brownson got himself into difficulties by trying to steer a middle course. The general consensus of opinion in Boston was that it was a good idea to bring the agrarians and infidels under some sort of religious influence—but that Brownson was the wrong man to attempt it, as he was too violent a democrat. He was imagined to be exciting the poor against the rich.[8] One of his sermons—that preached on July 10, 1837, was especially denounced as unchristian and blasphemous. But of this we have a fairly extended report made by Elizabeth Peabody. She sent Brownson her notes with a letter to say that she was much affected by his glowing faith and that a lady "of most careful religious education and of early piety" exclaimed to her afterwards, "this is preaching Christ!" [9]

It was hardly that; it was rather preaching faith in man. But Brownson held that to deny faith in man was "the most fatal of all infidelities, more fatal than scepticism in the Bible, or even in God. . . . Want of faith in man hardened the soul into selfishness, and made it inefficient for any good. He further asserted that "the doubt of being able to live Christ [is] the most fatal scepticism of our times . . . and that this fatal infidelity prevented all progress, for it not only belonged to the vicious, but the respectable, not merely to the uneducated, but equally to those who occupied the shining places of literature and science, so that it pervaded the clergy in the pulpits." It was this last phrase that brought the accusation of "blasphemy" upon him; but as Miss Peabody asked in a footnote to her report, "Is it not so?" [10]

Yet in spite of his radicalism—or because of the curiosity it aroused—he was invited to preach at the Park Street church, the citadel of "orthodoxy" in Boston. He was the only Unitarian who ever preached there. It is clear that he was making a great stir.

There are other indications of this. Harriet Martineau arrived at Boston about this time. The little Englishwoman had a habit of speaking her mind plainly, and threw herself into the abolitionist cause—which was none of her business—but showed herself a shrewd observer in writing her two books on America. Perhaps the fact that she had lost all sense of taste and smell and most of her hearing made her all the more tart—though Mrs. Trollope succeeded in being far more waspish without that excuse. Whatever the reason, Harriet Martineau offended many people. Her independence of judgment was shown by her printing Brownson's sermon, "The Wants of the Times," as an appendix to her *Society in America*. How much she could have heard of what Brownson said is questionable, but she studied the preacher's earnest manner and got hold of a report of what he had said, so she pronounced that "The rising-up of this new Church in Boston is an eloquent sign of the times." [11] She listened as best she could through her famous black ear-trumpet, sitting in the front row. That this made her a conspicuous figure did not trouble her at all. For she had a way of using her trumpet as a kind of sceptre, dropping it, as Hawthorne was to record, whenever anyone said anything with which she disagreed, and so silencing him. [12] But when she talked to Emerson, he gallantly told her that it acted as a chain between them, making them Siamese twins. And she was quite pleased when Dr. Flint wrote a sonnet on the instrument.

She was sufficiently caustic on the American habit of making speeches on the slightest provocation, and noted the absurd grandiloquence of the orators and the way they flattered their audiences. She noted also that Americans were much too intelligent to be taken in by such things, but thought that the speeches nevertheless did a good deal of harm by inducing a cynical frame of mind and that the listeners were too naïve not to give a kind of half-assent. [13] "For my own part," she said, "I remember no single instance of patriotic boasting from man, woman or child, except from the rostrum; but from thence was poured enough to spoil the auditory for life, if they had been simple enough to believe what they were told. But they were not." [14] All of which acid criticism made Miss Martineau's praise of Brownson the more significant.

She was by no means disposed to accept the estimate given Boston by its "first people" but added, "I certainly am not aware of so large a number of peculiarly interesting and valuable persons living in near neighbourhood, anywhere else but in London." [15] On first meeting Dr. Channing she was disappointed in him, saying that he had "an unfortunate habit of suiting his conversation to the supposed state of mind of the person he is conversing with, or to that person's supposed knowledge of a subject on which he wants information." [16] But she immediately recognized that Brownson was at least as forthright as herself and very much in earnest. Her younger brother, James, was already one of the leaders of English Unitarianism, and was to die in 1900 at the age of ninety-five; so she took a family interest in Unitarian ministers. She was never to meet one of whom she so fully approved as she approved of Brownson.

Dr. Channing also came to approve, though at first he had been a little distant. Brownson, when invited to preach for him, told the congregation that it was one of the Doctor's sermons that had saved him from infidelity. Yet at the one o'clock dinner that day Channing, who suffered from stomach trouble, gave his guest so very Unitarian a dinner that the tall Vermonter had to go out afterwards to a hotel and get another before he was sufficiently fortified for the evening service. He was in truth a rough and rustic figure among the fastidious and almost lady-like "liberal" Christians. On the ferry between Chelsea and Boston everyone knew the tall preacher in the swallow-tail coat who always carried a pile of books under his arm and a chaw of tobacco in his cheek. In his hearty way he used to get into conversation with strangers and, more likely than not, into a metaphysical argument. For the first time his astounded fellow-passengers would hear the outlandish names of Kant and Jouffroy and Constant and Saint-Simon and Cousin.

In order to have some sort of an organ, he had taken over the editorship of the *Boston Reformer*. It was not just the kind of magazine he really wanted, but for the moment it served as a further outlet for his flood of ideas. Those who took the trouble to read it, discovered that Brownson was against the working men joining the so-called Workingmen's Party. They would gain nothing by it, he told them; instead they would have their veins sucked by a new and more hungry swarm of demagogues.[17] Though he discussed politics freely enough, it was usually to deal with first principles; he held himself free to criticize political happenings as an independent. In a general way, however, he regarded himself as a supporter of the Democratic administration, detesting the Whig alliance with the financial interests. But so far from venting any extreme doctrine, even at this time, he wrote: "This is our democracy. We admit the sovereignty of the people when the question is of many or few; we deny it when we speak absolutely. The people are not sovereign. There is no sovereign, but the Infallible, that is, God, that is again, the Right, the Just. We dissent from the democratic party, therefore, and of course from the popular doctrine of the day, by denying the infallibility of the people, and the absolute sovereignty of their will. We make justice paramount to the popular will, and acknowledge allegiance to the popular only so far as it is in harmony with our convictions of the Just."[18] Yet while he thought that the commonly accepted notion of democracy fell short of this, he preferred Van Buren to General Harrison: "We cannot without pain think of him in connexion with the presidency."[19] George Bancroft wrote to him after the 1836 election, when Harrison was defeated, to tell him: "You are, (what so few are) rooted and grounded in the true doctrine . . . I am too familiar with your writings, not to know that our principles accord in many essential points."[20]

Bancroft went even further than that. When he was appointed by Van Buren to the post of Collector of the Port of Boston, he sought to secure Brownson to the party cause by offering him in 1837 the position of Steward of the Marine Hospital at Chelsea at a salary of $1,600 a year. It also meant a good stone house rent-free

as a residence.[21] The duties were largely nominal and Brownson
was sorely in need of a regular income, as he got very little out of
his paper or the Society for Christian Union and Progress. The
numbers who attended his services there were not very large—aver-
aging three hundred, says Hecker [22]—and they were mostly poor,
and little assistance was given by the well-to-do. Brownson had,
therefore, been obliged to do a good deal of Lyceum lecturing to
make ends meet. In spite of which, he at first declined Bancroft's
offer, fearing that it would hamper his freedom in political discussion. Only when assured that he would be allowed to say exactly what he thought and that Bancroft considered him all the
more useful as an independent whose general trend was in favor
of the Democratic party, could he be induced to accept.[23] Had he
been ambitious, a great political career was already opening for him.

It was at this time that he founded the *Boston Quarterly Review*.
What he had in mind was explained when he came to write *The
Convert:* "Whoever reads the five volumes of that Review . . .
with the view of finding clear, distinct, and consistent doctrines on
any subject, with the exception of certain political questions, will
be disappointed; but whoever reads it to find provocatives to thought,
stimulants to enquiry, and valuable hints on a great variety of important topics, will probably be satisfied." He knew he was often
being reckless, but even his dogmatism was deliberately intended
to excite thought. "The public," he confessed further, "read me
more or less, but hardly knew what to make of me. They regarded
me as a bold and vigorous writer, but as eccentric, extravagant,
paradoxical, constantly changing, and not to be counted on, not
perceiving that I did not want to be counted on in their sense, as a
leader whom they could safely follow, and who would save them
the labor of thinking for themselves." [24]

As editor and virtually sole contributor to his magazine, Brownson certainly showed himself the reverse of a politician. Instead, he
was a political philosopher—and in that capacity, as in every other,

he was at times given to impulsively following the dictates of his heart rather than his head. He was soon utterly to ruin himself politically, and without the slightest regret. In 1857 he wrote, "Almost the only blunders I ever committed in my life were committed when I studied to be politic, and prided myself on my diplomacy." [25] While one may wonder what these occasions were, it must be admitted that his notion of politics was itself an offense. He looked upon it as entwined with the highest metaphysical concepts, or as an application of religion to life. What the Parson said to William Cobbett would fit Brownson almost equally well: "Your religion seems to me altogether political." [26]

So closely were politics and religion related in his mind, that it is often difficult to distinguish between them. In attempting to bring into being the Church of the Future, Brownson was trying equally hard to establish a perfect political organism. In his special kind of theocracy—for it was at bottom that—it did not much matter whether one called the implementing institution the state or the Church. Yet he never regarded his Society as doing more than point in the direction of the institution he counted upon to arise when it had discovered its founder. "I saw clearly enough," he said afterwards, "that with more confidence in myself, a firmer grasp of my own convictions, a stronger attachment to my own opinions because they were mine, and a more dogmatic temper than I possessed, I might easily succeed, not in founding a new Catholic Church, but in founding a new sect, and perhaps a sect not without influence." [27] If that passage tempts readers to punctuate it with exclamation points, it only stated the fact. So far from trying to turn his Society into a sect, Brownson did all in his power to prevent it from turning into one. He wished to unite men, not to divide them still further. And dogmatic as he may often have sounded, he looked upon himself as "still a learner, a seeker after truth. I always told my congregation that I was looking for more light, and that I could not be sure that my convictions would be to-morrow what they are to-day." [28] When preaching, as in the case of what he wrote in his *Review,* all that he wanted to do was to throw out provocations to thought and investigation. In spite of his aggressive manner, he was a very humble man.

His *New Views of Christianity, Society, and the Church* appeared at the same time as Emerson's first little volume, *Nature.* Together they may be taken as representing what was in the air of Boston.

Of *New Views* Brownson might almost have said what he said of Hosea Ballou that, though none of his heresies were original, they were all original with himself. He modestly remarks in his Preface: "I believe my views are somewhat original," though he goes on to show that he had derived them largely from Heine, Saint-Simon, and Cousin. He writes as a professed Unitarian, but offers his opinions tentatively: "He who helps me correct my errors is my friend." [29] Nothing could be fairer than that.

He begins the body of his little book by postulating that the Church has failed. But he also postulates that "Christianity, as it existed in the mind of Jesus, was the type of the most perfect religious institution to which the human race will, probably, ever attain." [30] Equally striking is his insistence on the God-Man, though he gives this a meaning of his own.[31] What he is thinking of is the union of body and soul, the material and the spiritual. Catholicism represents, in his mind, a spirituality divorced from the material, and Protestantism—in so far as it *is* Protestant—the material divorced from the spiritual. Whatever of the spiritual it has retained, has been retained from Catholicism.

His central idea is that of the Atonement, the reconciliation effected between God and man—the function of the God-Man being to stand between spirit and matter.[32] But the Church, according to him, committed what he calls its "original sin" by changing the atonement into the redemption.[33] After that, as a consequence, it tended to be merely a spiritual institution, cut off from natural reason and the civil order.[34] Perhaps it was inevitable that he should think of that "spirituality" as something more or less Manichean. "Marriage was sinful," he naïvely tells us, "till purified by Holy Church. The song and dance, innocent amusements, and wholesome recreations, though sometimes conceded to the importunities of Matter, were of the devil. Even the gay dress and blithesome song of nature were offensive. A dark, silent, friar's frock was the only befitting garb for nature or for man." [35]

On the other hand, "This rebellion of Materialism, of the material order against the Spiritual, is Protestantism." [36] Such a rebellion was needed, but has erred by excess, so that now the spirituality of the Orient has come in to correct it once more—and is again swinging to the other extreme. "Some are becoming so spiritual that they see no necessity of matter." [37] At no moment does Brownson seem to have the faintest inkling of the fact that the very balance he is arguing for has been preserved—and with considerable difficulty, in the face of heretical extravagances—by Catholicism.

In his ignorance of history, he argues: "We must build a new Church" [38]—which was to be a synthesis of Catholicism and Protestantism. The Second Coming of Christ would occur when the concept of the Atonement had been fully realized. [39] Catholicism was the church of the middle ages, and so would not do; and Calvinism, apart from a few Protestant modifications, was only an extension of Catholicism. [40] Once he had hoped that the Universalists would offer the necessary basis for fusion, but he has come to find in it merely "a parallelism which has no tendency to union." [41] The one hope, therefore, is in Unitarianism, the only body that seeks to realize the Atonement. Whatever philosophy Unitarians have so far lacked had now been provided by Cousin. [42]

In all this, it need hardly be said, is a theory of history which disregards or distorts a good many historical facts. "The Church," Brownson tells us, "was the result of three causes, the Asiatic conquests of the Romans, the Alexandrian school of Philosophy, and the Christian movement of the people." [43] "The time has come for a new Church, for a new synthesis of the elements of the life of Humanity," [44] growing out of Unitarianism but by no means confined to it. "One man, however, stands out from this body, a more perfect type of the synthesis of Eclecticism and inspiration than any one else. I need not name him." [45] Going on, he makes it clear whom he has in mind by quoting from Channing's sermon.

The little book is not all abstract in argument. One passage that reveals Brownson's warm heart should be quoted; in it he rises to genuine eloquence: "The human mind, allied as it is to the Divine, is too valuable to lie waste or to be left to breed only briars and thorns. Those children, ragged and incrusted with filth, which throng our streets, and for whom we must one day build prisons, forge bolts and bars, or erect gibbets, are not only our children, our brother's children, but they are children of God, they have in themselves the elements of the Divinity and powers which when put forth will raise them above what the tallest archangel now is." [46]

What the book shows is that Brownson was, without knowing it, more orthodox than the ordinary Universalist and Unitarian of his time; that he was already more Catholic in feeling than the ordinary Protestant. Perhaps it is not a matter for great surprise that the Boston *Pilot,* the Catholic diocesan organ, in its issue for July 2, 1836, advised him to study the character and doctrines of the Catholic Church, and expressed confidence that he would find within it all that he was striving for outside. His reply was that he had immense respect for the Catholic Church, and did not share the Protestant hostility towards it, but that the mission and usefulness of Catholicism were ended. Though this was, in one way, more insulting to Catholics than raging bigotry, they smiled; from their vantage point Catholics are able to see who are walking towards the Church, and they recognized Brownson among them.

It was characteristic of the man that he should review his own book, though he waited until 1842 to do so. Then in the pages of the *Boston Quarterly* he wrote what was not so much a review as a long postscript which brought his views up to date. [47] He confessed again his debt to the Saint-Simonians, but differed from them in one important respect. They regarded Christianity as outmoded; Brownson thought the Church outmoded.

But now that he was actually nearer to Catholicism he seemed to be further away in his extraordinary interpretation of the Incarnation and Atonement. Precisely because he began to feel himself being drawn into the vortex of Catholicism, he struggled wildly against it and tried to escape by clutching at the straws of his fantastic theorizing. This was his view: "Not in Jesus alone does the divine ideal incarnate itself, but in every man, in all men. . . . This is the great truth which the Church must now accept and bring out, a truth which is nothing but the generalization of the particular truth she has always contended for. . . . The actual church is an organization for the worship of God as revealed in one individual; the church of the future will be an organization for the worship of God as revealed in all men." [48] Catholicism was true only up to the fifteenth century; now the philanthropist is the priest. The state is more Christian than the Church and its ministers are the politicians.[49] "The ideal will still be the Christian ideal, and [the new Church] will be a true Christian church, as true for the future as the old church was for the past." [50]

Then follows a characteristic attack on the "Church" as Brownson knew it: he understood by that term every form of organized Christianity. As he had said several times before, he said again: "She declares all men equal before God, and yet tolerates, nay, upholds the grossest inequality before society; she declares poverty a virtue, and riches a sin, and yet gives the chief seats to the rich and baptizes their means of gain. She declares that the poor are blessed because theirs is the kingdom of heaven, and frowns upon all measures likely to be effectual in securing them the possession of that kingdom on earth. She has no ideal. She looks back and sighs merely for her lost dominion." [51] Writing like that, he was not far from the kingdom of God.

Yet there were times when Brownson seemed to be—even according to his own definition—much too much of a Protestant. His

gospel was social rather than supernatural. In his public pronounc-
ments he appeared to think almost solely of man's felicity on earth;
heaven was something too far off and too uncertain for him to hold
up as a prize. The word "mystical" was to him then—and even during his Catholic days—a word to be used contemptuously. This was
because he used it in the sense of "poetical" or even "hazy"; he was
not thinking of mysticism as implying an experience of God. Perhaps this was because he was now encountering too much spurious
mysticism among the Transcendentalists, his associates at this period.
We know that Bronson Alcott set him down as unspiritual, finding
him too hard-headed for his taste. In spite of all this, however,
Brownson never quite lost sight of God as the soul's infinite satisfaction, or failed to perceive that this was something not to be
fully satisfied in man's mortal estate. One of the complaints he
brought against the Unitarians was his old complaint against the
Universalists: that the heaven they promised in the world to come
was only in the natural order,—"a sort of natural beatitude, such as
some Catholics have supposed might be enjoyed in the least unpleasant part of hell." [52] In its general plan it was not essentially
different from Mahomet's paradise, though it lacked the houris.

All the same, the foundations for whatever belief Brownson had,
even in his Universalist days, was in something akin to mysticism,
heartily as he disliked the term. He could never forget the col-
loquies he had had, when a child, with God, or the apparitions of
the Blessed Virgin and the archangel Gabriel. However much be
allowed for imagination, he still considered that they had some reality. In the *Gospel Advocate* he had written, "Intuition is undoubtedly
the strongest evidence we have." [53] That and his reaffirmation of it
in the *Philanthropist* in 1832 bear quoting again: "My own experience must count for something to myself. Theology . . . is
connected with all I remember of my early visions . . . I was never
alone. I felt the Deity with me. I loved his presence. A consciousness
of it created my joy and waked my holier and better feelings." [54]
Now in the philosophers he was reading—even in Kant—he was

discovering what he thought to be a sound psychological basis for what he had already divined. Vague and undependable as he came to recognize this as being, it nevertheless was for him an Ariadne's thread through a gloomy labyrinth.

It was his unquenchable religious sense that was the real theme of the novel he published in 1840. Written as a series of letters in 1834 and 1835, *Charles Elwood, or the Infidel Converted,* was recast in fictional form and given to the world. Considered as a work of art, it is of no great importance: Brownson admitted in his Preface, "I have introduced too much fiction for a serious work, and too little, if I intended a regular-built novel." [55] It is, as a matter of fact, hardly more than a series of dialogues, plus Elwood's own ruminations (which are sometimes complete essays) and long speeches from him or one of the other characters. The plot is most rudimentary: Elwood is engaged to Elizabeth, who has recently been converted at a revival. Worked upon by the adroit (and unpleasant) minister, Mr. Wilson, she feels it her duty to break with Elwood, upon which Mr. Wilson comes to the attack, feeling that he now has a lever against the jilted lover. Instead, Elwood is incensed against him (and religion) until he meets the cultured Mr. Howard, who has just returned from abroad; this new friend tries to show him that, as he believes in truth, he cannot be an atheist but is (without knowing it) a Christian, after all. Then another minister, Mr. Morton (who may stand for Brownson himself) completes what Mr. Howard has begun. But there is no characterization and no incident worth mentioning. Elizabeth herself is all but forgotten in the metaphysical disquisitions. By the time Elwood is at last converted, Brownson presumably found that it would take too long to round out the romance; so we are merely told of Elizabeth, "I have planted wild flowers on her grave and watered them with my tears." With that perfunctory sigh of dismissal the novel ends.

The "turn" of the story, such as it is, is reached when the rejected Elwood seeks an aim in life by reforming society. He had done his best to become a Lockian, relying solely on "enlightened self-interest," but "some how or other this was not enough. The truth is, I professed one system, but in fact demanded the results of another. No reform can be effected without sacrifice, and sacrifice comes not from selfishness." [56] Of the Church he was soon to join Brownson makes Mr. Howard say: "What now passes for Christianity is Catholicism. Protestantism, so far as it is Protestantism, is not a religion, and the religion we find connected with it in the minds and hearts of Protestants, is merely what has been retained of Catholicism. . . . But at the epoch of the reformation [the Catholic Church] had finished its work, fulfilled its mission, and since then it has been a mere cumberer of the ground." For this reason he still looks for a new religious institution, though without seeing so much as its nucleus in any of the existing sects. [57]

The true preacher Brownson regards as being a prophet directly inspired by God. [58] Taking over something of the Quaker notion of the "Inner Light," he advocates—very inconsistently with his demand for institutional religion—an extreme Protestantism. While asserting the authority of the Bible, he acknowledges that error has crept into its pages. The evangelists and the apostles have tried to interpret Christ, but the Christian must go to Christ directly. For as it is now impossible to determine just what was the doctrine which has to be postulated as having once existed, it is the Christ of today who has to be sought by each individual man as his teacher. [59] It is a Protestantism which assumes that each soul has its own access to revelation.

A kind of pantheism is admitted into this scheme, although Brownson is careful to tell us that it is not "low" pantheism but that of Spinoza, "which some people have been foolish enough to call atheism." [60] Again inconsistently with pantheism of any brand, miracles are defended,[61] to offset Elwood's formidable objections to them at the start of the tale.[62] The conclusion is that from each sect a man should take what he feels to be true. The Calvinist has a truth—that of the sovereignty of God; the Arminian has a truth—

the freedom of the will; the Universalist has a truth, despite his so exaggerating it as virtually to exclude the idea of justice; the Trinitarian has a truth, though he tends to overlook God's unity. It follows that all the truths of the various sects should be added together; then truth will be obtained.[63] "Beware of exclusiveness," Brownson says. "Beware of denying. Seek always to comprehend. Know that the human mind never embraces unmixed falsehood, and cannot believe a pure absurdity. Range freely over all doctrines, analyze them all, and what you find in them which accords with human nature, as you find it in your own experience, or in the records of the race, hold fast and cherish, for it is the truth of God and profitable to man." [64] Again he says, "The Christianity here set forth is the Christianity of the universal church, though presented perhaps in an uncommon light. I cannot persuade myself that a new Christianity is here presented, but the old Christianity which all the world has believed, under a new aspect, perhaps, and an aspect more peculiarly adapted to the wants of the present age." [65]

On Brownson's own admission, the case for Christianity was deliberately put at a minimum instead of a maximum. By 1840 he had already reached a firmer basis for faith than the one he indicates. But he felt that he would be more successful in getting people to become Christians if he whittled Christianity down as much as possible. Yet the vigor with which he put what he had to say carries the reader along, and perhaps further than Brownson intended. He was not cast for the rôle of the trimmer. That he had done so much trimming in *Charles Elwood*—without obtaining any appreciable results—was at least one of the reasons why, when he became a Catholic, he stated the Catholic case with an excessive rigor. He had tried the policy of concession, and it had failed.

The most telling criticism of *Charles Elwood, or the Infidel Converted* was made by Dr. Wayland of Brown University in the *Christian Review,* who remarked that it was misnamed and should have had the title of *Charles Elwood, or Christianity Converted.* When Brownson reviewed his own novel, which he did in forty-five pages in his *Boston Quarterly,* he criticized himself for his too great a dependence on Cousin. Dissatisfied with the novel, he refused to allow a second edition to appear, though it was reprinted in England. Edgar Allan Poe, however, writing in *Graham's Magazine,* pronounced that "in logical accuracy, in comprehensiveness of thought, and in the evident frankness and desire for truth in which it is composed, we know of few theological treatises which can be compared to it." [66]

What we may see in these first two books by Brownson is that he was an eclectic, taking his notions from various sources in order to make a new synthesis, but always giving to what he took a novel twist that made it his own. He was making a serious attempt to think things through. If his ideas are often crude, he has at least many ideas and applies what he has read to his own problems and to those of society. His paramount authority is the truth itself, as he sees it, and not that of the Church or the Bible. Always, too, he shows a great warmth of sympathy with mankind; man with him was more than the institutions he has devised. It was still in the service of man that Brownson proceeded to his next step.

[1] *The Convert,* pp. 164, 165.
[2] *Ibid.,* pp. 167, 169.
[3] *Ibid.,* pp. 171–172.
[4] *Ibid.,* p. 176.
[5] *Ibid.,* p. 177.
[6] *Ibid.,* p. 113. Brownson says this was true of all the time he was a Protestant.
[7] *Early Life,* pp. 146, 147.
[8] *Ibid.,* pp. 149, 151.
[9] *Ibid.,* p. 152.
[10] The report and her letter are in *Early Life,* pp. 152–158.
[11] Vol. III, pp. 284–285. His sermon is given in Vol. III, pp. 342–359.
[12] Julian Hawthorne, *Hawthorne and His Circle,* p. 111.
[13] *Society in America,* Vol. I, p. 146.
[14] Another English observer, Dickens in his *Martin Chuzzlewit,* made gorgeous fun of the same thing. But it is worth pointing out that Dickens's cultivated American, Mr. Bevan, was a Bostonian.
[15] *Society in America,* Vol. III, p. 30.
[16] *Ibid.,* Vol. III, pp. 73, 74.
[17] *Early Life,* p. 170. The Party had disappeared in New York State, but in Massachusetts it still had a feeble life.
[18] Quoted in *Early Life,* p. 182.

[19] *Ibid.*, p. 183.

[20] *Ibid.*, pp. 184, 187.

[21] *Ibid.*, p. 211.

[22] *Catholic World*, Vol. XLV (1887), p. 470. Henry Brownson, however, says that the average was five hundred. (*Early Life*, p. 140).

[23] *Early Life*, p. 212.

[24] *The Convert*, pp. 196, 197–198.

[25] *Ibid.*, p. 95.

[26] *Rural Rides* (Everyman Ed.), Vol. II, p. 114.

[27] *The Convert*, pp. 178–179.

[28] *Ibid.*, p. 179.

[29] *New Views*, pp. v, viii.

[30] *Ibid.*, p. 7.

[31] For that matter, so did many of the Unitarians of that time. Not all were outright Socinians; many were Arians; others were fairly sound in their Christology.

[32] *Ibid.*, pp. 12, 13.

[33] *Ibid.*, pp. 17–18.

[34] *Ibid.*, p. 22–24.

[35] *Ibid.*, p. 25.

[36] *Ibid.*, p. 27.

[37] *Ibid.*, p. 54.

[38] *Ibid.*, p. 57.

[39] *Ibid.*, p. 65. Here there are traces of the revivalistic Protestantism of the period. This supposed that with every soul brought to salvation, the Second Coming would be brought nearer.

[40] *Ibid.*, pp. 73–74.

[41] *Ibid.*, p. 78.

[42] *Ibid.*, pp. 79, 86–87.

[43] *Ibid.*, p. 82.

[44] *Ibid.*, p. 88.

[45] *Ibid.*, p. 93.

[46] *Ibid.*, pp. 99–100.

[47] This is reprinted in the *Works*, Vol. IV, pp. 57–78.

[48] *Ibid.*, pp. 64–65.

[49] *Ibid.*, pp. 68, 69.

[50] *Ibid.*, p. 75.

[51] *Ibid.*, p. 76.

[52] *The Convert*, p. 175. There was, however, no uniformity of belief here: some of his Unitarian friends believed in future disciplinary punishment, others in the annihilation of the wicked, but the majority—like himself—supposed that the future life would be merely a continuation of life on earth, under conditions more favorable for spiritual progress. (*Ibid.*, p. 174).

[53] Vol. VII, p. 37.

[54] Vol. II, p. 113.

[55] *Works*, Vol. IV, p. 173.

[56] *Ibid.*, p. 225.

[57] *Ibid.*, pp. 232–233.

[58] *Ibid.*, p. 257.

[59] *Ibid.*, pp. 259, 260.

[60] *Ibid.*, p. 276.

[61] *Ibid.,* p. 301.
[62] *Ibid.,* pp. 186, *et seq.*
[63] *Ibid.,* pp. 307, 308.
[64] *Ibid.,* p. 312.
[65] *Ibid.,* p. 315.

[66] Issue for November, 1841—January, 1842. Poe had an immense respect for Brownson's logical powers and actually went out of his way to bring them into two of his tales. In *X-ing a Paragrab,* referring to the New England editor who considered obstinacy not his foible but his forte, Poe says, "It would have required all the logic of a Brownson to convince that it was 'anything else.'" More critically in *Mesmeric Revelation,* when the hero wishes to bring himself to a belief in immortality, he remarks, "I had been advised to study Cousin. I studied him in his own works as well as in those of his European and American echoes. The 'Charles Elwood' of Mr. Brownson, for example, was placed in my hands. I read it with profound attention. Throughout I found it logical, but the positions which were *merely* logical were unhappily the initial arguments of the disbelieving hero of the book. In his summing up it seemed to me that the reasoner had not succeeded in convincing himself." This is a good indication of the reputation Brownson had among his best contemporaries before he became a Catholic.

CHAPTER VI

Horrible Doctrines

OF ALL THE SOURCES from which Brownson had so far taken his leading ideas—Constant, Cousin, Jouffroy, and Saint-Simon—it was Saint-Simon whom he considered "in our day the truest interpreter of the thought of Jesus." [1] But Saint-Simon merely confirmed the doctrine that Brownson claimed already to have discovered for himself. His "Christology was the unity, not union, of the Divine and human, and the Incarnation symbolized the unity of God and man, or the Divinity manifesting himself in humanity, and making humanity substantially divine." [2] Yet as a Catholic Brownson adds, "I imbibed no errors from the Saint-Simonians, and I can say of them as of the Unitarians, they did me no harm, but were, in my fallen state, the occasion of much good." The same thing was true of his other philosophical guides. The same thing was true of his association with the Transcendentalists—though, in their case, he borrowed nothing and benefitted only to the extent of receiving the stimulation of discussion. If any borrowing was done, it was rather that many of them borrowed from him. The severest of their future critics was at this time one of their leaders.

When he started the *Boston Quarterly Review* he was prepared to fill up most of the pages himself. He did, however, occasionally print articles by other people—Bancroft, Ripley, Margaret Fuller, Alcott, John S. Dwight, Theodore Parker, and Elizabeth Peabody: much the same set who were to become better known as writers for the *Dial*. And Emerson was invited to contribute. When it was proposed that the Transcendentalists have a magazine, Brownson offered [3] (through Bronson Alcott, with whom he claimed kinship) the *Boston Quarterly* to be their organ. But many of them did not like the argumentative and opinionated man, and Emerson feared that his expansiveness and truculence would swamp them all. Margaret Fuller, too, insisted on the *Dial,* writing, "Hearts beat so high, they must be full of something"—though as to just what that something was neither she nor anybody else had any very definite notion.

The Transcendentalists were, however, upon the whole well advised to bring out their own little magazine with its lilac cover, even if they never succeeded in pushing its circulation beyond three hundred copies. Transcendentalism was too sensitive a plant to entrust to the over-vigorous hands of a Brownson. Alcott described how Brownson and Jones Very, the poet, met and tried to talk to one another. They found themselves "sundered by spaces immeasurable. . . . Very was unintelligible to the proud Philistine." [4] It was so with others besides Brownson. And others besides Alcott, when pulled up sharp by Brownson's logic, tried to dismiss it as Philistinism.

Yet celebrated as the *Dial* was to become, several of its backers were disappointed in it and wondered if a mistake had not been made in rejecting Brownson's offer. Alcott, assuming his best Connecticut Swami manner, pronounced his judgment in his diary: "It satisfies me not, nor Emerson. It measures not the meridian but the morning ray; the nations wait for the gnomon that shall mark the broad noon." [5] Parker put the matter more bluntly when writing to Convers Francis on December 18, 1840, by comparing the *Dial* to "a band of men and maidens daintily arrayed in finery" and the *Boston Quarterly* to "a body of stout men in blue frocks, with great arms and hard hands, and legs like the Pillars of Hercules." [6]

Thoreau had written to Brownson on seeing the first number of the *Boston Quarterly,* "I like the spirit of independence which distinguishes it. It is high time that we knew where to look for the expression of *American* thoughts." [7] And William Henry Channing was to say when it ended: "Take it all in all, it was the best journal this country has ever produced." [8] But though Ripley wrote an article on "Brownson's Writings" for the first number of the *Dial,* and Brownson was counted among the leading Transcendentalists, he was only very loosely attached to the movement.

He did, however, attend some of the meetings of "the Club," and F. H. Hedge was not quite accurate in saying, "Brownson met with us once or twice, but became unbearable, and was not afterwards invited." [9] Actually this "club of the like-minded," as they first called themselves—"I suppose because no two of us thought alike," as James Freeman Clarke commented [10]—sometimes met in Brownson's house in Chelsea. What was true was that "they could only meet, these minds, by soaring up in the fog." [11] And Brownson, however queer some of his ideas may have been, was at least not foggy. He was, nevertheless, as much a member of the Club as most of those who attended.

As to just how much of a Transcendentalist he was is another question, as it is, for that matter, a question as to precisely what was a Transcendentalist. Mr. Goddard insists that to understand the New England movement it is necessary to understand Kant. [12] And he quotes Emerson's lecture, "The Transcendentalist," in proof. Yet about all that Emerson indicates is that the term was borrowed from Kant. There is no evidence that the Transcendentalists—except perhaps for Hedge and Parker and Brownson—knew much about Kant at first hand. It was Emerson who said, "I suppose all of them were surprised at this rumor of school or sect, and certainly at the name of Transcendentalism, given nobody knows by whom, or when it was first applied." [13] Something was no doubt taken over—mainly in the way of hints—from Kant and Fichte, Schelling, Hegel, and Schleiermacher, as also from Coleridge, Wordsworth, and Carlyle; but Emerson again let the cat out of the bag with, "Who has not looked into a metaphysical book? And what sensible man ever looked twice?" [14] By that standard nearly all the Transcendentalists were extremely sensible people. Lindsay Swift himself comments: "Their features were composed and their minds attuned

to the Immensities and the Eternities when this discursive sage
[Alcott] was asked 'whether omnipotence abnegated attribute.' Indeed, these Transcendentalists often found themselves enjoying
seraphic moods." [15] Yet perhaps the phrase of Schleiermacher, "The
soul's sense of things divine" summed up what they had of positive
content, though probably the best statement was that given by
Brownson of the "New School": "Some of them embrace the
Transcendental philosophy, some of them reject it, some of them
ignore all philosophy, plant themselves on their instincts, and wait
for the huge world to come round to them. Some of them read
Cousin, some Goethe and Carlyle, others none at all. Some of them
reason, others merely dream. . . . The movement is really of American origin, and the prominent actors in it were carried away by
it before they formed any acquaintance with French or German
metaphysics; and their attachment to the literatures of France and
Germany is the effect of their connexion with the movement, not
the cause." [16] In a later issue of his *Review* he explains: "By *intuition*
we understand merely the power of the soul to perceive ideas, and
by ideas we mean objects or realities of that world which transcends
time and space. All ideas—and we use the term in the original
Platonic sense—are transcendental. In asserting man's power to
perceive them, we coincide with the transcendentalists; but in
asserting, as we also do, that it is out of the soul, out of the *me* and
not in it, that they exist, and that we perceive them, we depart
from what we suppose is a characteristic feature of American transcendentalism." [17] Once again we find in his *Review*: "The dominion
of Locke is broken up, and he now has only a few adherents, and
they are men of yesterday, who can exert no influence on to-morrow.
The tendency is just now to an opposite extreme, to what among
us is called Transcendentalism, a system of philosophy—if that may
be called a system, which disdains all system—which builds on an
order of facts, proceeding from an origin which *transcends* the
senses and the operations of the understanding. The source of this
order of facts is called by some Instinct, by others Spontaneity, and

by others still Inspiration. They are intuitive and immediate." [18]
The truth is that the attempt to make Transcendentalism philosophically respectable, by finding for it a German origin, is something that did not belong to the time. All that the Transcendentalists
really agreed upon was the negative point of the rejection of the
sensism of Locke, who until then had been the ruling philosopher
in America.

Locke needed to be rejected, for though he had started with the
scholastic maxim, "Nothing is in the mind which is not first in the
senses," he interpreted it in such a way as virtually to rule out everything except sense knowledge. "From this grave peril," writes the
first historian of the movement, "the Transcendentalist found an
escape in flight to the spiritual nature of man, in virtue of which
he had an intuitive knowledge of God;" adding, "To the human
mind, by its original constitution, belongs the firm assurance of
God's existence." [19] Yet they were not ontologists, in the sense of
Descartes or Malebranche; they had no consistent body of thought,
and for system substituted aspirations. In its extreme form Transcendentalism was not so much "a deification of nature"—for its
adherents were not pantheists, even if Emerson's "Brahma" is the
most succinct expression of radical pantheism to be found—as a
deification of the soul.[20] Even so, as Frothingham admits, there
were relatively few thorough-going Transcendentalists, though
there were many people of all shades of opinion on the fringe of the
movement who were often grouped with it.[21] "As a philosophy," he
tells us, "it is abstract and difficult—purely metaphysical in character." [22] As a matter of fact it can hardly be said to have been metaphysical at all: if taken as a disconnected series of poetic hints, it
may be granted a good deal of value; it cannot be seriously considered
as a system of coördinated thought.

It was, however, poetry that had a religious character. Frothingham is quite correct in talking of the Transcendentalists' "Mounts
of Transfiguration"—on which he acknowledges that they usually
did not manage to stay for long.[23] But while Transcendentalism no

doubt "possessed the character of indefiniteness and mystery," it is too much to claim that it possessed all the chief qualifications of a gospel.[24] Frothingham calls Alcott the leader of the movement, not Emerson, and says that Alcott was a mystic where Emerson was a seer. Yet even he confesses that Alcott's "Orphic Sayings" would in ordinary prose sound like commonplace. They would, indeed. The man not only looked like Micawber, he often talked like Micawber. Thoreau complained that he was "forever feeling about vainly in his speech and touching nothing." Nevertheless, Alcott was in many ways genuinely impressive, this tall "sky-blue man"—to quote Thoreau again on his friend—with his springing step, his corn-tassel fringe of hair around his balding head, surmounted by strange-looking hats. He was perfectly ready to play the rôle of Messiah, and one day told Brownson "in a transcendental paroxysm": "I am God, I am greater than God. God is one of my ideas, I contain God. Greater is the container than the contained. Therefore I am greater than God." [25] About the same time, as complacently admitted by himself, he horrified Dr. Channing by attempting to prove the identity of the soul "in its diviner action," with God.[26] He talked very well—the one thing he could really do —and Miss Peabody had reason for thinking him the greatest teacher she had ever known.[27] He might be considered a humbug had he not been so transparently innocent, with a complete lack of knowledge of this wicked world. And he did have the "thin streak of genius" with which Odell Shepard credits him,[28] on the strength of which he rubbed along somehow—with the financial aid of his friends—until his daughter Louisa rescued him. It is very easy to laugh at such a man; what should be felt is a reverence for the goodness in him, as it was to a greater or less extent in all the Transcendentalists. If some of them—all of them at times—talked a vast quantity of nonsense, they also said many things that were illuminating and profound. To regard them as coherent thinkers would be absurd; it is not so absurd to regard them as saints.

Yet nobody could be quite so devastating about a Transcenden-

talist as another Transcendentalist. Elizabeth Hoar decided against
Thoreau, "I love Henry, but I do not like him." [29] To Emerson,
who admitted to having, like puss, a retractile claw,[30] if Alcott was
"the magnificent dreamer," "this wandering emperor," he was also
"a tedious archangel." [31] Thoreau was very fond of Alcott—"the
best-natured man he knew"; then came the shattering but—"but
the rats and mice make their nests in him." And much as Emerson
admired Margaret Fuller, he confessed that whenever they met he
could not repress a slight shudder. This may have been because
there was "something labyrinthine and glamorous" about her;
more likely it was because she was so distressingly plain. With her
bony face she talked incessantly, asking sphinx-like questions, but
being only too willing to answer all questions into the bargain.
Though she was not a good writer, and usually even a rather bad
one, she could now and then produce a fine sentence such as, "In
Egypt, too, the Sphinx, walking the earth with lion tread, looked out
upon its marvels in the calm, inscrutable beauty of a virgin's face,
and the Greek could only add wings to the emblem." [32] Not quite
right, but still grand. Emerson had to say of her—in criticism that
applied to all the Transcendentalists—"Margaret often lost herself
in sentimentalism. . . . [She] was really bent on truth, but too
indulgent to the meteors of her fancy."

Few of them were well read. Emerson did hardly more than dip
into books, fishing there for aphorisms to be thrown out glittering
in his lectures, or for names with which to besprinkle them. The
incongruity of their linking often reminds one of that masterpiece
of absurdity, Richard Alfred Milliken's "The Groves of Blarney":

> There's statues gracing
> This noble place in—
> All heathen gods
>   And nymphs so fair;
> Bold Nepture, Plutarch,
> And Nicodemus,
> All standing naked
>   In the open air.

It was for a long time the fashion at Harvard to talk in quotation marks about Emerson's "education"—sometimes even with an exclamation point or a query. But that did not matter; he was a man of unique genius, and the essay on *Nature* which he published in 1836 had the matter in it for a dozen poems. To the Ticknors and their like, who had returned with their German Ph.D.'s, he seemed of course an untrained man. For his part, he noted that intellectual science—by which he meant philosophy—"has been observed to beget invariably a doubt of the existence of matter"; therefore he refused to deal with metaphysics. Once for all, he dismissed logic with "The Soul holds itself off from a too trivial and microscopic study of the universal tablet." Even Idealism was to him no more than "a useful hypothesis." His was a beautiful spirit, full of religious sentiment of a kind—of the kind that Harriet Martineau sometimes found in the professed atheist. So far from affirming even the objectivity of nature, he decided to treat it *als ob,* as though it had objectivity—and to let it go at that. All he lived for was the burning instant of poetic insight, saying, "There is a depth in those brief moments which constrains us to ascribe them more reality than all other experience." Genius and religion were virtually identified in his mind, but so far from being arrogant, in the sense of asserting a special place for himself, he insisted that all men possessed genius, which he called "the fine innuendo by which the soul makes its exaggerated claims." The actuality of all else he was content to leave an open question.

If Emerson was no scholar, Theodore Parker was no philosopher. He had read more than any other man in Boston and owned more books than any other man—not so large a collection as Ticknor's but a better working library. Yet as a scholar he was half-baked, in spite of his enormous erudition; his guileless trust in the higher criticism of the *Theologische Jahrbücher* gave him away. When he asked in one of his early articles: "What scholarship can compare with the German? Where are the English classical scholars who take rank with Wolf, Heyne, Schweighauser, Wyttenbach, Boeckh, Herrmann, Jacobs, Siebelis, Hoffman, Siebenkees, Müller, Creutzer,

Wellauer, and Ast? Nay, where shall we find the rivals of Dindorf, Schäfer, Stallbaum, Spitzner, Bothe, and Becker, and a host more?" the irritated reader felt like asking why he should have these Teutonic numskulls thrown at him, and was inclined to reply by inventing Humpf and Krumpf and Stümpeldrinck and Schnotz.[33] Parker's literary ambitions came to little in the end. It was as a popular preacher that he attained his fame, and he was modestly sure that the version of Christianity he preached would be "the religion of enlightened men for the next thousand years." [34] With him, as with other Transcendentalists, the revelations of the soul were all that mattered. "If it could be proved," he declared, "that Jesus never lived, still Christianity would stand firm and fear no evil." [35] For him Christianity had dwindled into humanitarianism; as Brownson was to say later, he was not a heretic but an infidel.

Old-fashioned Boston Unitarians were shaken by such men. Even Dr. Channing thought that the Transcendentalists were falling into a kind of ego-theism. The danger besetting them, he told Miss Peabody, was that "they sometimes mistake their individualities for the Transcendent." [36] As for Andrews Norton, he was positively shocked. Sitting alone in his darkened study, he meditated the attack he soon made "On the Latest Form of Infidelity." It was nothing to him that the young men at Harvard, referring to another work of which he was the author, called his beauteous daughters "The Evidences of Christianity." What he saw was that Christianity was being undermined, and to protect it he brought his big guns into operation. He was answered by Ripley and Parker (who wrote under the name of Levi Blodgett), and Brownson also dealt with him—more cleverly than anyone else. His article in the *Boston Quarterly Review* on "Unitarianism and Trinitarianism" opened with "When we heard this work was announced as actually published, we trusted it would wipe out that suspicion of infidelity, which had long been attached to the author." [37] Here was a man who based his whole case on history and logic; how could one call this denier of religious intuition a Christian at all? Andrews Norton had commanded the last stand of the conservative Unitarians, and had been routed.

But people could, after all, be Transcendentalists and yet respectable. What Brownson did before 1840 came to a close outraged even most of the Transcendentalists who, though they might be liberals in theology—and even liberals in politics, so long as it was merely a matter of theory—hardly bargained for Brownson to appear in a more radical garb than any he had so far worn. Not that they were exactly surprised by what happened; at any rate they were not surprised after it had happened. This was the sort of thing that showed that he had been a leveller all the time. How right they had been in looking askance at his Society for Christian Union and Progress.

Democrats of course could be tolerated. They were not often to be found among the first Boston families. But some of the intellectuals inclined in their direction—George Bancroft, for example—though Emerson spoke for others when he said that, while the Democrats had the best cause, the Whigs had the best men. The Democrats, he decided, were destructive, not constructive.[38] Even intellectuals knew on which side their bread was buttered. One would have supposed that Brownson would have known that, too. While taking his own line in the *Boston Quarterly,* what he had been writing was, upon the whole, in the interests of the Democratic party; and he had obtained his position at the Marine Hospital under the Van Buren administration. That in itself should have been sufficient to restrain him.

But no. He now succeeded in shocking the Democrats even more than he shocked the Whigs, who were secretly delighted to see him come out in his true colors. In June, 1840, on the very eve of the presidential election, he published his article, "The Laboring Classes." It was the very worst moment to discuss such a matter, which had little or nothing to do with the respective merits of Van Buren, who was running for a second term, and of General Harrison, who was trying for a second time. That a prominent Democrat should write as Brownson did was taken as proof positive that the party was made up of "Marat democrats," as old John Quincy Adams confided to his diary.[39] On every side Brownson was denounced. His party repudiated him in an effort to undo the damage he had caused. All in vain: the Whigs reprinted his article and distributed it by the hundreds of thousands to show what it was the President and his party really held. After Van Bureau had been beaten by the hard-cider and log-cabin slogan and a song chanted by drunken mobs, he fastened the cause of his defeat upon Brownson.[40]

Mr. Schlesinger, who has written what is the best criticism of this aspect of Brownson—in which he may be presumed to have had the assistance of his distinguished father—says of Brownson's article: "As analysis or as polemic, it deserves a high place in revolutionary literature," and calls it "perhaps the best study of the workings of society written by an American before the Civil War." [41] As a precursor to Karl Marx, he thinks Brownson inferior as a thinker but superior as a pamphleteer. And Professor H. S. Foxwell, in his brilliant introduction to Anton Menger's *The Right to the Whole Produce of Labour*—which is almost as long as the body of the book—says of "The Laboring Classes," in the page he devotes to Brownson, "This is socialism of the true Marxian type." [42] There is, however, no evidence that Marx had ever read Brownson, though as Dr. Menger remarks, Marx often went to some pains to conceal his indebtedness to his predecessors,[43] and yet studied everything that might contribute grist to his mills. Had he come across Brownson he would have found a polemical method that might have provided him with useful suggestions; Brownson's specific proposals could hardly have been of much service.

The fact is that the economic part of what Brownson wrote does not seem particularly startling today. Brownson did, it is true, assert the doctrine of the Saint-Simonians (and of his former political bed-fellow, the agrarian Skidmore) that the right to bequeath property was not a natural right but merely part of municipal law. He therefore argued—while defending private property as something natural to man—that the right to bequeath property be abolished.[44] Instead property should be redistributed after the owner's death, until all men were not merely economically equal in their stake in the prosperity of society, but quite literally equal in the amount of private property they held. Possibly he intended no more than to throw out an idea for discussion, as was his usual way, but this is what he wrote: "If all men are equal before God, if God be no respecter of persons, then he must have designed the earth to be possessed by them in equal portions; and if, as democracy asserts, all men have equal rights, then it follows that all have a right to equal portions. That is to say, according to both Christianity and Democracy, every man has a right of property to a portion of the whole, equal to that of every other man." [45]

That was bad enough, but what raised the fiercest storm was his attack on the industrial system, and his arraignment of the clergy as the upholders of the existing order. He had said the same things before, but as *obiter dicta* which had passed almost unnoticed; here he gathered them together, and produced them just when they would be sure to attract attention. Contrasting the state of the laborer who worked for wages with that of the slave, Brownson declared: "As to actual freedom one has just about as much as the other. The laborer at wages has all the disadvantages of freedom and none of its blessings, while the slave, if denied the blessings, is freed from its disadvantages. We are no advocate of slavery, we are as heartily opposed to it as any modern abolitionist can be; but we say frankly that, if there must always be a laboring population distinct from proprietors and employers, we regard the slave system as decidedly preferable to the system at wages." [46]

Those who were horrified by the economic attack found a convenient handle against Brownson in his attack on the clergy. Here again he merely repeated what he had been saying for years: "Christianity is the sublimest protest against the priesthood ever uttered, and a protest uttered by both God and man; for he who uttered it was God-Man. In the person of Jesus both God and man protested against the priesthood. . . . The priest is universally a tyrant, universally the enslaver of his brethren, and therefore it is that Christianity condemns him. . . . It may be supposed that we Protestants have no priests; but for ourselves we know no fundamental difference between a catholic priest and a protestant clergyman, as we know no difference of any magnitude, in relation to the principles on which they are based, between a protestant church and the catholic church. Both are based on the principle of authority; both deny in fact, however it may be in manner, the authority of reason, and war against freedom of mind; both substitute dead works for true righteousness, a vain show for the reality of piety, and are sustained as the means of reconciling us to God without requiring us to become godlike. Both therefore ought to go by the board." [47]

When Brownson was condemned for his article, he was not in the least abashed. In the next issue of the *Quarterly* he defended himself, reiterating most of his arguments. Now he gave another twist to what he had to say about the clergy: as they were not to be trusted, he thought that the politicians should be regarded as the priests, and the State take the place of the Church. Or rather he argued that what was wanted was a realization not so much of the union but of the identity of Church and State. This may make him appear as a forerunner of totalitarianism; what he was really proposing was a theocracy. The name by which it was to be called—whether Church or State—was immaterial.[48] Which was, to say the least, strange coming from a man who had just had the best possible reason for being disgusted with politicians.

"This holy kingdom," he wrote, "which Christ came to found on the earth, has been mistaken for the outward, visible church; and the church has therefore been held to be a spiritual body, a body corporate, independent in itself, and distinct from the body politic, civil society, or the State. This has given rise to a double organization of mankind; one for material interests called the State, and under the control of the civil government proper; the other for spiritual purposes, called the Church, and governed by laws and officers of its own, distinct from those of the State. Now to this we strenuously object. We would establish the kingdom of God on earth; but we would not have a *double* organization of mankind. We would have but a single organization; and this organization we would not call the Church, but the State. This organization should be based on the principles of the Gospel, and realize them as perfectly, as finite man can realize them." [49]

Mingled with that almost fantastic hopefulness, was a streak of gloom. Many times before he had asserted that, in any contest between man and money, money would be sure to win.[50] But if that were actually the case, it would appear that Brownson was wasting his time in making any protest. His pessimism—but also his insight —came out in what he had to say regarding the Western Lands as a refuge for the badly paid working men of the East. "Few, comparatively speaking," he pointed out, "of the proletaries, in any of the old states, can ever become landowners. Land there, is already too high for that. The new lands are rapidly receding to the west, and can even now be reached only by those who have some little capital in advance. . . . Fifty years to come, if emigration go on at the rate it has for fifty years past, will leave very little for the new emigrant." [51]

It is evident that by now Brownson had little expectation of seeing the Church of the Future come into being. No longer did he look for a new religious institution, as such; and Dr. Channing had ceased to wear the aspect of a Messiah. But the Church of the Future had, after all, been no more than a means to an end—and that end was the Kingdom of Christ on earth. What if he had to use a new instrument, and look for a "providential man" outside the ranks of the clergy? He clung more than ever to this idea after

Harrison had been elected and had been succeeded by the nonentity, Tyler. Society would recover itself at the next election: Brownson already had his Messiah picked out—it was John C. Calhoun.

This was no new enthusiasm. As early as 1824, when he was in Michigan, Brownson had hoped that Calhoun would seek the Democratic presidential nomination.[52] Now Calhoun wrote to him, saying that in general he agreed with his articles, though he could not assent to his inheritance propositions. The same thing was true of Theodore Parker and Bancroft (who was now blamed for his patronage of Brownson) and Charles Sumner.[53] They rather enjoyed his fulminations against the clergy, but flinched from his economic ideas. Only Emerson, oddly enough, gave full approval, writing to Margaret Fuller: "The hero wields a sturdy pen which I am very glad to see. I had judged him from some old things & did not know he was such a Cobbett of a scribe. Let him wash himself & he shall write for the immortal Dial." [54] But Dr. Channing wrote to Miss Peabody that he considered Brownson to have exaggerated the hard lot of the working classes, who were, if they only knew it, better off than the professional and business men with their cares of which the poor knew nothing. The remedies proposed were "shocking, or absurd." "To me," he confided, "the matter of complaint is, not that the laboring class wants physical comforts . . . but that they live only for their physical natures." [55]

That was not Brownson's view at all. In his January issue, immediately after the election, he cast his comments into a biting parable: "The lamb is necessary to the wolf; for without the lamb the wolf might want a dinner; and the wolf is necessary to the lamb, for without the wolf the lamb might fail to be eaten. 'Therefore,' says the benevolent wolf to the lamb, 'do not be hostile to us, nor excite your brother lambs against us; for you see we wolves and you lambs are mutually necessary to each other. We are as dependent on you for something to eat, as you are on us to be eaten.' 'But I don't want to be eaten,' exclaims the lamb in great trepidation. 'Not want to be eaten!' replies the wolf. 'Now that's odd. You and I are far from thinking alike, and I must needs consider you very unreasonable, and radical in your mode of thinking.'" [56] If that shows Brownson utterly unrepentant, his article for October, 1840, was not a whit more conciliatory than his first article on "The Laboring Classes." For there he told his readers, "No matter what party you support, no matter what men you elect, property is always the basis of your governmental action." To which his readers might have made the rejoinder that, if such were the case, there was hardly any good reason for relying on venal politicians instead of a venal clergy to bring about social reform. It was, at all events, not a sufficient reason why they should go to the trouble to vote for Van Buren rather than Harrison.

Looking back upon it all, seventeen years later, Brownson confessed that he could not, even then, read his "Horrible Doctrines" articles without being shocked,[57] but that he considered his convalescence to have dated from that moment. As for his main argument, he declared, "I am unable even to-day to detect any unsoundness in my views of the relation of capital and labor, or of the modern system of money wages." [58] "For my party," he added, "the act was impolitic, for myself it was necessary and prudent." The more he came to be regarded as a leader of the Democratic party, the less he was able to insist on social reform. Already he was conscious of the workings in himself of political ambition, and he no longer dared trust himself. Had he gone on any further, he was likely to forget all his early purposes. Therefore, he decided, "the best and shortest way, because the honestest and most straightforward, is, now before I become deeper involved, to come out and publish in the most startling form possible my whole ulterior thought, without circumlocution or reticence." [59]

About his courage—amounting to moral heroism—there can be no doubt. What is open to some question is whether he really supposed when he wrote his October, 1840, article that it would close his literary as well as his political career.[60] Such things do not have that effect. If he was assailed, it was mainly because people were trying to strike at Van Buren through him. He might well have believed, however, that the Democratic party would be sure to regard him as unreliable because of his radical outburst. In writing as he did, he therefore thought of himself as signing his own political death-warrant. But so far from his literary career being endangered, he had enormously increased his literary fame. Almost overnight he had become a national figure.

O.B. becomes a national figure.

[1] *Works,* Vol. IV, p. 101.
[2] *The Convert,* p. 209.
[3] His offer was made on October 19, 1839. (Higginson, *Margaret Fuller Ossoli,* p. 148).
[4] *Journals of Bronson Alcott* (ed. by Odell Shepard), p. 130.
[5] Higginson, *Margaret Fuller Ossoli,* p. 160.
[6] Frothingham, *Theodore Parker,* p. 139.
[7] *Early Life,* p. 206.
[8] The *Present,* Vol. I (1843), p. 72.
[9] Lindsay Swift, *Brook Farm,* p. 7.
[10] Cabot, *Emerson,* Vol. I, p. 249.
[11] Brooks, *Life of Emerson,* p. 106.
[12] *Op. cit.,* pp. 1, 2.
[13] Swift, *op. cit.,* pp. 6–7. Brownson's name for the movement was "the Newness," and that name was, at first, used as often as that of Transcendentalism.
[14] Centenary Ed. of Emerson's *Works,* Vol. II, p. 438.
[15] *Op. cit.,* p. 10.
[16] *Boston Quarterly Review,* Vol. III (1840), pp. 270–271. A generation later Hecker said much the same thing when reviewing Frothingham's *Transcendentalism in New England.* (*Catholic World,* Vol. XXIII, 1876, pp. 528–537). He added, however, that all that was true and good in Transcendentalism could be found in the works of Catholic writers, centuries earlier.
[17] *Ibid.,* Vol. V (1842), pp. 152–153.
[18] *Ibid.,* Vol. III (1840), p. 11.
[19] Frothingham, *Transcendentalism in New England,* p. 190.
[20] *Ibid.,* p. 204.
[21] *Ibid.,* pp. 198–199.
[22] *Ibid.,* p. 302.
[23] *Ibid.,* pp. 221, 222. He might have added—though this was probably something he never suspected—that it was a high-brow substitute for the orgiastic emotions of revivalism.
[24] *Ibid.,* pp. 302, 304.
[25] *Works,* Vol. VIII, p. 594. One may doubt whether Alcott cast what he had to say in this syllogistic form. But he was quite capable of the sentiment.
[26] Shepard, *Pedlar's Progress,* p. 176.
[27] *Ibid.,* p. 211.
[28] *Ibid.,* p. 155.
[29] *Emerson's Journals,* Vol. VI, p. 371.
[30] *Ibid.,* Vol. V, p. 331.

31 *Ibid.*, Vol. VI, p. 472; Vol. V, p. 494.

32 *The Writings of Margaret Fuller* (Ed. Mason Wade), pp. 133–134.

33 Commager, *Theodore Parker*, p. 45. Of course I do not mean to suggest that all German scholars are numskulls, but merely that to be unduly impressed by such names and then to try to impress others with them indicates something deficient in scholarship.

34 Frothingham, *Transcendentalism*, p. 319.

35 Commager, *Theodore Parker*, p. 75.

36 Peabody, *Reminiscences of William Ellery Channing*, p. 365.

37 Vol. II (1839), p. 384.

38 *Journals*, Vol. VI, p. 311.

39 *Memoirs of John Quincy Adams* (ed. by Charles Francis Adams), Vol. X, p. 345. There Adams rather quaintly lumps Brownson together with abolitionism, phrenology and animal magnetism.

40 Or so Brownson said. It is not unlikely that in a petulant moment Van Buren blamed Brownson's article for his own defeat. But no historian gives "The Laboring Classes" that amount of historical importance; few of them even mention it in connection with this campaign. The truth is that Van Buren was not personally popular, even among Democrats, and the United States was having one of its fits of delusion that a soldier can make a good president. "Tippecanoe" being the soldier available, he was elected.

41 *Orestes A. Brownson*, pp. 95, 96.

42 Pp. lxxxix–xc. Menger himself points out that Marx was completely under the influence of the early English socialists (p. 101) and gives some account of these, to which Foxwell adds in his Introduction. A less exciting, but more fully informative study of them is in Esther Lowenthal's *The Ricardian Socialists*, William Thompson, John Gray, Thomas Hodgskin and John Francis Bray. As to how far Brownson was influenced by them is uncertain. He mentions only Robert Owen and Godwin.

43 *Op. cit.*, pp. 101–102 *et passim*.

44 *Early Life*, pp. 262, 263, 264. *The Convert*, p. 249.

45 *Boston Quarterly Review*, Vol. III (1840), p. 485. This is distributism, not communism, but in a form in which no later distributist has ventured to propose it.

46 *Ibid.*, p. 368.

47 *Ibid.*, pp. 384–385.

48 *Ibid.*, p. 437.

49 *Ibid.*, pp. 437–438.

50 He asserted it once more in *The Convert*, p. 227. This, however, is only to say that the greed of man is likely to be more powerful than the benevolence of man. Money, as such, cannot compete with man, being, like machinery, only man's invention (or convention), which man can use either for a good or an evil purpose. Money is nothing in itself.

51 *Boston Quarterly Review*, Vol. III (1840), pp. 473–474.

52 *Early Life*, p. 178.

53 Pierce, *Memoir and Letters of Charles Sumner*, Vol. II, p. 168.

54 *Emerson's Letters*, Vol. II, p. 373.

55 Peabody, *op. cit.*, pp. 415–416.

56 *Boston Quarterly Review*, Vol. IV (1841), pp. 35–36.

57 *The Convert*, p. 230.

58 *Ibid.*, p. 260.

59 *Ibid.*, pp. 262, 263.

60 *Ibid.*, p. 264.

CHAPTER VII

Brook Farm

WHEN BROWNSON TRIED to be tactful, he usually succeeded only in being more than ordinarily tactless. Or perhaps it would be more correct to say that in making his tactical dispositions, he tended to forget general strategy. This was so when he decided to call the new single human organization he had in mind the State instead of the Church. He explained, "It made no difference to the character of the organization itself. . . ; it remained precisely the same; but by calling it the State instead of the Church, I would obtain for it more support." [1] The judgment was completely fallacious: whatever he called it, it was recognized as the control of society by religion; yet he believed that in all this he was thinking only of a return to what he conceived to be the true concept of the American Constitution.

The truth is that Brownson was much less of a radical than he appeared to be. The change that people thought they saw in him was one rather of change of means than of change of ends. In fact, all through this reputedly wild man's career, such was the case. While Brownson said that he considered the French Revolution one of the most glorious events in history, and that he planned to write a novel about it sometime—he actually held (and always had held) a very conservative view of democracy. He disliked the word itself, because of the meaning that had come to be attached to it, and insisted that the United States was not a democracy but a republic. It was a view that he was to develop in his book *The American Republic*. But he had reiterated from his Fanny Wright days on— and in the teeth of popular opinion—that the people were not sovereign in any absolute sense. The only modification he made in his political doctrine when he became a Catholic was that, whereas before he had maintained that the ultimate sovereignty was Justice, and that Justice meant God, he came to hold that God's sovereignty had the Church for its instrument. In his statement of this he sometimes went further than most Catholic political philosophers, so that he gave (as he had in his Protestant days) a version of the doctrine that is not easy to distinguish from theocracy. It was as a theocrat that he had denounced the clergy in his "Horrible Doctrines" articles; it was as a theocrat that he showed himself prepared to accept the unity of the State instead of an ineffectual Church. If a year or so before his conversion, he reverted to the idea of the Church possessing all earthly sovereignty, it was again obviously as a theocrat.[2]

He alternately defended and denounced democracy; but in either event, he explained what he meant by democracy.[3] If it was government by the people, he was against it; if it was government for the people, he was for it. In one sense, he kept on declaring, he had never been a democrat; in another sense, he would always be a democrat. The mistake people made, according to him, was that of regarding democracy as a means; it was not a means at all but only the end of good government, for it meant justice—ultimately it meant the kingdom of God on earth.

It is sometimes said that the result of the 1840 election was such a shock to him that it threw him, disillusioned, into conservatism; and Brownson himself suggested as much. Yet what he held after the election was exactly what he had held before the election: that there was nothing sacred about a chance political majority. The only thing sacred was right—and as often as not the majority was not in the right. What the 1840 election showed (as did many another election) was that politicians could so engineer matters— especially at a favorable moment—as to becloud the real issues. All that had happened this time was that they had carried a man into the White House because he was popular as a soldier and could be "sold" to the electorate on the fallacious ground that he lived in a log-cabin and drank hard cider, whereas his opponent was (equally fallaciously) depicted as a worn-out fop. But Brownson could hardly have been surprised that the majority of any people should have had a moment of aberration. Writing in January, 1841, he merely remarked: "The people . . . have been deceived, woefully deceived; but the moment they become aware of the fact, they will lose no time in rectifying their mistake." [4] A partisan knows perfectly well that his party cannot always win. When he loses, he shrugs his shoulders and waits for the majority to reverse itself, confident that it will. His faith in democracy is not uprooted simply because his party has been defeated.

To imagine anything else of Brownson would be to set him down as an hysterical fool. What he saw in "Tippecanoe and Tyler too" was a confirmation of what he had never failed to assert—that majorities mean very little. But so far from finding himself politically eliminated by his "Laboring Classes" articles, we know from a letter Calhoun wrote him the following year that there was a prospect of his running for Congress.[5] Instead of despairing of politics, he more than ever worked for the nomination of Calhoun as Democratic presidential candidate for 1844. Calhoun himself wrote to Brownson about this, as did his political backers in Congress. Brownson was even asked to edit a pro-Calhoun paper in New York.

Concerning this he was approached by John Hecker, who had assisted in the formation of the Equal-Rights or Loco-foco Party. Henry Brownson says that the project fell through for lack of funds, but this is not indicated by letters that Brownson wrote to John Hecker's brother, Isaac. On September 18, 1843, he seemed decidedly interested: if the terms were good enough, he would be delighted to accept.[6] But on October 3rd, he wrote again to Isaac Hecker, telling him to stop all proceedings. "I have altered my plans and do not wish to become the editor of the paper." [7] He had decided to revive his *Review*. On it he could serve the Calhoun cause just as well.[8] Then when Calhoun was elected he would regain his pleasant sinecure at the Marine Hospital at Chelsea.

We hear no more about Brownson's political ambitions. The truth is that as a "practical politician" he was a notorious failure—which was probably greatly to his credit. If he had too little tact, he had too much honesty. Besides, he was only really interested in political theory, not at all in political manoeuvering. But he did believe that he had found in Calhoun the great political leader who would save America. "The cast-iron man, who looks as if he had never been born and could never be extinguished"[9]—so Harriet Martineau had described him after meeting him in Washington—was still Brownson's political hero, and even his political Messiah. "I am moving towards a single end," Calhoun had written to him on December 30, 1839, "to bring back the government, as far as constitutional measures are concerned, to where it was when it commenced."[10]

At this period Brownson thoroughly approved his theories and was an extremist with respect to "states' rights." He lost no opportunity of asserting that the states were severally sovereign and that the Federal government enjoyed no more than delegated powers— a position he was to abandon completely under the impact of the Civil War. Writing in 1843 he said, "I have no faith, as I have often said, in the intelligence of the people, and I have no assurance of good government when I have nothing but their intelligence and virtue, as *a consolidated mass,* on which to rely. But the pursuits and interests of the people are various—each of these interests has, as it were, an instinct of self-preservation and self-advancement."[11] Therefore, in order to prevent any one class that happened to be in possession of the Federal government from plundering another, he proposed what was virtually Calhoun's salutary check of "concurrent majorities."[12] In this way would the evils of absolutist democracy, as he saw them, be removed. As the Constitution was a compact between the several states, each remained as sovereign then as in 1787. It followed that any state had the right to nullify or veto any federal law of which it did not approve. But whether or not the individual states actually had this right—so Calhoun argued to Brownson in the course of a conversation in Washington in 1841—the Federal government would still find it impossible to enforce its will upon any recalcitrant state.[13] By such means the American Constitution was to be preserved in its pristine purity. In his hatred of industrialism Brownson made an alliance with the slave-owning aristocracy of the South.

If he escaped going to Congress in 1841, Brownson had also escaped becoming a professor at Harvard in 1838. Perhaps in neither case was there much danger—less of the professorship than of a political career. But it is interesting to note what happened.

His articles on Cousin had naturally delighted the French philosopher, who wrote to Brownson on January 10, 1837, and on December 10th of the following year.[14] He was pleased to have an American admirer, especially one of such penetration. The two men began to exchange their literary works, and Cousin had messages for Dr. Channing and Charles Brooks (whom he had met) and for Emerson, Ripley, and Bancroft. The fact that Eliza Robbins had been writing to him gave the Frenchman the opportunity to make a mild French joke: *"Malgré la galanterie française je repondrai une autre fois à cette dame et écrirai a M. Ch. Brooks."* Then he dealt out his French compliment: *"Aujourd'hui je n'écrirai qu'à notre philosophe en Massachusetts."* He took the opportunity in this second letter of denying the charge of pantheism so often brought against him.

In March, 1838, Charles Sumner, the future senator, then a young man of twenty-seven, called upon Cousin in Paris. He did not like him very much, but he was struck by the fact that Cousin brought round the conversation to Brownson whom he called "a man of great talent, and indeed a most remarkable person,"[15] adding that he thought that Brownson should be appointed to the professorship of philosophy at Harvard, which was then vacant. Brownson, he assured his visitor, was just the man for it. All of which impressed Sumner and was passed on to Judge Story,[16] who, as a member of the Harvard Corporation, might be able to assist in securing the appointment.

It is hardly surprising that Harvard did not act upon this suggestion but appointed James Walker instead. Brownson, after all, was a man of no formal education.

Other people, however, thought of Brownson as a professor. Alexander H. Everett, who had become President of a college in Louisiana, wrote in 1842 remarking, of his own accord, that he regretted that the means available did not permit him to offer Brownson the chair of philosophy.[17] And no less a person than the future Cardinal Newman, did offer Brownson a professorship in Dublin in 1853. What operated at Harvard was probably not so much Brownson's lack of a degree—such things did not count so much a hundred years ago as they do in America today—as that in the eyes of respectable Bostonians the demagogue of the Society for Christian Union and Progress would not have been eligible, even had he possessed a German doctorate. All the same, Cousin's idea was a brilliant one; as a philosopher Brownson undoubtedly stood head and shoulders above any American of his time.

Yet perhaps Harvard was right in not appointing him. Sooner or later Brownson would have been sure to have kicked over the academic traces. For a semester or two he would have been enormously stimulating; then the routine would have become intolerable. He knew very well what sort of work it was for which he was best fitted. Neither the halls of Congress nor the halls of Harvard would have been able to contain his fiery spirit for long. Even had he been offered the appointment, and accepted it, his "Horrible Doctrines" article of 1840 would have ruined him.

He went on preaching at the Masonic Temple and with the editing of the *Boston Quarterly Review*. Or rather he edited his *Review* until he received a letter in May, 1842, from John L. O'Sullivan, the editor of the monthly *Democratic Review*, suggesting that the *Boston Quarterly* "might be advantageously merged into" his own publication. Satisfactory terms were agreed upon, under which Brownson was to write a monthly article on whatever he pleased at rates considerably higher than O'Sullivan paid to Nathaniel Hawthorne—no less than three dollars a page.

Doran Whalen, who has a weakness for villains, says that "John L. O'Sullivan could bow very low. There were those who insisted that he could stoop even lower; but he got his way in most cases, and he was willing to attempt the capture of the greatest independent of nineteenth-century America." [18] Her insinuation is not borne out by the facts; there was no need for anybody to silence Brownson by a tricky manoeuvre; he had for some time thought of giving up the *Boston Quarterly Review*, as the strain was telling upon him. Indeed, he had announced that the Autumn issue of 1839 would be the last, and then had kept on. As for O'Sullivan—afterwards American Ambassador to Spain under the Pierce administration—he was a very decent fellow, according to the picture of him given by Julian Hawthorne and from all other accounts. [19] He merely thought that Brownson had enough of a following to be an asset to his magazine. No trammels were to be put on the expression of his opinions. What these opinions were O'Sullivan and everybody else knew perfectly well.

O'Sullivan's disappointment came when Brownson, instead of dealing with matters of general interest, started discussing metaphysics. Yet the editor put up with it for several months before writing to Brownson very tactfully asking if he could not supply something of a different type. "The greatest entertainment of the greatest number," he explained as his object—not an abstruse treatment of Schmucker's Psychology. Taking the hint, Brownson began to write on political theory—and that dismayed O'Sullivan still more. Nevertheless Brownson's articles were printed as written, although the editor felt it necessary to insert a note (really an article) disclaiming responsibility for Brownson's views.[20] When Brownson wrote a long article in reply, that too went into the *Democratic Review*.[21] In the end it was Brownson who withdrew of his own accord, and as the terms of his contract made it impossible for him to revive the *Boston Quarterly* under that name, he founded *Brownson's Quarterly Review* in 1844.

In the first number he led off by at once taking his readers into his confidence. "The name I have chosen, is not chosen from a selfish vanity, but because it is honest and appropriate. This is *my* review; I am its proprietor; its editor; intend to be its principal, if not its sole, writer, and to make it the organ of my own views of truth." He also said, "I have no fault to find with the conductor of the Democratic Review, Mr. O'Sullivan—a gentleman for whom I have a very high esteem. His conduct, so far as I am concerned, has been honorable, and even generous." But he added that he had never been at home on his paper and so was glad to go back among old friends.

He knew that he would regain his former following. "Never," he told them, "had a periodical a better list of subscribers than had the *Boston Quarterly Review*. . . . They were few, but they were serious, honest, earnest, affectionate. When a clamor was raised against me, which fetched its echoes from one end of the Union to the other, not one of them, to my knowledge, deserted me, or stopped his subscription, because he found me advocating offensive doctrines. I come into the circle of my friends, to exchange kindly greetings, and to allow my heart to expand, and to overflow with the warm sentiments, which have, since I went abroad, been pent up, struggling in vain for utterance."

He asserts again his independence and denies that he has in any way changed, though he may have advanced. "When I first began speaking to the public, I was young, inexperienced, ignorant, though perhaps not remarkably modest; my views were in the process of formation, rather than formed, and my mind, if not void, was at least in a chaotic state." It was soon to be firmly settled, but of that he gave no inkling, and did not himself guess where he would be before the year was out. Or if he guessed, he was as yet far from sure.

Those who had followed his writings closely already discerned a distinct Romeward drift. Isaac Hecker was to write about his services: "To a very acute observer it was evident that, consciously or unconsciously, he was aiming at Catholicity. It was also evident that his own difficulties were not settled; he was gradually settling them by this very preaching." [22] It had been apparent to him since he left the Presbyterians that the whole weight of logic pressed him towards the Catholic Church—the one place he felt entirely impossible as a habitation. But the thing that had once appeared so out of the question, was no longer quite that. Even the fact that he was a kind of Transcendentalist made him potentially a Catholic. For were not Catholics, with their disregard of reason, half-brethren to those in the "Movement"? At least it seemed so to many people at Brook Farm.

With the Farm he was closely associated as sympathizer and inspirer, but had no official connection with the undertaking. It was much the same as with his Transcendentalism: he was recognized as a leader, but one who was too individualistic to accept direct responsibility. It was not easy to say just how far his influence extended—though Ripley told Brownson that, had it not been for him, he would never have started the Farm. Afterwards it became convenient to pretend that his influence was of slight account. Because Brownson had become a Catholic there was an embarrassed silence at the mention of his name.

For a while a kind of æsthetic Catholicism had a vogue among the Farmers. It partly amused and partly disgusted Georgiana Bruce, who as Mrs. Kirby was to write in later life how she always suspected that rosaries and crucifixes were under the aprons of the girls with whom she worked. Some of the people at the Farm displayed their tendencies openly, and even flourished them—Charles Newcomb, for instance, "the quiet, retreating, demoniacal youth" [23] with the long, dark, lank locks of hair which he had to keep brushing off his forehead.[24] He had pictures of St. Ignatius and St. Francis Xavier in his room. One Sunday, when skating in his checked cotton blouse, he caught sight of a church spire. Unfastening his skates, in he went, and without paying any attention to the congregation, strode to the altar, where he said a prayer from Fénelon or Socrates—Georgiana could not quite remember which.[25] One day she asked him if he had been to see Fanny Elssler, the dancer, who was then performing at Boston. Charles was shocked and exclaimed, "Georgie, how *can* you, how *dare* you put such a question to me? Don't you know that she is a—vile creature?" A few days later, however, it was noticed that Charles had mysteriously disappeared, and after he came back Georgie found the vile creature's picture hung between those of Ignatius and Francis Xavier.[26]

Then there was William Henry Channing, the Doctor's nephew, who always visited them when he was in Boston from his church in New York. He would have joined the Farmers, had it not been for his wife. Even so, he was round them like a protecting spirit, preaching wonderful sermons to them in the woods when he came. On these occasions everybody present joined hands in a circle, as a symbol of the *at-one-ment*.[27] He, too, was one of those people who had long been on the road to Rome without ever actually getting there. He even had the pictures in his study arranged in the form of a cross. But somehow he could never quite convince himself that "Jesus Christ understood his own religion." [28] So those who knew him could cherish the shrewd hope that perhaps Mr. Brownson, in spite of all his loud vehement talk, would never get there either.

There were other people who seemed on the way. Mrs. Ripley and her niece Sarah Stearns; they got there in the end, and Miss Stearns even became a nun. And young Isaac Hecker, that excellent baker with the innocent face—they called him "Ernest the Seeker," because that was the name of a story by W. H. Channing in the *Dial*.

The nickname struck them as all the more fitting for Isaac because he had been attending Mr. Channing's sermons in New York.[29] When Brownson came over to the Farm he and Hecker would talk about nothing except religion—which with them meant Romanism.

One day one of the ladies flashed out sharply at the big booming man, who was "not the prince of gentlemen in debate," [30] "Do you approve of the priests of the Inquisition roasting off the feet of children under fourteen?"

"Certainly I do," he replied. "It was better for them to have their feet roasted off in this world than their souls to be roasted forever in the next." [31]

Georgie, being what was called in those days an "impressible female," was momentarily carried away in spite of herself and Mr. Brownson. Then she pulled herself together and concluded that, while "a little sentiment about crosses, rosaries, cathedrals and madonnas" might be all very well, she simply could not give up her reason and accept the spiritual tyranny of the Church. Think of the hair-shirt she would be obliged to wear! "For me, who had never worn a tight shoe, or glove, in my life, it is impossible!" [32]

Her good sense and her humor returning, she told the story of how Brownson, whose Latin was largely self-taught and full of false quantities, figured in one of George Ripley's nightmares. That exquisite latinist dreamed that he had become a Catholic and had confessed his sins to Father Orestes Brownson who said, "Now, my son, for a penance repeat after me the fifty-eighth psalm in the Vulgate." Upon which poor Ripley awoke in a cold sweat, trembling all over, and groaning, "O Lord, my punishment is greater than I am able to bear." [33]

But the good-natured and humorous Georgie could tell stories against herself as well. As a sedate old lady she used to smile at the way she gushed over Margaret Fuller whenever that loquacious Sphinx visited the Farm. Georgie claimed the privilege of giving up her own room at the Eyrie at such times, and she prepared it for

Margaret by burning pastilles in it as incense. In the morning it
was always Georgie who took her her breakfast in bed, using for
the object of her adoration the only decorated coffee cup and
saucer in the Eyrie's closet.[34] Having recovered from her girlish
infatuation, she recalled how Margaret's brother Lloyd, an unpleasant, loose-lipped lad of sixteen, kept a diary for the special
purpose of putting in it remarks about people whom he disliked
—and of then leaving the book around where those very people
would be sure to find it.[35] Even the kindly Mrs. Ripley wrote to
Dwight about Lloyd to say that he had "all the Fuller faults . . .
without their merits." [36]

Lloyd Fuller's was the only eccentricity of a disagreeable sort.
The chief characteristic of most of the Farmers was an almost milky
goodness. George Willis Cooke tells us, "There never were such
witty potato-patches and such sparkling cornfields before or since." [37]
If the habit of punning indulged in by everybody, with Ripley
setting the example,[38] and the small-change of small Transcendentalist jokes, may have been trying at times, this at least was the
clearest indication of that gaiety of heart which innocence gives.
The Farmers must have been harmless people to be so easily amused.
Laugh as we may at Brook Farm, we should feel as Dr. Johnson
did when he heard mention of a monastery—and want to kiss the
ground on hearing its name. It all seems an impossibly beautiful
dream—Paradise regained. Ripley, when writing to Brownson in
December, 1842, said of the young people there that, while it was
true they were "not quite free from nonsense"—due, he thought to
their unconsciously worshipping Emerson with too blind an adoration and so, like their master, expressing themselves confusedly—
added, with perfect justice: "They are pure, simple souls, apparently
without an erring instinct, and their beautiful divine lives would
seem to sanction their doctrine." [39] It is a matter of historical fact that
no breath of scandal ever touched the Farm, and that though
Ripley's scheme eventually failed, no man or woman who had been

among the Brook Farmers ever had anything but praise to give, or the kindliest of memories of their association.[40]

There was, of course, some criticism afterwards of the management. As is common enough in such enterprises, the financial resources were inadequate, some of those who had been counted upon for support giving no more than a sympathetic interest. Worse than this, Ripley selected the place chiefly because it was beautiful. How should he know anything about soils, or know that this soil was too gravelly for what he wanted to grow? But even that mistake he almost overcame by his good luck in finding in Minot Pratt, the ex-printer, a man who took naturally to farming, and in all his Farmers young men and women whose willingness made up in part for their lack of knowledge. The fire that eventually destroyed the phalanstery was perhaps providential, cruel blow as it seemed at the time. For when Ripley was persuaded to turn the Farm into a Fourierist association, the bloom began to be brushed from the peach.

Albert Brisbane, the father of the columnist, was responsible for this. He came to the Farm to translate Fourier, and he talked Ripley over. "In the mere name 'Phalanx'," says Frothingham, "he seemed to hear the trumpets of the angels." [41] Yet the enthusiast was a gloomy fellow in many ways, and Arthur Sumner related how one night, when a group of Farmers were lying on the grass and one of them exclaimed, "What a heavenly moon!" he got from Brisbane the growl, "Miserable world! Damned bad moon!" [42] But his enthusiasm for Fourierism overbore the reluctant Ripley. There was no resisting him, especially when he had an ally in Horace Greeley, with his colorless face and hair, accentuated by a white hat and light drab clothes.[43] They wanted Brook Farm to be a Fourierist Phalanx, and they had their way. From that moment the original spontaneity started to dry up.

The place was open to any visitor who cared to spend a day there, and these mixed freely with the Farmers. So many such visitors came—four thousand of them one year,[44] most of them out of curiosity—that Ripley was obliged to make a small charge to cover the cost of their entertainment. Many of them came disposed to be critical, but departed without finding much amiss. Alcott, it is true, thought the Farm not sufficiently austere, and so founded his caricature of it at Fruitlands. And Emerson, who had been too canny to take any shares, preferring safer investments, was mildly amused by what he saw. As Lindsay Swift puts it, he always conveyed the impression that someone was laughing behind the shrubbery.[45] He thought it funny that when the men danced in the evening, clothespins dropped out of their pockets.[46] But then, Emerson had a sly way of poking fun at people—especially those who were his best friends. It was he who told how Margaret Fuller said—and apparently perfectly seriously—"I now know all the people worth knowing in America, and I find no intellect comparable to my own."[47] And in his *Journals* he recorded how when Bronson Alcott's solemn English disciple, Charles Lane, took out paper and pencil from his pocket and asked Brownson to give him the names of the three profoundest men in America, Brownson gave him two—and then added his own for a third. Upon which Emerson's comment was, "Brownson never will stop and listen, neither in conversation, but what is more, not in solitude."[48]

Brownson, however, was observing things that escaped even Emerson's keen notice—things that Emerson ruled out from his consciousness. The fact of sin was one of these. Not that Brownson found sin at Brook Farm; in so far as any collection of human beings could be thoroughly good, here was that collection. As to this he satisfied Hugh Garland, the Clerk of the House of Representatives at Washington, who was thinking of sending his daughters there and who wanted to be sure of the morals of the place.[49] But it was all too clear to him that these admirable people ignored the patent fact of original sin. Even when Emerson wrote his poem "Grace," in which he reverted to a Calvinist terminology, the "preventing grace" turned out to be merely the checks of human prudence—
"Example, custom, fear, occasion slow."

Perhaps it was because of his acquaintance with the Romeward-bound Brownson, that Emerson, when in Baltimore in January, 1843, actually attended Mass at the cathedral. Writing to Margaret Fuller, he tells her, "It is a dear old church—the Roman, I mean—and to-day I detest the Unitarians and Martin Luther and all the parliament of Barebones. Ah, that one word of it were true!" At the same time he wrote to his wife Lidian, "It is well for my Protestantism that we have no cathedral in Concord. E. H. [Elizabeth Hoar] and I should be confirmed in a fortnight. The Unitarian church forgets that men are poets." [50] That sort of thing was to Brownson a trifling with the holy. The way these men patronized Christ was to him intolerable.

On this point the famous Methodist preacher, Father Taylor, of whom we get so unforgettable an account as Father Mapple in *Moby Dick,* agreed with him. He came to the Farm several times, and at least once attended a meeting of the Club. He was friendly enough to the Transcendentalists—this man who "walked his pulpit like a quarter deck" and who kissed all the babies he baptized—in which he was like Brownson, though he also kissed the bride after he had performed a marriage ceremony. Father Taylor commented, "What a beautiful being Dr. Channing is! If he only had had any education"; [51] and Channing said that Edward Taylor was quite right. There "Father Mapple" sat, with his green spectacles pushed up over his forehead, taking it all in. Of one Transcendentalist discourse he said, "It would take as many sermons like that to convert a human soul as it would take quarts of skimmed milk to make a man drunk." [52]

Brook Farm, however, was not really out to convert anybody; that people went there was a sign that they were already converted —to whatever doctrine or way of life prevailed in the place. In addition to its coöperative and community life for adults, it provided a school and a college; many went there just for that reason. Bancroft sent his sons, and Brownson put his eldest boy in Ripley's charge. If young Orestes was not much interested in books—thereby getting some harsh words from Charles A. Dana—that he was there at all proved his father's confidence in the Paradise Planters. In his case Brook Farm had a surprising effect. One of the girls—Ida Russell, whose father had been Minister to Norway and Sweden— aroused in him a passion for the sea by singing "A Life on the Ocean Wave," and Ripley had to write to Brownson telling him that he thought this inclination should be humored. As Captain Russell Sturgis came forward with a loan of forty dollars—which the boy might repay when he was able by spending the same sum on some other youth similarly disposed—and a gift of a sextant and a copy of Bowditch's *Practical Navigator,* the fourteen-year-old son of the philosopher went off to sea.[53]

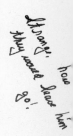

Isaac Hecker's career was very different. He had gone to Brook Farm on Brownson's advice in January, 1843, where he worked out part of his board and tuition by acting as community baker. Then deciding that the Farm was not sufficiently ascetic for him, he joined Alcott at Fruitlands. That should have satisfied all his yearnings for austerity. Not even milk or butter were allowed, though some depraved people kept them surreptitiously or munched cheese in dark corners. One young woman—Anna Page—who was convicted of having committed the mortal sin of eating fish at a neighbor's house, pleaded that she had taken only a little bit of the tail; her excuse was not accepted—out she went. Even of vegetables, only those of the "aspiring" sort were admitted to the Orphic table, or if potatoes were served, Mrs. Alcott had to mash them into aesthetic patterns.

The simple-looking Isaac was no fool. He soon saw through Alcott, whom he set down as an "innocent charlatan" and noted that he was vain and full of talk that had a "false air of profundity." Nor did he fail to see that the Sage's imposing aspect and bland self-confidence concealed an utter incapacity to deal with practical things.[54] He grouped him (perhaps a little unfairly to the others) with Emerson and Thoreau as "three consecrated cranks." [55] He could not fail to observe that Fruitlands was a place where Alcott looked benign and talked what he regarded as philosophy, while Mrs. Alcott and the girls did all the work. If Mrs. Alcott sometimes lost her temper and stormed at her husband, it never disturbed him. Placidly he went on with his interminable conversation.

Isaac before long left Fruitlands and the man whom Carlyle dubbed "the Potato Quixote"; but in the Spring of 1844 he was in Concord, this time to study Greek and Latin under the direction of George Bradford. He stayed with Thoreau's mother—a stone's throw away from Emerson—paying seventy-five cents a week for his room. "Never, surely" comments Lindsay Swift, "was the inward Light maintained at less cost to the lodger and at less profit to the landlady." [56] By now he had just about decided to become a Catholic and did his best to take Thoreau with him, offering to pay his expenses for a trip to Rome, choosing him because Henry could sleep on the ground and live on bread and water; such a visit would be sure to finish Henry off, he thought. [57] But Thoreau only growled, "What is the use of your joining the Catholic Church? Can't you get along without hanging on to her skirts?" Emerson and Alcott, too, did their best to rescue him, and (perhaps to distract him, or to give him a fearful warning as to the effects of an excessively enthusiastic religion) took him to see the Shakers. [58] Alcott showed himself positively inquisitorial. So, in his mild way, did Emerson, who caught up with "Ernest the Seeker" one day when he was out walking and opened fire. At last came the question, "Mr. Hecker, I suppose it was the art, the architecture, and so on in the Catholic Church which led you to her?" "No," he answered, "but it was what caused all that." They had to give him up as a hopeless case. He claimed afterwards to have been the first to break the Transcendentalist camp. [59]

Brownson was all this time getting nearer and nearer to Rome, and the nearer he got the more unpopular he made himself at

Brook Farm. It was all very well to discuss the Catholic Church in terms of aesthetics; one might even talk about Fénelon and Port Royal and Pascal. But Brownson insisted on talking philosophy and theology, and his iron mind made everybody uncomfortable, especially as the man in the badly fitting formal swallow-tail coat —it looked as though he went to bed in it, and he certainly studied in it till two or three in the morning—took what they considered an unfair advantage by being so big and roaring and loud in argument. Some of the Farmers hid themselves when he was there, and Marianne Dwight wrote to her friend Anna Q. T. Parsons, "Mr. Brownson is expected to be here next Sunday, in which I don't rejoice." [60] His was the offence of being remorselessly logical. James Russell Lowell admitted that his was "transparent and forcible prose," but he too wilted before the barrage of syllogisms. When he published his *Fable for Critics* in 1848 he took his revenge with:

> The worst of it is, that his logic's so strong,
> That of two sides he commonly chooses the wrong;
> If there *is* only one, why he'll split it in two,
> And first pummel this half, then that, black and blue;
> That white's white needs no proof, but it takes a deep fellow
> To prove it jet-black, and that jet-black is yellow.

By now it was only with George Ripley of all the Transcendentalists that Brownson had much in common. Parker, though he was preaching many of the things that Brownson had said before—so much so that Brownson accused him of plagiarism—had drifted into what his friend considered infidelity. For Emerson Brownson retained still, as he did to the end, affection and respect—recognizing his genius and nobility—but he saw little of him now, as he saw little of Alcott or Margaret Fuller, except when they happened to be at the Farm when he was on a visit. Hawthorne and he could never make much of one another, and indeed Hawthorne was not much interested in philosophy, and as spreading manure was too much for him, he had left the Farm. Dr. Channing had recently died, getting

the singular honor on the day of his funeral of having the bells of the
Catholic churches in Boston tolled by order of Bishop Fenwick.
That he came as near as any Protestant could to being a saint was
acknowledged. Nor was his friendship with Bishop Cheverus forgotten.[61] Now Brownson, even if he continued occasionally to print
articles from Transcendentalists in his new *Quarterly,* was a somewhat lonely figure. He grew all the more lonely as his Catholic
tendency increased.

Yet he still enjoyed a good deal of influence, both because of his
meetings at the Masonic Temple and through his *Review.* The influence need not of course be exaggerated, and some of Brownson's
admirers—who relish his logic more than they have any means of
estimating the literary and intellectual currents of the time—are disposed to see in him the main root for the Flowering of New
England. Such a notion is of course quite absurd, though it is true
that had Brownson not become a Catholic, he would not have
suffered the neglect which was to be his fate. What was happening
in New England—particularly in Boston and Concord—if it had
any origins, had them in the English Romantic Movement, and
only to a minor degree was affected by German and French metaphysical speculation. But these happenings are never to be adequately
accounted for on the basis of "origins" or derivations. It is the
heightened and quickened mood that sends men out to seek what
intellectual fodder they can find; when that mood is not present,
the fodder is allowed to lie around in great heaps all untouched.
The best that one can say is that during the 'thirties and 'forties—as
in the 'fifties—something was "in the air." It was as mysterious as
electricity, whose effect can be felt but whose nature cannot be
analyzed. To try to find any one person who may be regarded as
the energizer of the group is a waste of time. The most typical
Transcendentalist was poor loquacious Alcott; the most resplendent
Transcendentalist genius was Emerson; the most strenuous popular-
izer of the Movement was Margaret Fuller. That Brownson contributed something—and even contributed a great deal—is doubtless

true. But so did Dr. Channing, and William Henry, his nephew, and William Ellery, another nephew and a namesake, and Ripley and Bancroft, and Miss Peabody. So, too, did Cranch and crazy Jones Very and Theodore Parker and Bradford and Dwight; even the clash of intellect brought by Andrews Norton and the fervor of Father Taylor's preaching at the seamen's mission brought something to Transcendentalism—though these last two men were not Transcendentalists at all. Moreover, several of the best writers were hardly Transcendentalists—Thoreau, for example—or were outside of the group, or had not yet quite arrived on the scene: Hawthorne and Melville and Lowell and Holmes. And when we remember the writers, we must also remember that the audience contributed more than can be easily measured. New England was, in truth, in a state of ferment. Many people were particles of the yeast, and all worked upon one another.

The case of the friendship between Brownson and Ripley may be taken as exemplifying the situation. Ripley it was who in 1834 had encouraged Brownson to come to Boston and found what eventuated a couple of years later in the Society for Christian Union and Progress. But Ripley's reciprocal indebtedness to Brownson was handsomely acknowledged in a long affectionate letter, dated December 18, 1842, the occasion being an article by Brownson defending Brook Farm. Then Ripley wrote: "We have truly sympathized as few men have done; you have always quickened my love for humanity; and for no small share of what mental clearness I may have, am I indebted to the hours of genial, pleasant intercourse I have enjoyed with you." Then follows a still stronger statement: "If I had never known you, I should never have been engaged in this enterprise [the establishment of Brook Farm]. I consider it as the incarnation of those transcendental truths which we have held in common, and which you have done much to make me love." [62] Now that is definite, so far as it goes, as was Thoreau's saying that his stay with Brownson in 1836 meant for him a new *"Lebenstag."* But Thoreau had only that one brief encounter, and was too thorny an individualist to allow anyone to influence him. In the case of Brownson and Ripley we know that there had been long discussions between the two men. There was stimulation on both sides, and because of that stimulation Ripley conceived the idea of Brook Farm. That is all we positively know; it is not safe to assert anything more.

[1] *The Convert*, p. 243.

[2] What he wrote in one of his articles for the *Democratic Review* in 1843 was "The real sovereign on earth, representative of the divine sovereignty, the Sovereign of sovereigns, was the Christian church. . . . Civil governments were held to be not *co*-ordinate governments with the ecclesiastical, but *sub*-ordinate. . . . I confess that I have a strong predilection for this theory." (*Works*, Vol. XV, p. 348). That it very much overstates the Catholic position, which he imperfectly understood at the time, need not concern us. What matters is his opinion.

[3] In 1838 he wrote: "[The Americans] are conservatives, and to be a conservative in this country, is to be a democrat." (*Works*, Vol. XV, p. 1). But on the very next page he said "We do not call ourselves Democrats in a party sense"— which was all the more strange coming from a man who was holding an appointment given by the Democratic party.

[4] *Works*, Vol. XV, p. 114.

[5] *Early Life*, p. 303. We know this, however, only from Calhoun's letter. Brownson could not have treated his candidacy very seriously, for on the same page Calhoun makes reference to the metaphysical work Brownson was proposing to write at this time.

[6] *Hecker Papers* in the Paulist Archives.

[7] *Hecker Papers*.

[8] There are many passages or letters bearing on this matter in *Early Life*—pp. 305, 326, 328–332, 334, 339, 340–341.

[9] *Retrospect of Western Travel*, Vol. I, p. 247.

[10] *Early Life*, pp. 321–322.

[11] *Works*, Vol. XV, p. 293.

[12] *Ibid.*, p. 290. "This theory of government . . . is not mine," he explained, after having quoted an exposition of it given by Calhoun. (*Ibid.*, pp. 293, 294).

[13] *Works*, Vol. XVII, pp. 243–244.

[14] *Early Life*, pp. 394–396, 406–409.

[15] Pierce, *Memoir and Letters of Charles Sumner*, Vol. I, pp. 264–265.

[16] *Ibid.*, Vol. I, p. 295. This was in a letter dated May 21, 1838, after a second visit to Cousin.

[17] *Early Life*, p. 235.

[18] *Granite for God's House*, p. 183.

[19] Hecker added his testimony in the *Catholic World* (Vol. XLV, 1887, p. 470).

[20] He did perhaps a little more than that, for he declared Brownson's doctrine to be essentially that of the divine right of kings "united in unblessed alliance with the old papal doctrine of the spiritual-temporal supremacy of the Church." (*Democratic Review*, Vol. XIII, 1843, p. 657). The whole article reveals O'Sullivan as kindly but muddle-headed and without much literary ability. His own doctrine of democracy,

however, was not particularly extreme, and the phrase quoted here at least shows that even at this date some of Brownson's contemporaries perceived where his political theories were leading him.

[21] It is reprinted in the *Works*, Vol. XV, pp. 281–296.

[22] *Catholic World*, Vol. XLV (1887), p. 471. But in a letter to his family, dated January 19, 1843 (it is among the *Hecker Papers*) young Isaac notes that the hymns sung were Methodist and the tone of the services was Methodist.

[23] *Emerson's Journals*, Vol. VI, p. 374.

[24] Codman, *Brook Farm*, p. 49.

[25] Kirby, *Years of Experience*, pp. 158–159.

[26] *Ibid.*, p. 106.

[27] Codman, *Brook Farm*, pp. 71, 72.

[28] Swift, *Brook Farm*, p. 218.

[29] He wrote on September 6, 1843, to tell Brownson that Channing was "Catholic in heart, Protestant in head." (*Early Life*, p. 337).

[30] Kirby, *op. cit.*, p. 147.

[31] *Ibid.*, p. 147. That is Georgie's story and must be taken for what it is worth. She was not the most reliable of historians. And she liked neither Brownson nor the Catholic Church.

[32] When she wrote her book in 1887, she had to remember that not only Brownson but Mrs. Ripley and Miss Stearns and Sumner's younger brother and Isaac Hecker, as well as Brownson, had become Catholics. She explained that they had given their vigor "born of Protestantism" to "the feeble old mother at whose breasts no man or woman had been nourished for the last hundred years." (*Ibid.*, p. 182).

[33] *Ibid.*, p. 146. In some versions of this story Bradford figures as the penitent.

[34] *Ibid.*, pp. 101–102.

[35] *Ibid.*, pp. 95–96.

[36] Haraszti, *The Idyll of Brook Farm*, p. 18.

[37] Introduction to the *Early Letters of George Wm. Curtis to John Dwight*, p. 9.

[38] Codman in his *Brook Farm* (pp. 172–176) gives a number of deplorable examples of these puns.

[39] *Early Life*, p. 314.

[40] As to this, Hecker gives his testimony through the mouth of his biographer, explaining that the Brook Farmers were further off from Puritan beliefs than Puritan discipline. So as not to set their goodness outside the supernatural, he pointed out that these people, after all, had the grace conferred by baptism. (Elliott, *Life of Father Hecker*, pp. 47, 52–53). An undated memorandum among the *Hecker Papers* reads, in part: "It was the grandest, noblest, bravest dream of New England. Nothing greater has been produced. . . . Brook Farm was the realization of the best dreams these men had of Christianity, it embodied them."

[41] *George Ripley*, p. 174.

[42] Swift, *Brook Farm*, p. 272.

[43] Amelia Russell, *Home Life of the Brook Farm Association*, p. 39.

[44] Codman, *Brook Farm*, p. 80.

[45] *Brook Farm*, p. 52.

[46] *Ibid.*, p. 54. See also *Early Letters of George Wm. Curtis to John S. Dwight*, p. 21.

[47] Emerson, W. H. Channing and Clarke, *Memoirs of Margaret Fuller Ossoli*, Vol. I, p. 234.

⁴⁸ *Journals,* Vol. VI, p. 297. The local judgment upon Lane and the other English-man at Fruitlands, H. G. Wright, was that, while Alcott might be a bit daft, they were *clean* daft. (Canby, *Thoreau,* p. 179.) The daftness momentarily descended even upon Mrs. Alcott when she wrote: "The dear English-*men,* the good and true. Welcome to these shores, this home, to my bosom!" (*Journals of Bronson Alcott,* p. 148). Later, when Lane expressed his disapproval of the institution of matrimony, Mrs. Alcott changed her opinion of him. (Shepard, *Pedlar's Progress,* p. 146).

⁴⁹ *Early Life,* pp. 308–311.

⁵⁰ Cabot, *Emerson,* Vol. II, pp. 471, 472.

⁵¹ Peabody, *Reminiscences of W. E. Channing,* p. 277.

⁵² Cabot, *op. cit.,* Vol. I, p. 328 fn.

⁵³ *Early Life,* pp. 315, 316, 317.

⁵⁴ Elliott, *Hecker,* p. 76. After Alcott's death in 1888, he said, "I don't believe he ever prayed. Whom could he pray to? Was not Bronson Alcott the greatest of them all?" (*Ibid.,* p. 81).

⁵⁵ *Ibid.,* p. 82.

⁵⁶ *Brook Farm,* p. 102.

⁵⁷ Hecker to Brownson, August 1, 1844 (*Brownson Papers*). Also a letter dated August 17th, in which he tells Brownson that he has not yet heard from Thoreau.

⁵⁸ *Emerson's Journals,* Vol. VI, p. 523.

⁵⁹ Elliott, *op. cit.,* p. 89.

⁶⁰ Marianne Dwight Orvis, *Letters from Brook Farm,* p. 38. She added, however, that many *were* glad at the prospect of his coming.

⁶¹ Miss Peabody in her book on Channing (pp. 98–99) reports him as telling her one day: "I must say I was somewhat *disappointed* in finding the Roman Catholic worship such a moral inanity; for I knew and loved Cheverus." This was his comment on a strange religious ceremony in which, he said, Cheverus took part, when a group of priests, the Bishop among them, held hands in a circle before a picture of the Madonna. Channing thought they "were expressing symbolically a very sublime idea" until, right in the middle of the proceedings, the saintly Bishop took a pinch of snuff! Could the "Grandmother of Boston" but have foreseen it, her own niece, Hawthorne's daughter, was to become not only a Catholic but a nun!

⁶² *Early Life,* p. 313.

CHAPTER VIII

Conversion

Brownson's frequent insistence upon his consistency has sometimes been taken as a mark of his vanity. Nobody, it is said, had less steadiness than "Weathercock Brownson." Yet, he did not assert too much for himself. Every step he took since leaving the Presbyterians—and his joining them he describes as the act of an intellectual desperado, a retrogression—was in the direction of the Catholic Church. Almost all the books he had studied influenced him in the same direction, though none of these was a Catholic book, with the exception of Milner's *End of Controversy* and the *Catechism of the Council of Trent,* both of which he may have borrowed from Hecker.[1] Though these are the only Catholic works mentioned by Henry Brownson,[2] and though Orestes Brownson was presumably referring to Milner when he said, "One or two modern Catholic controversial works had fallen into my hands . . . but they did not impress me favorably,"[3] towards the end of his life the convert declared that "The writer who first turned my mind in the direction of the Church was the Abbé Maret . . . by his work *Le Panthéisme en la Société Moderne.*"[4] Yet even allowing for Maret, whom Brownson forgot to mention in his autobiography, it is hardly too much to say that it was an ecumenical council composed of such queerly assorted figures as William Godwin, and Robert Owen, and Benjamin Constant, and Saint-Simon, and Cousin, and Leroux—all presided over by Dr. Channing—that gave Brownson his faith, in so far as this came from natural sources.

Henry Brownson remarks that his father always considered it a great advantage that, as a self-educated man, he had escaped

123

what college so often does in the way of destroying originality. But he adds that "books did him almost as much injury and tyrannized almost as absolutely over his mind as professors could have done." There was, however, one important difference: the authority of the book could be more easily shaken off than that of the professor; [5] and, to do Brownson justice, he was under no writer's domination for very long. At the first impact with a new philosophy there may have been unmeasured enthusiasm; but critical second thoughts soon came in, and then it was the philosophy that was dominated and not Brownson. He was almost ruthless in taking just what he wanted and no more out of a book, and of twisting even that to his own requirements. This was the case with all the illustrious names that have been mentioned.

To say that Channing "presided" over the process of Brownson's acquisition of faith is of course no more than a fashion of speaking: the Doctor did not read much in the philosophers who influenced Brownson; he was more influenced by Coleridge and Wordsworth. But he, more than any other man, had a personal influence over Brownson. Here was direct contact with a holy man of God—something much better than books. The fervent, delicate little preacher with the large eyes and the beautiful voice made a deep impression on all who met him—even if he sometimes repelled them at the first encounter. None owed more to him than did Brownson. He was one of the few people who looked upon Brownson's changes, "not as fluctuations, but as steps of rational progress." [6]

Had Channing been an ordinary Unitarian this effect would not have been made. But Channing was not properly a Unitarian at all. He disliked the terms "unity" and "trinity" as applying to God, because they seemed to him cold and abstract and conveying little of the divine Fatherhood. This point of theology he considered no more than verbal. "Men," he told Miss Peabody, "are not mere spirits of reason, they are sensibilities of heart as well. Sentiment is not mere feeling, it is feeling penetrated with thought." [7] He objected to Congregationalist "orthodoxy" and threw in his lot with the new denomination mainly out of his hatred of Calvinism which, as early as 1812, he said would make existence a curse if it were true. While holding that the Scriptures were a record of inspiration rather than plenarily inspired, he believed in the miracles and said of the resurrection that it was "a fact that comes to me with a certainty I find in few ancient histories." Upon Transcendentalism he looked with a friendly eye because he thought it a quickening of the spirit. But he was not a Transcendentalist himself, except in a very loose sense. He often told Brownson, "There is a higher form of Christian truth and love needed and to be revealed than the world has yet seen, and I look with hope to the discussions and movements in the midst of which we live to elicit and realize it for mankind." [8] Brownson soon gave him up as the Messiah of the Church of the Future,—as soon as he discovered that Channing's mind was far from being settled—but he continued to reverence him for his spirituality. It was Channing's catholicity of general outlook that did much to prepare Brownson for the acceptance of the Catholic faith.

In June, 1842,[9] Brownson wrote Channing a long letter, which was afterwards published as a pamphlet entitled, "The Mediatorial Life of Jesus." It is a remarkable document.

Addressing the good Doctor as "my spiritual father" and saying that it was his writings that had brought him to a "living faith in God," he admits that "discovering that I was not understood, or rather, that I was misunderstood, I have from time to time changed my point of view and my phraseology, with the hope of being able to communicate my real thought. All in vain. I have only gained a sneer for my versatility and frequent changes of opinions. I have at times wondered at this; but I am satisfied that it was owing to the contrary tendencies at work in my mind, and to the fact that I had not fully mastered what I wished to say, and therefore had only lisped and stammered, instead of articulating clearly and distinctly." [10] But now at last he thinks he has finally attained to the key to all religious problems—it is that of the world's salvation through Jesus as Mediator. "I think, sir," he continues, "I am able to show that the doctrine that human nature became depraved through the sin of Adam, and that it is redeemed only through the obedience of Christ; that the doctrine which teaches us that the Mediator is truly and indissolubly God-man, and saves the world by giving literally his life to the world, are the great 'central truths' of Christianity, and philosophically demonstrable." [11]

Acknowledging that he had derived his hint from Leroux' *L'Humanité,* Brownson claims only the originality of applying that hint to theology. With a touch of asperity he points out that "men have gained great credit in this city since I have been here, by doing little more than echo the doctrines which I then put forth, or which may be found at least in germ in what I, an untutored backwoodsman, then wrote and published." [12] It was a palpable hit at Theodore Parker.

As for Channing's own views, Brownson says that he finds in them only an assumption of man's *natural* likeness to God and a denial of the doctrine of man's depravity. [13] Brownson believes he is now able to present what were called the "orthodox" doctrines in such a light that Channing will not refuse to accept them, despite the fact that the Doctor had himself given some measure of support to "that deification and worship of the human soul, which has within a few years past manifested itself among our transcendentalists." [14] In short, he is about to show Channing that "orthodoxy" could be liberalized.

Brownson admits that he has much to recant: he had, for example, taught that Christianity did not stand or fall with the historicity of Christ. And he still thinks of baptism as being merely a symbol of that unity of the redeemed race "which is, to my understanding, rejected by all those who admit only baptism of adults." So also, "the same doctrine of the transmission of the life from man to man in time and space, by what I have termed spiritual generation, is borne witness to by what is termed apostolic succession. Without meaning to accept this last doctrine, in its episcopal sense, I must say that I see a great truth which it covers." [15]

The great truth is that "the human race lives . . . *in solido;* all are members of one and the same body, and members one of another. There is a oneness of life which runs through them all. . . . Consequently, the very moment that this new life of Jesus was communicated to the disciples, it was communicated virtually to the race." [16] Or again, "The coming of Jesus communicated a new life to the race, which by means of *communion* of man with man shall extend to all individuals." [17] Here is Brownson's great key word —"Communion": "The doctrine that man lives by communion with man, and through the life derived from Jesus with God, will bring us together on one platform, in the unity of life itself, and the church will become one in Christ." [18]

Channing replied congratulating Brownson upon the peace and confidence he had found, but gave the warning: "Some passages of your letter would lead an incautious reader to think you a thorough-going Universalist and as asserting the actual appropriation of the life of Christ to the whole human race, past and present, will they or nill they." [19] Then, lest Brownson feel too dashed by the suggestion that he was, on this point, saying what was not, after all, particularly new, he concluded: "God made you for something better than to scatter random shot, although these shot may sometimes be grand ideas and hit old errors between wind and water." Emerson, however, after having read the letter when it was published as a pamphlet, wrote in cold contempt to Miss Peabody: "With such questions I find myself unrelated. They are for those whom they concern. It is all positive, local and idolatrous." [20] He could not but recognize that "The Mediatorial Life of Jesus" was Brownson's repudiation of Transcendentalism.

At the same time that he was writing to Dr. Channing, Brownson was also writing his article, "Leroux on Humanity" for the *Boston Quarterly Review.* There he says that though Leroux is a Saint-

Simonian—and "Saint-Simon will be to the church of the future very nearly what St. Augustine has been to the church of the past" —he himself has no sympathy with the errors of the school. For it has confounded Christianity with the Catholic Church.[21] The Saint-Simonians have called for a new Christianity, whereas what should be called for is a new Church. Then he goes on to Leroux' theory, or his own application of it: "The true Christian redemption is . . . that of humanity, and of individuals only so far forth as they exist in humanity, and because it is in them only that humanity lives and is actualized. . . . This new life was not actually communicated to individuals, but it was communicated to the race, and through the race to all individuals *virtually,* because all exist virtually in the race, and *actually* to all who commune with regenerate humanity."[22]

Leroux, he declares, has freed him from the doctrine of Transcendentalism, which regards man as his own object.[23] Instead, "the church must enlarge its ideal, and propose, not the progress of isolated individuals—but the progress of men in their union with humanity."[24] Brownson similarly reinterprets other Christian doctrines. Transubstantiation he more or less equates with his newfound "Communion." "The Catholic doctors are less untrue to it than the Protestant," but still they have not got quite the right idea, though they are on the track of it. God is not to be loved or known except mediately, through humanity; and we attain to God only by loving—or entering into communion with—one another. Leroux' statement of the thesis, on the other hand, has to be rejected as pantheism.[25] The only sound view, of course, is Brownson's version of Leroux—purged of the Lerousian errors—and with the traditional Christian terminology used in a Brownsonian sense.

Purgatory Brownson defends in the same way. He believes as his Universalist and Unitarian friends do, that the individual has a personal immortality; but there is something they have missed. Those who have passed from us still commune with us. "The secrets of the country lying on the other side of that dark river death, are not so well kept as is sometimes alleged." On this ground he sets forth "the great truth the church has shadowed forth under her doctrine of purgatory." It is also "the basis of the doctrine of the Communion of Saints . . . [which] authorizes us to offer prayers for the dead, to make efforts for their sanctification, as we would were they still with us." [26]

Delightedly he presents all this as "a perfect synthesis of philosophy, politics, including ethics, and theology." It is a "universal solvent," [27] almost a magic formula, which could include everything—so at least it seemed at moments—because anything could mean anything, once it was sufficiently ingeniously explained. It was, it need hardly be said, all very far from being Catholic or from containing the Catholic doctrines he indicates. If it comes to that, it was not precisely what Leroux taught. But what of that? Leroux could call himself a pantheist if he liked; by the time Brownson had done with him, he would perceive depths in his own teaching he had never suspected.

Yet so far from merely amusing himself with his own intellectual dexterity, Brownson was desperately in earnest. The gist of it all is: "The profound truth of the solidarity of men in humanity, and of humanity, through Jesus, in God. . . . [It] is only by a living communion of the individual with humanity, through humanity with Jesus, and through Jesus with God, that he can be redeemed and sanctified." [28] The thing that matters now is not whether or not this curious amalgam of metaphysics and mysticism was tenable, but that it appeared to be so at the time to Brownson, and that it was by this tenuous thread that he was to find his way into the Catholic Church. In an article written in 1855, as two years later in *The Convert,* he calls Leroux the occasion of his conversion, and still asserts that his doctrine of Communion is the natural counterpart of the supernaturalism of Catholicism.[29]

Perhaps the clearest exposition of his own doctrine of Communion (as derived from Leroux and modified to suit his own

needs) is to be found in *The Convert*. There he explains that,
according to Leroux, man lives by communion with his object—
with nature, with his fellow-man, and with God. He communes
with nature through property, with his fellow-man through family
and the State, and with God through humanity. But having indicated what Leroux held, he at once largely demolished it by remarking: "In the third statement he adds nothing, for to commune with
God through Humanity is nothing else than to commune with
our own kind, or with other men in the family and the State." [30]
On the next page he adds, "The communion with God through
Humanity . . . was in effect simply no communion at all." Yet
it was by means of Leroux that Brownson was brought to the truth:
"I was obliged to give up all my hopes of progress, or abandon my
doctrine of no God but the God in man, or the identity of the
human and the Divine." Though still far from the truth, "I . . .
was headed, for the first time in my life, in the direction of real
Christian beliefs."

Several objections may be made to all this. Does man commune
with nature only through property, or even most effectively through
property? What about the man who has no property? Is he excluded
from the scheme? And is not the concept of communion with the
race only an abstraction, and even as such hard to conceive, unless
it be put in a Hitlerian racial myth? And is the notion of "Providential Men"—individuals elevated by the Creator "to an extraordinary or supernatural communion with himself," by which they
could live a divine life in which all men, by communion with them,
would partake—much more than the Carlylean doctrine of Heroes
and Hero Worship? [31] But whatever objections may be made to
Brownson's system of thought at this time, or however fantastic or
confused it may be, it was by this means that Brownson was working
closer to establishing a harmony in his mind between nature and
Grace, reason and revelation—a harmony denied by Calvinism and
indeed by all forms of Evangelical Protestantism. [32] It was for the
same reason that he had lost all sympathy with the Transcendentalist

concept of a natural origin for what Transcendentalists called revelation. He never wearied of quoting as heresy Emerson's lines:

> Out from the heart of Nature roll'd
> The burdens of the Bible old;
> The Litanies of Nations came,
> Like the Volcano's tongue of flame,
> Up from the burning core below,—
> The Canticles of Love and Woe.

Of which it is sufficient to say that fine poetry as they are, they postulate what is simply historically untrue, and that that untruth lay at the bottom of Transcendentalism.

If Brownson had taken anything from Carlyle in his idea of "Providential Men," he never acknowledged it. In any event he derived from this notion a conviction of Providence—a special as well as a general Providence [33]—and, in gaining it, he found that most of his obstacles, real or imaginary, to belief, had been removed at a stroke. Always he insisted that "to believe is normal, to disbelieve is abnormal," [34] and that belief would always come to the candid mind once the obstacles to belief were removed. Pointing out that we always believe what a man tells us, unless we have reason to doubt his veracity, he went on: "Truth is [the mind's] object, and it seeks and accepts it instinctively, as the new-born child seeks the mother's breast. . . . Place the mind and truth face to face, with nothing interposed between them, and the truth evidences itself to the mind. . . . The assent termed knowledge follows immediately from the joint forces of the intelligible object and the intelligent subject." [35] "Whenever the truth is immediately present, and reason looks it full in the face, it knows that it is truth without further evidence." [36] It was the idea that Dryden had expressed in *The Hind and the Panther*, the poem in which he defended his Catholicism:

> For truth has such a face and such a mien,
> As to be lov'd needs only to be seen.

This immediate and intuitive process (as distinct from the logical one that followed it) Brownson strongly affirmed. For it had been from the beginning at the very heart of all his religious experience. He did not deny the value of logic—no man ever could have denied it less—but he was aware that we do not always reach truth by logic; in fact, as logic often calls for a long and carefully constructed chain, we should be virtually excluded from knowledge did we not have an intuitive process to precede logic.[37] This, Brownson argued, applied to the supernatural at least as much as to the natural order. But he guarded himself with: "The understanding does not assent to [the propositions of faith] because it sees immediately their truth, as in the case of science or of knowledge, but because it sees the sufficiency of the authority or testimony affirming them."[38]

Here he came to his "ontologism" which, at this stage, as he afterwards admitted, was of the kind that was to receive Papal disapprobation. His later version of it was, he believed, disentangled from philosophical error. When he was accused of having derived it from Gioberti, he met the charge by saying that he had never so much as heard of Gioberti at this time. "Cousin and Leroux had held something like it, but made it . . . a pantheistic doctrine. They did not distinguish with sufficient care between the human reason and the reason of God, and while they made the immediate presence of God in the soul the condition of our intelligence, they did not regard that presence as creating our reason, or faculty of intelligence, and becoming immediately in the act of creating it, its light and object."[39] By this he clears himself from a possible charge of pantheism—a doctrine he had never really held at any time.

His realization of God as Creator, and exercising a special providence, removed from his mind what he saw was to so many people an obstacle to the acceptance of Christian faith. Here was a belief in the freedom of God. In asserting Providential Men, he felt he had risen above this difficulty, and in a noble passage concludes: "I was no longer fatherless, an orphan left to the tender mercies of inexorable general laws, and my heart bounded with joy, and I leaped to embrace the neck of my Father, and to rest my head on his bosom. I shall never forget the ecstasy of that moment, when I first realized to myself that God is free." [40]

Fourteen years later, writing in the *Ave Maria,* he again tells of it: "I shall never forget the singular emotion, I may say rapture, I felt one day, while wandering in the mazes of error, when suddenly burst upon my mind, for the first time, this great truth that God is free. . . . It struck me as a flash of light in the midst of my darkness . . . and changed almost instantaneously not only the tone and temper of my mind, but the direction of my whole order of thought. Though years elapsed before I found myself knocking at the door of the church for admission, my conversion began from that moment. I had seized the principle which authorizes faith in the supernatural." [41] This, of course, did not give Brownson Catholic dogmas, but it did prepare him, by the grace of God (which he was always careful to acknowledge in this connection), to receive the Catholic faith.[42] When writing *The Convert* in 1857 he still considered that, though his doctrine of Communion was much less than Catholicism, there was nothing in Catholicism "opposed to that doctrine, or which makes it necessary for a Catholic to exclude it." [43]

Many factors had contributed to bring him this far, some of them rather strange ones. For instance, when Theodore Parker (who was at that time one of his closest friends) began to preach Brownson's Religion of Humanity in 1841, Brownson was repelled when he heard the Parker version of it. He later had some hard words to say of this former friend: Parker's greatest defect was lack of loyalty; he might be a fanatic, and die in the defence of his opinions, but never a martyr to the truth. In short, "His boldness, firmness, courage, and independence were striking, and would have deserved very high reverence, if they had been exhibited in the cause of truth, not simply the cause of Mr. Theodore Parker." [44] He found himself murmuring, "There, but for the grace of God, go I!" He saw that though he and Parker held apparently much the same doctrines, there was a radical difference between them—the difference between naturalism and supernaturalism. As for Parker, he commented on Brownson in the spring of 1843: "He seems tending towards the Catholic Church. God bless him, wherever he is! He has a hard head." [45]

The progress Brownson was making was shown when in 1843 he wrote a series of articles for the *Christian World* on "The Mission of Jesus." The first two pleased the Unitarians, the third was praised by a Puritan journal, the fourth "threw the Tractarians into ecstasies," and the next three were commented upon favorably, and in part reprinted, by some Catholic periodicals. But the eighth, which was to answer the question, "Which is the True Church?" the *Christian World* declined to publish, and though a Catholic editor offered to do so, Brownson would not let him have it.[46]

When he began this series he had no idea of ever himself becoming a Catholic, but when he saw his articles being reprinted in Catholic papers, he began to entertain, for the first time, the possibility that the Church would prove his final goal. He saw that to be logical—and who more logical than himself?—he ought to accept the Church, and for an enthusiastic moment was on the point of doing so then. But grounds for hesitation occurred to him: he had a poor opinion of such Catholics as he had met; such Catholic writings as he had seen had not seemed to him very powerful; he thought of the Church as unprogressive, and remembered how all the energetic nations were Protestant; worst of all, he peopled the Church "with all manner of monsters, chimeras, and hydras dire." To enter it would be a committal for life, and that was something he did not dare. Therefore, he says, "I recoiled, and set my wits to find out, if possible, some compromise, some middle ground on which I could be faithful to my Catholic tendencies without uniting myself to the present Roman Catholic Church." [47] He was prepared to accept Catholicism without the Pope—the very compromise attempted under Henry VIII and proved to be so impossible. Or if Brownson was not precisely Henrican, he did his best to concoct a Unitarian variant.

He had been receiving letters from Protestant ministers who had read his articles and who confided that his ideas were very similar to their own. They, too, were dissatisfied with Protestantism and were in search of a new kind of Catholicism. Perhaps he exaggerated when he wrote: "The secret history of my own country for several years prior to 1844, would reveal a Catholic reaction in the more serious portion of the Protestant sects that would surprise those who look only on the surface of things." [48] But it was at least true that there was a kind of high-church movement among the Mercersburg group,[49] paralleling the Oxford Movement. Feeling that he was not alone but in a strong current, Brownson devised a theory which would make all sects part of the Catholic Church. "All communion of the sects," he thought, "with one another and even with the Roman Church, has not been absolutely interrupted. . . . They all belong, in some sort, to one and the same family, and all, in a measure, live the one life of Christ." [50] That this is to some extent —and in a certain sense—true need not be denied. On this assumption Brownson believed that, while the Roman Catholic "fragment" of the Church had its special advantages, those not of the Roman communion should, instead of uniting with it, "labor, from the point where Providence has placed us, to effect in the surest and speediest manner possible the reunion of all the fragments, and thus restore the body of Christ to its original unity and integrity." [51]

For his own guidance he posed a number of questions which he specifically answered. He could not join the Episcopalians, though he felt them to be doctrinally closest to him, as that would involve reordination and thus a denial that "the Congregational communion is an integral part of the church Catholic." Indeed, he felt he could be more Catholic as a Unitarian than as an Anglican. "From my Unitarian-congregational pulpit, I proclaim, as best I may, the faith and discipline of the holy Catholic Apostolic Church, out of which there is no salvation." His solution was that he should continue to preach as he had been doing, in the hope that an ecumenical council would be called to adjust the basis of reunion. The several sects might be so many branches torn from the Vine, but they were not dead branches. As for schism, "We who live now are not and cannot be partakers of the guilt of it, though we may suffer from its effects, unless we seek to perpetuate it, or refuse to labor to effect a reunion." [52]

Brownson indicated in the memorandum he wrote for himself that he did not look upon his view as final but as provisional.[53] In the first number of *Brownson's Quarterly Review* he set it forth, for what it was worth, mainly in order to stimulate enquiry. "The outward form of our Lord's Body," he said there, "has been broken into fragments; but it was an IMMORTAL body, and each particular fragment, however small, or however far the adversary may have cast it abroad in the earth, is still quick with its original life, and can not die." What should be done was to gather all the fragments together, as Isis gathered the torn body of Osiris together, "to be moulded anew into one homogeneous and lovely form of perfection." "The true church, the Holy Catholic Apostolic Church," he explained, "does still exist, . . . *but exists at the present time in a fragmentary state.*" [54]

All through this period of uncertainty Brownson's closest confidant was Isaac Hecker. This young man was still attending W. H. Channing's church in New York, and concerning that Brownson wrote to him on November 8, 1843, "[Channing's] theory of Christian union is very beautiful, very true; but he will fail. For to succeed he must institute a new Church, and to do that he must be a new Christ, and even greater than Christ . . . The principle of union, he says, is love, nothing more true. [But] so far from seeking Christian love as the basis of the union of the Church, we must seek the union of the Church as the condition of creating Christian love." Continuing, he wrote: "I hope you will find that you can now associate yourself with Mr. Haight's congregation. I cannot myself go with any of the fragments. My mission and destiny is [*sic*] fixed; but I believe, in the present state of the

Christian world, no denomination should be more acceptable to the soul yearning after union & Catholicity than the Episcopal. If I was in I would not go out of it, but being as I am I cannot go into it. But you, young man, it seems to me, might find a home and a sphere of action in it. I say to all my friends who consult me on the question, join the Episcopal Church, if you can with a good conscience." [55]

In later life Hecker used to tease Brownson about this letter, declaring it to be the one illogical act of Brownson's life. But that Brownson's view was quickly modified is evident from another letter to Hecker, written on the following March 11th. In it Brownson says: "My own feelings and convictions, in spite of my struggles to the contrary, carry me to the Catholic Church, and I foresee plainly that I must sooner or later become a member of it. There is no help for it. I seek, however, to maintain my position for the present." Now he cannot encourage Hecker to join the Episcopalians, though he still does not actively discourage it. What he does feel very strongly is that Hecker has a vocation to the ministry—whether Catholic or Episcopalian. In this letter he tells his young disciple, who was now outstripping him, that he is "plunged head and ears in Greek," and he advises Hecker to master Greek and Latin— "They are indispensable to you." [56] It was because of this advice that Isaac went the following month to Concord to study under George Bradford. About the same time Brownson gave up preaching at the Society of Christian Union and Progress.[57] He had been using his sermons as a means for clarifying his own thought. Now he had reached the point when silence was necessary for the reaching of a decision.

The first clear intimation that the readers of *Brownson's Quarterly Review*—there were only six hundred subscribers, but with that the editor seems to have been satisfied as a start [58]—got as to what was to happen was in the July number. In January he had told them: "There is no truth in the report, that I have joined, or am intending to join, the Roman Catholic Church. I am free to confess, that I accept the general theory of that Church, as the true theory of the Church of Christ, but that theory itself prevents me, *in the present state of the religious world,* from seeking to unite myself to the Roman Catholic Communion." [59] Hecker was later to account for matters: "[Brownson] was occupied in working out that problem philosophically and for the universe. I was looking out for number one. . . . He told me once that he was like the general of an army born in rebellion, and his duty was to carry as many back with him to the true standard as he could." [60]

In the April number he had had an article that had shown the direction he was taking. This postulated the necessity of a church as the only means of social reform. Man could not raise himself; and just as Archimedes said he could lift the world if he were provided with a fulcrum, so the dynamic law must be applied to moral conditions. He concluded: "Either there is already existing the Divine Institution, the Church of God, or there are no means of reform." [61] At that time, however, he was not prepared to say that the Catholic Church was the divine institution he had in mind; he was still trying to cling to his own notion of the Catholic Church as made up of scattered fragments.

Between April and July the whole thing had broken down. In the July issue Brownson told his readers bluntly: "The church in communion with the See of Rome is the one holy catholic apostolic church, or the one holy catholic apostolic church does not exist. We have tried every possible way to escape this conclusion, but escape it we cannot. We must accept it or go back to the no-church doctrine. Our logic allows us no alternative between Catholicism and Come-outerism . . . We are thoroughly convinced in mind, heart, and soul, that Christ did institute a visible church; that he founded it upon a rock; that the gates of hell have not prevailed, and cannot prevail, against it; and that it is the duty of all of us to submit to it, as the representative of the Son of God on earth." [62]

In the July issue he also had an article on "Come-outerism." In it he asserted, as he was so often to assert again, that he was no longer a radical but a conservative. And he explained, "We frequently find the man, who in his youth was a flaming radical, a stanch conservative in his maturer years." [63] "For ourselves, we have made our choice. We began our career with the radical tendency . . . and followed it till we saw where it must necessarily lead. We recoiled from its consequences. . . . Nothing remained but to take our stand on the conservative side." [64] Yet how little he had really changed—or had needed to change in this respect—is indicated by his reaffirming: "Our industrial system is working gradually, but surely, the subjection of the great mass of the operative classes; and when our new lands shall have been exhausted, and the price of land become so high that the laboring man can no longer hope to be a proprietor . . . we shall find established all over the country an industrial feudalism, of which the military feudalism of the middle ages was but a faint prelude." [65] As he was to write in *The Convert* thirteen years later, "I had, after all, less to change on becoming a Catholic than was commonly supposed at the time." [66]

From his hatred of industrialism he did not deviate; all he ever changed was his concept as to the means of reform. Even there he had long been essentially a conservative, in the sense of denying the effectiveness or the validity of revolution. It was as a Calhoun "Constitutionalist" that he had been waging his war against the oppression of the poor. In Calhoun he found another hand that pointed in the direction of the Catholic Church.

Brownson had not taken his doctrine directly from Calhoun. It was rather that, seeing in Calhoun an exponent of his own constitutional theories, he had backed him for the presidential nomination in 1840. He was now backing him again for the nomination in 1844 —this time more openly. Though in this Brownson failed, he had something to do with Van Buren's not being chosen as the Democratic candidate. To the last he hoped that Calhoun would be picked by the Baltimore convention. Then one morning one of his sons came in with the morning papers. At once his father asked eagerly, "Well, have they made a nomination?" "Yes, sir," the boy replied; "it is James K. Polk." "And who is James K. Polk?" roared Brownson, dashing the bundle of papers to the ground.[67]

It was another proof that men were simply not to be counted upon to act with intelligence. He had received another such proof when he was in Washington about this time. He was sitting talking with Calhoun and Buchanan, and the subject turned to religion. Brownson was arguing that, if one wanted to be saved, one should join the Catholic Church. Daniel Webster just at that moment joined them and Buchanan repeated what Brownson had said, adding that he agreed. "Have you just found that out?" said Webster. "Why, I've known that for years."[68] Or so goes the story. It is too bad that all these famous politicians should have plumped for hell.

It was not the first time that Webster had talked like this. Some years before Brownson had run into him in a Boston book-store, and Webster, observing that Brownson had picked up a Catholic book, took it from him and glanced through it, saying, "Take care how you examine the Catholic Church, unless you are willing to become a Catholic, for Catholic doctrines are logical." Upon which Hecker, who told the tale, comments, "How little appreciation of the philosophical mind did that remark reveal!"[69]

Hecker, referring to Brownson's conversion, was to write: "When a man without guile is brought face to face with truth he spontaneously desires union with it. Appetite proves the existence of food, and the food affirms itself by satisfying the appetite." One of the grudges he and Brownson had against Calvinism was that it affirmed that the human heart, because it was totally depraved, was not to be trusted. In their case they discovered that "the affections of the heart are guides to truth as certain as the logic of the understanding."[70] Isaac, perhaps because he was younger and more impulsive than Brownson, had preceded him into the Church, having been received in July, 1844.

After leaving Brook Farm and then Fruitlands, he had continued to write to Brownson about his spiritual condition. In March "Deiner Sohn Isaac," as he signed himself to Brownson, had seen Bishop Hughes in New York; but the interview was not satisfactory, and he was still wavering between Catholicism and Episcopalianism. The following month he went to Concord to study Greek and Latin under Bradford. That he sorely needed some education is evident from the way he told Brownson about this: "He will take an interest in learning me the languages in the shortest time, but *none the less thorough*." [71] The experiment, however, did not turn out well. Bradford, Hecker wrote in his diary on May 6th, went to see him only after he was tired out from his school and did no more than listen to him recite. If he had known that Thoreau was so good a scholar—one who had learned his Greek at Harvard from the poet, Jones Very—he would have gone to him instead. A few moments conversation with him gave the eager student "more instruction and delight" than all that George Bradford had ever said on the subject.[72] Isaac did not remain long at Concord.

On the way up, he had visited the genial Dr. Seabury, the Episcopalian editor, who had warned him: "We cannot accept the church of Rome as she now is, and I am afraid that the influence of Brownson upon the Roman church is such as to make her cling to her exclusiveness and her practices which are not catholic." This was in a letter to Brownson dated April 7th but which should have been dated the 9th.[73]

On his way back to New York Hecker stayed with the Jesuits at Holy Cross College at Worcester. Concerning this also he wrote to Brownson at the end of June. Isaac found them well enough educated but considered that "their method is a very short one in settling difficult points—scripture and the church—not appreciating any other method, however important and profound it may be, to the welfare and success of the church, but a new generation must take their place if Catholicism is to be established in the world. I feel so in their presence that if it was to them that I was to be united I should shrink, but it is not to them, but the church. Understand me, I believe these men have many private virtues which if I knew would command my deepest respect and reverence for their individual characters; but I wish they did not take so much snuff, and that too even in the midst of that holy awful sacred sacrifice, the Mass." [74] But by July Isaac had seen "Bishop McClosky" [*sic*], Hughes' coadjutor and the future cardinal, who pleased him much better than the snuff-taking Jesuits had done. Before the month was out he had not only been received into the Church but accepted as a postulant by the Redemptorists.

By that time Orestes Brownson was himself under instruction, and had been since May. There had been a long period of hesitation and delay, about which those who set him down as precipitous and rash knew nothing. Actually he had done his best to find some middle ground, on which he could be faithful to his Catholic tendencies without joining the Catholic Church. [75] That effort had come to nothing. In the end there was no resisting logic.

It is interesting to compare the comments the two friends made upon one another. In his diary, under June 29, 1845, Hecker wrote of Brownson: "Though he is a friend to me and the most critical periods of my experience have been known to him, and he has advised and frequently given me his sympathy, yet he never moves my heart. He has been of inestimable value to me in my intellectual development. He is too a man of heart. But he is so strong and intellectually active that all his energy is consumed in thought. He is an intellectual athlete. He thinks for a dozen men. He does not take time to realize in heart for himself. . . . He has not the temperament of genius, but more of a rhetorician and declaimer. He arrives at his truths by a regular and consecutive system of logic. His mind is of a historical rather than a poetical mould. . . . He never will be charged with holding two doctrines, one esoteric and the other exoteric. As a man, we have never known one so conscientious and self-sacrificing. This is natural to him. His love of right is supreme,

A description by a dear friend of Brownson's character. B

and his great [abomination?], the thing he detests, is bad logic. This makes him peevish and often riles his temper. He defeats but will never convince an opponent. . . . No one loves to break a lance with him, because he cuts such ungentlemanly gashes. He is strong and he knows it. He has more of the Indian chief than of the chivalrous knight in his composition. . . . His art is logic but he never aims at art. He is a most genuine and true man to his nature. None so much so. . . . There is a pure and genuine vein of poetry running through his nature, but not sufficient to tincture the whole glow of his life. . . . He is an anomaly among scholars, writers and divines. He is not thorough on any one subject, though at home on all. . . . He is genuine, we love him for this. This is the crown of all virtues." [76]

It is clear from this careful analysis of Brownson's character that the disciple has become sufficiently detached to see his master just as he was. It is even a question as to whether at this time Hecker could still be called Brownson's disciple. Ten years later, Brownson, in reviewing Hecker's first book, was to acknowledge: "We owe personally more than we can say to our long and intimate acquaintance with him. How often, when neither of us knew or believed in the glorious old Catholic Church, have we talked together by our own fireside, on the great questions discussed in the volume before us, and stimulated each other's endeavors after truth and goodness! His modesty and docility made him in those times regard us as his teacher as well as his senior, but in truth we were the scholar. . . . Each perhaps was of service to the other, but he aided us more than we him." [77] From which it is clear that to the list of qualities drawn up by Hecker in his diary, the quality of magnanimity should have been added. Hecker, not to be outdone, referred to this passage at the end of the last of the series of articles he wrote on his friend and insisted: "He was the master, I the disciple. God alone knows how much I am indebted to him. To the channels of thought opened to me by Dr. Brownson I owed, more than to anything else, my conversion to the Catholic faith." [78] From which we may safely conclude that they acted upon one another; perhaps neither man would have come into the Catholic Church had it not been for this providential friendship. In the quest itself, Brownson supplied most of the thought, Hecker most of the feeling.

Brownson called on Bishop Fenwick, a Marylander and a Jesuit, for the first time during Holy Week, a bad time to call, because the Bishop was busy. The conversation did not touch the question of Brownson's admission to the Church but was carried on "in a lively and half-sporting strain." The visitor thought Fenwick a very pleasant man but of no remarkable ability. At least none had manifested itself during those twenty minutes. However, he saw him again in May, and then came to the point.

The Bishop said he had been reading the *Review* and had observed that Brownson was approaching the Catholic position, but asked, "What can be your objections to the Pope?"

"I do not object to the Pope," Brownson told him. "Some time ago I was foolish enough to say that the problem of the age is Catholicism without papacy; but I no longer entertain that notion. The Church without the Pope would be to me no church at all."

"Why then, are you not a Catholic?"

Brownson explained that he would be one except for wanting to discover some ground for becoming a Catholic without at the same time declaring Protestants all wrong and that they could not be saved. To which the Bishop answered, "God is just, and you may leave your Protestant friends in His hands. If they break the order He has established, that is no good reason for you to remain where you are and to neglect to make sure of yourself." [79]

Subsequent visits were made and books were lent; then Fenwick turned Brownson over to his young coadjutor, Bishop Fitzpatrick, Boston born and educated at Montreal and by the Sulpicians at Paris. By now Brownson had reached the conclusion that, though to become a Catholic was an unpleasant step, "To be eternally damned would, after all, be a great deal unpleasanter." [80]

The process of instruction was, in many ways, distinctly disagreeable. Fitzpatrick started with a prejudice against a man whom he set down as "proud and conceited." [81] To understand the situation we must go to Hecker. He says that while Fitzpatrick had "a native ability far above the ordinary, . . . his knowledge did not embrace the intellectual trend of the present age nor take in the signs of impending changes among men outside the Catholic Church." [82] Hecker lets a blacker cat out of the bag by expressing the opinion that Fitzpatrick was "the hierarchical exponent of all that was traditional and commonplace in Catholic public life." [83]

The coadjutor was, moreover, a little difficult to talk to consecutively, his ironic habit of mind making it almost impossible to argue with him. He was, says Hecker, who had consulted him about his own difficulties, one "who continually flashes back and forth between first principles and witticisms. When I would undertake to grapple with him on first principles he would throw me off with a joke, and while I was parrying the joke he was back again upon first principles." Partly it was the difference between the Irish and the German mind. Yet it was really more than that. When Hecker had gone to Fitzpatrick, expecting to be asked, "What truths were the stepping-stones that led you here?" his mind was probed instead for the errors it might still contain. This mode of procedure was, so Hecker considered, especially bad in Brownson's case, "for he was one who had come into the possession of the full truth not so much from hatred of error as love of truth." [84] Brownson, for his part, let the Bishop down tenderly by saying, "I have met men of bolder fancy and more creative imaginations; but I have never met a man of clearer head, a firmer intellectual grasp, a sounder judgment, or a warmer heart. . . . Though I have found men who made a far greater display of theological erudition, I have never met an abler or sounder theologian." [85]

The main difficulty Brownson found was, not in accepting Catholic dogma—*that* he accepted without question, once he had accepted the authority of the Church to teach—but in Fitzpatrick's

attitude. It was several months before they could come together.
The fact is that the genial Bishop John (as Boston Catholics loved
to call him) had not the slightest interest in what had brought
Brownson to the Church. If he ever understood the convert's
"Doctrine of Communion," he probably looked upon it as a lot of
nonsense. But Brownson's position in the beginning was, "if I rejected or waived it, what reason had I for regarding the Church as
authoritative for natural reason, or for recognizing any authority
in the Bishop himself to teach me?" [86] Eventually Brownson re-
linquished his theory—to the extent of putting it in cold storage
for later use—and consented to follow the ordinary lines of Catholic
apologetics. He even brought himself to believe for a time that he
had given it up entirely and wrote to Hecker, "Many of the notions
I threw out on the doctrine of Communion I look upon now as
false and even hurtful. It is best for us to take the Church in the
old way, without studying to find a philosophical basis for what it
teaches. We want a logical basis rather than a philosophical basis.
The notion of Communion I formerly advanced, and which wrought
such a revolution in us, both, served its purpose, but, if extended
far, it is dangerous and heretical." [87] Now that Leroux had brought
him so far, he was not going to let Leroux (or even Fitzpatrick)
keep him out of the Church. Yet despite what he told Hecker, his
conviction revived that his own method—while no doubt not one
that would supersede the accepted method of instruction—had its
use as a preparation for that preparation. A little loftily he says in
The Convert: "This new process or method I found was as satisfactory to reason as my own," adding, "What would have been its
practical effect on my mind, had I encountered it before I had in
fact become a believer, and in reality had no need of it for my personal conviction, I am unable to say, though I suspect it would never
have brought me to the Church." [88] With which, like Brownson himself, we may let it go for the present.

Fortunately for Brownson, there were no domestic complications
over his conversion. Sally, who had grieved deeply, if silently, dur-

ing the early years of their marriage, at witnessing his growing unbelief, now encouraged him to become a Catholic, and her own candid heart readily accepted the faith to which he had attained only with so much struggle. As for the children, they were not only Brownsons but Brownsonians, and they prattled around the meal-table of the *me* and the *not-me,* and *das reine Seyn* and *das Ding-an-Sich.*[89] All except Orestes Junior, who was living his jolly life on the ocean wave and who knew nothing of what was happening at home until it was all over and he was back from Calcutta. Then he was at first so shocked that he left home and went to live with some relatives in Ohio. But he, too, after a while entered the Jesuit college at Cincinnati to complete his interrupted education, and there he was baptized by Bishop Purcell. All the other members of the family entered the Church together.

On the other hand, Brownson's effect upon his brothers and sisters was almost nil, though he remained on affectionate terms with them. We hear of his eldest brother, Daniel, obtaining some local celebrity as a public speaker, and of his sisters as Methodists even in old age. His other brother, Oran, came to visit him in 1851. He had become a Mormon, for the same reason—so he wrote on April 5, 1846—that Orestes had become a Catholic, a belief that it was the Latter Day Saints that possessed proper spiritual authority.[90] Now he and Orestes had long arguments about religion. George Parsons Lathrop describes the scene, though of course not at first hand, and misspelling Oran's name.[91] "Orrin," he wrote, "would put a question, which Orestes would answer with uncompromising, unsparing force. Then Orrin, without saying a word, would dart out of the house and walk a long time in the hot sunshine; after which he would return and put another question. The same process was repeated: Orrin still making no rejoinder. When this odd dialogue ended, there was no summing up: Orrin went away in silence. After nine years, during which the brothers had not met again, Orrin wrote to Orestes that he had become a Catholic. From Dublin, Ohio, he had gone to Dublin, Ireland, where he was received into the Church."[92] Possibly if Orestes Brownson could have seen more of Daniel and his sisters, the same thing would have happened to them.

Joseph Henry Allen, who was upon the whole rather friendly to Brownson, tells a story about him which had best be taken with a grain of salt. Allen asked him one day what would have happened to him had he died on the 19th of October, 1844, the day before the one set for his reception into the Church. He says that Brownson answered "instantly and grimly": "I should have gone to hell." [93] The grimness may of course have been merely grim humor; Brownson was rather given to making such jokes. But it was quite in keeping with what Brownson seriously believed, even if he deliberately put this particular remark in an exaggerated form. His own comment on his conversion, made in 1872 and embedded in an article on "Catholic Popular Literature," was: "The question with me came not in the shape, What shall I believe? but in this other shape, What shall I do to be saved? . . . I came to the question of the church as a sinner in need of a Saviour. . . . I never sought the truth; it came to me, . . . and I believed as the child believes the father or mother, and for thirty years have never doubted." [94]

[1] We know from Elliott's *Life* (p. 162) that Hecker took this Catechism with him to Concord to study. And Brownson wrote to him in December, 1843 (so dated from internal evidence): "I want to see the Scotus Erigena you have been reading." (*Hecker Papers*). There is no indication that he actually did see it, however.

[2] *Middle Life*, p. 2. The brilliant and attractive Félicité de Lamennais cannot be counted in this connection, as he was an apostate, though he may have put some Catholic notions into Brownson's mind. Brownson had certainly studied him closely and he wrote to Cousin in 1838 asking for his address, which, however, Cousin was unable to supply, though he did refer Brownson to Lamennais' publisher. (*Early Life*, p. 409.)

[3] *The Convert*, p. 356. He adds that they were written in a dry, feeble, and unattractive style, and abounded in terms and locutions which were to him totally unintelligible.

[4] *Latter Life*, p. 555.

[5] *Early Life*, p. 369.

[6] *Early Life*, p. 477.

[7] Peabody, *Reminiscences of Channing*, pp. 153–154.

[8] *The Convert*, p. 170.

[9] Brownson makes the slip in *The Convert* (p. 332) of saying that it was in June, 1843.

[10] *Works,* Vol. IV, pp. 142–143.

[11] *Ibid.,* pp. 143–144.

[12] *Ibid.,* pp. 144–145.

[13] *Ibid.,* pp. 151, 152.

[14] *Ibid.,* p. 150.

[15] *Ibid.,* p. 162.

[16] *Ibid.,* pp. 161–162.

[17] *Ibid.,* p. 167.

[18] *Ibid.,* p. 170.

[19] *Early Life,* p. 444.

[20] *Letters,* Vol. III, pp. 63–64.

[21] *Works,* Vol. IV, p. 101.

[22] *Ibid.,* pp. 106–107.

[23] *Ibid.,* p. 119.

[24] *Ibid.,* p. 120.

[25] *Ibid.,* pp. 123, 124, 126, 129.

[26] *Ibid.,* pp. 135, 136.

[27] *Ibid.,* p. 139.

[28] *Ibid.,* p. 124.

[29] *Works,* Vol. X, p. 527.

[30] *The Convert,* p. 289.

[31] Carlyle's book was published in 1841.

[32] *The Convert,* p. 295.

[33] *Ibid.,* p. 305.

[34] *Ibid.,* p. 306.

[35] *Ibid.,* p. 307.

[36] *Ibid.,* p. 308.

[37] *Ibid.,* pp. 309, 310.

[38] *Ibid.,* p. 310.

[39] *Ibid.,* pp. 312–313.

[40] *Ibid.,* p. 318.

[41] *Works,* Vol. VIII, p. 262.

[42] *The Convert,* p. 337.

[43] *Ibid.,* p. 338.

[44] *Ibid.,* pp. 344–345. In this connection George Santayana's aphorism might be quoted: "Fanaticism consists in redoubling your effort when you have forgotten your aim." (*The Life of Reason,* Vol. I, p. 13.)

[45] Weiss, *Life and Correspondence of Theodore Parker,* Vol. I, p. 353.

[46] *The Convert,* p. 353.

[47] *Ibid.,* pp. 359, 360.

[48] *Ibid.,* pp. 364–365.

[49] As to this see the letters from Drs. Philip Schaff and J. W. Nevin (*Middle Life,* pp. 361–362, 369–372). They arose out of one of the articles written by Nevin in the *Mercersburg Review* which are listed in my bibliography, part of a controversy on a very high plane. These, however, were subsequent to Brownson's conversion. What previous letters or confidential conversations he had in mind it is impossible to say. The gist of Brownson's contention was that though the theologians of the Mercersburg

school were tinged with a large number of heresies, Dr. Nevin, at least, "has caught some glimpses of certain important Catholic truths, not much regarded by Protestants generally, and which he wields with murderous effect against vulgar Protestantism. But he only partially apprehends these great truths, and he combines them in his own mind with principles utterly repugnant to them . . . [But] he clasps the errors to his bosom, because he does not see how, without them, he can hold the Catholic truths which he sees in connection with them, and which really enrapture his heart." (*Works*, Vol. III, p. 102.) In subsequent articles he wrote as though he quite expected Nevin to become a Catholic. Though Nevin's personal letters to Brownson somewhat encourage such a hope, it does not seem to me that the *Mercersburg Review* articles do so. I fear that the passage in *The Convert* about the "secret history" of America, does not have anything much more substantial to support it than the Mercersburg affair.

[50] *Ibid.*, p. 362.

[51] *Ibid.*, p. 363.

[52] *Early Life*, pp. 455–463. This is especially interesting in view of a similar movement, which attracted many very able men of various denominations in England from about 1910–1920, and which, for all I know, may still be in existence. Among its leaders were Drs. Lloyd Thomas and W. E. Orchard—who is now a Catholic priest. As a Congregationalist, Dr. Orchard obtained schismatic ordination and so said a genuine Mass. A somewhat similar convert was my friend Dr. George Hitchcock, who after being a Catholic priest for a few years, reverted to Unitarianism, though (so I understand) continuing to preach Catholic theology and to say Mass. He died some years ago.

[53] *Ibid.*, p. 459.

[54] *Brownson's Quarterly Review*, Vol. I (1844), pp. 60, 77.

[55] *Hecker Papers*. The Mr. Haight referred to was the pastor of All Saints Episcopal Church on Henry Street, New York City. He lived only a few blocks away from the Heckers on Rutgers Street and was also a professor at the General Theological Seminary.

[56] *Ibid.*

[57] *Middle Life*, p. 1.

[58] Brownson to Hecker, March 11, 1844 (*Hecker Papers*).

[59] Vol. I (1884), p. 15.

[60] *Catholic World*, Vol. XLV (1887), p. 472.

[61] *Brownson's Quarterly Review*, Vol. I (1844), p. 193.

[62] *Works*, Vol. IV, p. 559.

[63] *Works*, Vol. IV, p. 545.

[64] *Ibid.*, p. 556.

[65] *Ibid.*, p. 542.

[66] P. 197.

[67] *Early Life*, p. 360.

[68] *Early Life*, p. 467. Webster's law partner was J. P. Healy, a cousin of Brownson's wife.

[69] *Catholic World*, Vol. XVI (1887), p. 4.

[70] *Catholic World*, Vol. XLVI (1887), pp. 222–223, 231.

[71] *Early Life*, p. 520.

[72] *Hecker Papers*.

[73] I quote from the letter as it is given in *Early Life*, pp. 527–529. As to the correct dating see Father Holden's *Early Years of Isaac Thomas Hecker*, p. 204 fn.

[74] *Early Life*, pp. 533, 534. Henry Brownson made an error in transcription—the phrase he renders "moral virtues" should be as I have given it.

[75] *The Convert*, pp. 354, 355, 360.

[76] *Hecker Papers.*

[77] *Works*, Vol. XIV, pp. 538–539. On March 28, 1851 he wrote to Hecker: "I am more indebted to you for having become a Catholic than to any man under heaven, and while you supposed I was leading you to the Church, it was you who led me there" (*Hecker Papers*).

[78] *Catholic World*, Vol. XLVI (1887), p. 235.

[79] *Works*, Vol. XIV, p. 474.

[80] *The Convert*, p. 372.

[81] *Ibid.*, p. 374.

[82] *Catholic World*, Vol. XLV (1887), p. 1.

[83] *Ibid.*, p. 7.

[84] *Ibid.*, pp. 2, 3.

[85] *The Convert*, pp. 373–374. The reader should be warned, however, that though Brownson meant every word of this praise, his autobiography was written by way of valedictory to Fitzpatrick from whom—it would hardly be too strong to say—he had escaped. *The Convert* was dedicated to the Bishop, but was (as we shall see later) written largely to justify himself against Fitzpatrick.

[86] *Ibid.*, pp. 375–376.

[87] *Hecker Papers*. Letter conjecturally dated July 3, 1845. In the same letter he warns Hecker of his dangerous tendency to mysticism. "Here is the rock on which many a great saint has been wrecked." In another letter (also among the *Hecker Papers*) dated June 25, 1845, Brownson advises Hecker to join the Jesuits, and adds as a compromise, "Your disposition, I should think, would lead you to the Carthusians, but could you not be content yourself with the Dominicans?"

[88] Pp. 376, 378.

[89] *Early Life*, p. 413.

[90] This letter, which is among the *Brownson Papers*, is quoted, in part by Mr. Schlesinger in a footnote to page 187 of his book.

[91] So does Doran Whalen (*op. cit.*, p. 5).

[92] *Atlantic Monthly*, Vol. LXXVII (1896), p. 779.

[93] *Our Liberal Movement in Theology*, p. 88.

[94] *Works*, Vol. XIX, pp. 582, 583.

CHAPTER IX

No *Salvation Outside the Church*

WHEN BROWNSON CAME INTO the Catholic Church he was at the peak of his fame. Somehow he had lived down the obloquy that had been thrown upon him for his articles on "The Laboring Classes," written in 1840; in fact, these articles had increased his celebrity. Since then his increasing conservatism had attracted to him many who had once looked upon him with suspicion. Though he probably did not have, as yet, over a thousand subscribers for his *Review*,[1] they included most of the best minds in the country. He was now able to say, "For the first time I had the sentiments of the better portion of the community with me." [2] Yet it was just then—just when he had recovered a position he had imagined to have been lost forever— that he threw it away again by becoming a Catholic. There is the measure of the sacrifice he was prepared to make for truth.

It was not only his position he was prepared to give up, but his means of livelihood—a dreadful prospect for a man of forty-one with a large family to support. But it did not distress him unduly: he was conscious of his powers and thought of becoming a lawyer; the profession would be useful to him if a political career opened in spite of everything; if not, he could still practice law.[3] In it his logical powers would have stood him in good stead, and he was already an authority on constitutional theory. Even so, it would not have been easy for him to make such a change at his time of life.

That he continued *Brownson's Quarterly Review* we owe, at least in part, to Fitzpatrick. The Bishop told him that he should not hide his light under a bushel, upon which Van Wyck Brooks's comment is, "As well urge a bull not to pretend to be a lamb!" [4] The difficulty was that Brownson was as yet unprepared to deal with the theological and philosophical subjects upon which he had been writing—at any rate if along other lines than those he had so far followed, and Fitzpatrick definitely discouraged any others. For a time it seemed to him, that if the *Review* was to continue, it could not with advantage be conducted in Boston. We may infer what it was he wrote to Hecker from what Hecker wrote to him on September 5, 1844: "You would find the heads of the Church more to your mind in New York than in Boston, it seems to me, and more able, and with greater enthusiasm to second your plans. . . . They feel much stronger, and are more disposed to break the silence which the church has suffered herself to keep. If you are disposed to restart your Quarterly under different auspices I think it would be well for you to see the Bishops of this diocese prior to the undertaking. I think it is very probable that Bishop Hughes will write to you soon by what Bishop McCloskey said to me." [5] It may well be that the zeal of the convert and the affection of the disciple led Hecker to say too much. That he said it at all is clear evidence that Brownson was somewhat worried about living under the jurisdiction of Fitzpatrick.

Whether or not Hughes ever did write to him we do not know; probably he did not. In any event Fitzpatrick succeeded in persuading Brownson to continue his *Review* in Boston. Reasons against what Hecker proposed occurred to the editor, who replied to Hecker on September 24th: "I do not like the project of a Catholic Review, at New York. Such a Review would necessarily be confined almost exclusively in its circulation to the Catholic population. It is better to let mine go on as it is. If the Catholics will support it, it will live, and go among protestants also." [6] It was a decisive argument with Hecker, who believed as much as Brownson did, that his mission was to his former associates. They both had visions of thousands being led into the Church by the newly-converted apostle. [7]

The Catholic Church in America already had a number of periodicals, but none of them was of any great intellectual importance or appealed to the kind of people who had been reading Brownson. These periodicals all addressed themselves exclusively to Catholics and took a defensive tone. Fitzpatrick saw that there was need for Brownson's positive and aggressive methods. The new-comers were mostly ignorant; the descendents of the old American Catholics were all timid, doing their best to make themselves inconspicuous. Even in England Newman, preaching his sermon "The Second Spring" in 1852, described how cowed Catholics had been almost within living memory: "Here a set of poor Irishmen, coming and going at harvest time, or a colony of them lodged in a miserable quarter of the vast metropolis. There, perhaps, an elderly person, seen walking in the streets, grave and solitary, and strange, though noble in bearing, and said to be of good family, and a 'Roman Catholic.' An old-fashioned house of gloomy appearance, closed in with high walls, with an iron gate, and yews, and the report attaching to it that 'Roman Catholics' lived there; but who they were or what they did, or what was meant by calling them Roman Catholics, no one could tell;—though it had an unpleasant sound, and told of form and superstition." In America things were in some ways even worse, for there there was active antagonism. Only ten years previously the convent at Charlestown had been burned to the ground by a mob; even while Brownson was under instruction at Boston, there had been a three-day riot in the streets of Philadelphia, in which cannon had been used, several churches destroyed, and thirteen men killed and fifty others wounded.[8] There was certainly need for Brownson's powerful journalism.

Yet not all Catholics welcomed it. Many were seriously alarmed by the truculence of their new champion. It extended not only to his style of writing but to his personal behavior. And indeed there was really no need for him to roar at the inn-keeper at Andover who served him meat at the common table on a Friday, "Why don't you have something in your house a Christian can eat?" When the landlord, quite unaware of his offence, and supposing merely that the guest did not care for the particular dish before him, began to suggest steak or—he was cut short with another roar for the benefit of everybody in the dining-room: "Why don't you have fish? No Christian eats meat on a Friday." [9] And when in the office of Benjamin Greene, the publisher of his *Review*, a man called Hoover attacked the Catholic Church, Brownson simply took hold of him by the coat-collar and the seat of his trousers and tossed him over the stove.[10] Greene himself got it one day, though in a mild and humorous form, when he asked Brownson what his reward would be in the after life for having as a Protestant published a Catholic Review. Brownson answered, "Well, let me see. You will get a reward of course. It will be that once every million years you will be allowed to put your foot for the millionth part of a second on the coolest spot in hell." [11] Another man, who insulted him by telling him that by becoming a Catholic he had turned traitor to his country, he quite literally floored.[12] Brownson was determined, like the character in *Hudibras,*

> To prove his doctrine orthodox
> By apostolic blows and knocks.

There was no doubt that from the start he made himself felt.

If he had been fortunate in having no domestic upheaval as a consequence of his conversion, he could also congratulate himself in old age, when he looked back on what had happened, that he did not have very many or very close social ties to break, as he had lived so much alone.[13] All the same a man of his warm-hearted disposition must have felt it hard that friends withdrew, and a writer must have missed the stimulating companionship of his own kind. No doubt he would have agreed with Kant—at least on this point—that the society of mere literary men is detestable. But his own literary friends had been, with few exceptions, philosophers rather than creative artists. He had been mixing on familiar terms with many of the leading spirits of the age, and to have given them up must have cost him a great deal. Ripley himself became estranged. When he took his position on the New York *Tribune* Brownson made a last effort to win him over, but Ripley told him that he would lose his job if he became a Catholic, and so would have to wait until he retired.[14] After that, he and Brownson drifted further apart.

There is no hint of regret over this lost companionship in anything that Brownson wrote, and certainly no whine of complaint. He was so completely satisfied with the Faith that he was content to forgo his former friends, and seems to have dropped them quite as much as they dropped him. In 1870 he said, "It is not easy to describe the sensations of relief a convert from Protestantism feels on coming into the church and learning that he has now a religion that can sustain him instead of needing him to sustain it."[15] He signalized his conversion by beginning to put on weight, and when he met in the street a couple of lean Protestant ministers whom he had known, one of them asked him, "How is it, Brother Brownson, that you who used to be as thin as we are, have grown so big?" To which Brother Brownson replied, "All very simple. Become Catholics and go to confession and get your sins off your conscience; then you will grow fat and laugh."[16] It was assuredly not due to his having an easier life as a Catholic; only after his reception into the Church did his real battles begin. Of these the fiercest had to be fought with fellow-Catholics. Whatever else he found in the Church it was not comfort. Asked some years later whether his life among Catholics had been a bed of roses, he did not hesitate: "Spikes, sir— spikes!"[17]

It was well worth it for the sake of the intellectual satisfaction he obtained. Some of his former acquaintances not unnaturally supposed in the beginning that Brownson had joined the Catholic Church to find a snug harbor where he could be at peace. They looked upon what he had done as a form of intellectual suicide. It did not take very long to disabuse them of that idea. One had only to open the pages of *Brownson's Quarterly Review* to see that his mind had lost nothing of its force, but had gained a greater breadth. Then they had to console themselves with the thought that his Catholicism could not possibly last long. He had changed so many times; he would be sure to change again. It was no doubt fun for the moment to defend the indefensible, but as soon as the novelty had worn off, he would be shooting off into some other form of extravagance. He was obviously far too intelligent a man to remain submissive under the dull despotism of priests. To the very end those who had known him in Boston, and who wrote about the Transcendentalist movement, showed that they were looking for the return of the prodigal.[18]

His position was not very secure even among Catholics. They too remembered his many divagations. And they did not like his manner or his manners. They believed he was doing them harm by being so belligerent. Converts are nearly always under a little cloud of suspicion to the day of their death. It was resented that Brownson set himself up at once as a leader of the Church [19]—and many of his co-religionists kept a weather eye cocked for his heresies. Not a few questioned whether it was possible for a Yankee to be a genuine Catholic—whether, if it came to that, anybody could be a genuine Catholic who was not an Irishman. This bluntly tactless man rasped their nerves. He was never to become popular among them. It troubled him not a whit.

What caused him a good deal of disappointment, however, was that he was much less successful than he had expected to be in winning his former associates to the Faith. At first he largely addressed himself to them, until he saw that it was useless, that they were not going to be won. It was evident that they were determined to ignore him, and to forget him if possible. After that he wrote directly for Catholics. Though a few friends followed him into the fold—Mrs. Ripley and Miss Stearns and young Arthur Sumner and two of the many former Unitarian ministers who had been at Brook Farm, William J. Davis and George Leach—his general failure at the very point where he had been most confident was undeniable.

It was to some extent his own fault. It was also, perhaps, to some extent the fault of Bishop Fitzpatrick—only it should be added that, even in the most fortunate circumstances, Brownson could not have accomplished all he had hoped for. Already he should have learned that triumph in dialectics does not invariably (or even very often) mean that conviction is obtained. And he used the wrong type of argument.

As this is a matter we are going to meet many times in the course of Brownson's career, a preliminary word or two had better be said at this point.

People who had met him, or who had heard him in the Society for Christian Union and Progress, or who had read his books and articles, were accustomed to his knock-down-drag-out style of controversy. Some sensitive souls were distressed by it, but everybody by now had come to recognize it as part of Brownson's make-up. As for his formidable logic, they had discovered in Boston that the only safe way to argue with him was to deny everything he postulated. "If you admitted anything," they said, "even the most simple and obvious, that he proposed, you were lost: he would proceed logically and prove his point triumphantly." [20] The thing that now bewildered them was that there was no discernible nexus between what Brownson had said in the past—even in the very near past— and what he was saying now. They had seen—the more acute among them—that for years his face had been turning more and more in the direction of Rome. Some of them knew of the arguments he had derived from Constant and Saint-Simon and Cousin and Leroux, and how he had modified their ideas in such a way as to bring himself to a new kind of Catholicism—a kind that they did not object to, and could even sympathize with, so long as it did not involve submission to the Papacy. Now the chain was broken and they could perceive no connection between his former and his present positions. [21]

They can hardly be blamed. There was of course a connection, and it is to be hoped that it has already been shown here. But

Brownson did not indicate what it was—not at that time, not until many years afterwards; and his friends were confused. This last sudden change struck them as wholly irrational. They acknowledged that he was defending his new position with his old skill,—but they set this down to his ability to defend any position. What he had failed to do was to account for taking it up.

In *The Convert,* when he came to write it, he did trace his own intellectual processes very clearly, but by then it was too late to do much good. By then he had lost the ear of his non-Catholic following. Worse, he seemed to be accusing men who were no more confused than he had been—and were as sincerely groping for the truth as himself—of an actual preference for error, giving them the impression that all ideas not absolutely Catholic were to be abhorred, and that they were fools for not reaching in an instant what it had taken him twenty years to find. By this he not only bewildered but antagonized them.

They were now certain that he was only a special pleader, or that —as soon as he came to recognize that there was no real bridge between what he had been and what he was—he would be forced to return or proceed to some wilder intellectual eccentricity. What they were getting from him was only the stock arguments for Catholicism—put indeed with admitted cogency but telling them no more about Catholicism than what they knew already. They considered that they had the right to a good deal more than this from him. A man of Brownson's gifts ought to be able to offer an interpretation that was richer and more imaginative and more up-to-date than the one they were offered. They regarded it as aridly scholastic and, at bottom, conventional. James Russell Lowell in 1848 expressed the general view in the concluding lines on Brownson in *A Fable for Critics:*

> He offers the true faith to drink in a sieve,—
> When it reaches your lips, there's naught left to believe
> But a few silly- (syllo-, I mean) -gisms that squat 'em
> Like tadpoles, o'erjoyed with the mud at the bottom.

For this Father Hecker, writing after Brownson and Fitzpatrick were both dead, roundly blamed Fitzpatrick. After quoting a long passage from *The Convert,* the founder of the Paulists remarks: "These extracts reveal plainly how Dr. Brownson, by shifting his arguments, shifted his auditory and lost, never to regain, the leadership Providence had designed for him. I always maintained that Dr. Brownson was wrong in thus yielding to the bishop's influence, and that he should have held on to the course Providence had started him in. . . . Had he held on to the way inside the church which he had pursued outside the church in finding her, he would have carried with him some, and might perhaps have carried with him many, non-Catholic minds of a leading character." [22] In another article he presses the same point: "If Dr. Brownson's reasons for becoming a Catholic were put into a formula it would be this: He found that he could not solve the problems of human destiny in harmony with reason without the aid of Catholic teaching and discipline. But this applied only after he had settled the philosophical question of objective reality of the facts of consciousness. These two branches of philosophical controversy were the providential theses of his life. By means of them he could have cleared away passion, prejudice, ignorance in the minds of his fellow-countrymen, especially in New England, and brought them to a decision in a multitude of cases as correct and inevitable as his own. What Dr. Brownson was best able to do he was not called upon to do enough of." [23]

What Hecker means is not merely that Brownson was "not called on" to do this, but that he was positively prevented from doing it. "He was switched off the main line of his career by the influence of Bishop Fitzpatrick, who induced him to enter upon the *traditional line of controversy against Protestantism* at a time when the best minds of New England had long given up belief in the distinctive errors of that heresy." Again he says: "I told him at the time that in confining himself to the historical proof, and in pointing out that road alone to the truth, he had forgotten the bridge by ·which he himself had reached it, if, indeed, he had not actually turned about and broken it down. And when, shortly after my conversion, I went to Europe, all the letters I wrote to him were filled with complaints that he had given up his first principles, or at any rate ignored them." [24] Finally to quote Hecker: "That as a controversialist of the old school he so greatly distinguished himself only showed his versatility, and his versatility was in this his misfortune." [25]

That has special weight, coming from Brownson's life-long friend and earliest disciple, a man who had been led into the Church largely by the method Brownson had himself followed. Yet while the Bishop may have shown undue caution, he realized better than Brownson could at the time the possible dangers of trying to prove Catholicism true on the basis of the theory of Communion. Though the convert might have made a huge haul of Transcendentalists, he would have certainly puzzled—if not scandalized—the majority of American Catholics. Fitzpatrick knew that, after the hosannahs for the reception of so celebrated a man had died down, suspicion and envy were all too likely to show themselves. Perhaps he already caught sight in the shadows of the smiler with the knife under his cloak. Had Brownson been permitted to follow his own devices immediately after his conversion, while he was still distrusted, he could not have hoped—even had he avoided heresy—to have avoided being so misunderstood as to have had his usefulness destroyed. So long as Brownson used the method of argumentation to which Fitzpatrick was accustomed, Fitzpatrick could guide him; not otherwise.

Moreover, Brownson had to learn his theology while he was expounding it.[26] He had the journalist's facility in getting up a case, but this case was too important and intricate for him to proceed without expert assistance. Brownson came to see and to acknowledge that it was a pity that he was obliged to become a Catholic controversialist before he was thoroughly prepared for the rôle.[27] Many a time he had to bang away and make a loud noise concerning matters of which he was not fully informed; many a time his air of learning concealed the fact that what he had written quite exhausted his store of knowledge. Fitzpatrick would himself have been completely at sea had he been asked to act as Brownson's advisor and censor if some mode of apologetics outside the Bishop's comprehension had been attempted.

There is, however, another side to the question: Hecker found, when he consulted Fitzpatrick early in 1844, that he was much less interested in discovering what imperfectly grasped truths were leading young Isaac to seek further enlightenment than he was in seeking to eradicate all traces of lingering error. His was, in short, a negative rather than a positive mind. Under his influence, Brownson tended to become negative too—and made it his object to confute rather than to convince. Yet this, after all, accorded with his natural constitution: the logician is prone to seek for fallacies that he may expose them, and Brownson was a logician. Recognizing that fact, Fitzpatrick encouraged him to follow what must be said to have been at least one bent of his mind, and to discard speculative novelties. In this, even if he was not right by good judgment, he was assuredly right by good luck; but some credit should be given to the Bishop's judgment in this matter.

Hecker himself laid a finger on a very important consideration, which he omitted from his discussion of Fitzpatrick, when he said of Brownson, in a passage which has been already quoted at some length, "He has not the temperament of a genius, but that of a declaimer. . . . His mind is that of a historical rather than a poetical mode. . . . He defeats but will never convince an opponent." [28] While at Brook Farm Hecker learned two lessons he never fogot: one was that human nature, even at its best, has its defects; the other was that the people he had met there—and Americans in general— offered a marvellous field for the apostle.[29] In the abstract, he was correct enough in believing that there was an apologetic method, other than that commonly used, that could be used. In the concrete case of Brownson, he may not have been so correct. Hecker had singled his friend out to play a part desirable in itself, one that Hecker himself, to a large extent, succeeded in playing, but that

Brownson would defeat, but not convine an opponent.

Brownson was temperamentally unfitted to play. It was as a logician that he had to do his work, or not at all. Brownson was aware with Pascal that the heart has its reasons of which reason knows nothing; he would have admitted the justice of St. Ambrose's sentence, *"Non in dialectica complacuit Deo salvum facere populum suum."* In *Charles Elwood* he had written, "As a general rule, would you gain the reason, you must first win the heart," [30] and he repeated this often. But to admit that much did not mean that logic could not render a great service by removing the factors prohibiting belief. In any event, he knew that he was not richly endowed with the gift of persuasion. He had to use what weapons he could. And nobody has ever used these weapons better. It is senseless to complain that Brownson was not somebody else.

But having granted all this, it is still rather curious that a man who had discovered truth in so many unexpected places, who knew that there is no doctrine that does not contain at least some germ of truth, and who knew that most of the people he had met— whatever their eccentricities and absurdities—sincerely desired the truth, and were even eagerly searching for it, should have been so severe with anybody who had not yet reached the completion of truth which was now his. There was, in fact, something not a little harsh and forbidding in his treatment of opponents. Instead of trying to show these confused but earnest souls that what they were fumbling after was to be found in its fulness in the Catholic faith, he fell back upon telling them in effect: "This is what the Church holds. I will now demonstrate it so clearly that even your thick wits will be able to grasp it. But if you do not accept it to the last iota, you must understand that you are headed straight for hell." This was really what was in Hecker's mind when he objected to Fitzpatrick's influence. And yet the objection was not wholly just, for Brownson had shown much the same intolerant temper before he ever met Fitzpatrick. Therefore in comparing the two friends, we might perhaps say that Hecker was too sanguine about human nature, and that Brownson was not sanguine enough. In politics and sociology he had developed into something very like a pessimist; without changing his fundamental views, he came to despair of people having, except in isolated instances, sufficient intelligence to act as they should. Yet that he argued with them at all—and when did he stop arguing?—shows that he never completely despaired. In his irritation he might sometimes talk as though he did; his hammering away proves not merely that he trusted logic, and his own capacity to use it, but that he had an unshakable confidence in human reason.

This fundamental trust in the reasonableness of men appeared in his controversial writings directed against Protestants. He had some right to boast that "Many a man may find in our pages his objections to our views put in a clearer and stronger light than he had himself put them." [31] His honesty forbade him to misrepresent an opponent's position. All he had to do was to point out to Protestants how illogical they were, and then they would of course all become Catholics. Especially would they hasten to the Church if he showed them their personal spiritual danger—that if they did not accept the Church they had no hope of salvation. If it often seemed as though—as was customary with him—he over-emphasized his case, the case itself was—in its general features—not new with him. He had seen even in the days when he hoped he could find a new basis for Catholicism [32]—something which did not involve building on the Rock of Peter—that Catholicism was necessary for salvation, and he had said so clearly enough. Now he was stating what was only axiomatic—though stating it with a greater decisiveness.

Another factor operated. He had done his best, when a Universalist and Unitarian minister, to win men to Christianity by presenting Christianity in its lowest possible terms. He had supposed that he could make men believe by asking them to believe very little —less than he himself even then believed. But he had come to perceive that this apologetic method was ineffective. The infidel in *Charles Elwood* did not change his views; all that happened was that he allowed himself to be persuaded that he might retain his views (because they were sincere) and call himself a Christian. Therefore Brownson determined upon an unequivocal straightforwardness. Georgiana Bruce expressed notions current in the circles in which she moved when she wrote: "The Catholic Church . . . is ready to accept those who disbelieve the most horrible parts of the creed and doubt the remainder."[33] Such people could be convinced that Catholics really did believe everything in the creed only by dealing strongly with them. On the other hand, Brownson had to meet the kind of venomous attack on the Church that was so prevalent in the 'forties and 'fifties. Disdaining to be bothered with vulgar calumny, and above wrangling over alleged scandals, he saw that what was needed was the setting forth of principles plainly.[34] If he occasionally overstated the Catholic argument, that was perhaps unavoidable under the circumstances. He had to outroar the mob that was trying to howl him down; he was the only man who could outroar it.

Something like this, at all events, is the defence sometimes put up for Brownson. It would have more force if it were true that Brownson had always to meet the rowdier and rougher type of antagonist; only that is not quite the case. The people for whom his *Review* were written were fastidiously cultured; the people with whom Brownson had his controversies were, as compared with the Nativist agitators of the period, refined and polite. Though controversy with them was less polite than the same sort of controversy as conducted in Europe, it was still reasonably gentlemanly. Nevertheless, there were times when Brownson wished that he were in a position to write as Cardinal Wiseman had done against the Oxford Movement. "We cannot read these essays on the Oxford controversy," Brownson said in 1853, "without something like envy of their illustrious author,—not, of course, for his talents, his genius, his erudition, his courteous manner, and his graceful and dignified style, for these are above our humble aspirations, but for his public, for the men he had to refute, and to bring within the pale of the truth. He had a great and important movement setting towards the church to deal with, conducted by men of mistaken views indeed, advocating, in itself considered, an absurd and ridiculous theory, but sincere, honest, and loyal, well-bred, cultivated, eminent for their abilities and learning, who were too much in earnest to be cavillers . . . and respectable enough to enable one to address them in gentle and hopeful terms. . . . One could so treat these men as to refute their errors and retain their respect, and even secure their affection." [35] But even in that passage, it will be noted, Brownson tosses out a gratuitously offensive phrase about their absurd and ridiculous theory; not even when sighing for polite opponents could he himself be polite. He therefore obtained no affection, even while his polemic prowess exacted respect. In short, he was enormously irritating, and this largely offset the good he accomplished. An acute and friendly critic described him as a "Puritan Romanist." [36]

Nor is this all. Although he was scrupulously fair in stating his opponents' position, in another sense he was unable to be fair at all. He was simply unable to see any good in Protestantism. What he should have recognized and fully acknowledged was that Protestantism, at its best, is a sincere attempt to emphasize personal religion against what it considers formalism. He could also have said that there are many good Christians who while, indeed, cut off from the unity of Catholicism, yet derive what they retain of Christian doctrine and what they enjoy of Christian life from the Catholic Church—however unconscious they may be of this fact. Protestantism is not merely negative, or to be regarded as nothing but a historical remnant of Catholicism; it may be regarded as a kind of parasite living upon the Church—one that would die should the Church die, one also that draws all its nutriment from the Church. To that extent it is positive; to that extent it is Catholic. Without doing any harm to anybody, Brownson might have made the concession that, in individual instances, Protestants have a higher spiritual life than some Catholics—by making the most of their meagre stores where lax Catholics neglect their abundance. To reverse the parable: it not infrequently happens that the man who is given ten talents buries them, while the man with the one talent puts it to good use.

Brownson would make no such admissions. His logic therefore, though impeccable, often defeated his main purpose. He would not have been less of a Catholic had he been more catholic. Instead of extending a helping hand to honest and earnest seekers, he cracked them over the skull—and then wondered why they did not instantly enter the Church. And yet he came (at least for a time) to see that he was on the wrong controversial track. Then—it was in 1859— he wrote: "[Our opponents] feel that in our reasoning against them, we combat by rigid logic what is not purely logical in its nature or origin . . . Hence, though we silence their logic, we do not convince them; we convict without convincing them . . . In most men there is something besides logic. . . . The fact is, we refute them from the point of view of the Catholic, but not from the point of view of the non-Catholic, or fail to show the non-Catholic that the truth he sees . . . we also see and retain." [37]

This, however, was Brownson's later judgment on his apologetic method, made at a time when he came to call his own method— that of logic—the worst of all.[38] In these early years his method was that of shouting at the top of his voice, and though there are occasions when a shout is necessary, it has its limitations if it is a matter of conveying a somewhat complicated truth. The dictum, *Extra Ecclesiam nulla salus,* like most of the truths of Catholicism, is somewhat complicated and calls for delicate statement if it is to be correctly understood. Yet this was the very point that Brownson stressed most often and most vigorously and (it should be added) most crudely. For though, as he said perfectly correctly, truth should never be the subject of compromise, it must also not be forgotten that truth *is* compromised when it is so put that the necessary distinctions or qualifications are ignored.

The trouble here, and in so much else of Brownson's controversial writings, is that he thought that by being emphatically logical he had done all that needed to be done. It is, however, notorious that life lays a trap for logicians. The more logically sound they are, the less psychologically sound they may be. And Brownson's psychology regarding this question was very faulty. He said over and over again that if the slightest admission was made that perhaps it was possible for a man who was not actually and formally a member of the Catholic Church to be saved, then all attempt to get anybody to become a Catholic might as well be given up. But this is simply not so: those who become Catholics become such because they are convinced of the truth of Catholicism and not primarily in order to escape hell. Of course a man who is unfaithful to his intellectual light and the leading of his conscience will lose his soul; there is no question about that. But the love of God is always a stronger motive than the fear of God; indeed, perhaps it is hardly possible to fear God unless one also loves him. The brandishing of threats over the heads of those whose faith is imperfect is hardly the most effective way to win them to perfect faith. By telling them that they will be damned if they do not become Catholics, one is all too likely to draw the retort, "I'll be damned if I do!" When a minister said precisely this to him one day, Brownson did not make the situation much better by replying, "Well, take your choice!" [39]

Brownson considered that any Catholic who did not hold the doctrine that there is no salvation outside the Church in his own stringent sense was a "latitudinarian." He was quite accurate in affirming that a man could not deny the doctrine and be a Catholic. But no Catholic did deny it; most of them merely wanted to make the ordinary theological distinctions—and these Brownson rejected, against the weight of accepted theological opinion. He told them that they were watering Catholicism down; though all that was involved was a perception that the truth was by no means so simple as Brownson supposed. He was contemptuous of the Catholic theologians who "by their explanations open wide the door of salvation." [40] He would not allow that a Protestant could be, in a certain sense, a Catholic without knowing it, or have any vital connection with the "Soul of the Church," drawing upon God's grace; nor would he admit the plea of "invincible ignorance" or that the theory of "intention" could possibly apply. Baptism of desire, according to him, can have validity only to declared catechumens who die before they complete their probation. Though he grudgingly grants that a Protestant may conceivably be saved, this is, according to him, only because we have no means of knowing what may have passed between his soul and God at the moment of death.[41] It was nothing to him that a great deal may have passed between that soul and God during that person's life.

The worst feature in this is that the reader derives from Brownson the idea that he presses his point so fiercely because he fears that any sort of concession is liable to be misunderstood—not because concessions are not, in themselves, desirable and necessary. To be less than blunt would be to appear to be weak. Therefore the whole thing becomes not so much a question of what is theologically correct but tactically advisable. And once such a tactical purpose is discovered, or even suspected, the value of the tactics is at an end. Logic has a way of turning into a boomerang.

It is not being suggested that anything said by Brownson was false, even if it called for the kind of "explanations" he so despised. But it *is* being suggested that the telling of the full truth is not an easy but an immensely difficult matter. Brownson's notion that the truth to be convincing must be put baldly, or that a man could not be telling the truth unless he bellowed it, caused much more damage than he realized. Where the scalpel was called for he insisted on using the pickaxe. That he did so was not due to his Catholicism, for it had always been his way. But when he obtained a dogmatic religion he was able to give freer rein to his temperament. Well might Father Hewit, Hecker's associate, in the obituary article he wrote, say that though Brownson's power lay in his grasp of first principles and the ability to follow them out logically, "his defect was in subtlety of thought, fineness of discrimination, completeness of induction, and minute, accurate analysis." [42] What he called "The Great Question" was his "King-Charles'-Head." From the time that he wrote that article in 1847 to the day of his death he was forever parading it. And we have yet to hear of anyone whom he succeeded in scaring into the Church by such dialectics.

This criticism has been frankly made at the outset, because it seems to me necessary to make it. The very strength of Brownson was so frequently his main weakness. But now having made this reservation, it is possible to go on to speak of his strength. He brought to his business of controversy a style that was one of the clearest and most forceful that English literature has seen. Without attempting any graces, and sometimes making grammatical slips, he yet wrote very well. Not so well as Cobbett, against whom he had a prejudice, [43] but certainly better than Godwin, whose literary style he rated too highly. There are places, too, in which he reminds the reader of Swift, whom he greatly admired, and other places where he reminds the reader of Dr. Johnson. There are also many touches that suggest Paine and a few that suggest Carlyle. But his style was his own—plain and unpretentious and immensely serviceable. Ripley expressed the opinion to Father Hecker that "there were passages in Dr. Brownson which could not be surpassed in the whole range of English literature"; [44] and Lord Brougham is said to have pronounced him to be the best magazine writer in America. [45]

Perhaps as good an instance as can be found of his journalistic effectiveness is in the articles he wrote about the Transcendentalists. Here he claims to be, "The first in this country to set forth . . . the doctrine we have ascribed to them." [46] He thinks that "Transcendentalism is virtually the ground on which the enemies of the church, generally, are rallying and endeavoring to make a stand, and the ground on which they are to be met and vanquished." [47] He proceeds to give an excellent analysis of the intellectual confusion of the system, showing that under it man is the measure of all things and the ideal is regarded as superior to the real. He says he has actually heard the Transcendentalists contend that "the unintelligible is more intelligible than the intelligible, that nothing is less known than the known, that only the unknown is known, that more is to be seen by night than by day, in the dark than in the light. We exaggerate nothing. We have heard all this said, and seriously maintained." [48] Transcendentalism, he points out, logically leads to the triumph of passion over reason, and the flesh over the spirit.[49] If it did not do so, this was only because the Transcendentalists happened to be very high-minded men who were saved by their inconsistency —also by their artistic gifts. He brought forward in exemplification Emerson, "the first poet of his country," who "in his own character, is a striking proof of the falseness of his theory. . . . In the very tempest and whirlwind of his passion, in the very access of his madness, uttering the most incoherent ravings, the wildest extravagances, Mr. Emerson is eminently himself, perfectly cool and self-possessed, and proceeds as deliberately as a mathematician solving his problems, or a stone-cutter in squaring his blocks of granite. We dissent from his doctrines, we shrink from his impiety and his blasphemy, but we see and feel his intense personality, that he is master of his thought, that he knows what he says, and intends it. . . . Here is a man to whom Almighty God has given ability and genius of the first order, and of whom he will demand a large account." [50] In short, Brownson makes for Emerson the same excuse that Joseph Henry Allen was to make for Brownson, when he quoted with approval what he calls "the finest sentence of all he ever wrote": it is the one in which Brownson spoke of "that glorious inconsistency which does honor to human nature, and which makes men so much better than their creeds." From Allen himself comes a description of Brownson which deserves to be remembered. He calls him "the strong, stormful, rude, yet tender-hearted man." [51] The tender-heartedness has been generally overlooked.

Parker, whom Brownson was often afterwards roundly to term an infidel,[52] he says "retains something better than transcendentalism, and has not quite lost all sense of religion." Yet with him, as with the rest, "religion is voluntary obedience to our nature,—which means, in the last analysis, that it is the surrender of ourselves up to our instinctive nature, to do simply what it moves or impels us to do." [53] He still had some hope of his friend.

In a later article than those from which these quotations have been made, Brownson declares "Transcendentalism a much more serious affair than they would have us believe . . . but is in fact the dominant error of our times." [54] On the same page he argues that it is "the fundamental principle of the Protestant reformation itself. . . . The Protestant who refuses to accept it, with all its legitimate consequences, however frightful or absurd they may be, condemns himself and his whole party." It is "the last stage this side of *nowhere*," he concludes; "and when reached, we must hold up, or fly off into boundless vacuity. In its prevalence, then, we may trust to see the signs of a change near at hand; and any change must certainly be in a better direction." [55]

All this was very acute. Yet the Transcendentalists resented it as a caricature of themselves, although they must have perceived that half the people in the "movement" were caricatures enough without any need from Brownson's pen. As for Catholics, they were not greatly interested in the Transcendentalists, whom they set down as freaks. Therefore little good was accomplished. Readers were more entertained than enlightened by the *reductio ad absurdum:* "We have been led through tomes of metaphysical lore; we have been allured by the brilliant promises of a recovered Eden; we have been flattered by glowing descriptions of our godlike powers, affinities, and tendencies; we have been transported by the assurance that we may dispense with priests, prophets, intercessors, and mediators, and of ourselves approach the Infinite One face to face, and drink our supply at the primal Fountain of Truth itself; but now, having lingered till the ascending sun has exhaled the dewdrops and exhausted the gems and precious stones which sparkled in rich profusion at our feet, what is the real and positive value of what has so long detained and charmed us? Things are what they are; man

is what he is, and by a right use of his faculties may be, do, and
know all he can be, do, and know. So far as we are wise, good, and
loving, so far we have and know wisdom, goodness, love. . . . He
who knows more of these knows more than he who knows less.
If the possession of wisdom, goodness, love be inspiration, then he
who has the most wisdom, goodness, love, is the most inspired—
and to be the more inspired, he must get more wisdom, goodness,
love. To be more inspired, he must be more inspired. If white be
white, then white is white; if black be black, then what is black is
black; if two be two, then two are two. Or, in two grand formulas
from Mr. Parker, 'Goodness is goodness,' and 'Be good and do
good,' and—you will be good and do good! If that is not the whole
of transcendentalism, when divested of its denials, its blasphemy,
and its impiety, and reduced to its simple dogmatic teaching, then
we have given days, weeks, months, and years, to its study to no
purpose." [56]

Funny as that is, it left Brownson open to the rejoinder that he
did his intelligence something less than justice; surely so clever
a man would not have had to take all that time to discover that
Transcendentalism was nothing but what he now pictured it as
being. Reading this in the Redemptorist novitiate in Belgium,
Isaac Hecker must have winced. Of course there was a great deal of
truth in Brownson's criticism; the trouble was that it was negative
and not the constructive criticism that might have shown the
Transcendentalists like St. Paul that "Whom ye ignorantly worship,
him declare I unto you," or told them, with Pascal, "That thou
dost seek me is a sign that thou hast found me." They were seeking
something—these men—as nobody should have known better than
Brownson. It achieved nothing to alienate them by deriding them
in this fashion.

The same thing happened when Brownson engaged in controversy with "orthodox" Protestants. Many—perhaps most—of these
were bigoted, or at least strongly prejudiced against Catholicism.

But they had kept large elements of Catholic dogma. The right method of apologetics in their case would have been to have shown them that they did not fully value those elements because they did not fully understand them; that only in Catholicism was the religion of Protestantism—which they clung to with a steadily weakening grasp—firmly asserted. That, however, was not Brownson's way. He says finely, "He who sacrifices the truth sacrifices charity, and he who withholds the truth needed—the precise truth needed— by his age or country does sacrifice it. If that truth be offensive, and he tells it, it will offend, whatever the soft phraseology in which he may tell it." [57] But the inference we are allowed to draw is that the truth is bound to be offensive—this despite the fact that Brownson's whole life was a proof that truth was more beautiful and to be desired than rubies.

It is not, after all, a choice between sugar-coating the truth and ramming it down people's throats. This was what Brownson never saw. He made of course the formal admissions: charity was never to be forgotten, and he who contends for the Gospel must do so in the spirit of the Gospel. "Undoubtedly, vituperation and abuse are as impolitic as they are unchristian; but we must be careful not to mistake liberality for charity, the natural meekness or amiability of our own dispositions for the meekness and tenderness of religion." [58] But it was not very wonderful that his readers did not always think him conspicuously meek or amiable. Even when he gave them what he supposed was a playful tap on the head, the huge paw descended, they thought, with force enough to bash out their brains. He was genuinely puzzled by it all, for he regarded himself as restrained and never putting out his full strength.

Even when he tried to be polite honesty demanded that he explain that it was only "conventional" politeness which made him refer to Protestants as "our separated brethren." They must understand that he did not consider them Christians. He must not call them heretics "in anger" because in anger "even the truth spoken for unlawful ends is libellous." All the same, he wished to make it clear that they *were* heretics; in fact, he said, "There is not the least sense or propriety in addressing the great mass of Protestants, especially in this country, as if they were . . . sincerely and honestly Christian . . . and only in intellectual error as to the true form of Christianity." [59]

He could be very irritating, too, with his logic-chopping. The following passage comes out of *The Two Brothers; or Why Are You a Protestant?*, one of those quasi-novels of his that are no more than dialogues. The Catholic brother says to the Presbyterian brother: "*If* Protestantism be Presbyterianism, none but Presbyterians can be Protestants. Is this your belief?"

"Not exactly," replies the Presbyterian brother, "for there are Protestants who are not Presbyterians."

"These, of course, differ more or less from Presbyterians, or else they would be Presbyterians. Consequently Protestantism must differ more or less from Presbyterianism."

"In non-essentials, but not in essentials. All who embrace the essentials are Protestants."

"Do Catholics embrace the essentials?"

"According to the general opinion of Protestants, they do."

"Then, according to the general opinion of Protestants, Catholics are Protestants." [60]

That sort of thing gets nowhere. Not even the most rigid Presbyterian would assert more than that he believes his to be the purest form of Protestantism and that Protestantism is a purer form of Christianity than Catholicism. The true line of Catholic apologetics is to show that all forms of Protestantism are nothing but eccentric or attenuated or impoverished forms of Catholicism; there is no use in denying that Protestants are Christians. What they should be shown is that Protestants are merely incomplete or deformed Catholics. Then there is something to build on. It was the argument Brownson most abhorred.

He always denied that he was an extremist, and was correct enough in his denial, if it is only a question of what he believed, not of how he expressed what he believed. "Orthodoxy," he declared, "is a definite quantity, and one has it, or has it not. . . . You are bound to go as far as your religion requires you to go, or you sin by defect; and if you go beyond what it permits, you sin by excess." [61] Quite so. Brownson was the most orthodox of men—and also the most tactless. Perhaps he even felt he could dispense with tact because of his orthodoxy.

All the same, a greater finesse might have accomplished less than his tactlessness—especially in the days of the Breckinridges and the Lyman Beechers. The narrow man—if you will, the fanatic—has always, if it comes to that, an advantage over the man who is broad; by pursuing one line and leaving aside all the qualifications, he puts a deeper mark on those he encounters. Many people are confused by the admission that there may be another side to the case than the one presented. By hammering away at a single theme Brownson accomplished more than would have been possible to a subtler mind. He had little to say to the mystic and the poet; his appeal was to what is called the plain man. His energy was canalized so that none of it was lost. He kept to essentials; he stripped every issue to its pith; everything else was disregarded.

For many, however, his over-simplifications had always been un-satisfactory—as unsatisfactory as his remorseless logic. In 1836 Bronson Alcott had complained, after an evening spent with him and James Walker, that "the high works of poetic genius, the marvels of holiness, are beyond their grasp." [62] Theodore Parker, smarting under the attacks of his former friend, called him "intel-lectual always, but spiritual never; . . . not a Christian, but only a verbal index of Christianity—a commonplace book of theology." [63] Stern ratiocination was distasteful to such men, and to many others, and Brownson retorted that his critics regarded "all mental clear-ness, distinctness, and precision of thought as scholastic subtleties, to be despised by every man of common sense." [64] But when anyone was so bold as to try, as sometimes happened, to trip Brownson up logically, he came to grief. Then, having disposed of the challenger,

Brownson would rub his hands together with fiendish joy and roar, like Goliath, "Give me a man, that we may fight together!" An opponent who was greeted with the compliment, "It gives us pleasure to meet a Protestant who has a beard on his face," [65] *he* had a special need to look to himself; it was a warning that the champion was about to make his kill.

The core of Brownson's controversial method is revealed in an article he wrote in 1850 by way of reproof to the English convert, J. M. Capes. "His statements are generally under the truth, and appear to the Catholic weak and tame. The author's motive has been a good one; he has believed that a calm, deliberate, and reserved statement will have more weight with Protestants than one in which he suffers his Catholic heart to speak out in its own unrestrained warmth and energy. But in this we believe he is mistaken. Heretics do not in our days doubt our ability, our learning, or our logic. What they doubt is our sincerity. . . . They look upon the intelligent Catholic defending his religion as a lawyer speaking from his brief. In a word, they doubt our honesty." [66] That is all very well. Yet some people still believe that, if a man is sure of his case, he can afford to put it temperately. Lawyers speaking from their briefs have been known to put on a great display of passion for the benefit of the jury. If vigor and noise overwhelm some men, others regard such things with suspicion. The fact that Brownson rarely encountered an antagonist who was his match was all the more reason for handling gently those whom he did encounter. Again there was a psychological mistake on the part of the logician. And his assumption that he set the Catholic standard—when he said "the Catholic" thinks this or that, he meant that Brownson thought it—was not pleasing to men who had the Catholic cause as much at heart as himself, even if they advocated it in a somewhat different way. During this early period—and to some extent all through his Catholic life—what Brownson gained on the swings he lost on the round-abouts.

Brownson had a way of inserting into his articles, whatever their subject, purely personal matter. This often gave them unexpected charm and color, even if it was sometimes a little quaint. The man who was so forbiddingly gruff in a personal encounter, seemed to be able to unbend only when he had a pen in his hand. His address to his readers in the opening number of *Brownson's Quarterly Review* has already been drawn upon, and quotations will be made at the appropriate places from similar pages, which culminated in the noble and moving Valedictory he wrote at the close of 1873. At this point a few extracts might be made from the Postscripts he usually appended each year to his January issue. They were very characteristic of him.

For 1848 he wrote: "Some have complained that the Review adopts a tone unbecoming a recent convert and a layman, but without justice. The editor of this Review is indeed a recent convert and a layman, but he is nobody, and should not be taken into account, because the question is not what it is or is not becoming in him to say, but what is or is not becoming in a Catholic Quarterly Review, and because it is well known that in religious and theological matters he does not speak from his own head, but under the revision of those who are neither laymen nor converts. . . . If the doctrine is sound, it must be held, let who will advance it; if it is unsound, its unsoundness is a sufficient reason for not holding it." [67]

That is put with studious moderation. The following year he permitted himself to crow over his former associates. "We enter now upon the fifth year of our Catholic life; we have, through the grace of God, falsified the predictions of our friends that we should turn back to Protestantism in six months, and rendered it idle for people to repeat their old nonsense about 'changing with every moon.' . . . We have had no wish to return to what we have abjured, are satisfied with where we are, and wish, from our heart, all our old and new friends A HAPPY NEW YEAR." [68] Two years later he crowed even more loudly, adding, "We have almost forgotten that we were ever

Brownson could often in writing

any thing but a Catholic." Then he turned on those who had criticized him for his belligerent tone: it had never been his intention, he explains, to be severe or discourteous, but merely to be orthodox and bold and independent in his statement of Catholicism. "During the greater part of the time we have been conducting this Review," he goes on, "we have had to combat latitudinarian and revolutionary tendencies among Catholics, as well as error and heresy outside of the Church. Many *liberal* Catholics have been liberal in their abuse of us." However, he feels that times have changed. "The Catholic press of the country has come nobly to our aid, and all the Catholic journals in the country now appear to speak with one heart and voice. We believe our most painful trials are over." [69]

He spoke a little too soon. His worst trials were about to begin. In 1854 he stirred up a new hornets' nest by his articles on the Irish immigrants. Yet his personal postscript (this time inserted in the October issue) makes little allusion to the attacks made upon him, except to say: "We apprehend no serious injury to the future prospects of our Review from the passing squall." He does not expect that everything he writes will please everybody. But he has confidence in the fair play of American Catholics and has been consoled by the number of letters he has received expressing agreement with his views. Still more he is encouraged by the letter Bishop Fitzpatrick had brought him from Pope Pius IX, which he proudly printed both in Latin and English. Looking back over the eleven years of his *Review,* he notes that at the end of 1845 the circulation fell off so drastically that he was saved from failure only by the support that had come to him from Canadian Catholics and the letter of approbation given him by the American hierarchy. The difficult corner had now been turned.

The most interesting passage is the one in which he lets his readers still further into his confidence by confessing that when he began his career as a Catholic editor he knew very little of theology or Catholic tastes and habits of thought. "We had much to unlearn, and everything to learn. We had Catholic faith, Catholic fervor, and Catholic docility, and scarcely anything else to qualify us for our post. We did not dare trust our previous philosophy, our previous reading, or our previous knowledge, any further than we could review it in the light of our Catholic faith, and the teachings of approved Catholic doctors. We had to study day and night, and to task both our physical and mental powers to the utmost . . . We felt our incompetency, but we felt that we had been placed by legitimate authority in the position we held, and we looked for help to the only Source from which real help ever comes." [70] That he made so candid a confession shows that he felt another difficult corner had been safely turned. Confident that he has at last mastered what he needed to learn, he looks serenely into the future.

The *Review* during those days had many articles on politics—mostly on political theory. Even when specific measures were discussed, they were dealt with in the light of principles. Such a method of treatment Brownson felt to be all the more necessary now, because he had a reputation as a radical to live down, and also because the Irish Catholics tended to a view of democracy of which he disapproved. One of the best of these articles—in fact, one of the best articles Brownson ever wrote—was "Catholicity Necessary to Sustain Popular Liberty." It was directed equally to his co-religionists and to the general public that clung (as it still does) to the fallacious notion that the American idea stems from Puritanism. "By popular liberty," Brownson explains, "we mean democracy; by democracy, we mean the democratic form of government; by the democratic form of government, we mean that form of government which vests the sovereignty in the people as population. . . . The thesis we propose to maintain is, therefore, that without the Roman Catholic Religion it is impossible to preserve a democratic government. . . . Infidelity, Protestantism, heathenism may institute a democracy, but only Catholicity can sustain it." [71]

Having so stated his thesis, Brownson immediately proceeds to make qualifications. "Our government, in its origin and constitutional forms, is not a democracy, but, if we may use the expression, a limited *elective* aristocracy." The government framed by the Founding Fathers has virtually ceased to exist, except in name, and since 1828 has become "pure democracy"—the thing Brownson most hates. This, however, was no suddenly acquired bugbear of his. He had long declared that "democracy" was the end of government, not its means, as was commonly supposed. This removal of political form from the essence of democracy was not due to his disillusionment over the 1840 election; that had done no more than to substantiate his contention that the mass of the people could not be trusted to vote intelligently, and that the *vox populi* was not necessarily the *vox Dei*. Here was an old thesis of his advanced with new power.

But one wonders who had ever seriously maintained a theory of democracy in the sense in which Brownson condemned it. O'Sullivan had indeed talked about the "people's right and might," yet it is doubtful whether O'Sullivan or anyone else had meant that the people are infallible—for Americans had decisively proved that they were not infallible by electing Harrison. All that even the most extreme democrat really believes is that the democratic form of government is, upon the whole, to be preferred to any other form. Brownson, by denying that democracy had anything to do with the form, was saying in effect that the direct rule of a monarch—should he happen to be a saint and a sage, or perhaps even a man above the average—would be more democratic, in the Brownsonian meaning of the term, than the democratic rule of the best of societies. Even in such a society fools abound, and venal politicians can cajole fools into electing them to office.

By belaboring the weakness of the democratic method, Brownson was doing no more than belabor the obvious. Every form of political machinery is liable to be used against the very purpose for which it was originally intended. No perfection is attainable by imperfect men, even when the wisest among them take all due precautions.

Brownson was over-stating his case when he asserted, "The reign of great men, of distinguished statesmen and firm patriots, is over, and that of the demagogues has begun. Your most important offices are hereafter to be filled by third- and fourth-rate men." [72] The only hope he could see for his country was in electing Calhoun to the presidency. As for Van Buren, he was "serpentine and crooked," "the *beau ideal* of a true party man, riding . . . on the storm, but *not* directing its course." [73] And the extent of Brownson's disappointment with "practical politics" may be measured by the fact that, writing in 1873, he was able to look back to Van Buren's administration as almost a golden age, and to consider Van Buren "the last first-class man that sat, or probably that ever will sit, in the presidential chair of the United States." [74]

However strange are some of Brownson's judgments of individual men and particular political measures, he had a great deal of value to say regarding general principles. His contention was that democracy can be preserved only under Christianity and that Christianity and Catholicism are identical. "If democracy commits the government to the people to be taken care of," he points out, "religion is to take care that they take proper care of the government." But if religion is to depend on the people—as under Protestantism—"if the people are to take care of it, to say what it shall be, what it shall teach, what it shall command, what worship or discipline it shall insist on being observed, we are back in our old difficulty." [75] For just as the first stage of Protestantism was "to place religion under the charge of the civil government," the second stage of Protestantism "is to reject, in matters of religion, the authority of the temporal government, and to subject religion to the control of the faithful," while the third stage is irresponsible individualism, which "leaves religion entirely to the control of the individual, who selects his own creed, or makes a creed to suit himself . . . and submits to no restraints but such as are self-imposed." [76] It follows that, as Protestantism will not serve the purpose, only Catholicism is adequate to sustain popular liberty, "on the ground of its being

[margin, handwritten: Democracy and Christianity]

exempted from popular control." He therefore demands Catholicism as a political necessity, but "as a religious, not a political power." [77] All this is a very neat piece of argumentation. It might have been more conclusive had Brownson recognized that democracy—though by no means the only form of government with which the Church is willing to coöperate—is the form most consonant with its own spirit. Apparently he did not know that the democratic institutions of the United States were largely based upon the theories of Catholic political philosophers, and that even the Puritan rebels against the English monarchy drew (as Sir Robert Filmer perceived) their arguments from a Catholic source. What Brownson did assert, when reviewing a volume of his friend Bancroft's great *History* in 1855, was that the Calvinist system was "of all systems . . . the least favorable to that liberty and equality which he so eloquently and energetically asserts." [78] Brownson's political doctrine, in short, beautifully dovetailed with his theology. Intellectual security, and reason itself, could be obtained only by external authority; and liberty was safe only on condition that there was a sovereignty higher than that of the people. The authority in both cases operated in much the same way—there was no salvation outside of the Church.

Despite his alliance with the Southern Democrats and his grudging support of the Polk administration, Brownson followed his own line regarding the imperial expansion which his country, and more particularly the slave-owning section of it, was now seeking. He denounced the war with Mexico as "uncalled for, impolitic, and unjust." [79]

The war itself, however, drops into a minor place in his 1847 article compared with the larger issues raised. Here Brownson separated himself from the Massachusetts liberals, with whom he had so recently associated, by declaring again and with new emphasis that he was no abolitionist. In this matter, as on the constitutional question, he reaffirms: "[The abolitionists] are the worst enemies of their country, and the worst enemies, too, of the slave. They are a

Brownson and Slavery.

band of mad fanatics, and we have no language strong enough to express our abhorrence of their principles and proceedings." [80] He even announces that he is ready to maintain that man may have property in man. All that he will concede is that "many of the laws of the slave-holding states on slavery are unnecessary, unjust, cruel, and disgraceful." [81] In any event, the question is one for the individual states to decide. He agrees with Rhett and Calhoun that "the federal government is a simple agency created by the states," [82] and he attacks the position of John Quincy Adams that the sovereignty rests in the Union because Americans were "one people from the beginning, and that the division into colonies was only for the purpose of administration." Against this notion Brownson opposes the doctrine that "each colony held immediately from the crown, and each, under the crown, contained in itself all the legal authority it recognized, or to which it was subjected." Therefore it follows that "the sovereignty in the constitution vests in the states severally— not in the Union, which is their creature." [83] It was this position he steadily held until he reversed himself under the pressure of the Civil War. It was all recanted when in 1866 he published his book, *The American Republic.*

Brownson denied that Congress had any constitutional right to exclude slavery even from the territories of the United States and remarked, very truly, that in any case, "the refusal of congress to admit a slave-holding state into the Union would have little practical effect," as that territory, once it was a state, could become slave-holding, just as Massachusetts might reëstablish slavery. [84] He deplored the war with Mexico mainly because it was impolitic "in consequence of the slave question, already threatening the Union." [85] It is evident that Brownson was arguing for the extreme theory of state sovereignty primarily as a means for effectuating the Calhoun check of "concurrent majorities," and that he would quickly enough abandon his constitutional theory if it were necessary to do so in order to preserve the Union.

Four years later he had to write on the expeditions to Cuba, which he rightly called piratical, but he regretted that those who opposed the Cuban adventure did so on the collateral issue of slavery instead of on principle.[86] He was particularly scathing on the protest made by Clayton, the Secretary of State, against the threatened punishment of the pirates by Spain. Clayton had written, "Tell the Count of Alcoy to send them back to the United States, where they will find a punishment worse than he can inflict on them, if they are honorable men, in the reprobation that they will meet from all right-minded persons." Brownson's comment is that "This is in some respects no less amusing than grandiloquent. The supposition that men enlisted in a piratical expedition are *honorable* men is somewhat comical, and the suggestion that they would meet a heavier punishment for their crimes than any the Count of Alcoy could inflict on them, when that public opinion was in favor of their enterprise . . . is original, and shows that the late secretary of state has one of the qualities, if not of a statesman, at least of a poet." [87] He concludes, "We cannot shut our eyes to the dangerous and utterly immoral and dishonorable career upon which the American people to a fearful extent have entered." [88]

These articles brought him into close contact with the Spanish Ambassador, Calderon de la Barca, and three years later Brownson was writing even more blisteringly on the same subject: "A more cruel, barbarous, and vindictive people than our own, when their passions or interests are excited, it would perhaps be hard to find among civilized nations. We are vain boasters, and boast always of the virtues which we lack." [89] As though that were not enough, he raged: "We love our country, but we blush for the immorality of our countrymen. . . . The active mass of our people, those who influence public affairs, and give tone and character to the country, we believe to be utterly destitute of all sense of religion and morality, and capable of any iniquity. . . . Let us, my countrymen, cease boasting, and endeavor to see ourselves, for once, as we really are." [90] It was the kind of violence that defeated its own object, as was so often the case with Brownson. He had many of the marks of a great pamphleteer, perhaps, but he missed a magnificent opportunity for satire and restrained understatement, such as he had shown in his earlier passage on Clayton.

What he had to say about England pleased his Irish audience, who at last began to think that he might be a good Catholic and almost one of themselves. The American government, he declared, "is preparing to enlist in a Jacobinical war for the propagation of democracy, under the pretext that the sovereigns of Europe are preparing to attack our principles—a pretext without the slightest foundation." The only exception made was one in favor of the "quasi-monarchy of Great Britain." [91] Spain he declared was being attacked because it was a country at once monarchical and Catholic.[92] Recently an American Catholic priest has gone to the trouble of collecting Brownson's anti-British *obiter dicta* and of writing an article about them.[93] What he presented has not much point, except perhaps as isolationist propaganda, and neglects to take into adequate account Brownson's often expressed general views. The fact is that Brownson was immensely proud of his English ancestry, and that he asserted—perhaps a little too strongly—the close relation between American and British political institutions. He always denied the hatred of England of which he was sometimes accused in that country and declared: "We like England as the land of our ancestors. We like the English people, and perhaps have more points of sympathy with them than with any other European people. But both as a Catholic and as a patriot, we do dislike English preponderance, and we would rather, for the best interests of mankind, see any other European nation supreme than Great Britain." The root of his criticism immediately follows: he is "opposed, heart and soul, to the British industrial and mercantile system." [94] Though he had given up all hope of seeing it destroyed, now that it had fastened itself upon America, and could think of no means of restraining it except by balancing the South against the industrialist North, he was still essentially as much of a radical as he had ever been. That is, he never ceased to reiterate that capitalism was the prime material evil of the modern world.[95]

If this sort of thing delighted his new audience—who were almost willing to condone his anti-democracy for the sake of his anti-Britishism—they had not forgotten how, in the very first issue of his *Review* brought out after his reception into the Church, he had said some plain words about the Irish immigrants. While disclaiming any sympathy with the "Native Americans," he touched the Irish on the raw by asserting that the right to the suffrage was a municipal and not a natural right, and that therefore they must not complain of injustice if they were not accorded it.[96] It was anything but tactful of him to tell the Irish that the Yankee, even if only a hod-carrier, thought that " 'Paddy' hardly belongs to the human family." [97] It was unavailing that he said that he did not share this contempt himself, or that he stressed the anti-Catholic outrages of the Nativists; the fact remained that he lost no time in going on record with the opinion that Nativism was political and economic quite as much as it was anti-Catholic. He reminded the Irish that some of them—Thomas D'Arcy McGee, for example —"show occasionally an offensive want of respect for American feelings," and that by doing so they only provoked antagonism.[98] Moreover, he seemed in their eyes to be as bad as any Nativist by rejecting their claim to the vote. When, the following July, he expressed his hope "that the time is not far distant, when all traces of Ireland's conquest by or subjugation to Great Britain will be wiped out," [99] his kind words were forgotten. All that many of the Irish ever read or remembered were less kind remarks which, especially when quoted out of their context, struck them as decidedly anti-Irish. It was to do him a great deal of harm before long and was one of the main causes of the unpopularity he had in certain quarters throughout his life.

Even when reviewing an unimportant Irish novel he gratuitously commented on "the melodious wail of Moore, exciting compassion, but killing respect," and "the voice of bombastic orators and ignorant

editors, turning even Irish virtue and nobility into ridicule." [100]
That, too, was taken out of its context and used against him. John
McCaffrey, the president of Mount St. Mary's College, wrote to
warn him: "I'm afraid that, touch the Irish as you will, unless you
tickle their vanity, you will stir a hornet's nest. . . . Their nationality
is intense, touchy, suspicious, unreasoning, morbid—as irritable and
as easily hurt as a patient in inflammatory rheumatism." [101] The
warning went unheeded. Brownson had a wonderful gift for treading on sensitive toes; tactlessness with him was raised to a fine art.
If he found the Catholic Church a bed of spikes, the spikes were
often of his own making.

[1] When he began *Brownson's Quarterly* he had only 600, which he considered
a good start. (*Hecker Papers*, Brownson to Hecker, March 11, 1844). In 1840 the
Boston Quarterly had had less than a thousand; in 1850 its successor had reached
a circulation of about 1,400. Probably *Brownson's Quarterly Review* never had more
than 2,000. But it was immensely influential. In 1853, so Brownson noted in his
personal postscript to the January issue (p. 136), the interest in his *Review* was
great enough to bring about an English edition. This was almost, though not quite,
the first instance of such a thing happening to an American magazine.

[2] *The Convert*, p. 366.

[3] *Middle Life*, p. 3.

[4] *The Flowering of New England*, p. 248.

[5] *Early Life*, pp. 546–547.

[6] *Hecker Papers*.

[7] Yet in the letter from which quotation has just been made, Brownson also
writes: "I was at Brook Farm last Sunday & preached a discourse to them. Two or
three will become Catholics. Mr. Ripley, I fear, is worse than an infidel. The
atmosphere of the place is horrible. Have no faith in such associations. They will
be only gatherings of all that is vile, to foster and breed corruption." It was hardly
the frame of mind likely to appeal to Brook Farm and the Transcendentalists.

[8] Billington, *The Protestant Crusade*, pp. 220–237.

[9] *Middle Life*, p. 98. This looks like (and probably was) calculated truculence.
But it must be remembered that Brownson ate vast quantities of meat—which was
probably the cause of the gout from which he suffered in later life. Therefore the
Friday penance was so great as to make him irritable; he did not have a Catholic
stomach.

[10] *Ibid.*, p. 635. Henry Brownson adds that because of this incident the verb
hooverize for a time became part of the language.

[11] *Ibid.*, p. 638.

[12] *Ibid.*, p. 534.

[13] *Works*, Vol. XIX, p. 582.

[14] *Middle Life*, p. 96. Ripley's wife became a Catholic and Ripley had a kind of
understanding with Hecker that he was to be received into the Church when dying.

But long before that his Catholic wife had died and he had married again. So when Ripley was sinking, Hecker got the message too late, and arrived only to find his old friend unconscious. Hecker's comment was: "Ripley was a great man, a wonderful man. But he was a complete failure." (Elliott's *Hecker*, p. 90).

In extenuation of Ripley it might be said that he heroically addressed himself to paying off all the debts of Brook Farm, and even to reimbursing the stock-holders. Starting with $5 a week for his work on the New York *Tribune*, he eventually became one of the most successful of literary journalists, working night and day until everybody was paid. (Codman, *Brook Farm*, pp. 237–238).

[15] *Works*, Vol. XIII, p. 181.

[16] *Middle Life*, p. 634.

[17] *Princeton Review*, Vol. XXX (1858), p. 392. The story is told there against him by Reuben Smith, who had been his minister at Ballston during his Presbyterian days.

[18] A curious echo of this idea occurs in Gilbert Seldes' *The Stammering Century*. Taking leave of Brownson and about to begin a discussion of "new thought" and Christian Science, Mr. Seldes remarks: "Had he waited a few years he might have been seduced into the newest [Christian Church]. It was just around the corner." (P. 347). But Brownson had accepted—and rejected—the Transcendentalism from which the still hazier modern cults degenerated.

[19] In Brownson himself this idea emerged. Writing in January, 1847, hardly more than two years after his own conversion, he comments on that of Henry Major (who was afterwards to be one of his chief journalistic enemies): "We are also pleased to see that Mr. Major is a simple-minded convert, who comes to the church to be taught, not to teach, and is willing to take the church as she is, and on the grounds on which she has hitherto been taken. He brings her no theory or ingenious hypothesis of his own." (Quoted in a footnote on p. 43 of *Middle Life*). These are curious words coming from the exponent of the Doctrine of Communion.

[20] So a "well-known Boston man" told George Parsons Lathrop. *Atlantic Monthly*, Vol. LXXVII (1896), p. 779.

[21] *Middle Life*, p. 8.

[22] *Catholic World*, Vol. XLV (1887), p. 5.

[23] *Catholic World*, Vol. XLVI, p. 233. Concerning what he calls "The peculiar ontological views of Dr. Brownson," he merely remarks, "What these were I have never been able to satisfy myself." (*Catholic World*, Vol. XLV, p. 5). They will be touched on later; at this time they were not fully developed.

[24] *Catholic World*, Vol. XLV (1887), pp. 6, 7.

[25] *Catholic World*, Vol. XLV (1887), p. 208.

[26] *Middle Life*, p. 32.

[27] *Brownson's Quarterly Review*, Last Series Vol. I (1873), p. 197, also Vol. II of the Third Series (1854), p. 538.

[28] Lord Acton, however, who knew and admired Brownson, speaks of his "unhistorical mind." (Gasquet, *Lord Acton and His Circle*, p. 289).

[29] Elliott, *Hecker*, p. 54.

[30] *Works*, Vol. IV, p. 241.

[31] *Works*, Vol. VII, p. 455.

[32] *Early Life*, p. 458, for one instance.

[33] Kirby, *Years of Experience*, p. 29.

[34] Later in his life he said that, so far from having read the *Awful Disclosures*

of Maria Monk, he had not even seen a copy of that book. He did, however, show great interest in Maria Monk's Catholic daughter, and reviewed her autobiography in the Last Series of his *Review*, Vol. III (1875), pp. 43–75.

35 *Works*, Vol. X, pp. 452–453.

36 J. W. Nevin in *Mercersburg Review*, Vol. II (1850), p. 39.

37 *Works*, Vol. XII, pp. 190, 191.

38 *Latter Life*, p. 60.

39 *Works*, Vol. XIII, p. 167.

40 *Brownson's Quarterly Review*, Vol. II of the Last Series (1874), p. 226.

41 *Ibid.*, pp. 227, 228.

42 *Catholic World*, Vol. XXIII (1876), p. 371.

43 What he says of Cobbett's *History of the Protestant Reformation* (and he does not appear to have read much else by this author) is worth quoting, because it could almost be applied to Brownson himself. "Cobbett wrote an idiomatic, racy, and nervous English style, but his spirit was coarse, pugnacious, and savage, and whoever undertakes to imitate him is in great danger of catching and exaggerating his spirit without attaining to the excellence of his English." (*Works*, Vol. X, p. 451).

44 Elliott, *Hecker*, p. 182.

45 I do not know where Brougham said this, but the opinion is often quoted. The earliest reference I can find to it is in an article in the *Catholic Magazine*, Vol. IV (1845), p. 152.

46 *Works*, Vol. VI, p. 78.

47 *Ibid.*, p. 83.

48 *Ibid.*, p. 23.

49 *Ibid.*, pp. 30–32.

50 *Ibid.*, p. 29.

51 *Ibid.*, p. 88.

52 *Works*, Vol. VII, pp. 260–261, 265, 267, 274.

53 *Works*, Vol. VI, p. 73.

54 *Ibid.*, p. 115.

55 *Ibid.*, p. 134.

56 *Ibid.*, pp. 111–112.

57 *Works*, Vol. V, p. 542.

58 *Ibid.*, p. 541.

59 *Ibid.*, pp. 549, 553.

60 *Works*, Vol. VI, p. 250.

61 *Works*, Vol. X, p. 286.

62 Sanborn and Harris, *Alcott*, Vol. I, p. 266.

63 Weiss, *Life and Correspondence of Theodore Parker*, Vol. I, p. 28.

64 *Works*, Vol. X, p. 296.

65 *Works*, Vol. X, p. 329.

66 *Works*, Vol. XX, p. 4.

67 *Brownson's Quarterly Review*, Vol. II, New Series (1848), p. 136.

68 Vol. III, New Series (1849), p. 136.

69 Vol. V, New Series (1851), pp. 135, 136.

70 Vol. II, Third Series (1854), pp. 537, 538, 539.

71 *Works*, Vol. X, p. 1.

72 *Works*, Vol. X, p. 2.

73 *Works*, Vol. XV, p. 470.

[74] *Works,* Vol. XVIII, p. 224. See also Vol. XX, p. 384.

[75] *Works,* Vol. X, p. 5.

[76] *Ibid.,* pp. 6, 7.

[77] *Ibid.,* p. 13.

[78] *Works,* Vol. X, p. 541.

[79] *Works,* Vol. XVI, p. 51.

[80] *Ibid.,* p. 26.

[81] *Ibid.,* p. 27.

[82] *Ibid.,* p. 40.

[83] *Ibid.,* pp. 41, 42, 43.

[84] *Ibid.,* pp. 46, 47.

[85] *Ibid.,* p. 58.

[86] *Works,* Vol. XVI, p. 283.

[87] *Ibid.,* 291.

[88] *Ibid.,* p. 297.

[89] *Ibid.,* p. 319.

[90] *Ibid.,* pp. 324–325.

[91] *Ibid.,* p. 323.

[92] *Ibid.,* p. 320.

[93] This is my friend, the Rev. Thomas Ryan, C.PP.S. (*Catholic World,* Vol. CLIV, 1942, pp. 426–429). He explains in a letter to me—received while correcting my proofs—that his article was written before the Pearl Harbor attack but candidly admits that he is still strongly anti-British.

[94] *Ibid.,* Vol. XVI, p. 536. In "Conversations of Our Club" he balances this with: "Victory for the British civilization will not result in making the world more heretical, but will help make it more Catholic, by removing the principal obstacle which now prevents the return of the nations to unity." (*Works,* Vol. XI, p. 548). As this is put into the mouth of Father John, the "moderator" of the discussions, it may be taken as representing Brownson's own opinion, even if we did not have other utterances of his along the same lines. Brownson's point of view may be summed up by saying that he held (as do many other people) the British industrialist system to be a disastrous model for the world, but the British political system a great offsetting advantage. Especially he saw that political system as the one that would give Catholicism an advantage wherever it prevailed.

[95] There were, however, defenders of slavery in the South who argued that the planters should make an alliance with the Northern capitalists to defend interests that were fundamentally the same. The argument had too much force in it not to recoil upon those who used it. (A. C. Cole, *The Irrepressible Conflict,* p. 55).

[96] *Works,* Vol. X, p. 20.

[97] *Ibid.,* p. 22.

[98] This was in April, 1845. (Quoted in *Middle Life,* p. 113).

[99] *Works,* Vol. XV, p. 574.

[100] *Works,* Vol. XVI, p. 146.

[101] *Middle Life,* p. 142. McCaffrey, however, showed astonishingly little discernment in believing that the Irish-born bishops, Hughes and Purcell (whom he had known well at Mount St. Mary's, Emmitsburg) and O'Connor of Pittsburg, would join Brownson "in an effort to save their countrymen from demagogues and their own folly." For though they were opposed to a certain type of Irish demagogue, they were themselves Irish enough to be very angry with Brownson. In later years they were to become his bitter enemies.

CHAPTER X

Nativism and Newman

MR. VAN WYCK BROOKS HITS the matter off neatly by remarking that Brownson was too Catholic for the Yankees and too Yankee for the Catholics.[1] If he is not so correct in saying that Brownson "stormed against the Irish domination" of the Church, the comment at least shows the impression made upon one of the few people of our time who have read the twenty volumes of his *Works*.[2] Brownson never stormed against the Irish ecclesiastical domination, or was anything but friendly towards the Irish as a people. But he was a too candid friend. And candid friends are not liked. By coming to the defence of the Irish—which was what he supposed he was doing—he made many enemies among them. In truth, even people less touchy than the Irish might have taken offence. Brownson should have borne in mind that the Irish are sensitive because of the warm-heartedness that gives them their special charm; also that a race that had suffered oppression in its own land was all the more hurt when it encountered attack in the New World. He did not bear this in mind. Instead, with the best of intentions of course, he talked to the Irish for their own good; and they considered themselves a better judge of that than a Yankee radical turned Catholic and conservative.

It is to be hoped that these matters may be safely discussed after the lapse of nearly a hundred years.[3] In any event, they must be discussed, for there is no way of writing an honest book about Brownson without bringing them in. It should be understood, however, that what is given here is an exposition of Brownson's views,

192

and that they do not necessarily, on this point or on others, coincide with my own.

He had little to say about Protestant bigotry as such. Soon after his conversion he summarily dismissed the "No-Popery" agitation by saying that it was something cooked up by the ministers, because they were losing their influence. "What," he asked scornfully, "avails it to prove the pope to be antichrist, to populations that do not even believe in Christ? What avails it to thunder at Catholicity with texts which are no longer believed to have a divine authority?"[4] He understood very well that the Nativist disturbances would pass. What interested him far more was what lay behind the disturbances.

When Bishop Fitzpatrick visited Europe in 1854 his ten-year-old censorship over *Brownson's Quarterly Review* came to an end. A priest—Father John Roddan—was, indeed, appointed to act for the Bishop, and Brownson read his articles to him before publication; but Roddan's, being only a delegated authority, probably could not be very strictly exercised. And on what Brownson wrote about the Irish, Roddan happened to agree with him.[5] In any event, as it did not touch upon theology, no theological exception could be taken. Had Fitzpatrick been in Boston, he probably would have told Brownson that what he was writing was inadvisable; he could not have done more. But he was not in Boston, and the mouse accordingly played while the cat was away. When the Bishop returned, Brownson no longer submitted his work for ecclesiastical approbation.[6] He had obtained his liberty, and he did not mean to give it up again. It seems safe to infer that some coolness between himself and Fitzpatrick sprang up on this account, for soon afterwards Brownson decided to move to New York where, he hoped, there would be no question of any censorship.

The gist of what he wrote in 1854 may be stated in a sentence. While Brownson condemned the excesses of the Native Americans in their new guise as "Know-Nothings," he stood firmly on his own Americanism and told the immigrants that, if they were regarded with hostility, it was because they often acted in such a way as to give Americans offence. It was an opinion that had at least a great deal of truth in it, but as usual Brownson put it tactlessly. What many readers got out of his articles was that he was defending, or palliating, Know-Nothingism. And they took this as an attack on the Irish.

It need hardly be said that it was nothing of the kind. It was only an attempt to make the immigrants understand their relation to America, and that it was for their own best interests to accept America and to become assimilated as soon as possible. They would not have been so irritated had Brownson not started with the assumption that the typical American was the Anglo-American; to this Anglo-American civilization he told the Irish that it was both their duty and privilege to conform. What he hardly guessed was that the Irish had a special mission in the process of Americanization. Though he argued that the Church would aid in the process, this was because he perceived that American liberties had a safeguard in the Church; he did not know that the Church would be able to do this particular work so effectively precisely because it was already being captained for the most part by Irishmen.

In the first article, "The Native American," Brownson distinguished between the spirit of nationality (which he admired) and the methods of the so-called Nativists, which he repudiated. At the same time he rebuked the newcomers, who were taking their revenge by talking derisively about "naytivism" and the "naytives." [7] Nativism, in the sense of nationality, he pointed out, was a good thing in itself—as nobody should know better than the Irish, who were so "sensitive to remarks derogatory to their national characteristics." What they ought to accept was the fact that "whether it be for good or for evil, the American nationality is and will be determined by the Anglo-American portion of our population." The American was right in insisting that the immigrant conform to him; that the immigrant commonly refused this conformity was "the secret of the native American hostility to foreigners naturalized amongst us." [8]

Brownson granted that the Native American feeling was "to some extent" anti-Catholic, but for this he blamed the immigrants, whose refusal of assimilation, "although they may have violated the letter of no positive law of the country," was nevertheless an abuse of American hospitality.[9] Therefore he said, "We speak to warn our foreign-born population against provoking a contest with native Americanism, which most assuredly will not result to their advantage. They must beware of confounding the proper American feeling with the anti-Catholic feeling," and added that when he first became a Catholic he had fallen into the same mistake.[10] Native Americanism and anti-Catholicism were only accidentally allied; that they were allied at all was the fault of the Catholics.[11] Such generalities might have been allowed to pass. The trouble was that Brownson, after saying that the Irish had often been vilely slandered, went on to talk about "a miserable rabble . . . a noisy, drinking, and brawling rabble," and further seemed to bear out the Nativist contention by remarking that the Irish, because of never having regarded the laws of England as legitimate, often lost their respect for all law.[12] As for the Germans, because they had been accustomed to regard their princes as the law, they tended upon escaping this authority, to become "wild democrats," socialists or anarchists. "It must be conceded," he stated flatly, "that the great body of foreigners naturalized or simply resident among us are not republican in their spirit, their interior habits, and their interior life and discipline."[13] Though the Germans were worse than the Irish, in the matter of radicalism, the Irish had "that ribald sheet," the *Irish American,* and "that Protestant radical, John Mitchell."[14] As might be expected, the "bombastic orators and ignorant editors" did not forgive these remarks, which gave so much help and comfort to the Nativists. Here "right out of the horse's mouth" came a Catholic admission that the chief Know-Nothing accusations against Catholics were justified.

When Irish readers got as far in Brownson's article as that, they usually had had enough. They did not read any further, which was a pity. For they would have found Brownson condemning the

Know-Nothings as un-American and as being "hand in glove with foreign radicals." He said that Know-Nothingism did "not direct its opposition to foreigners in general, but to Catholic foreigners in particular, that is, against the only class of foreigners from whom very little if any danger is to be apprehended. The really Catholic portion of our foreign population, whether Irish or German, are at present the most conservative body in the country." [15]

If any Irish or German Catholic was mollified by this interlude, he was soon touched again on a very raw spot—the naturalization laws. Arguing, as he had done in 1845, that naturalization is a boon conferred at discretion and not a natural right—this at a time when the Nativists were trying to make those laws more stringent, so as to keep out the Irish—Brownson suggested that the Catholic newcomers would be well advised voluntarily to forgo citizenship if by doing so they could exclude the foreign born radicals from the suffrage.[16] He was careful to say that he did not himself "advocate" this; it was only that he would not "oppose" it, if a kind of tacit deal could be effected, under which there would be "no discrimination against us" and immigrant Catholics would withdraw their claim to the vote. The whole argument was somewhat questionable: the good Catholics among the immigrants certainly vastly outnumbered the foreign radicals who were arriving, so nothing would have been gained, and much lost, by the suggested abstention from citizenship. And of course no "deal" could have been made with the Know-Nothings. The whole thing struck the Irish as a bit disingenuous.

To the Nativists he pointed out that their hostility to the newcomers because of their Catholicism virtually forced them into segregation and a retention of their old national characteristics. However, he qualified this by declaring that the Catholic immigrants manifested in general little disposition to be naturalized.[17] The answer should have been patent to the logician's mind: if the facts were as he stated, what was the point in the Nativist attempt to make the naturalization laws more stringent? And if the Catholic should forgo citizenship, why should he be expected to become assimilated? Indeed, how could he be completely assimilated unless he were naturalized?

Another Nativist contention found some support in Brownson when he said that Catholic immigration had given the Catholic Church a foreign aspect in the United States.[18] This was something that could not be denied, though it was something which time would cure. "As for our Irish Catholics," he wrote, "we are willing to treat them either as simply Catholics and Americans, if they will permit us, or as simply Catholics and Irishmen, if they prefer; but we insist that they shall make their election, for we cannot, even if we would, treat them as both at once, because the national type they bring with them from Ireland—that is, those of them who are called *the Irish*—is different from the American type, and unity is possible only by the assimilation of the one to the other." [19] These Irish Catholics, he declared, had created such a conviction in the American mind that Catholicism was incompatible with Americanism, that he himself was beginning to be accused of lack of patriotism on the grounds of his criticism of the Mexican War and the Cuban expeditions; and that suppositious lack of patriotism was set down to his Catholicism.[20] On the other hand, some Catholic editors, such as "our highly gifted friend, Bakewell," editor of the late *Shepherd of the Valley,* had thrown the blame on him as "a poor convert" and had tried to make him responsible for the hostility manifested towards Catholics.[21] Brownson, for his part, accused Catholics of being ready to sacrifice him to appease the Know-Nothing anger, and the Know-Nothings of attacking him in order to get the Catholics to disown him.[22] Yet all he had done had been to maintain that Catholicism is Catholic and not a foreign religion anywhere and that it is not hostile to American institutions. The danger, as he saw it, was that "the more prominent we make the Irish nationality, and the more we identify it with Catholicity, the more do we confirm the prejudices of the American people against our religion." [23] In all of which there is much that is true and much that badly needed to be said. The only question is whether Brownson said it in the right way.

The date of the articles from which these quotations have been made must be remembered. They appeared in *Brownson's Quarterly Review* for July and October, 1854. With that fixed in our minds, we can now go on to the Newman affair.

During the time he was in retirement at Littlemore, John Henry Newman wrote the book which was published after his conversion to Catholicism. He called it *An Essay on the Development of Christian Doctrine.* Upon its appearance in 1845, Brownson thought he perceived in its certain heretical propositions; with the consent of Fitzpatrick—and egged on by Archbishop Purcell—he severely criticized the work.

Newman wrote the book primarily to clarify his own mind and to discover some ground on which he could become a Catholic. After his reception into the Church he published what he had written in the belief that it might provide others who had his own difficulties with sufficient reasons for acting as he had done. It must be borne in mind that the audience he was addressing was a highly educated one of men who, like himself, were steeped in the Greek and Latin Fathers. William George Ward was to tell Brownson [24] that Newman had read the entire Patrology at least three times before setting to his task. Because he had once been held back from the Church by seeing—or thinking that he saw—in the writings of the Fathers discrepancies from the Faith as held in his own day, he attempted to formulate a theory to account for this fact. He did not deny that the deposit of faith had been *implicitly* held by the Church from the moment of its foundation, but as to whether it had been held *explicitly* was another matter. He said in his book: "It is the general pretext of heretics that they are but serving and protecting Christianity by their innovations; and it is their charge against what by this time we may surely call the Catholic Church, that her successive definitions of doctrine have but overlaid and

obscured it." [25] He therefore made it his business to try to account
historically for these definitions, as they seemed to show a development of doctrine. "Modern Catholicism," he wrote, "is nothing . . .
but the legitimate growth . . . of the doctrine of the early church." [26]
In this development he saw a proof of life. [27] "An idea," he pointed
out—by way of analogy—"grows in the mind by remaining there." [28]
More definitely, he added, "All great ideas are found, as time goes
on, to involve much which was not seen at first to belong to them." [29]
The deductions made by the Church were not "made at random"
but were "all along on definite and continuous principles." [30] To
make things worse, in the judgment of the plain and unsubtle
Brownson, Newman argued (quoting the Anglican Bishop Butler)
that "a collection of weak evidences makes up a strong evidence" and
that "the truth of our religion, like the truth of common matters, is to
be judged by all the evidence taken together." [31]

This point of view infuriated Brownson, who could not admit
that certainty was to be obtained by the mere accumulation of prob-
abilities, and still less that there had been any development in
Christian doctrine. It was the faith once for all delivered to the
saints, and what Newman was doing seemed to him to cut at the
foundations of Christian belief. Newman had written, "It may
almost be laid down as a historical fact, that the mystical interpretation [of Scripture] and orthodoxy will stand or fall together."
Yet he meant no more than that these "mystical" interpretations
were a drawing out of what was not on the surface. Even Christ
had told His disciples, "I have yet many things to say to you, but
you cannot bear them now."

Newman never held that anything needed to be added, or could
be added, to the original deposit of faith, but only that the understanding of that deposit was something that called for time and
the operation of the Holy Ghost. It was a psychological development
of believers rather than the material development of dogma itself.
But what he had to say in his book was widely quoted by Unitarians
as proof that the Trinitarian doctrine itself was not "primitive."

And Wilfrid Ward remarks that "an outcry followed—the narrow and vigorous Dr. Brownson taking up the matter in his Review," with the result that many of Newman's opinions of his Anglican period were now brought up again in an attempt to discredit him.[32]

In Rome fortunately a less serious judgment was taken of the matter. Perrone, who was the leading theologian there, made some criticisms but only by way of stating what the Catholic position was and not charging Newman with holding the opposite. In fact, between him and Newman a great friendship was struck up.[33] The well-known English Jesuit, at Rome, Father Thomas Glover, was also asked for his opinion and replied that most of what Brownson had said was sound and could not easily be refuted. He went on: "There can be no doubt that the Apostles were enabled, on the day of Pentecost, to expound, or develope, explicitly, any dogma to its utmost extent, if there had been any need of it, as well as their successors at any subsequent period. But it does not appear that they did so, whereas their successors have developed explicitly many truths, which were implicitly contained in the original deposit."[34]

Now in 1845 Brownson could have known virtually nothing about the Fathers. Subsequently he gained some knowledge of them, though it could never have begun to approach Newman's long and minute familiarity with the Patrology. When he wrote as he did he was armed with little except his famous logic, and a convert's zeal. Yet he accused Newman of having written a Protestant book, though he acknowledged the genuineness of Newman's conversion. What is rather strange is that he failed to perceive that Newman's theory of development played much the same part in his conversion that the "Doctrine of Communion" had played in his own. Rather, while understanding this, he refused it any validity.[35] Newman had tried to account for the seeming variations of doctrine by saying that "time is necessary for the comprehension and perfection of great ideas." To Brownson the word "perfection" appeared to convey that doctrine had had a material development. Therefore with belligerent orthodoxy he informed Newman—somewhat unnecessarily—

that the Church "denies that she has ever added a new article to the primitive creed" [36] and declared that, however much Newman's doctrine may have been of service to him, it was one "which for years kept us out of the Catholic Church, as it now keeps out the greater part of our former friends and associates." [37] It looks as if there were some degree of wilful misunderstanding in all this: it could not have been Newman's theory that had kept Brownson out of the Church so long—and there is no indication in Brownson's writings that it had ever bothered him when on the road to the Church. If he had been held back, it was by the very misapprehension that Newman essayed to remove. The most that could be said is that, by seeking to remove the difficulty, Newman acknowledged its existence; Brownson's simple method would have been to have denied the difficulty. All that Newman was trying to say was that the Christian revelation "is not and cannot be taken in all at once by the human mind," not that it had not existed in an inchoate form in the Church from the beginning. [38]

It would be wearisome, except perhaps to professional theologians, to follow this controversy—which was mainly one-sided—through all its ramifications. In an article written in 1863 Brownson admitted that he might have misunderstood Newman. [39] But afterwards he reverted to his former attitude, and from first to last wrote about the theory of Development enough to make several volumes. But Cardinal Wiseman upheld Newman, getting from Newman the reply, "I have not allowed Dr. Brownson's rudeness to annoy me, yet it is a very great satisfaction and comfort to receive such an assurance as you have written to me." [40] And Richard Simpson, another Oxford Convert, wrote with some amusement to Hecker to say that he thought "posterity will judge of their quarrel as it has done of that between Plato and Aristotle; that the latter, though the most acute and formally logical, has failed to see what the former intended." [41]

Newman, despite what he told Wiseman, was very much hurt by Brownson's attack, and William George Ward came to his defence in the *Dublin Review,* writing to tell Brownson that he was the anonymous contributor.[42] In this letter he protested against Brownson's treatment of his friend, saying, "I cannot but feel it an *extreme injustice and cruelty* that Catholics who were silent when he was searching in their direction for some way of escape, should afterwards, when he had found a way . . . be loud in their objections to the legitimacy of that way." [43] Brownson himself is exculpated; he was not a Catholic at the time. But should he— *per impossibile*—succeed in proving his contention, he was told, "you would only throw him back on his original perplexity and shake his whole Catholic faith to the foundation." [44] To which the dialectician did not lose the opportunity to make the rejoinder, "Well, if Newman's faith is so easily shaken as all that . . ."

The controversy is perhaps not particularly important in itself. It is dealt with here because of the light it throws upon the relations between the two men. It must be remembered because of what is to follow.

What must also be remembered is that a healthy and hearty human prejudice lay behind Brownson's strictures on Newman. Even if we could not discover this from the criticisms themselves, Henry Brownson lets it out that this was so and that he himself shares his father's prejudice. Orestes Brownson, he says, "rarely, if ever, reviewed a publication by the converted Puseyites without finding more or less fault with it." He always read them with a presumption against them.[45] Oh yes, Henry admitted—and how far he speaks for his father and how far for himself is not very clear —oh yes, the Tractarians were all "nice men," highly cultivated and refined, and probably they had always been very moral. But they had come into the Church for "aesthetic and intellectual reasons" and because they were so presumptuous as to wish to attain to heroic sanctity—this last seemingly being their worst offence.[46] Orestes Brownson did not like the tone of their voice, or their "insular arrogance," or their inability to construct a syllogism without either a faulty major or minor. (This of "logical Ward!") Being Englishmen was bad enough, but being Oxford men was quite unpardonable. For a dozen pages Henry lets himself go, mingling his acrid steam with that of his father.

Six years after he had written his first article against Newman, Brownson was still snorting, "Our tractarian friends, brought up to look upon contemporary Catholics as an ignorant, feeble, cunning, credulous and superstitious set of mortals, far inferior in learning, talent and morals to themselves, and accustomed to regard the scholastics as dealing mainly in vain subtlities and distinctions without a difference, very naturally passed from the study of their jejune Anglican theology to the study of the fathers, whom they were forced to read through the spectacles of their more famous Anglican divines. They thus not only had not the requisite preparation for studying them, but had views and habits which wholly unfitted them for studying them, with even passable success. They have come from the fathers down to the scholastics, whom they have studied not profoundly, and have interpreted them by the fathers, instead of interpreting the fathers by them. Hence their theory of development, and other errors, adopted to reconcile the fathers and the later theologians." [47] The truth is that Brownson resented the Oxford manner and the cultured air of those whom he delighted in calling "ex-Puseyites." [48] Like other logicians he had illogical moments that serve to endear him to people who lack his virtuosity in the syllogism.

Newman was not so urbane as not to be annoyed over Brownson's attack.[49] But instead of replying himself, he allowed William George Ward to do so in the *Dublin Review*. Then, because Brownson complained that the rebuttal had not been entrusted to a priest, Ward retorted tartly: "Surely what a layman and a recent convert is at liberty to write, a layman and a recent convert is at liberty to answer." Brownson contrived to escape the logical noose by saying in his turn: "Unquestionably; yet a certain layman and a recent convert may be *competent* to write what another may not be competent to answer. The question is not as to the liberty, but as to the competency." If he had asked for a "Catholic doctor" instead of a layman it was because the point was of such importance that it called for an authoritative decision.[50]

This was in April, 1848. On October 15, 1852, he wrote to the editor of the *Dublin Tablet*: "Dr. Newman, when he wrote his Essay on Development, was not a Catholic, and when I first wrote against it he was only a layman like myself. He had, indeed, been a Protestant minister, and so had I, and there was nothing in our respective positions that made it improper for me to review his book . . . I am, I very well know, a layman, and write on religious and theological subjects, which no layman of himself has the right to do. But I do so at the request of the ecclesiastical authorities of my country, and I never publish an article, written by myself, on theological questions, without first submitting it to my own Bishop, or a competent theologian approved by him. I do not presume of myself to teach, for I well know that I have no authority to teach." [51] About the same time, when reviewing a book by J. M. Capes, he remarked, "If the layman cannot write on theological topics with exactness, both of thought and expression, he has no business to write on them at all." [52] And twelve years later he declared: "Even the theological judgment of a layman is entitled to more weight than that of a priest or bishop, if he be a man more richly endowed by nature, and has superior theological learning and science." [53] It all turned on the question of competency—obviously something not very easy to decide.

Newman's own position was put in a letter to Capes, dated January 19, 1857: "I am opposed to laymen writing theology, on the same principle that I am against amateur doctors, and still more lawyers— not because they are laymen, but because they are αὐτοδίδακτοι. For this reason I am disgusted with Brownson." But at once he added, "I don't exclude myself. I have not written on dogmatics or asceticism since I have been a Catholic." [54] Yet even that did not quite meet the point: in any field the amateur is occasionally to be encountered who is superior to the professional. The most that anyone can say is that as a general rule the professional is likely to be superior to the amateur. Self-educated as Brownson was, and suffering from the defects of self-education, he was, within limits, an extremely able theologian. It was useless to try to brush him aside as a "mere layman"; the only thing to do was to disprove his arguments. And though in his controversy with Newman's friends he was probably wrong, one can hardly say that he was worsted.

That Newman, despite his expression of "disgust" in 1857, thought highly of Brownson's competence, is shown by an extraordinary offer he made him at the end of 1853, as soon as he had been appointed Rector of the new university in Dublin. It shows a few other things as well: it shows, for example, that Newman was a most magnanimous man, even if Cardinal Manning used to say, "Poor Newman! He was a good hater." It also shows that the men of Oxford, though they seemed to have insufferable airs of superiority, did not really feel any superiority. It was only the English manner that had irritated Brownson, as it still irritates most Americans. Behind it—at all events in this case—there was a discerning mind and a generous heart. Newman invited Brownson to accept one of the chairs in his university.

Father Neville, who writes the introduction to the posthumously published *My Campaign in Ireland,* says that Newman would not sacrifice the interests of the University by allowing his resentment against Brownson to affect the issue. He recognized that Brownson would confer distinction upon his project.[55] By proposing that he become one of his professors he at once conferred honor upon himself and honor upon Brownson. It was perhaps the highest and handsomest tribute that Brownson ever received.

The first letter Newman wrote to Brownson was dated December 15, 1853. In it he asks him whether he would care to lecture for a year, beginning in the autumn of 1854, and saying that he was also going to invite Döllinger. What he proposed was—of all things in the world—a course on Geography. What a fertile subject of thought it would be! "Viewed under its different heads, as physical, moral, and political, it gives scope to a variety of profound philosophical speculations"—which was a sufficiently broad hint that under that nominal heading Brownson would be free to talk about whatever occurred to him. And he concluded with, "You are the first person to whom I have applied." [56]

In June, after Brownson had demurred on Geography, Newman wrote again to reassure him. Theology and metaphysics, he said, were subjects which the Irish bishops wish assigned to priests, but "It has struck me you would not be disinclined to take the chair of Philosophy of *Religion,* or the evidences of Xtianity, or of the Notes of the Church . . . Would not the subject you mention of *Civilization* come into it, without going into the subjects of theology or metaphysics, which, as I have said, the Bishops will reserve for Ecclesiastics?" [57] And from Lord (then Sir John) Acton arrived a long enthusiastic letter saying, "I am quite certain that they would be too happy to let you lecture on opossums if you choose to communicate your good things in that way. The vast field of philosophy will be yours, and you will have an opportunity of making philosophical questions familiar to a nation hitherto barely acquainted with them, and I thank God for the good fortune of my countrymen in being initiated in that magnificent science by you of all men living. . . . I can speak with perfect confidence of the facilities which will be given you to choose your own subject, for I am intimately acquainted with Newman's closest friends, and I know the immense price they attach to the prospect of an alliance with you in this work. . . . We Catholics have no philosophy: no philosophical writers exist among us. . . . You alone can prepare us for the great controversies by founding among us a school and arming it with the principles of a sound philosophy. . . . Your intercourse will be as an infusion of new blood in many societies, in Dublin, in London, in Paris, and in other places." [58]

Something must perhaps be allowed in all this for the ebullience of youth. In 1854 Acton was only twenty. The year before he had met Brownson in Boston and had heard him denounce the dangerous doctrines of Newman; at the same time he had arranged to join Brownson at Emmitsburg, Maryland, where the philosopher was to lecture. If Acton did not hear the lecture it was because at the hotel at York, Pennsylvania, he was provided with such astounding sherry cobblers that he was unable to get to Emmitsburg in time.[59] But in his letter he refers to the happy hours he and Brownson had had together at Emmitsburg and Boston.[60] If he was young, he was already moving in the best intellectual circles in Europe. No better testimony to the power of Brownson can be found than the admiration of this extraordinarily gifted stripling.

The university appointment was not to be. In July, 1854, Brownson's article on the Know-Nothings had appeared and the Irish were incensed against him. What forces were put to work we do not positively know—except that Brownson suspected Archbishop Purcell of Cincinnati [61]—but on August 23rd Newman had to write to Brownson to tell him, "I am urged . . . now for the first time, in quarters to which I cannot but listen, to ask you whether it would be inconvenient to you to postpone your visit here, on the ground of some offence which happens to be taken *just now,* in America, and, I believe in Ireland, at something you have lately written." [62] To which Brownson, who knew better than Newman what the trouble was all about, replied on September 12th to say that it would be advisable if instead of "postponing" the matter, he at once definitely declined the offer. He went on: "I need not tell you that what I call the *Irish* party both here and in Ireland, here especially, are by no means pleased to see an Englishman at [the University's] head, and they would in no manner consent to have me connected with it as lecturer. They would raise the cry that the University is intended simply to Anglo-Saxonize the Irish. . . . I assure you that the Irish party, for whom in a great measure the

University is designed, have always disliked me, and will never accept me. The storm which recently broke out here, is only the expression of long pent up feelings." Then he thrust at Purcell: "I am censured severely by a distinguished prelate, who appears before the public as your most ardent admirer, for having written against your Essay on Development, when he himself urged me through the Bishop of Boston to do so." [63] To which Newman answered that he was not going to announce a definite refusal, but that he still hoped that, when things had quited down, Brownson would be able to come. In the meanwhile he was not going to fill the professorship. [64]

The blow was severe, for the prestige that would have come to Brownson would have been enormous. If the American-Irish must be pardoned for their anger against him, he must also be pardoned for his momentary bitterness against them. It did not last. He was never a man to harbor a grudge. But it was all the harder for him because this disappointment came at the very moment that he was thinking of leaving a Boston that had grown too hot for him and of betaking himself elsewhere. In Europe he would have obtained complete rehabilitation.

Yet it may have been just as well that he was never attached to Newman's university. For one thing, he could hardly have lived on the salary. None was mentioned in the correspondence, but we know that a full professor was paid only £300 a year—and that precisely two men received it. Counting some part-time men who were paid less than £100, the average salary was £185. [65] And Brownson had still to get to Ireland.

Newman himself soon ran into difficulties. He was badly treated in the matter of the bishopric *in partibus* he was promised and which would have given him standing in what he eventually found an impossible position. He was humiliated by letting his friends know he was to receive the mitre and by accepting a gift of a pectoral cross from them to celebrate the elevation that never occurred. [66] It was blocked by the Irish bishops who, he was to say, "regard any intellectual man as being on the road to perdition." [67] And the calibre of the first students was such that Brownson could hardly have found a very fertile field for his labors among them.[68]

The personal encounter of Newman and Brownson might have shown the two men that they had, after all, much in common. Father Neville tells us that Newman, when planning a household in Dublin for himself, had included in it a suite of rooms for Brownson, with whom, and two or three other professors, he meant to live *en famille*.[69] On the other hand, the sensitive Newman might have found it unbearable had Brownson started to bellow and pound the table in argument. But at least we may suppose that, while the terms Brownson might have used would have been different, he would have felt some kinship with the man who was to write in his *Apologia*: "If I am asked why I believe in a God, I answer that it is because I believe in myself, for I feel it impossible to believe in my own existence (and of that fact I am quite sure) without believing in the existence of Him, who lives as a Personal, All-seeing, All-Judging Being in my conscience." To both men God was a being luminously self-evident.

How much Brownson would have got out of Europe is another question. He was a man of books and he could obtain all the books he needed. He never felt any need to see foreign lands, though he had perhaps more foreign interests than any American of his time. But they were limited to politics and philosophy. It would have been pleasant, of course, for him to have met his early philosophic mentors; Cousin was still alive in 1854. But the closest Brownson ever got to Europe was by way of introducing some chapters about European travel—obviously in order to drag in Gioberti—in his novel, *The Spirit-Rapper*. There may be some significance that he was writing this book at the time he was expecting to go to Ireland. European "culture," however, in the sense of wandering about picture-galleries and cathedrals, guide-book in hand, never had the slightest attraction for him; nor would he have made any pilgrimages to literary shrines. His whole work lay in America, and if he studied European politics it was only to apply its lessons to conditions at home. From Europe he asked no more than the knotty metaphysical treatises he so eagerly devoured. All the more firmly because of this set-back was he fastened to his distinctively American vocation.

[1] *The Flowering of New England,* p. 248.

[2] In a letter to me Mr. Brooks (to whom this book is dedicated) writes: "Brownson's is altogether a very curious case, and of course his career was badly 'timed,'—I mean for a controversialist of his type. In England, Ireland or France, for instance, what a great influence he would have had! . . . But I don't suppose he ever had the kind of opponents, on his particular ground, who might have brought his great powers into full play. I never got such an impression as in reading his 'Works' of an intellectual dynamo running in a void. I don't believe that at that time the American Catholic public either needed or knew how to use the kind of mind he brought them. . . . He was geared, so to say, for a learned society, and his later range of sympathies lay wholly outside the learned society of the country. But I really think he presents an extraordinarily interesting problem."

[3] My hope is slight, however. Even my *Story of American Catholicism* has made some people charge me with anti-Irish prejudice, though my thesis there (in so far as I had one) was: "Upon the whole it is incontestable that the guiding hands of the Church in the United States have been Irish. That this is so may be considered providential. The Irish were at once the men most capable and of the race most assimilable by America." (P. 507).

[4] *Works,* VI, p. 132.

[5] In the Boston *Pilot,* which he edited, Father Roddan had expressed much the same views. His comments aroused less animosity because they were not those of a convert and were made by a priest. Also of course they were less vigorously put than Brownson's and attracted much less attention. (*Middle Life,* p. 536).

[6] *Middle Life,* pp. 635–637.

[7] *Works,* Vol. XVIII, p. 281.

[8] *Ibid.,* pp. 283, 284.

[9] *Ibid.,* pp. 284, 286.

[10] *Ibid.,* p. 285.

[11] *Ibid.,* p. 286.

[12] *Ibid.,* p. 289.

[13] *Ibid.,* p. 291.

[14] Brownson's misspells his name, which should have only one "l." Yet Mitchel was a man not very unlike Brownson himself in many ways, except of course for his Fenianism. His *Jail Journal* is one of the masterpieces of lucid English prose. He died in 1875 after being elected to Parliament.

[15] *Works,* Vol. XVIII, p. 294.

[16] *Ibid.,* p. 311.

[17] *Ibid.,* pp. 297, 298.

[18] *Ibid.,* p. 302.

[19] *Ibid.,* p. 315.

[20] *Ibid.,* p. 320.

[21] *Ibid.,* p. 329.

[22] *Middle Life,* p. 587.

[23] *Ibid.,* p. 323.

[24] *Ibid.,* p. 45.

[25] *Development of Christian Doctrine,* p. 419.

26 *Ibid.*, p. 169.

27 *Ibid.*, p. 186.

28 *Ibid.*, p. 190.

29 *Ibid.*, p. 207.

30 *Ibid.*, p. 324.

31 *Ibid.*, pp. 107, 108.

32 *Life of Cardinal Newman*, Vol. I, p. 160.

33 *Ibid.*, pp. 184, 185.

34 *Early Life*, p. 69.

35 *Works*, Vol. XIV, pp. 2–3.

36 *Ibid.*, p. 11.

37 *Ibid.*, p. 14.

38 *Ibid.*, p. 19.

39 *Works*, Vol. VIII, p. 4.

40 Wilfrid Ward, *The Life and Times of Cardinal Wiseman*, Vol. II, p. 41.

41 *Middle Life*, p. 396.

42 Vol. XXIII (1847), pp. 373–405.

43 *Middle Life*, p. 46.

44 *Ibid.*, p. 48.

45 *Middle Life*, pp. 376, 379. In part, however, Brownson's prejudice against all Oxford converts stemmed from his prejudice against Newman.

46 *Ibid.*, p. 381.

47 *Works*, Vol. XIV, p. 182. Later he was accustomed to compare the Fathers of the Church and the later Doctors and theologians, very much to the disadvantage of the latter. (See *Works*, Vol. XI, p. 223). The theologians might subject a particular point to a bright hard light, but the Fathers were those who had integrity of view. The line of degeneration, according to Brownson, was this: Fathers, Doctors, theologians who gave compendiums of the Doctors, and finally the modern professors who "content themselves with giving compendiums of the compendiums . . . and have fallen as low as possible without falling into nothing and disappearing in the inane." (*Works*, Vol. XX, 181).

48 It should, however, be added that English Catholic controversy was sometimes fierce enough to satisfy anybody. A writer in the *Rambler* for August, 1849, complained that "compared with other classes and religious bodies, Catholics attack one another with a virulence, an uncharitableness, a reckless imputation of motives and an ungentlemanly coarseness of language, which can be paralleled in no other society professing to be guided by religious principles and restrained by the laws of common propriety." (Quoted in Gasquet's *Lord Acton and his Circle*, p. xlii). Twenty years later the *Saturday Review* explained the reasons: Catholics had got into the way of hitting so hard because their nerves were on edge after long years of being dominated over, and they took out on one another what they would have liked to say about Protestants but found it inadvisable to say. Therefore some outlet for their pugnacity was necessary. (*Ibid.*, p. xliii).

49 Newman, *My Campaign in Ireland*, p. xxxv.

50 *Works*, Vol. XIV, pp. 122, 123.

51 *Middle Life*, pp. 387, 388.

52 *Works*, Vol. XX, p. 3.

53 *Ibid.*, p. 225.

54 Gasquet, *Lord Acton and His Circle*, p. xxiv.

55 P. xxxiv. The book was published in 1896, six years after the Cardinal's death.

It is not included among his *Collected Works* and has, in fact, not only on the title-page but the cover: "Printed for Private Circulation Only." Though most of it consists of confidential reports that have no immediate interest here, it contains some matter that has bearing on Brownson. This will be drawn upon.

⁵⁶ *Middle Life,* pp. 470, 471. Actually Newman did appoint a professor of Geography—J. B. Robertson. The importance of the subject has at last been recognized in our geopolitical age—another indication of Newman's large and luminous mind.

⁵⁷ *Ibid.,* p. 480.

⁵⁸ *Middle Life,* pp. 472–474.

⁵⁹ "Lord Acton's American Diaries," *Fortnightly Review,* Vol. CXI (New Series), 1922, pp. 66, 82–83.

⁶⁰ *Middle Life,* p. 475.

⁶¹ Hughes of New York may have had a hand, but this seems unlikely from the fact that he expressed directly to Brownson his disapproval. A letter to the Archbishop from Brownson dated July 3, 1854, and in the New York Archdiocesan Archives, has this in it: "To say that the letter has given me inexpressible pain is simple [*sic*] saying nothing. I certainly wrote the articles of which you complain." He goes on to accept full responsibility, but says that he had submitted what he wrote to the censor appointed by Fitzpatrick. "I did not write them with any thought of concession to the Know Nothings & I am not aware of anything in my article on Native Americanism that differs from what has been the uniform doctrine of my Review from the first . . . I am an American, and I write as an American. I could not do otherwise, and I am sure that you would not wish me to do so."

⁶² *Middle Life,* p. 481.

⁶³ *Ibid.,* pp. 482, 483. Henry Brownson quotes only the first draft and says that this passage may have been omitted from the letter as sent to Newman. The letter actually sent was dated September 13th, and is quoted in part in *My Campaign in Ireland.* There Brownson added what was not in the first draft, a complimentary reference to Newman's *Loss and Gain.* "If I had seen that work at an earlier date," he says, "many things which I have written concerning you and your friends, the Oxford Converts, would never have been written. . . . Forgive me, Reverend Father, whatever injustice I may have done you, and ask them in my name to forgive me also. Believe me, I was moved by no personal considerations, but thought I was only doing my duty." (P. xxxiii).

⁶⁴ *Middle Life,* p. 484.

⁶⁵ *My Campaign in Ireland,* pp. 152, 153.

⁶⁶ Ward, *Newman,* Vol. I, pp. 331, 332, 356.

⁶⁷ *Ibid.,* Vol. I, p. 355.

⁶⁸ The report from the Professor of Ancient History for 1857 reads, in part: "A University Professor has the right, under ordinary circumstances, to take for granted that his hearers have *some* knowledge, however imperfect, of the matter upon which he lectures. This has *not* been my good fortune, at least as regards an important portion of my hearers, and it would have been idle to have plunged into an abyss of historical erudition, or to have indulged in the flights of speculation, in presence of gentlemen who have yet to learn such elementary truths as that Jerusalem is not in Africa, that the Helots did not dwell on the shores of the Red Sea, and that the Patriarch Jacob lived and died before the Babylonish Captivity." (*My Campaign in Ireland,* p. 202).

⁶⁹ *My Campaign in Ireland,* pp. xxiv–xxv.

CHAPTER XI

Temporal and Spiritual

AT THE SEVENTH PROVINCIAL COUNCIL of Baltimore, held in 1849, the presiding Archbishop suggested to the other bishops that they give Brownson a mark of their approval. Accordingly a letter was signed by twenty-four prelates and this was printed on the cover of each issue of *Brownson's Quarterly Review*. It did two things: so unparalleled an indication of episcopal favor brought him many new subscribers; it also made other Catholic editors very jealous. As conductors of diocesan magazines, they could not, of course, expect more than the support of their own Ordinary. But that Brownson was acknowledged to be in a class by himself, scarcely increased their good-will towards him. Those who had not already attacked him when they could, now lost no opportunity for doing so.

This professional envy he could afford to treat with disdain; it was the compliment of mediocrity. The letter of the bishops, so proudly displayed, more than offset the malicious digs he got from time to time. And it came at the right moment. For though some of his subscribers of 1844 remained loyal to him, most of them dropped away. Without the Bishops' backing his *Review* might not have been able to survive. Even with that backing he had many difficulties to surmount.

Apart from the damage his lack of tact did him, he was somewhat deficient in business instincts. Or rather, while he was shrewd enough, when he took the trouble to look into practical affairs, he was careless. He had involved himself by going surety for a friend who had started another magazine in Boston, and lost a good deal more than he could afford over that venture.[1] Moreover, he was not very prompt in answering letters and sometimes completely forgot his lecture engagements.[2] Yet his lecturing was an important source of income, and he received what were, for those days, substantial fees.

But this was only indifference to his personal interests. He was fortunately quite devoid of the neuroticism which is called the artistic temperament, except in the sense that he was inclined to be explosive and irritable. In his writing he was at once indefatigable and fertile. Nearly all the pages of his *Review* were filled by himself, and though he frequently rewrote his long articles from beginning to end, the labor of the pen never tired him. Once he returned home from a lecture tour at the beginning of March with nothing written for the April number. Yet within three weeks he had produced and corrected the copy for 136 pages.[3] He was indeed blessed with a powerful frame and steady nerves, as well as enormous facility.

A good deal of his former eccentricity had worn off by now. He was still ready enough to get into an argument with strangers, but he did not thrust himself on people as he used to do in the butcher shop, or the barber's, or on the ferry.[4] Nor did he make scenes any more when innkeepers failed to give him fish on Friday. He had settled down comfortably into his Catholicism and was a better-balanced man because of his religion—also because of his domestic responsibilities and his domestic happiness. That he was putting on weight was perhaps due to that as well as to going to confession and so having a good conscience. Whatever crosses came to him he accepted lightly or with no more than a passing growl. To Count de Montalembert he wrote in 1851: "I have had all my life-time to fight against powerful odds, but I have never seen any way to do, but to keep on fighting. No man ever yet stood up for truth and justice, God and heaven, but he had to complain of opposition from all quarters." [5] Though he never let the slings and arrows of outrageous fortune worry him too much, they at least removed the need for any self-imposed asceticism. When Isaac Hecker came back from London as a Redemptorist Father, he presented his former master with a knotted cord to use as a discipline, and promised him a hair-shirt as soon as he could obtain one. The hair-shirt never turned up, which was perhaps just as well: the knotted cords remained ever unclotted with the philosopher's blood.[6] It was enough that he had his work to do; Brownson's was an immensely busy and fruitful life.

A great deal of space in the *Quarterly* was devoted to the criticism of books. In fact, books that dealt with political or philosophical or religious questions provided him with most of the grist that came to his mill. Sometimes he examined the book in detail, as in the case of John Henry Newman's Unitarian brother Francis, who had in his youth been a missionary in the Near East for the Plymouth Brethren, and whose versatility was shown later by his Latin translation of Longfellow's *Hiawatha*. Brownson set out to demolish his *Natural History of the Soul, as the True Basis of Theology,* when it fell into his hands. He triumphantly met its two chief assumptions: that "philosophy is an independent discipline" and that "reason by her own light and energy, without the aid of tradition or the light of faith" is fully competent to construct it.[7] A similar piece-meal refutation was given by Brownson to the social ideas of his former friend William Henry Channing,[8] or to Protestant theologians, whatever the school to which they belonged. Quite as often, however, the book was taken, in the way of those days, as the excuse for an independent disquisition that hardly refers to the work supposed to be under consideration.

Purely literary criticism with Brownson was rather haphazard. He reviewed such books as happened to come his way, but these were often of no great importance. His references to the leading writers of his time are not very many, nor are they very just. Yet sometimes, even when not very just, he says things that are worth hearing, if only because they are things so different from what everybody else says. Take, for example, the conclusion of his review of Emerson's Poems. "There are passages in them," he says, "which recall all too vividly what we, in our blindness and unbelief, have dreamed, but rarely ventured to utter. We know these poems; we understand them. They are not sacred chants; they are hymns to the devil. Not God, but Satan, do they praise, and they can be relished only by devil-worshippers." [9] That might seem an instance of complete insensibility to the beauty of the poems; it is only a keen (if you like, a morbid) sensitiveness to their literal substance. As a former Transcendentalist he understood more about their implications than do those of us who are content to enjoy them for their verbal felicity and the imagery. But the advantage is not all with us.

Brownson makes it clear in this article on Emerson that he is not blind to the beauty of his poetry. They are "wonderful productions," and Emerson is the first poet of America. But his comment on the "Threnody," being made by one who knew both the poet and the child lamented, has a special point. "The saddest part is the consolation it offers. . . . The author speaks in his own character, his own grief over the early death of his own son—a son of rare sweetness and promise. It was a lovely boy, one a father might well love, and be pardoned for weeping. The grief is natural. The stern pride of the father gives way to it, and the stoic becomes wild, all but frantic, and blasphemes nature, his only god after himself." [10] That is, no doubt, not all that needs to be said, but nobody else said it; nobody else, apparently, thought the meaning of the poem worth dwelling upon. As for its loveliness, that and Brownson's memories united to make him weep while reading it to a visitor. [11]

For Wordsworth he always expressed vast contempt, partly because of his pantheism and platonism, but still more, it would seem, because of his glorification of the infant mind in the "Intimations of Immortality." And, after all, this glorification may be considered slightly silly, like the fundamental idea of Coleridge's "Ancient Mariner." Many fine poems can be made somewhat foolish if approached with the touch-stone of too cold a common-sense. Personally, I am, as are most people, ready in such cases to accord the necessary "willing suspension of unbelief"; Brownson was not. He could not disabuse his mind of the meaning, the philosophic sense —something the majority of readers too readily forget.

Yet, when all allowances are made, it must be said that this narrow test, though a useful one, led Brownson to what often seems to be an inability to appreciate a literary work as literature. When he said that, for him, English poetry "died with Byron," [12] he might have added that he had read very little poetry since his youth. The great Victorians made no impression on him, except that he regarded them as an "affliction"; [13] nor did Poe or Whitman. On the other hand, he dealt severely with Lowell's *Vision of Sir Launfal,* finding in it the sentimental morality, "No matter what we give, if we give from a sense of duty, we merit nothing"; our alms must be on impulse and without motive.[14] And he praised Longfellow's *Evangeline.*

It was for fiction, however, that Brownson reserved his greatest scorn, although he wrote several novels himself and was a great reader of such things. The popularity of Dickens he considered "one of the worst symptoms of the age in which we live" [15]—a judgment which seems to have been due, at least in part, to Dickens's criticism of America. Because of him, "we have never been able to hear of an international copyright since, without a certain nausea at the stomach" [16]—a fine instance of a logician's illogicality. Hawthorne is denounced for condoning sin in *The Scarlet Letter,*[17] but is placed, as an artist, at the head of American writers. Summarily Brownson decided that he and Irving have "imagination, though not of the highest order; Bancroft has fancy, a rich and exuberant fancy, but very little imagination." Bancroft, too, is accused of writing history to make facts fit his theories: "His method . . . is manifestly a disingenuous method, defensible on the score neither of morals nor of art." [18] Prescott is "gentlemanly, but monotonous, and occasionally jejune." [19] The English writer Brownson refers to most often and with most respect is Carlyle, but of course with reservations. Motley he does not deal with at all, and he ignores

Thoreau. Whatever may have been Brownson's faults as a critic, he was not given to puffing the works of his friends.

If he dealt so severely with the books written by people whom he liked, it could not be expected that he should bear more easily upon those by people whom he did not like. And Margaret Fuller was a woman for whom he had a strong distaste. Even so, when reviewing her *Summer on the Lakes,* he admits her talents before proceeding to execution. "Miss Fuller," he wrote, "is a woman of more than ordinary abilities, and, we are told, of rare attainments. She is said to possess remarkable conversational powers, and her conversations . . . are represented by her friends to be in the highest degree brilliant, instructive and inspiring. . . . Her writings we do not like. We dislike them exceedingly. They are sent out in a slipshod style, and have a certain toss of the head about them which offends us." He goes on to call her a "heathen priestess. Though of what god or goddess we will not pretend to say. She is German, heart and soul." Moreover nobody has appeared in Boston whose conversation and morals have done more to corrupt the minds and hearts of the community. She has read much, "but her notions are crude, and the materials she has collected lie fermenting in her intellectual stomach, and generate all manner of strange and diseased fancies." Yet in spite of himself he relents at the end. "All she needs, to be the ornament of her sex, and a crown of blessing to her country, to be at peace with herself and the world, is the firm, old-fashioned Catholic faith in the Gospel." [20] Possibly this brought forth another toss of Margaret's head. She could hardly have relished such a lecture from the recently converted Catholic. Nor would she have been prepared to admit that this was acute criticism, or plead guilty to the mysterious charge of moral corruption.

When dealing with women novelists, whom he detested on what are usually called "general principles"—which means for no reason at all—Brownson never mentions Jane Austen. Probably he never read her. But he decided that Charlotte Brontë in *Jane Eyre* shows that women "can enter into and describe with minute accuracy the grossest passions of man's nature, . . . which men could not describe to their own sex without a blush." This proves men to be more modest than women! [21] Poor Mrs. Gaskell is called the "mistress of the positivist Lewes." [22] "In general," he announced, "we do not like modern novels." Those by women are the worst because they "have the grave fault of tending almost uniformly to degrade women." [23] When depicted by women, women are painted as "heartless, coquettish, intriguing, artful, tyrannical, abusing power whenever they have it, or as weak, puny, whimpering, broken-hearted things." [24] On the next page he informs us that "women, like children, need a master," that "the most corrupt periods of history are precisely those in which women's influence is greatest," and that "they can be harder-hearted, more despotic, more cruel, and less scrupulous in effecting their purposes than men."

When it was a case of a Catholic novel written by a woman, he grew savagely angry for other reasons. Despite his belief that "all that is profane, or not religious, is hurtful to a greater or lesser degree," he so often denounced religious fiction as "wretchedly dull as novels, and miserably defective as moral essays or theological treatises" [25] that it became almost a mania with him. One of these Catholic novels—made worse in his eyes by having been written by a woman—was Lady Georgiana Fullerton's *Grantley Manor*. "Mere Puseyism!" he snorted—and proceeded to pull it to pieces.[26] Later, however, when she had strained out the leaven of the Pharisees, he conceded, "Lady Georgiana is a gifted and highly cultivated Christian lady, who knows and loves her religion, and whose very presence is a joy and a blessing." [27] Mrs. Dorsey's work also met his approval.

It might seem from all this that Brownson was of little consequence as a literary critic. Such is not the case. Imperfect as was his acquaintance with general literature—even Dante he does not seem to have known except for such summaries as might have been found in an encyclopaedia—he brought to criticism what so few critics bring, a philosophical judgment and a highly acute intelligence. He could have been remarkable in this department had he chosen to use his gifts in the appraisal of first-rate books. Unfortunately he largely wasted them, and his own time, by attempting to survey the ephemeral stream of American Catholic literature, which was then a rather pallid affair. But that he said so, helped to improve it, or should have helped. His mission was regarded by him as primarily one for Catholics. He was completely free from the humbug of criticism; especially the humbug of Catholic criticism. Never would he praise a book simply because it happened to be written by a Catholic, and he was scorching about those who did. On one, written by the famous Sister Mary Francis Clare ("the Nun of Kenmare"), he commented: "We would, before going hence, do something to elevate the tone and standard of Catholic popular literature, by making it more thoroughly Catholic. . . . Our dear Sister Mary Francis Clare, whose books sell by the hundreds of thousands, should not feel it any thing more than a useful mortification, if there happens to be one old man who stands aloof from the crowd of her flatterers, and refuses to puff what he regards as her light-weighted wares." [28] Similarly he gave a single deadly thrust at a book by "an Oxford Convert," entitled *For Husks, Food,* by remarking that it ought to have been entitled, *For Food, Husks.*[29] He did not like Oxford Converts.

Though it was not altogether a question of personal prejudices, when he did happen to have such prejudices they extended far and wide and without any reference to what might be prudent. Thus he was so imprudent as to attack a fellow Catholic editor, when reviewing a novel by J. V. Huntington. Yet how entertaining this passage is: "We think it repugnant to the laws of true art for a writer, every time he has occasion to introduce a woman, to stop and give us a full-length portrait of her, the color of her hair, the form of her eyebrows, the cast of her features, the pouting or not pouting of her lips, the shape of her bust, the size of her waist, with remarks on the flexibility of her limbs, and the working of her toes." He continues with: "The author, we are sure, means well, but he is a little fussy where women are concerned, and is too fond of adjusting their corsages, tying on their slippers, or smoothing the folds of their petticoats, and not content with indulging his fussy disposition, he looks you very innocently in the face, and tells you there is nothing improper in all this, for he means nothing. Perhaps there is not, but he would do better not to challenge us to discuss it." [30] He did not realize, or did not care, that criticism of this sort only added to his enemies. And this, though he could describe himself as being "as thin skinned as a flayed eel." [31]

The same thing applies to his casual remarks in conversation. For instance, when the young priest Sylvester Rosecrans visited him, after returning from Rome with a degree of Doctor of Divinity, Brownson, quite unawed, told him in the friendliest fashion, "You have the muddiest head on metaphysics that I ever met with." [32] The remark was unlucky; the young man, the convert of his brother, the General, was nine years later created a bishop. Brownson could never understand why what he called "grave pleasantry" should be taken as "bitter sarcasm." "I am not aware," he wrote to Dr. Corcoran, editor of the *United States Catholic Miscellany,* "of a single sentence in the whole series [of the *Review*] that has been written in anger, in bitterness, or a sarcastic spirit." [33] Unfortunately his little harmless jokes often inflicted serious wounds that never healed.

The brilliant Benedictine monk, Virgil Michel, whose untimely death so many of us deplore, writing his doctoral dissertation on *The Critical Principles of Orestes A. Brownson,* credits Brownson with an æsthetic theory which the evidence hardly justifies. Brownson did not, indeed, neglect the question of artistic form, but his emphasis was nearly always utilitarian or sociological, and not æsthetic at all. It was the content of a book that he was almost exclusively interested in; and while this is an aspect that modern criticism neglects for the sake of babbling about "significant form," it is, after all, only one aspect of any work of art. Brownson stated his own critical object: "The reviewer may, for reasons of his own, pass over the literary and purely artistic merits of a book sent him, and speak of it only under its doctrinal or moral character; and in doing so no one has the right to infer that he recognizes no such thing as literary merit, or has no appreciation of merely literary, artistic, or poetic beauties." [34] Quite so; that kind of criticism is permissible; it may even be very valuable. But it is also permissible for us to object that it is not completely rounded criticism. A work of art, in truth, was dealt with by Brownson only for what it might contain of supernatural value; that its natural value might suggest the supernatural was an idea that escaped him. With all due respect to the analysis that Dom Virgil has offered us, Brownson did not produce a body of critical doctrine—though it may have been within his power to have done so; he was a reviewer and did not pretend to be anything else.

His detestation of the sentimental and the insincere made him an excellent corrective of humbug—in which he suggests an H. L. Mencken born out of due time. His best things are his *obiter dicta,* as when he remarks of Oliver Wendell Holmes, "He is like many of the descendants of the old Puritans, who, having lost all faith in the Calvinism of their ancestors, still identify it with Christianity. . . . Those outside of the church, and who credit not the evangelical cant against her, identify her teaching with Jansenism [and] regard Jansenists as the better class of Catholics. . . . It would, perhaps, relieve them a little if they knew that not only the Jesuits condemned Jansenism, but the church herself condemns it, and Jansenists are as much out of the pale of the church as are Calvinists and Lutherans themselves." [35] The wise and witty and kindly Autocrat supposed he had exploded the doctrine of original sin when he wrote *Elsie Venner,* but this was because he understood that doctrine in the sense of the total depravity of the Calvinism from which he had escaped. Never for a moment did men like Holmes suspect that in Catholicism was all that they were unconsciously seeking. This was where Brownson missed his opportunity; his method was that of finding error and of then smashing it under the sledge-hammer of his logic. His strength, here as elsewhere, lay in his power to detect the sham and the fallacious; his weakness was that of over-simplifying the issue and of over-stating the case against it.

Brownson had appeared before the public in 1840 as a novelist with his *Charles Elwood*. At intervals during his life he was frequently to use the fictional form again, though he usually carried it no further than setting a group of people to arguing over religious or philosophical or political questions. He had done so in *The Two Brothers,* which ran through several issues of his Review during 1847–1848. He had done so in *Conversations of an Old Man and His Young Friends,* which had been published in the same way in 1850. He did so again in 1854 in *Uncle Jack and His Nephew*. But none of these was reissued as a separate volume. In fact, not until his *Liberalism and the Church* (1870) did he bring out any of these more or less Socratic Dialogues between the covers of a book.

In 1854, however, he published a work which has to be classed as a novel, though Brownson himself acknowledged in his preface that he hardly knew what to call it. "It is not a novel; it is not a romance; it is not a biography of a real individual; it is not a dissertation, an essay, or a regular treatise; and yet it perhaps has some elements of them all, thrown together in such a way as best suited my convenience, or my purpose." He further confessed, "I [am] not, properly speaking, a literary man." All that he claims is that he has "read some" on his subject—which is that of spiritualism, under which heading he groups the spiritualism and mesmerism which were having a vogue at the time. The book was *The Spirit-Rapper*.

Though deficient as a story, and bearing all the marks of having been hurriedly tossed-off, the work is not without considerable interest, if only because he introduces some of his friends, or other living people—now under fictitious names, and again under their own. Thus Fanny Wright sat for the character "Priscilla" and Emerson appears as Mr. Egerton, "a thin, spare man, with a large nose, and a cast of Yankee shrewdness in his not very handsome face." The notorious spiritualists, the Fox Sisters, appear undisguised, as does Dr. Poyen, who had already been brought into *The Convert* as the one who had introduced him long ago to "animal magnetism." [36] Gioberti is dragged in—the episode of a European tour being invented to provide the machinery—and so are Proudhon, Mazzini and Fourier. Alcott, Garrison and Theodore Parker are to be recognized; and Brownson writes of Joseph Smith—familiarly referred to as "Joe"—in such a way as to give the impression that he had known him in his own youth.[37] He even goes out of his way to refer to and quote from the play *Mohammed,* which had been written by George Henry Miles, a professor at Mount St. Mary's College and an occasional contributor to his *Review*. It was an opportunity for discussing Mohomet as a case of satanic possession.[38]

The thesis of the book is that he who denies the existence of Satan also denies the existence of God.[39] "Prove to unbelievers," he says, quoting Bayle, "the existence of evil spirits, and you will by that alone force them to concede all your dogmas." [40] It has the merits of being, at all events, a novel mode of apologetics, but is surely a rather dubious one. The Christian may well hold that, when spiritualism is not fraudulent, it must be demoniac. But only the convinced Christian can be approached on Brownson's grounds; and of Christians the majority are likely to think, like most other people, that spiritualism has been too often proved to be fraudulent to be anything else.[41] Therefore an air of unreality hangs over the whole book; we are never quite persuaded that Brownson is perfectly serious. And the heavy humor he sometimes uses accentuates this. He strikes the reader as exhibiting what is no more than a *tour de force*.

Carlyle, he thinks, had hold of a truth and has exposed "the shallow philosophy and absurd theories of our popular historians." But his "Heroes" nearly all turn out to be possessed. "The nature he bids us worship is the devil, the dark, subterranean Demon, that seizes us, blinds our eyes, and carries us onward, whither we know not, and by a power which we are not. It is the demon of the storm, the whirlwind, and the tempest, the volcano and the earthquake, and the Carlylean heroes are energumenes, Bersekirs, who spread devastation around them, who quaff the blood of their enemies, from human skulls, in the orgies of Valhalla, and leave us their monuments in the ruins of nature." [42] That is not merely a fine passage of criticism; it is one that almost persuades us of Brownson's thesis —when we remember Hitler.

But I have to come back to my former complaint against Brownson: he presses his case too far when he argues that all history is to be explained in terms of the conflict of the satanic powers with God. In a certain broad sense this may be admitted, but only in the sense that in all history—as in the life of each individual—there are crosscurrents of good and evil. The difficulty is that of tracing these forces clearly and of making sure in such a tangle just what is good and what is evil. They are, in the historical process and in personal experience, mingled and confused. Not even in the cases Brownson specially cites—those of the Protestant Reformation and the French Revolution and what had happened in Europe in 1846 and 1848— can anybody be sure precisely what the devil had to do with the matter. It does not greatly enlighten our minds to be told that Mesmer and Cagliostro were more responsible for the French uprising than anything written or said by Voltaire, Rousseau, D'Alembert, Diderot and Mirabeau.[43] And when we are invited to believe that criminals should be punished for that yielding to Satan which has resulted in their possession by him—even though this has all the appearance of insanity—the most enthusiastic Brownsonian must see that at least this time he has overshot his mark. Had the whole book been written with the passionate conviction which is in the passage on Carlyle, it might have succeeded as a work of art even while failing in its polemic object. But the labored jocularity only lessens the total force, and Brownson's knowledge of his subject

itself can only be described in his own words: he has "read some." [44]
Of all his books this is without doubt the worst.

Yet during the early 'fifties he did some of his best work, and was
already pointing to a further development. For one thing, he began
after 1849 to take up the study of philosophy again, although he
was at first somewhat cautious as to how he wrote about it. This
study had had to be neglected because for the five years following
his conversion he had as much as he could undertake in the study
of theology—the matter most immediately important to a convert
who was obliged to become a controversialist. Now the impact of
Gioberti upon his mind gave a new direction to his thinking and
modified many of his ideas.

In so far as this resulted in the formulation of Brownson's famous
ontologism, it had better be left until a later chapter. All that need
be noted here is that he took from Gioberti an assortment of hints
which he applied to politics—sometimes in a way that would have
greatly surprised Gioberti. If Brownson in the years that were to
follow seemed to become at once more liberal and more reactionary,
it was because under this new stimulation his intellect acquired a
new acuteness and a new range. There was often enough little
formal connection between what he thought and what the Italian
philosopher had held.

For the moment the only thing that need be discussed is the
change in Brownson's political views. The slavery issue can be put
to one side, as that was something forced upon him by events; it
may be dealt with more conveniently when we come to the Civil
War. What needs to be said at the moment is that by degrees
Brownson had shifted his constitutional theory until he ceased to
be one of Calhoun's men and had come to call himself in 1849—the
year before Calhoun died—a "Conservative Whig, with a dash of
Federalism." [45] So engrossed was he with the consideration of general principles that many important contemporary events in America
were passed over almost in silence. This was so with regard to the

uproar caused by the visit of Archbishop Bedini as the Pope's emissary to the United States in 1853; Brownson covered that matter adequately enough for his purposes by his discussions of Know-Nothingism. Kossuth interested him a little more,[46] for he came to America as the incarnation of the European revolutionary spirit, and was hailed as such by Americans. Even so, Brownson did not treat him very seriously. He prophesied shrewdly that Kossuth would leave no lasting impression and said, "We shall have a good time with him, feast ourselves, have our own jollification, let him laugh a little at us in his sleeve while we laugh a good deal at him in ours, and then—cast him off." [47] It was precisely what happened.

What was of much more significance to Brownson was the *coup d'état* of December 1, 1851, by which Louis Napoleon Bonaparte passed from being the President of the French Republic to being the Emperor Napoleon III of France. It was an event hailed by the vast majority of American Catholics as one that would greatly strengthen the French Church. Brownson very soon took up a different attitude, in which he was almost alone; he saw that it merely meant absolutism and that absolutism meant Gallicanism.[48]

Brownson saw even more than that; he saw that Americans who were already firmly convinced that the Catholic Church and absolute monarchy were natural allies would find a fresh confirmation of their belief in the accession of the French Emperor. They would view it simply as one more instance of the suppositious Catholic inclination for despotism and the Catholic dislike for political liberty.[49] But American Catholics refused to listen to Brownson's warnings: Napoleon had taken the Church under his protection, and with that momentary advantage they were satisfied. For them Louis Veuillot of the *Univers* was an infallible political guide.

Not so with Brownson. On this subject he exchanged many letters with Montalembert, whom he afterwards came to consider too liberal but with whom on this matter he thoroughly agreed. Montalembert put it all in a nut-shell when he told Brownson: "The Emperor is, I believe, a sincere well-wisher to the church, but he knows little about her real interests, and is exclusively devoted to his own. In this respect I cannot blame him, since the church herself, by her official organs, asks for nothing but what she has got— *protection*." [50] Brownson, writing in the same issue of his *Review* that contained his article on the Know-Nothings, further offended Catholics, even those not Irish, by telling them: "Under Louis Philippe, and especially under the republic, the French church spoke with a free, bold, earnest, and commanding voice. She was the admiration and glory of the Catholic world. She has been dumb since the *coup d'état,* or eloquent only in eulogies on her new master. . . . The church in France prospers most when thrown back upon its own resources, and grows weak and helpless as it is petted by the secular government. . . . The Emperor . . . is the last sovereign in Europe, in communion with the church, that we should rely on to make any sacrifice for religion, or to promote Catholic interests any further than he can make them subservient to his own secular ambition." [51]

Brownson's views regarding this absurd little man are perhaps of no great importance in themselves, after this lapse of time; what is of considerable importance still is the basis of his judgment, the principle by which he measured Napoleon III and found him dangerous, almost in spite of himself, as representing an upsurge of despotism and an indication of the all-too-facile Catholic readiness to make an alliance with autocracy. He saw with a very clear eye that all history shows how the kind of union of Church and State Napoleon wanted could only mean the domination of the Church by the State. This is what has to be borne constantly in mind when we come to Brownson's many elaborate discussions during the next few years of the relation between the spiritual and the temporal. If sometimes he seemed to state his case in terms so excessive as almost to recall his old theocratic tendencies, and to lead incautious readers to imagine that he advocated putting the State under the control of the Church, this was because he wished to make his warnings as emphatic as possible.

Stripped of incidental exaggerations and excrescences, about all that Brownson said was what St. Peter said to the High Priest's Council: "We ought to obey God rather than man." He did not deny that the State had its own proper province of authority. He merely asserted that over both State and Church stands God and that, as the State receives its sanctions from God, it should, in the event of any conflict of opinion within the field over which religion claims authority, yield to the Church as the representative of God on earth. It is a proposition which, so stated, cannot but be accepted by everybody who really believes that there is a Church. It must be accepted even by Erastians, including the Erastian who virtually accords the monarch the kind of powers claimed by Queen Elizabeth —those of a quasi-Papacy. It has been strenuously fought for throughout history by many a dissenting Protestant minority, as no country should know better than America itself. But because, under the Puritan experiment, a theocratic system nearly came into being, there was a violent reaction which made most Americans feel that complete political secularity was preferable to the spiritual tyranny under which they had groaned. Logically, however, the principle is beyond dispute: we ought to obey God rather than men.

To expand this a little: Brownson made it clear that he did not claim temporal jurisdiction for the Church but merely her right to define the moral law. "Whatever pertains to morals comes, by its nature, within the jurisdiction of the spiritual order." [52] The "liberal" error, on the other hand, is that of supposing that the temporal order is the teacher, though it should be added that no political system except that of National Socialism—which claims to be a revelation—ever formally asserted its superiority to the moral law. And if Hitler does so it is because for him the State has no value except as the empty shell to contain the sacred teutonic blood. [53] Under whatever formula, to declare the temporal independent of the spiritual in all matters is to declare that God has no dominion. [54]

If the primacy of the spiritual is denied by any non-Catholic who calls himself a Christian, it can only be because he perceives that by admitting it he would also have to admit the authority of the Church, and that the authority of the Church would in turn call for the admission of the authority of the Pope. Therefore to save his face he has to be illogical. Yet the acceptance of the authority of the Church does not involve accepting the Church as the civil authority; not even Brownson held more than that the Church should exercise restraint where morals are involved, over the temporal sovereign.[55] But of course he did not flinch from asserting that, when it was a question of defining the boundary between the two jurisdictions, this had to be done by the Church, and that this constituted the Church the judge of its own cause.[56] But here there was only a speculative difficulty—and therefore really no difficulty at all—for the Church is the direct representative of God, while the State is only His representative indirectly. In actual practice the Church never interferes except in the last extremity and then merely to deal with general principles.

Throughout history the shoe has been on the other foot. Even in the United States, where constitutional safeguards are provided, there have been efforts from time to time to make the State dominant over the Church. In 1871 there even came into being a movement to amend the First Article of the Constitution so as completely to change its meaning. Leaving the first part of the article as it stood, the proposed amendment would have added, "But Congress may enact such laws as it shall deem necessary to control or prevent the establishment or continuance of any foreign hierarchical power in this country founded on principles or dogmas antagonistic to American institutions." That there was nothing in Catholicism antagonistic to republican institutions, or that Catholicism could not be "foreign" anywhere, would have been urged in vain, had this constitutional modification been made. It was aimed at the suppression of the Catholic Church in America. As Brownson pointed out, "The only arguments we could use to prove it lie in an order of thought which they are not familiar with." [57]

It is in his articles, "The Secular Not Supreme" (1871) and "The

Papacy and the Republic" (1873) that Brownson gives his full, final and most closely reasoned presentation of his position.[58] His earlier statement of the same case was open to the objection that it was belligerent and provocative and a deliberate treading on the coat-tails of Protestants. Later he took the sounder line that Americans generally understood the union of Church and State in a Protestant sense and with the Anglican Establishment in mind.[59] Though the Founding Fathers were not altogether inspired by liberality in removing the disabilities of Catholics—for, being deists, they regarded Catholicism as moribund and as such harmless—there was nevertheless in America "a real union of the church and state in our sense of the term," which, if not perfect, was as near perfection as it had ever been elsewhere. Indeed, the Church was freer in America than in any country since the time of Philip the Fair of France. "The state with us," he declared, "recognizes the independence of the spiritual order, and its own incompetency in spirituals." It even recognizes the supremacy of the spiritual order, for "it recognizes what it calls the rights of man, holds them to be inalienable, confesses them to be anterior and superior to itself, and acknowledges itself bound to respect, protect and defend them. And the courts will pronounce any law repugnant to them, that denies or abridges them, contrary to justice, and therefore null and void from the beginning." [60] That the State thinks of these rights as "natural rights" makes no difference, since "without God there is no right." "It is not true, then," he concludes, "that under the American system the state is totally separated from the spiritual order." [61] On the contrary, if we give the state only a human basis, it will have only a human authority—which will mean that it has no real right to govern, and that we are under no real obligation to obey. To compel us to do so would only be intolerable tyranny.[62]

This, after all, was what he contended for in his more truculent articles of the 'fifties. Had he put his case in such terms then, he would have said what would have found more general acceptance. But he chose to raise what was, under the circumstances, the academic question of the Pope's deposing power, and with such vigor that nobody would suppose the discussion to be merely academic. Yet even then, his actual words did not have the meaning that was read into them. What he wrote in 1853 may be taken as a summary of what he maintained: "The church . . . in deposing a sovereign and absolving his subjects, does not abrogate the law of nature, but simply administers it. She really only declares the law, or pronounces judgment under it. It is not her judgment that makes the forfeiture, or that releases the subject; she only declares a forfeiture already incurred, and releases subjects already virtually released by the [misconduct] of the prince." [63] He felt it necessary to insist on this doctrine, because if Catholics should attempt to whittle it down, their sincerity would be doubted. All of which was by way of rebuttal to what Brownson considered the Gallicanism of Père Gosselin, the Superior of the Sulpician seminary in Paris. It was directed to the correction of the Gallicanism rather widespread at the time among the American clergy. His own orthodoxy, he used to boast, was more offensive to them than the heresy of non-Catholics.[64] As to that, he wrote in 1854, "We have heard some very loud whispers about ultra-Catholicity, and have received some significant hints that we are ultra-Catholic. But we venture to hint, in reply, that there is and can be no such thing as ultra-Catholicity, and that the charge is absurd. Catholicity is a definite system of truth, and to be more or less than Catholic is simply not to be Catholic at all. Catholicity, so long as it continues to be Catholicity, cannot be carried to excess." [65] Brownson did not say that the deposing power of the Pope applied to America. Indeed, he admitted that it did not apply to any modern state, as it was constituted. All that he maintained was that the Pope had the right—not to depose a prince—but to make a judicial declaration when a prince had forfeited his right by acts of outrageous tyranny. Even this—which was the indirect rather than the direct deposing power—he upheld as no more than a corollary to the supremacy of the spiritual over the material, of God over all men.

It was quite enough very seriously to alarm many of the American bishops. For twenty years the Catholic Church in the United States had been assailed by the Nativist movements, and was at that very moment being assailed by the most virulent of them all—Know-Nothingism. And here came Brownson, the best known Catholic publicist in the country, the editor of the Quarterly which, by printing the letter of approval signed by twenty-four bishops,[66] seemed to claim an official standing; here he was saying the very thing they least wanted to have said. While some of them no doubt considered that, in the abstract, Brownson's theory was sound, nearly all of them considered that to trumpet it abroad was to call the attention of the enemies of the Church to matters which, if they had to be discussed at all, should be touched on only in seminary class-rooms. The Know-Nothings, of course, quoted Brownson as proving what they had always contended was the case—that Catholics regarded their allegiance to the Pope as weighing more, even in secular concerns, than their allegiance to the United States, and as being a temporal allegiance.[67] Here, in short, was proof positive that no Catholic could be a good American. Brownson had demonstrated this already (to the Know-Nothing satisfaction) in his articles about the Irish immigrants; now he was demonstrating the same thing of himself. Clearly it was no simple question of race; perhaps even the Irish would be loyal citizens if they were not Catholics. It was a question of religion; and the Catholic religion was now shown to be opposed to the American Republic.

It is hardly to be wondered at that Brownson's views gave a good deal of offence and caused a good deal of alarm. Even those who understood what it was he was trying to say, feared the effect it would have on the public mind—especially on those who chose to misrepresent him and to instance him as an "official" exponent of the Catholic position. There was no denial that, even though Brownson was pressing his arguments further than was customary with Catholic political philosophers, he had a right to his opinion,

Remember that OB set this forth at a time when there lay in the offing virulent anti-Catholic attack.

Was it necessary that OB speak thus at this particular time?

for he was doing no more than draw out principles admitted by all Catholics to conclusions which a man was free to derive from those principles. It was only that to do so was extremely impolitic. And mingled with that objection there were objections to Brownson on other grounds.

Archbishop Hughes wrote to tell him that he thought what he had written about the deposing power of the Pope was "inopportune"—only to get from Brownson the retort that the very fact that the assertion of a truth aroused opposition was an indication of its opportuneness.[68] Bishop O'Connor of Pittsburgh went a good deal further, and made public attacks on Brownson. Catholics seemed almost as eager to repudiate him as the Democratic party had been in 1840.

It seemed all the more ungrateful in O'Connor's case, because he had appealed to Brownson, as recently as 1852, for help when, as he put it, he had got himself "into a regular scrape" in a controversy.[69] Now through the *Metropolitan Magazine,* which was edited by Brownson's enemy, Huntington, he denounced him for pressing the doctrine of the temporal power, which he correctly declared not to be of faith. Brownson replied—but only because Bishop Fitzpatrick told him that he must reply to criticism coming from such a quarter [70]—that what he maintained was a logical deduction from the doctrine of papal infallibility. His only concession was that "One who denies it [may] not be a heretic; for the church does not hold a man to be a heretic because he happens to be a bad logician." [71] At the same time he wrote privately to O'Connor complaining that a controversy between a layman and a bishop could not be on equal terms. "You can bring popular and national prejudice to bear against me, and I can avail myself of no extraneous help. . . . My character, my reputation, my means of subsistence are threatened. . . . The doctrine I have defended, if not precisely of faith, is one which I am at liberty to hold." [72] He added that the Bishop of Boston had approved his article.

O'Connor did not treat Brownson's private letter with the confidence it should have received. Instead he sneered in his diocesan paper that Brownson was hiding behind Fitzpatrick's skirts, and that he should not throw "the whole odium which attaches to this, or any other article, on his bishop, who, we think, never meant to assume greater responsibility than might arise from the assurance that the Review contained nothing contrary to faith or morals." [73] At the same moment a Protestant paper found in all this an admission that when Brownson "took upon himself the yoke of Rome, he surrendered the free spirit with which he was imbued, and voluntarily placed the stamp of bondage upon the divinity that stirred within him." [74] Brownson had worked himself into a position in which he was attacked, on the one hand, for dangerous intellectual eccentricity, and, on the other, for intellectual servility. And this merely for exercising a legitimate freedom of discussion. It impelled him to write again to O'Connor telling him that prudence defeated itself: "I know something of the American people, and I am confident that you will never make them believe that my doctrine . . . is not the true Catholic doctrine. All the bishops in the universe may disclaim it, and they will still believe it. You may silence me, but you will get no credit with them, and only lose a portion of their respect, both for yourselves and for Catholicity." [75] In brief, as Catholics were believed to be wolves, there was no use in their trying to behave like lambs.

The attack Archbishop Purcell of Cincinnati made upon him was of a similar sort. He had told Brownson in conversation, as Brownson afterwards reminded him, "You cannot go too far for me." Yet now Purcell was declaring that Brownson ought to be excommunicated. On which Henry Brownson comments: "As to the Archbishop's opposition, no one can believe that it was caused by the advocating of doctrines he had himself desired put forth, . . . but must be attributed to the same cause as that of the Irish Catholics generally of the period." [76] In other words, what was described as Brownson's "ultraism" on the subject of the Pope's deposing power might have been allowed to pass, had it stood alone; but it was used as a pretext to club Brownson for what he had said about the Irish. All through his life he was to have similar experiences: half the criticism brought against him was disingenuous, and he was belabored on one ground when the real reason for the objection was on another.

Brownson might have been silenced had he not had in such men as Archbishop Kenrick of St. Louis, and his brother, who was Archbishop of Baltimore, and Bishop Miège, firm friends. Fitzpatrick, who should have befriended him, preferred to take a neutral attitude. Rather bitterly, Brownson wrote to Huntington, the editor of the *Metropolitan,* "The course which some Catholic prelates who approved my doctrine to myself personally, have taken, has not given me so high an opinion of their Catholic honor as of their policy." [77]

The editors of some Catholic magazines gleefully joined in the hue and cry, Huntington and McMaster (who had been a fellow novice among the Redemptorists with Hecker) and Henry Major of Philadelphia, especially distinguishing themselves by their animosity. They had old grievances against Brownson. Huntington was still smarting from the review of his novel. And McMaster's feelings were further ruffled when Brownson loftily informed him: "Not to be a metaphysician is no sin; it is only an inconvenience when one insists on writing or talking about metaphysics." [78] Perhaps it was not quite so strange as Brownson supposed that, as he put it when writing to the Pittsburgh *Catholic,* "My brethren, who differ from me, usually express their difference in a harsh, sneering, contemptuous tone . . . and refuse me the ordinary courtesy due from one gentleman to another." [79] They resented his superiority to themselves; still more they resented the treatment they got at his hands.

None of the editors that have been mentioned was an Irishman, in the accepted sense. McMaster, as a converted Ulsterman, retained a low opinion of the Irish from the South of Ireland, and Huntington shared his prejudice. But McMaster, who had often been rubbed the wrong way by Brownson, found a convenient cause for offence in his onslaught on Ulster radicals.[80] He thought this an opportunity too good to miss for settling old scores. And the Catholic Irish—those who considered themselves the "real" Irish—ranged themselves against their too candid friend for what he had said about them in relation to the Know-Nothing movement.

The fiercest of his critics was the Protestant Fenian, John Mitchel, who was then editing the *Citizen,* which had a circulation of 50,000. The policy here, as in several of the Catholic periodicals, was that of trying to appease the Know-Nothings by repudiating what Brownson had said about the papal power. Mitchel whipped himself into a frenzy and wrote: "Doctor Orestes, *you* more than any one living man, have aroused and kindled this strong anti-Catholic, and therefore anti-Irish spirit in America, by your ultra-Catholic and anti-republican teachings and writings. . . . On the part of my Irish fellow-countrymen, I accuse you of so misrepresenting them and their church before the American people, that any republican nation could not but look on them and all their ways with suspicion and abhorrence." [81] That Brownson had caused the anti-Catholic outburst was, of course, simply untrue. As Professor Billington has conclusively shown in his richly documented book, *The Protestant Crusade,* the attack on both the Church and the Irish—on the Church, largely because in the East it was for the most part composed of Irishmen—had been going on for more than twenty years. Charlestown Convent was burned in 1834, and ten years later the most violent of the anti-Catholic and anti-Irish riots (those in Philadelphia) had occurred. Both things had happened before Brownson entered the Church. And if he soon succeeded in antagonizing the Irish, his views on the temporal power had not been formulated until about 1850. The most that can be said is that Brownson unintentionally supplied the Know-Nothings with ammunition, equally because of what he said about the Irish and because of what he claimed for the Church.

As to the supremacy of the spiritual, on October 8, 1855, he explained his position to a group of Marylanders who asked him a number of specific questions. One passage will be enough: "I have never asserted, out of the Papal State, any civil authority or jurisdiction for the pope, or any other than spiritual allegiance to him as the duty of Catholics. . . . Nevertheless, I have maintained and maintain that this spiritual authority extends to the morality of temporal things, in so far, and only so far, as they are spiritually related or have a spiritual character." [82] As for the Irish, all he had done was to advise them not to give Americans gratuitous offence by insisting upon preserving their distinctive Irish character in a new land.[83] He warned them that when they talked, as some of them did, as though Catholicism and Irishry were synonymous terms, they played into the hands of the Know-Nothings. "I think," he wrote to a correspondent early in 1855, "they are as much bound to respect my American nationality as I am to respect theirs. I do not like their claiming the right in their organs to run down all nationalities but their own, and then cry out as if a great wrong were done them, if the calumniated nationalities remind them gently that they who live in glass houses, etc. It is impossible for you to conceive how offensive in this respect they are to the American convert, who is discarded by his own countrymen because a Catholic, and distrusted and abused by his Catholic friends, if he deems it his duty to retain his American sympathies and not make himself a foreigner in the land of his birth." [84] It was a misunderstanding all round; the Irish were hardly admonished "gently" by the Know-Nothings, or by Brownson himself; and he should have made allowance for the fact that, if some of the Irish indulged in absurd boasting, it was provoked by the attacks being made on them, so that the more they were slandered, the more they flaunted their nationality.

In spite of his private and public comments on their shortcomings, Brownson liked the Irish—as men, even if not always as politicians—and looked upon himself as their truest friend in America.[85] He had, however, adopted an attitude that was offensive to nearly all parties: that he was the type of the genuine American; that Anglo-American civilization was the norm to which all should conform; and yet that that civilization could continue to exist only on condition that the supremacy of the spiritual was acknowledged, which meant conceding that the Pope had the powers asserted for him by Brownson.

Alarmed by the situation, Archbishop Kenrick of Baltimore wrote to Brownson early in 1855 suggesting that, as his essays on the temporal power were being "brought forward to prove that we profess principles at variance with our civil duties," it would be as well if the editor "voluntarily" remove from the cover of *Brownson's Quarterly Review* the letter he had received from the Bishops in 1849. "Your own prudence," he wrote again twelve days later, "will dictate the best course to be adopted to meet the effort which is made to convert our letter of encouragement into approval of every sentiment or view which you may express." [86] In September Bishop O'Connor wrote peremptorily requesting that his name be withdrawn.[87] There was nothing to do but to remove the whole letter. The action of the hierarchy was not a condemnation; there was nothing that *could* be condemned: but the Bishops had no such love for Brownson as to be willing to get themselves into hot water on his account.

The removal of this letter need not be given any undue importance in relation to what followed. Brownson's decision was no doubt affected by it to some extent, but he does not seem to have taken the suggestion from Archbishop Kenrick as more than what it was—one more sign that his position was becoming difficult. Another sign—and this bore more immediately upon his case—was that Fitzpatrick did not back him up. After his return from Europe Brownson's articles were not read to him as formerly. What was the use of inviting his censorship, when the Bishop would assume no responsibility? It is likely that Fitzpatrick found that he was busy when Brownson offered to show him what he had written.

In any event Brownson, as he now was obliged to act according to his own judgment, thought that he might accord himself a greater freedom of expression than he had so far permitted himself. He had been docile; he was now glad to have his liberty. Nobody ever again should be able to sneer at him for hiding behind his Bishop. He would come out boldly and say what was in his mind.

It would seem that for some time prior to this he had been thinking of moving to another city, though his son says this began when Fitzpatrick ceased his censorship.[88] At the time of his conversion Hecker had suggested that he go to New York, and though Hecker was now against Brownson's doing so—presumably because such a change would not be advisable in the middle of a tempest—Brownson was anxious to leave Boston.[89] On August 29th he wrote to Hecker: "I think I should be with you more in the midst of friends, and I could exert far more personal influence than here. . . . This diocese is becoming more and more Irish. I think I could now get along with his Grace the Archbishop without any serious difficulty, and I think I could breast the storm still raging and likely to rage for some time against me better in New York under his patronage than here."[90] On October 1st Hecker replied: "This afternoon I called on the Archbishop. In the course of our conversation he mentioned that he had heard that it was your desire to come to New York. I told him it was, with his approbation. He replied that 'he would be quite pleased at your coming, and that if I wrote to you I should tell you so.' These were his words."[91] They were enough. As soon as the October, 1855, number of the *Review* had gone to press, Orestes Brownson and his family packed up and transferred themselves to New York City.

[1] *Middle Life,* pp. 193, 194. The $500 he lost fell especially heavily on him by coming in the middle of the summer, when he had to wait until the lecturing season to replenish his coffers. There was nothing for it but to borrow from friends.

[2] *Middle Life,* pp. 127–128.

[3] *Ibid.,* pp. 137, 138.

[4] Dr. C. H. Leonard, the President of Tufts College, wrote to Henry Brownson in 1890 to tell him how he remembered often seeing twenty people around Brownson on the ferry. (*Middle Life,* p. 640).

[5] *Ibid.*, p. 335.

[6] *Ibid.*, p. 277.

[7] *Works*, Vol. III, p. 134.

[8] *Works*, Vol. X, pp. 137–206.

[9] *Works*, Vol. XIX, pp. 201–202.

[10] *Ibid.*, p. 196.

[11] George Parsons Lathrop, *Atlantic Monthly*, Vol. LXXVII (1896), p. 780.

[12] *Brownson's Quarterly Review*, Last Series Vol. II (1874), p. 277.

[13] *Works*, Vol. XIX, p. 338.

[14] *Ibid.*, pp. 311–312.

[15] *Brownson's Quarterly Review*, Last Series, Vol. I (1873), p. 63.

[16] *Works*, Vol. XIX, p. 217.

[17] *Middle Life*, p. 256–257.

[18] *Works*, Vol. XIX, p. 387.

[19] *Ibid.*, p. 367.

[20] *Brownson's Quarterly Review*, Vol. I (1844), p. 546.

[21] *Works*, Vol. XIX, p. 548.

[22] *Ibid.*, p. 545.

[23] *Ibid.*, p. 547.

[24] *Ibid.*, p. 601.

[25] *Ibid.*, p. 146. See also pp. 143, 144, 225–226, 253.

[26] *Ibid.*, pp. 247, 257, 258, 261.

[27] *Ibid.*, p. 549.

[28] *Brownson's Quarterly Review*, Last Series, Vol. I (1873), p. 287. This came all the harder on her because on January 23, 1873, she wrote to congratulate Brownson upon the reappearance of his *Review*. Already he had brushed her aside in his January issue (pp. 53–54), but she had not seen that when she wrote. Therefore she wrote to him again on February 8th, saying: "It matters very little to me personally, and will not in the least injure the circulation, now over 200,000, of my works. . . . To attack any lady's private character is bad enough, but it is surely worse to attack a nun." One effective point is made by her: "It will of course lessen the value of any criticism, when it is observed that the work written by your daughter is the only one selected for enthusiastic and unlimited praise. . . . I fear your feeling against any woman (except one) who holds a pen will hardly allow you to receive this as it is meant." (*Brownson Papers*). The trouble was not merely that she was a woman but had been what Brownson called a "Puseyite." Some years later she received permission to leave the Poor Clares and to found another order, the Sisters of Peace. It did not prosper, and she got herself into some trouble with bishops. Her autobiography, which was published in 1889, was dedicated to the Pope and was her defence. Mary Frances Cusack was a clever and amusing woman, but one also who was vain and unstable.

[29] *Brownson's Quarterly Review*, Last Series, Vol. II (1874), p. 425.

[30] *Middle Life*, pp. 403, 404.

[31] *Ibid.*, p. 195.

[32] *Ibid.*, p. 509.

[33] *Ibid.*, pp. 584–585.

[34] *Works*, Vol. XX, p. 91.

[35] *Works*, Vol. III, p. 300.

[36] *The Convert*, pp. 202–203.

242 ORESTES BROWNSON: YANKEE, RADICAL, CATHOLIC

[37] *The Spirit-Rapper,* pp. 164 *et seq.* It is not impossible that he had met the founder of the Mormons, who came from the same part of the country as himself. But if so, he gives no other indication of it.

[38] *Ibid.,* p. 369.

[39] *Ibid.,* p. 393.

[40] *Ibid.,* p. 155. I must confess that this does not strike me as having the axiomatic force that Brownson believed; but it may be one—only one, however—of the inferences to be drawn from a demonstration of the reality of satanic powers.

[41] Catholic investigators are divided on this question. Some, like the late Godfrey Raupert, conceded nearly all spiritualistic manifestations to be genuine—and diabolic; others, like the Jesuit Father Heredia, offered to match any manifestation by ingenious machinery, and his view was supported by Dr. James J. Walsh. Father Herbert Thurston, who wrote what is perhaps the best book on the subject, takes a middle ground.

[42] *The Spirit-Rapper,* p. 378.

[43] *Ibid.,* p. 160.

[44] That Brownson was sincere in this book is shown, however, by his advancing his theory again, though then with rather more restraint, in an article in the *Catholic World* in 1869. (*Works,* Vol. IX, pp. 332–351). There he does not try to find in the ouija-board and the elevated table the clue to all history. He is content to take the more reasonable position that spiritualism (or spiritism as he called it) is satanic when genuine.

[45] *Middle Life,* p. 204.

[46] See *Works,* Vol. XVI, pp. 187, 213, 229, 246, and Vol. X, p. 548.

[47] *Middle Life,* p. 422. "Our people," he said, "have shown their usual bad taste in attempting to make him the object of their hero-worship. . . . In Kossuth they have selected a second-rate revolutionist." (*Works,* Vol. XVI, p. 213).

[48] *Middle Life,* p. 438.

[49] *Ibid.,* p. 447.

[50] *Ibid.,* pp. 616–617.

[51] *Works,* Vol. XVI, pp. 423–424.

[52] *Works,* Vol. X, p. 315.

[53] *Mein Kampf* (Reynal and Hitchcock edition), p. 189.

[54] *Works,* Vol. XI, p. 10.

[55] *Works,* Vol. XI, p. 33.

[56] *Works,* Vol. XI, pp. 460, 461, 465.

[57] *Works,* Vol. XIII, p. 312.

[58] *Works,* Vol. XIII, pp. 303–326, 326–351.

[59] *Ibid.,* p. 330.

[60] *Ibid.,* p. 331.

[61] *Works,* Vol. X, p. 129.

[62] *Ibid.,* p. 332.

[63] *Works,* Vol. XI, p. 87. He maintained that civil allegiance was a religious duty until the right of the ruler had been declared forfeited by spiritual authority (*Middle Life,* 599). On this principle it is hard to see how the American revolution could be defended by him.

[64] *Works,* Vol. XI, p. 344.

[65] *Ibid.,* p. 110.

[66] The printing of their letter had become very embarrassing to the bishops. For

example, the *Mercersburg Review* (Vol. II, 1850, p. 38) described it as "in truth, a solemn *imprimatur*." It was not that at all, but people can hardly be blamed for thinking it was.

67 He answered these charges in *Works*, Vol. VII, pp. 508–566.

68 *Middle Life*, p. 521.

69 *Middle Life*, pp. 434, 435.

70 *Middle Life*, p. 488.

71 *Ibid.*, p. 489.

72 *Ibid.*, p. 490.

73 *Ibid.*, p. 498. Brownson's answer—made to the editor of the *Catholic Telegraph* of Cincinnati—was that by citing his bishop he was not attempting to hide behind him, or to prove his own freedom from error, but merely was trying to show that he was not bringing out the "vagaries" with which Archbishop Purcell was charging him. (*Ibid.*, p. 504).

74 *Ibid.*, p. 500.

75 *Ibid.*, p. 505.

76 *Ibid.*, p. 510.

77 *Ibid.*, p. 605.

78 *Ibid.*, p. 454. Henry Brownson notes (*ibid.*, p. 83) his father's inability to reconcile McMaster's public animosity with his private professions of friendship. Huntington, on the other hand, says Henry Brownson, at least tried to be fair. (*Ibid.*, p. 598).

79 *Ibid.*, p. 492.

80 *Ibid.*, p. 533.

81 *Middle Life*, p. 549.

82 *Ibid.*, pp. 555, 557.

83 *Ibid.*, p. 578.

84 *Ibid.*, p. 583.

85 *Middle Life*, p. 584. The Irish faults, he says, were no greater than, if as great, as those of Americans; "only they are precisely the faults the most offensive to Americans."

86 *Middle Life*, pp. 589, 590.

87 *Ibid.*, p. 592.

88 *Ibid.*, p. 636.

89 *Ibid.*, p. 637.

90 *Hecker Papers.*

91 *Middle Life*, p. 637.

CHAPTER XII

Uneasy Haven

WRITING TO THE COMTE DE MONTALEMBERT, Brownson, after he had been in New York a year, told him: "I think I shall be here more free to advocate our old constitutional doctrine," [1] under which heading he included all that he had been saying about the Americanization of the immigrant and even (by implication) all that he had said about the Pope's range of power. But that he was even then not quite sure that he was going to obtain the freedom he had hoped to find peeps out at the end of the same letter: "Our Catholics have been cast in the mould of absolutism, and our Irish clergy confound obedience with servility. They cannot understand the submission of a people to the church from love and intelligent conviction. All manliness and independence is heresy or schism, or what is worse than either, un-Irish." [2] He had not been born a Yankee for nothing. Though upon the whole he was far more docile than might have been expected, he retained a very rugged individualism. He stood for moderation, even if his defence of moderation often seemed to be truculent in expression. Yet so far from obtaining peace in New York, he only got embroiled in acrimonious controversies.

Some of the Irish—those who might be called the professional Irish, especially their editors and demogogues—continued to attack him, if not for what he wrote about them, then on account of his political or papal theories. In those days it must be remembered that, as Henry Brownson put it, "The Catholic religion had for Irishmen very much the character of a national religion." [3] There were Irish writers who even argued that Protestantism might be suited to the

244

Teutonic race as Catholicism was suited to the Celts and the Latins. This was a thesis Brownson had no difficulty in demolishing in his article on "Romanic and German Orders." [4] He simply pointed out that it did not fit the facts.

On the other hand, what is almost equally open to question is his counter-theory: that the long subjection of the Latin nations to the Roman Empire had moulded them to an acceptance of absolutism, whereas the freedom of the Germanic races from that empire had fitted them for political liberty. He denied that it had anything to do with blood or religious belief, and to that extent he was quite correct. [5] At the same time, his notion of absolutism as the legacy of the old Roman Empire leaves far too much history out of account, as any such theory is bound to do. Ingeniously he contrived to find a resemblance between "the spirit and institutions of the Celtic and Teutonic families. . . . Nowhere have we found the Celts, whenever unromanized, the friends of despotism." [6] It was about all the comfort he gave the Irish. Upon the whole they preferred that to any formal defence Brownson made for them.

He had a way, too, of irritating them by his *obiter dicta*. The sensitive Gaels naturally did not greatly relish hearing that it had been an advantage for the Church in the United States that the Catholic immigrants were for the most part laborers and servants, poor and illiterate. His thesis was that Protestants would tolerate such people, where they would not tolerate men of position and influence. [7] Whether or not the thesis was sound, the Irish did not like to be reminded of the facts upon which it was based. A former acquaintance of his in Massachusetts, Father John Boyce, now gave them their revenge.

He had a personal resentment because of a review that Brownson had written of a novel he had published in 1848. Now he serialized in the *Metropolitan* a work of fiction into which he introduced, under the character of "Dr. Horseman," a gruff, tobacco-chewing Yankee editor with spectacles and a loud voice who was instantly recognizable as Brownson. So far from Brownson minding the caricature, he reviewed the novel when it was reissued in book form and only deplored that "Dr. Horseman" had been changed into "Dr. Henshaw," a Scotch reviewer. While Brownson said that he knew he had been pilloried in order "to prejudice him as much as he could in the minds of Irish Catholics," he suggested that Father Boyce "let us have back the Yankee reviewer." "So here is our hand, Father John, only give us back our friend Dr. Horseman, and remember for the future that Jonathan can bear with good humor a joke, even at his own expense, if it lack not the seasoning of genuine wit." [8]

Good humoredly as Brownson took Father John's picture of him, he was aware that this was one more indication of the fact that he was not popular. Under the most fortunate circumstances he could hardly have escaped attack, for he was a convert, a Yankee, a layman (and a layman who was presuming to teach) and a superior man. This last offence alone would have sufficed to arouse what might almost be called the "Catholic" vice of envy.[9] But apart from these general reasons for animosity, Brownson provided American Catholics with ample reasons for feeling offended, reasons which were perhaps all more or less entwined with the irrational prejudices that have been indicated.

That he was often attacked gave him matter to write about. And he enjoyed argument for its own sake. Fertile though he was, he would have found it hard to have filled up single-handed the hundred and fifty pages of his *Review* each quarter, had it not been for his obliging enemies. Yet those who took him to be pachydermous were mistaken; he wore his skin inside out. Archbishop Purcell (still very friendly towards him) wrote on January 25, 1849, admitting that he had himself written in his diocesan paper the piece of "severe censure" of which Brownson had complained to him, said: "If *it* caused you any pain and regret, as indeed you assure me it did, I myself feel pain and regret as far as God sees I have done wrong in writing or inflicting it; and, in this view, sincerely humble myself and ask your forgiveness." Only he explained that he had not meant what he had written as censure at all, and he expressed some surprise that one who had felt "free to find fault with Bishop Kenrick's not having taken stronger ground in a former edition of his work on the Primacy, was himself so sensitive." He even mildly suggested that Brownson had departed from the gentleness Boston had known from Bishop Cheverus, and that his Review "was likely to revive, though infinitely its superior in talent, the 'Jesuit' of unhappy memory." [10] The fact is that Brownson considered his own hard hitting to be mere abstract logic (as it usually was) and other people's hard hitting to be personal abuse—which also was too often the case. But though he did not indulge in abuse, he was inclined to use sarcasm. Both in print and in private conversation, when anybody failed to follow his line of reasoning, he was likely to get very angry with him for being so stupid. He hurt others quite as often as he was hurt himself.   /3

Especially was he hurt with the treatment he received from some of the bishops, among whom (after the early 'fifties) had to be included Purcell. This was all the more galling because he had to be polite to such high ecclesiastics. Perhaps that was why, when in 1863 reviewing Archbishop Ullathorne's strictures on the *Rambler,* he introduced an oblique reference to his own difficulties with bishops. Previously Brownson had had his disagreements with Richard Simpson, the *Rambler's* editor, now chiefly remembered not for his Shakesperian Studies but his life of Blessed Edmund Campion. And again he indicated his dissent from some of Simpson's views.[11] Yet it must have relieved him somewhat to have been able to make a general observation that applied to his own case, as to the way some bishops have of misstating or misapplying or mutilating a meaning, and about their unfairness and high-handedness. "Mr. Simpson," he wrote, "makes it evident that the bishop ascribes to him views he does not entertain, and censures him for opinions he does not hold and has not expressed." [12] Brownson was not a vindictive man, but he surely may be pardoned for making a personal defence in this round-about way. By the time he wrote it he had added Archbishop Hughes to his list of episcopal enemies.

A clash between Hughes and Brownson had been inevitable from the first, which probably was why Hecker, who had tried to bring Brownson to New York in the 'forties, was, in the 'fifties, not enthusiastic about his coming. "Anyone," says Henry Brownson, "who knew the two men, knew that [they] could never labor in the same cause unless at a distance from each other and without ever coming into contact together." [13] If temperamental differences did not suffice, there was enough active conflict of opinion. The sorest point of all may well have been Hughes's expectation of playing the rôle that had been played by Fitzpatrick, and his chagrin at learning that Brownson intended to act on his own responsibility. According to Brownson, the Archbishop said to him hotly: "I will suffer no man in my diocese that I cannot control. I will either put him down, or he shall put me down." [14] Whether or not Hughes ever used these precise words, Brownson certainly wrote to Bishop Elder of Natchez in 1860, "I cannot accept the Archbishop of New York as my consultor. His advice I cannot respect." [15] The stage was therefore set for a clash. It came in the most public manner possible.

Brownson was asked to give the address at the commencement exercises of 1856 at St. John's College, the nucleus of the present Fordham University; and of course, as Archbishop, Hughes presided. The "drift" of the orator's remarks, as embodied in a letter Hughes wrote to Brownson, was "to the effect [that] if the Catholic religion had been or could now be presented to the American people through mediums and under auspices more congenial with the national feelings and habits, the progress of the Church and the conversion of Protestants would have been far greater." Hughes added, "This is pure speculation. But it is a view in which I do not and cannot concur." [16] We shall soon come to Brownson's presentation of the same ideas in his *Review,* but for the moment Hughes's summary of them will suffice.

All this, whether or not "a pure speculation," or well founded, was at least something Brownson was free to hold. As a matter of fact, Hughes told him, as soon as he had sat down, that while he did not like the spirit of the speech, nothing had been said inconsistent with the Church's teaching. The spirit, or tone—if we may judge from the manner Brownson often adopted—was in all likelihood truculent. Yet after he had made his private comment to Brownson, the Archbishop gave a final address—as is customary on the part of the presiding dignitary—in which he made a number of "hostile and ironic allusions" to the speaker, "vastly to the entertainment of the audience," according to Hassard.[17] This Brownson considered very unfair, especially as they came after a private admission that what had been said was perfectly permissible. The Archbishop himself was a rather truculent man, with a gift of sarcasm; quite probably he was led on to say more than he had intended— led on by his audience.

The tone of his remarks was promptly commented upon by Thomas D'Arcy McGee,[18] the editor of the *American Celt,* a man who did not particularly like Brownson but who liked Hughes even less, and who may have thought he could kill two birds with one stone. This made Hughes write to Brownson protesting that a "malicious construction" had been placed upon his remarks, and that he had intended nothing disrespectful.[19] The letter concludes with three pieces of advice: Brownson would do well if he carefully avoided "every censorious allusion to the nationality of our Catholic brethren"; he should also "not write or say anything calculated to represent the Catholic religion as especially adapted to the genius of the American people as such"; and that he should ignore the unkind articles about him in small Catholic papers. "We have all looked upon you," the Archbishop flatteringly explained, "as belonging to the whole Catholic Church."

This advice was offered in a friendly way and was, upon the

whole, very sound. But of course Brownson had never said that the Catholic religion was "especially" adapted to America; he had merely affirmed that in no country did it have a more favorable opportunity. He had always insisted that Catholicism, being universally true, must be equally suited for all men; but he had stressed, for the benefit of the general public, the fact that Catholicism was eminently consonant with the American scheme of things. What he would have been wise to have done, however, was to have treated the criticism of the "small Catholic papers" with contemptuous silence. Had he been the proud man he was often accused of being, this is what he would have done. But he was constitutionally incapable of prudent silence; he never lost a chance for an argument —even if it was only an argument with a fool.

Brownson replied to Hughes saying that he was surprised to hear the public condemnation just after he had been told that the Archbishop's criticisms had been intended only for his private ear. "It was taking an unfair advantage of me," he declared. "It was opposing to me, a layman, the opinions of an archbishop . . . It was crushing me with the weight of authority, in a matter of simple opinion . . . Your remarks, however intended by you, were an episcopal censure upon me, and I can see no reason why the 'American Celt' had not the right so to consider them." [20] If this was not very gracious on his part, he had reason, after all, to feel aggrieved—for such public criticism from an archbishop, and on a matter regarding which Brownson was admittedly at liberty to hold his own views, was calculated to undermine his influence, which had already been sufficiently threatened.

Characteristically he reiterated all he had said in the next issue of his *Review* in his article, "The Mission of America." There he told his fellow-countrymen: "We look upon ourselves as a providential people, as a people with a great destiny, and a destiny glorious to ourselves and beneficent to the world. . . . There is more than meets the eye in the popular expression, 'Manifest Destiny.' . . . The manifest destiny of this country is something far higher, nobler, and more spiritual,—the realization, we should say, of the Christian ideal of society for both the Old World and the New." [21] As for Protestantism, there was "an inherent antagonism" between it and the American order; and "our Protestant ancestors founded the American order, not on their Protestantism, but on the natural law, natural justice and equity as explained by the church, long prior to the Protestant movement of Luther and his associates. . . . Protestantism is outgrown, and has fallen into the past. . . . But the church of the future exists, and already exists in our country." Therefore "the responsibility of Catholics in this country is greater than that of any other class of citizens. It is only through Catholicity that the country can fulfill its mission." [22] He did not claim that "the American people have as yet realized the Christian ideal of society," but he did think that they had already laid its foundations. At the same time he expressly repudiated the "false liberalism" represented by Kossuth and Mazzini and the "superb gentilism" sometimes met with in the writings of Gioberti. "You may, if you will," he concluded, "add a nation, a nation destined to rule the future, to your church, and to the world a new civilization." [23]

Hughes was not at all pleased with this article, though he wrote a pamphlet in which he made a show of praising it. At the same time he charged Brownson with being too hopeful about America's conversion, wrong in believing that Catholic progress would be greater when immigration had ceased or diminished, and wrong again in making an uncalled-for appeal to youth. It was not so much what Brownson had actually said that was offensive to him, but what Brownson had implied: that a new sort of leadership was necessary for the Church in the United States. One could hardly expect the Irish Archbishop of New York to relish being instructed on this point by a Yankee convert.

Hughes was even more annoyed by an article written by Dr. J. W. Cummings, a priest who had been living under the same roof with himself. Its thesis was that the Irish and German seminarians who were coming to the United States were very often young men of rather undesirable qualities. He did not charge them with being unworthy men, but only with having an attitude or cast of mind out of place in America. What he wrote had much truth in it, as everybody knew, but when he described the seminaries as "cheap priest factories" he flung out a phrase that stung and that might have been left unused. The case of Brownson and Cummings was, that if America was to be won to the Faith, American priests would be needed. Cardinal Gibbons was to perceive this clearly, and he told the seminarians at Baltimore in 1891: "If the Church is to take deep roots in the country and to flourish, it must be sustained by men racy of the soil, educated at home, breathing the spirit of the country, growing with its growth, and in harmony with its civil and political institutions." [24] But of course when Cummings wrote it was impossible to supply American Catholics with American-born priests; the bishops were compelled to recruit their clergy very largely from abroad, and it was inevitable that many of those who came to America should not be of the highest calibre. Hughes must have realized all this very well, but the criticism of Cummings did not appear to him very helpful. His retort was to accuse Brownson of belonging to a club (which did exist in New York, though Brownson was not a member of it) which had for its object "the carrying of Americanism into the Church." [25]

Brownson threw further fat into the fire by writing an article on education, a subject of which he was often to treat. Though he came to modify his views later, at this time he was disposed to put more faith in the public schools than at all suited Hughes's ideas. As Hughes had fought a great battle to have the parochial schools supported out of the public funds, it was anything but discreet of Brownson to maintain that a good public school was preferable to the somewhat inefficient parochial schools which in those days were far too prevalent. And those who were struggling to establish a Catholic higher education did not like being told that the teaching of philosophy was disgracefully bad in their institutions. Yet again it was no more than the truth. Bishop O'Connor had confided to Brownson his opinion that philosophy, as taught in Catholic colleges, was, for the most part, "some fragments of theology badly proved." As Henry Brownson explains the situation: "When a priest is one year on the mission, the next, teaching the rudiments of Latin, and then, professor of philosophy, it can hardly be expected of him that he should have thought out for himself a whole system of philosophy." [26]

All these plain words—to which may be added Brownson's article, "Archbishop Hughes on the Catholic Press" [27] totalled up to relations with Hughes which were those of increasing strain. It was not that Hughes and Brownson disliked one another; on the contrary, when they met and there was not at the moment any issue between them, they got along well enough together. They always expressed respect, and perhaps in a queer confused way felt much more affection than either would admit. But each rasped the other's nerves, and except for their devotion to the Catholic cause, they looked at nearly everything from divergent points of view. Upon the publication of Hughes's *Collected Works* Brownson wrote an article in which he said: "We were no blind admirer of his during his life, and we confess that we often did him injustice in our thoughts and words too freely spoken. . . . Though we never fell under his official censure, we did fall under the lash of [his] unofficial criticism, which was not at all pleasant, and the perfect candor and impartiality of our judgment may reasonably be distrusted." [28] But while indicating his differences with the Archbishop—and still contending that all he had ever tried to assert was that "an American on his conversion to the Church is not required by his religion to renounce his American nationality, and that foreign nationalities, domiciled on American soil, should treat his nationality with respect," [29]—Brownson handsomely acknowledged that "time and events have proved that he was right in many things in which we thought him wrong, or at least injudicious, at the time, and it is not for us to say that he was not always right, wise, and judicious. We are laymen, and not judges of episcopal administration." [30]

As Brownson's opinion of Hughes in 1874 has been anticipated, the story of their later relations might as well be anticipated at this point, so as to round the story out, except for leaving his clash with the Archbishop on the subject of slavery to a later chapter.

In 1861 Brownson was again the Commencement orator at Fordham, and again Archbishop Hughes presided. That Brownson should have taken the theme of American patriotism was only appropriate at the time of the Civil War. But Brownson's views as to what constituted Americanism were too well known for the audience not to draw all the inferences, even supposing that so blunt a man would allow anything to be merely inferential. Hughes interpreted the speech as a challenge to himself. When his turn came to speak, he severely criticized Brownson and his "school." Again the Catholic Club came in for castigation, and the Archbishop insisted that Brownson was one of its members—though even had he been one, there was no justification for the diatribe. As Henry Brownson says, "It was a bolt out of a clear sky. There was consternation on every side." In his indignation Brownson rose and attempted to contradict Hughes on this point, but Hughes ordered him to sit down. After the ceremony was over, the Jesuit Fathers took the Archbishop and the other big-wigs to the banquet that had been prepared for them—and left Brownson sitting alone in the auditorium until the time for him to catch his train. [31]

Henry Brownson notes that after his father went to New York in 1855 his health was at first good. But he missed the hills and the bracing New England air, and did not like either the narrow quarters he had to occupy or the social life that wasted much of his time. The only recreations he cared for were the gardening, of which he was now deprived, and an occasional game of whist or chess—the chess still a fierce passion. He did not move much in what are called literary circles, and the few literary friends he might have made in New York who even approached his own stature he managed to antagonize. He wrote to J. V. Huntington on August 25, 1855, saying that he had decided to make no advances to John Gilmary Shea because he regarded Shea as the aggressor. The historian had taken offence at having one of his books inadvertently ignored by Brownson. The letter continues: "I am ready to receive any advances from him, and to forget his uncalled for hostility to me. I accept all you say in his favor, and really believe him far more deserving than I at first thought him. Nothing in the past will affect any notice I may have occasion to take of any of his works. He can and will, whatever course I take, be my enemy and injure me. . . . He is a Celt, and a Celt once an enemy is never a friend afterwards. I wish him well, and if it is ever in my power to do him a service, I shall do so, most cheerfully." [32] On second thoughts he decided to make an effort at reconciliation with Shea. Nothing came of it, though the two men were soon to be living in the same town, Elizabeth, New Jersey. Shea revenged himself on Brownson by giving him only a line or two in his *History of the Catholic Church in the United States*. His cold malignity was something far more reprehensible than Brownson's stormy temper. The pity is that these two laymen, who were intellectually head and shoulders above most of their Catholic contemporaries in America, should have been estranged over so trivial an incident as an unwritten review. As for Ripley, now on the New York *Tribune,* he and Brownson had long since drifted apart.

Brownson did, however, have many friends among some of the leading New York priests. The chief of these of course was Hecker. But next in importance was Dr. Cummings, who had taken upon himself in past years to arrange Brownson's lectures on his visits to New York, and Dr. Manahan, both of whom were members of the "Club" so detested by Archbishop Hughes. Others were Dr. Pise, the only Catholic priest who had ever been Chaplain of the Senate at Washington, Dr. Forbes and Fathers George McCloskey

and Sylvester Malone.[33] Henry Brownson holds them—especially
Hecker—responsible for the change that he said now gradually
came over his father and deplores that their influence was substituted
for that of Bishop Fitzpatrick. Yet on the very next page he contradicts himself by remarking that to his father's assertion of intellectual freedom "we owe the profoundest and sublimest of his
writings." [34]

Whether or not the intellectual climate was bad for Brownson, his
physical health certainly worsened. We now begin to hear for the
first time of the gout from which he was destined to suffer for the
rest of his life. Father Hecker sent him to a convert doctor whose
somewhat strange method of treatment he believed "was inspired by
the Holy Ghost and was to the body what baptism was to the soul."
It consisted in bleeding the patient and prescribing quantities of
whiskey—for which he charged from fifty to a hundred dollars,
paid in advance. It did no harm perhaps to a man who had so
much blood in his burly body as Brownson, but it did no appreciable
good. Soon afterwards, fortunately, the inspired Dr. Watson, having
collected all the fees he was likely to get, left New York, and
Brownson found a better physician in Father Hewit's brother.[35]

The gradual change of tone that began to be noticed in Brownson's articles was not so gradual as Henry Brownson would have us
believe. It really began the moment that Bishop Fitzpatrick sailed
for Europe in 1854. What is significant is that in his *Review* for
April, 1855, Brownson took up again his "doctrine of communion"
which had lain on the shelf unused since his conversion. Writing
in 1849 on his old friend, W. H. Channing, he had mentioned the
doctrine, as stated by Channing, only to condemn it.[36] Six years
later, however, he said that the writings of Pierre Leroux "revolu-
tionized our own mind both in regard to philosophy and religion,
and by the grace of God became the occasion of our conversion to
Catholicity." [37] Later in the same article he declared, "The thought
we developed [the doctrine of communion] does not rise to the

order of Catholic dogma, and at the highest remains in the natural order. Yet the doctrine is substantially true. . . . Man has a three-fold nature and lives by communion with God, man, and nature. He communes with God in religion, with man in society, and with nature in property." [38] It was an idea to which once more he came to attach enormous importance. Though I have never heard of anyone who was ever brought to the Catholic Church by this particular road,[39] except Hecker and Brownson himself, some exposition of the point, because of the weight that Brownson gave it, must be attempted.

What nobody seems to have pointed out is that Brownson wrote *The Convert* with the primary intention of justifying this doctrine as a mode of approach to the Church—not simply as the mode he had found serviceable but as a mode that would work wonders in the case of others. He deals with it in the last seventy pages of that book, of which it constitutes the real thesis—a point which everybody who has written on Brownson seems to have missed.

I think I can explain how this is. Henry Brownson, like all the other biographers, went to *The Convert* as the principal source for the years 1803–1844. But when people reach what is the dramatic climax of that work—Brownson's reception into the Church—what follows strikes them as a long-drawn-out redundancy. They have already been told something about Leroux and the doctrine of communion—about all they want to know. What remains, if read at all, is therefore read hurriedly. It was so with me—at my first reading of *The Convert*. Only later careful readings brought me to see what had been Brownson's object.

With sincere gratitude and affection he had dedicated his autobiography to Bishop Fitzpatrick; but whether or not Fitzpatrick ever discovered the fact, the book is a declaration of independence of Fitzpatrick, who had dismissed what was to be its central idea as not having any apologetic value and who had insisted, during the ten years that he had been Brownson's advisor, that the ordinary apologetic methods be used. For a time he even brought

Brownson to believe that the doctrine of communion was dangerous if not actually heretical, as appears in the letters of this period to Hecker, from which quotation has already been made. Now Brownson took his discarded notion up again.

Of scholasticism he says in *The Convert*, "I have never found the method effectual, in the case of any non-Catholic not already disposed to become a Catholic." [40] On the other hand, he claims that his method, "though it can by no means supersede [that of the scholastics], might be advantageously used as a preparation for theirs." [41] He had dropped it "for the time" in deference to Fitzpatrick, because he attached "for the moment" no great importance to it. "It did not comport with the modesty and humility of a recent convert to be obtruding theories of his own on the Catholic public." [42] He indicates plainly that it was this temporary shelving of his theory that put him in a false position towards his non-Catholic friends. "They were thrown all aback the first time they heard me speaking as a Catholic, by finding me defending my conversion on grounds of which I had given no public intimation, and which seemed to them wholly unconnected with those I had published." [43] He also says that the doctrine of communion was the connecting link that had so long been kept concealed. Now he wishes to clear himself "of an unfounded suspicion of having acted capriciously" and thinks he can do a real service to a large number of people who still remember him as a Protestant veering towards the Church.[44]

Though it was first developed and applied while he was as yet outside the Church, Brownson holds that the theory "is not repugnant to any principles of Catholic faith or theology"; on the contrary, he believes that "a philosophy of this sort has become indispensable." [45] He gives his reasons: "[The age] distrusts reasoning rather than reason. It has no confidence in the refinements and subtilties of schoolmen, and though often sophistical, it is in constant dread of being cheated out of its wits by the sophistry of the practised logician." [46] The ordinary motives of credibility do not move non-Catholics to believe, and Catholic apologetics, as ordinarily practiced, do not touch their real objections. "I repeat again and again, that philosophy did not conduct me into the Church, but just in proportion as I advanced towards a sound philosophy, I did advance towards the Church." [47]

The non-Catholic attributes the plausibility of usual Catholic arguments to "some logical sleight-of-hand"; therefore "an external refutation of the unbeliever's objections effects nothing, because the real objection is internal, and the refutation leaves the internal as it was before." Brownson's contention was that "there is little use in arguing against the objections of non-Catholics, or in laboring directly for their refutation." What must be done is to bring "the age back, or up to a philosophy which conforms the order of knowledge to the order of being, the logical order to the order of reality. . . . Such a philosophy is the desideratum of the age, and we must have it, not as a substitute for faith, but as its preamble . . . or we cannot recall the non-believing world to the Church of God." [48]

Brownson further points out that "The greatest and most serious difficulty in the way of the unbeliever, is his inability to reconcile faith and reason, that is, the Divine plan in the order of grace with the Divine plan evident in the order of nature." "What is wanted is not argument, but instruction and explanation." "I believe the process by which I was conducted towards the Church is not only a legitimate process in itself, but one which, in these times, in abler hands than mine, may be adopted with no little advantage. . . . I hope it is no presumption or lack of modesty on my part, to recommend it to the attention of the schools." [49] He is able to add: "I have found, on reviewing my past life, hardly a single positive conviction I ever held that I do not still hold, hardly a denial I ever made that I would not still make, if divested of my Catholic faith. I fell short of Catholicism, but in no instance, where I faithfully followed reason, did I run counter to it. The change I underwent was in taking on, rather than in casting off, and my Catholic faith was, under the grace of God, the slow and gradual accumulation of twenty-five years of intense mental activity." [50]

From his defence of reason he turns to the reasonableness of authority. "Nothing is more reasonable than to believe God at his word, but we cannot believe even him by reason that his word is a command; we do so only by reason that his word is the word of eternal, immutable and absolute Truth. It is overlooking this distinction, and taking authority in the sense that it commands, and not in the sense that it enlightens and convinces, that has excited the hostility to belief on authority, we so frequently encounter." [51] He further explains: "Authority for believing is always necessary, and nothing is more unreasonable than to believe without authority. Belief without authority is credulity . . . ; not an act of reason, but an act of unreason." [52] Again speaking out of his own experience, he declares: "I have, as a Catholic, felt and enjoyed a mental freedom which I never conceived possible while I was a non-Catholic." Certitude is freedom; therefore he says, "I have not had even the slightest temptation to doubt." [53]

The concluding chapter of *The Convert* does not directly bear on this. What I have given will suffice. It is, as will be seen, not a summary of Brownson's ideas on apologetics but a string of specific quotations. From these it will be amply evident what store he put on his mode of approach—the doctrine of communion. Whether or not it is quite as valuable as he considered it, what must be patent is that he had not been employing what he considered the best mode of apologetics while working under Fitzpatrick, and that he was now announcing that he proposed to try a new method. In an article written in 1862, he tells us that during his Boston Catholic period, "We used our own logic and language, but we ventured to utter no thought of our own. We wrote the best we could from the premises given us; . . . and what was set down to pride, to an overweening confidence in our own judgment, was due to an excess of self-abnegation." He goes on to fix the moment when he began to recover his personal identity as January, 1850, but the process was completed only after his removal to New York. "We were *not* mistaken as to the principle which conducted us to the church of God, as we were afterward led to believe,—an error which has caused us so much trouble, and lost us so much time; and if we had known better how to interpret the analytic language of scholastic theology, we should never have been induced to lay aside, or hold in abeyance, our original conviction." [54] It is an underscoring of the concluding chapters of *The Convert*. Grateful as he is to Bishop Fitzpatrick in this article, as in his autobiography, he makes it perfectly clear that Fitzpatrick obliged him, against his better judgment, to use the old apologetic methods when he had something so much better at his command. He regarded it, as did Hecker, as the story of a lost opportunity.

Brownson did not have much immediate chance to bring his new methods into play, so engrossed was he in his controversies. But what he was intending to do was made apparent in a letter he wrote on March 17, 1856, to Father Augustine Hewit (who like Hecker was still a Redemptorist) [55] to express his agreement with the apologetic mode the future Paulists were already using. "My own conviction," he said, "is that our true policy in dealing with the American mind is to study first to ascertain, not its errors, but the truth it still maintains, and to show it that that truth can find its unity and integrity only in the Catholic Church. We must find the *point d'appui* in the sound principles it still holds, and lead it by arguments, drawn from those principles, of the justness of which they can judge without going out of themselves, to the conclusion to which we wish them to come. . . . My own method, I believe, is the worst of all, that of logic." [56]

That Brownson had set out in 1844 with high hopes of bringing numbers into the Church is certain; it is equally certain that he came to give up that hope. Then, instead of changing his methods, he changed his audience and began to say that he regarded his mission that of confirming the faith of Catholics and of quickening their intellectual life. In this of course he had remarkable success. But he was always troubled in mind that he had failed in his first purpose, and now that he was free to work along his own lines, he returned to his former hope. At last he could use the instrument Fitzpatrick had virtually forbidden him to use.

He realized by now that his brilliant *tour de force* of logic was only a *tour de force,* or that it seemed so to his old friends among the Transcendentalists. It irritated men without persuading them, and so left them in worse case than before. He saw that he should find another means of approach, and he believed that he had it in the theory he had discarded—his doctrine of communion. Whether this particular theory was the master-key he and Hecker imagined it to be is questionable, but they were assuredly right in believing that the traditional Catholic apologetics made little appeal to the minds it was their hope to reach. The fault was not, it need hardly be said, in the mode of apologetics, considered in the abstract, but in the fact that Protestantism had reached such a state of confusion as to be all but impervious to logic, at least logic of the formal sort. The trouble was that Brownson was temperamentally unfitted to use anything but formal logic. And even had this not been so, his change of tactics came too late to do much good. His old audience of non-Catholics had drifted away, and if he was read by people outside the Church, it was only by those who rummaged through his writings to see if they could not find something that could be used against Catholics. That it was wrenched out of its context did not matter at all; Brownson's only interest to them was that he provided them with ammunition. As for Catholics themselves, they were often puzzled by him. They had looked upon him as a "wild man" who put the case for Catholicism in so extreme a form as to be alarming; now he alarmed them for a different reason. They could not make head or tail of all his talk about foreign philosophers, and they suspected that he was playing with novelties likely to lead him out of the Church. In the years that followed he therefore lost something of his standing among Catholics without winning back what he had lost when he became a Catholic.

Yet what he had got hold of—the need for a new method of

apologetics—had much to be said for it, though he was perhaps not the man best equipped to utilize it. There was, however, in America a man who was already doing something like the work Brownson envisaged; and this was Isaac Hecker. Early in 1855 Brownson wrote him a letter, otherwise undated, "I think as you do. The simple truth is our old controversialists have their method, and they will look with distrust on our new method, and fancy it full of danger. Very few of them have any suspicion that times have changed and that old errors are to be refuted under new forms & from a different stand-point." [57] Why he could successfully wield the weapon Brownson now tried to take up is explained by Brownson himself in his delineation of Hecker's character: "Few men really know him, few even suspect what is in him; but no one can commune with him for half an hour, and ever again be precisely what he was before. . . . His modesty and docility made him in [times past] regard us as his teacher as well as his senior, but in truth we were the scholar. . . . Each perhaps was of service to the other, but he aided us more than we him, for even then his was the master mind." [58]

What he has to say about Hecker's apologetic methods casts a good deal of light upon his own—both upon those he had been using and those he had now made up his mind to use. "All our controversial works have been written for a state of things which has passed or is passing away in this country. They do not meet our American mind; they fail to recognize to that mind the truths which it unquestionably has, and attack its errors under forms that it does not recognize as its own." [59] Still more surprisingly he asserts: "We are best represented by those who have outgrown all the forms of dogmatic Protestantism, and are looking, like Emerson and Parker, for something beyond the reformation, and have glimpses of a truth, a beauty, a perfection above it, to which they long to attain. . . . These are the real American people." [60]

Having so expressed his confidence in the receptivity of the American people to Catholicism, he goes on to expound Hecker's ideas, which he has now made his own. "We shall, with the grace of God, find our account in proportion as we address the heart, and the intellect through the heart. The fulcrum of our lever is in the natural craving of the heart for beatitude, to love and to be loved. We shall do well not to slight the mystic element of the soul, an element perhaps stronger than any other in our American nature. Hitherto our Catholic authors, very naturally and properly, have confined themselves, when addressing those without, either to the defence of Christianity against the objections of Protestants, or to the refutation of the errors of non-Catholics. We have confined ourselves personally, in our discussions, mostly to the latter object, for it suited best our peculiar temperament. But, after all, we in this way present Catholicity mainly on its negative side, and silence the logic rather than win the heart of non-Catholics. . . . There is another way of presenting it, which we have as yet hardly tried, that of presenting it in its purely affirmative or positive character, as the adequate object of the heart, which Tertullian says is naturally Christian, frankly recognizing its natural wants and activities, and showing it that Catholicity is that unknown good that it craves. . . . [Father Hecker] makes no apologetic defence of Catholicity, and no polemical assault on Protestantism; . . . he presents Catholicity as the answer to the Questions of the Soul. . . . In this consist the originality and peculiar merit of his method." [61]

Two and a half years later, when Brownson reviewed another book by Hecker, *Aspirations of Nature,* he seemed to correct himself to some extent. But it was only that he was now looking at Hecker from a different point of view—a habit of Brownson's that so often made people mistake a new angle of vision for a fundamental change of opinion. The aim of the second book was much the same as that of the first: "to show that all men naturally aspire to religion, and that the aspirations of their nature can be satisfied in the Catholic Church, and nowhere else." [62] Again Hecker addressed himself to "that class who have cast off Protestantism, fallen back on simple nature, have become earnest seekers after religion, and are prepared to accept it the moment they see it meets their intellectual and moral wants, and that they can embrace it without denying the plain dictates of reason or forfeiting the rights and dignity of their human nature." [63] This means of course the Transcendentalists; only Brownson now declares that they were never very numerous or powerful and have all but disappeared.

His main criticism of Hecker is that he overestimates the radical power of reason and nature, "confounding what reason and nature have the power to do with what they actually accomplish." "He has so expressed himself that the unlearned reader may regard him as maintaining, when asserting reason and nature against Calvinists and Jansenists, what he denies when asserting revelation against rationalists and transcendentalists." [64] Though only a confusion of terms is involved, Brownson thinks there is some danger of the unwary reader getting the idea that Hecker lays too little stress on original sin and the supernatural. He puts it all very gently, for him, but it is important to note that Brownson explicitly declares: "We are . . . opposed to every thing that looks like accommodating Catholic teaching to the tastes and temper of the age or country." And, as he may have been misunderstood in this matter, he adds with greater emphasis: "There is scarcely a trait in the American character as practically developed that is not more or less hostile to Catholicity." [65]

This second review was intended as a clarification of Brownson's own position. He had often said that American institutions derive from Catholic political philosophy and that therefore the Church has a naturally fertile field in America; but he did not wish to be understood as saying that Americans, merely by virtue of being Americans, are incipient Catholics. But having made that much plain, he wandered off into a consideration of Know-Nothingism—which was now virtually dead—and protested against the sneers that had been directed at him in the Catholic press as a convert who presumed to teach. He protested, "We publish our *Review* because originally invited to do so by the prelates of the church." [66] And by way of asserting his orthodoxy in a test case, he gave a thrust in passing at a writer in the *Rambler* who had suggested that "the upper regions of hell," or limbo, will contain not only unbaptized infants but the heathen and the greater part of "our dissenting brethren." He still affirmed *extra ecclesiam nulla salus* without any qualification and commented on the *Rambler* man, "He seems to think the only use of hell, properly so called, is to punish bad Catholics." [67]

These two articles, taken together with *The Convert,* embody most completely what Brownson was trying to say on the subject of apologetics during his middle period. But at any period of Brownson's life we can reach what he really held by, so to speak, adding up everything he said and then striking an average. His habit was always that of discussing a subject first from one side and then from the other—each time with the utmost emphasis. Therefore anyone who reads what he says on only one side is likely to get a wrong impression. Henry Brownson explains that his father regarded his *Review* as a continuous work, "and never completed on any one subject as long as that subject was before the public for discussion." [68] He was continually denying that he had ever held this or that proposition which he was accused of holding, and even expressed the greatest astonishment that anybody should have ever thought he did. There are times when his denials even appear to be a trifle disingenuous; and there can be no doubt that, in spite of all his rashness, he had a good deal of Yankee wiliness. But the fact is that he always expected his readers to balance one utterance against another and thus arrive at his rounded doctrine.

This was especially true with regard to the ontologism with which he was beginning to be charged—his chief contribution to metaphysics and the thing which has given his enemies their chief handle against him. The other causes of offence disappeared in time: either because they ceased to be annoying, on account of changed circumstances, or because Brownson was admitted to have been right, or because he recanted. What he never recanted was his ontologism, which remains the ground for a certain distrust with which he is still regarded in some Catholic circles.

Ontology, perhaps I should explain—lest anyone should suppose that it has a connection with ontologism—is that branch of philosophy which investigates the nature of being as such, though Brownson tended to extend the meaning to being, considered both absolutely, as God, and in the relation of other beings to God. Ontologism, on the other hand, is a modification of the Cartesian system, through Occasionalism, which made an effort to explain how the mind can reach reality; and it propounded a theory of intuition instead of the more strictly rational process of the scholastics. Here perhaps it would be as well if, instead of making my own explanations, I quote from a modern scholastic philosopher. The Dominican, Father D. J. Kennedy, defines ontologism as teaching that "the first idea formed in the human mind is a direct knowledge of God. Without that idea we can have no scientific knowledge; with that idea we can have a certain and infallible knowledge of all things. We do not see the essence of God as He is in Himself, but we see that essence as it represents all things, which were first conceived in the mind of God and were then created in accordance with the idea of the Divine Architect of the world." [69]

Brownson's position was somewhat different. As against the scholastics who correctly asserted that ontologism, defined in this sense, logically led to pantheism by failing to differentiate clearly between the knowledge of the creature and the knowledge of God, he affirmed that it was scholastic philosophy that had failed to deal adequately with the problem of being, and that therefore those who were dissatisfied with its explanations were liable to fall back upon pantheism. He believed that his special brand of ontologism—which he strenuously and steadily denied was ontologism at all—really did solve the old problem. It is perfectly true that he had rejected and written against the ontologists, Rosmini, Hugonin and Branchereau, and the Louvain professors who had voluntarily submitted a number of propositions to the Holy See—which improbated them—and that this was in advance of the decision of the Holy See. The ground of that decision was that philosophy is competent to demonstrate by its own rational principles the existence of God, as well as His nature and attributes.

Prior to 1849, Henry Brownson tells us, his father had called himself an ontologist, though the qualification is quickly made that "ontologism may be understood in several senses." [70] But after that date, when he began reading Gioberti, he at last evolved his own system which, while borrowing from Gioberti, avoided, so he maintained, all the Giobertian errors. It was so with all the philosophers from whom he borrowed. He claimed to have reached their doctrine—even if perhaps in an inchoate fashion—independently, and that what he afterwards read served no more than to sharpen his perception of what he already held. Certainly in borrowing from a philosopher he always transformed what he took—sometimes almost beyond recognition.

His extravagant praise of Gioberti only fastened the more firmly upon him the charge that he was himself a Giobertian. "Aristotle," he wrote in January, 1863, "was a great master of reason, but, as we judge, inferior to Plato, and both he and Plato were inferior to St. Augustine or to St. Thomas. We dare also to be known to hold that in intellectual power and philosophic genius and attainments, the Abbate Gioberti may rank as the peer of any one of the four." [71] Instantly that was seized on by William George Ward in the *Dublin Review,* who pointed out that Gioberti was not only on the Index but had received the rare distinction of having all his works condemned, in whatever language they were written.[72] To which it may be replied that anyone, supposing him competent to distinguish between what is true and what is false in a condemned author's work, is free to admire it for what it contains that is admirable. Brownson's admiration of Gioberti did not mean that he accepted Gioberti's system as a whole, or was himself an ontologist, though that was the inference often drawn. About all he actually took from Gioberti, so he claimed, was the formula: *Ens creat existentias*—in other words, that Absolute Being creates contingent beings. This of course saved him from the pantheistic conception of "being" as inert; it was personal, absolute and all-powerful. What matter that Gioberti interpreted this in a pantheistic sense? That only showed that Gioberti—like Cousin and Leroux—did not fully understand the implications of his own philosophy.[73]

As for the process of knowledge, though Brownson by no means denied that it was logical, he pointed to the plain psychological fact that it was also intuitive, and from this possible intuitive knowledge of God he was assured by his own experience that he had derived more than from the more strictly rational method of procedure. But when he proceeded to elaborate, he either used scholastic Latin terms in a special sense of his own, or he invented English terms that were unfamiliar to scholastic philosophers and which they interpreted in the light of the terms to which they were accustomed. This, it is obvious, could easily be a source of honest misunderstanding. It is to be feared, however, that there were some who wilfully misunderstood him. The easiest thing in the world was available to such people: all they needed to do was to take Brownson's terms in the ordinarily accepted meaning, and then convict him out of his own mouth. Clever malice and simple stupidity worked in combination. Brownson's enemies, by finding they could charge the great defender of Catholic orthodoxy with philosophical heresy, enjoyed the sweetest kind of revenge.

I need hardly say that I am incompetent to decide in so highly technical a matter about which there is still so much controversy. But so far as I can understand what was at issue, it seems to me that Brownson's denials of being an ontologist were justified. He was indeed an ontologist, but it was—as usual—in a sense of his own, and not the sense in which the ontologists lie under the disapproval of the Church. What was unfortunate was that he chose the moment when for a variety of reasons he was most under attack to bring forward philosophical novelties which would have been suspect, whoever had advanced them, but were altogether unacceptable as coming from Brownson. Worst of all, he contrived to set the Jesuits against him by the sarcasm he directed against them as the chief upholders of what he considered an outmoded scholasticism. Here, as elsewhere, he showed himself, to say the least, completely devoid of tact.

What must be admitted is that he was animated by a desire to be of service to his fellow-Catholics. Whether or not he was right in believing that his metaphysical theories were the only possible guarantee against pantheism, whether or not he was right in believing that his doctrine of communion was the best mode of apologetics, there can be no doubt that he wanted to be useful. He had his share —and perhaps more than his share—of human vanity, and he was proud of his discoveries. Yet his pride was only incidental. Far more than his little vanity was his vast longing to serve humanity. Everything with him had a practical object, and always the practical object was the apologetic one. He was, indeed, a metaphysician because he could not help himself, and he may have had too high an estimate of Orestes Brownson as a metaphysician. Nevertheless metaphysics was with him not an end but a means to an end, not something to provide the scholar with the delights of private speculation but something to be put to service. Unpractical as he might be in his handling of men, he was practical in the purpose he had in mind.

What remains a question is of what practical use pure metaphysics is to ordinary people. Most of them have no interest in such matters, or even the ability to comprehend them. The average man contrives to rub along fairly well without any sort of philosophical system; for that matter, it was Brownson's contention that even perfectly orthodox theologians are not infrequently heretical as philosophers. If this be true of them, it would seem that those who are not theologians may usually be trusted to go through life tolerably safely without a knowledge of scholastic or Brownsonian philosophy. Usually, perhaps, but not always; those of a metaphysical turn—and all men are, after all, to some extent philosophers, just as all men are to some extent poets—if not properly grounded in truth (however abstract and remotely related to life that truth may appear to be) are only too liable to be entrapped by the specious. Should they happen to be logical, they are likely to proceed from a false philosophical premiss to the rejection of that dogmatic truth necessary to their salvation. Should they happen *not* to be logical, they are in grave danger of being affected by false speculations which infiltrate downwards—often after they are abandoned by those on higher intellectual levels. It was for these that Brownson did his work. He knew that philosophy is enormously important. If he fancied that there were more metaphysicians than actually exist, no harm was done. A great deal of harm might be done by neglecting to provide for their needs.

His first important article on ontologism was that which appeared in the *Review* for October, 1855—another sign of his intellectual independence. This was the famous "Problem of Causality," which Henry Brownson says "marks an epoch in [his] intellectual life." [74] But already he had touched upon his theory, a little cautiously, in 1850, when he wrote: "In God we live, move, and are; and therefore it is only in him we can see, know, or conceive at all, as Malebranche has shown in his theory of *Vision in God,* whatever we may think of the theory itself. Every conception of which we are capable, whether of the actual or possible, conceals at bottom, connotes, or implies the conception of God, as actually existing, living God. The idea of God logically precedes all our other ideas, and in fact chronologically, although not distinctly, or as distinguished from our other conceptions; for to distinguish implies reflection, which belongs to a later period of life. This idea, the idea of God,—not of pure abstract being, as Rosmini, if correctly reported to us, maintains, —is the *forma,* or formative principle, of the intellect, or faculty of the intelligence. It is the light by which the faculty is constituted intelligent faculty, and by virtue of which we see all that we do see." [75]

"The Problem of Causality" is an analysis and historical survey of the problem rather than an argument for Brownson's own position. But at the end he says: "Our solution . . . differs in only one respect from that of the so-called Thomist school, a school which has not wholly broken with the past, and which retains many of the traditions of the ancients, the greater Fathers and the more distinguished scholastics. This difference is, that we begin intellectual life,—not philosophy,—with the intuition of the principle of things, and it begins it with a sensible fact, and ascends, by way of demonstration, to that principle. But the principle once attained, we proceed alike, and come to the same conclusion . . . Certainly St. Thomas teaches that God can be known, though not *per se;* but this does not necessarily imply that we cannot have intuition of real and necessary being, which is God, or of real and necessary being creating existences, which is at once the principle of things and the principle of science. No doubt this judgment, though intuitive, becomes clear and distinct to reflective intellect only by a process of reasoning. What St. Thomas really does, is to clear up and render this judgment distinct, by what he calls demonstration. . . . But if he had been asked its origin, it is not to be believed that he would have said we obtain it from demonstration. . . . The pseudo-Thomist seems to us to confound the method it is necessary to follow in *teaching,* with the method the mind follows in its intellectual life. Whoever teaches philosophy must follow the Thomist method, but it will not do to confound it with the method of that which the teacher has to explain and systematize." [76]

In subsequent articles Brownson wrote more profoundly and at greater length upon his alleged ontologism; but I do not quote from these because they are often very technical. The passages just given will serve to illustrate his meaning, as they are simple and give Brownson's doctrine in a nut-shell. His son's comment on his theory is that here—as always—he avoided extremes and was as moderate as he could be with logical consistency. He continues: "In philosophy, under the point of view from which he discussed it, the extremes are pure rationalism and pure traditionalism, pure psychologism and pure ontologism; and it is well known that he rejected all these extremes, and started from a primitive synthesis which avoids them." [77]

A closely reasoned and richly documented study—one addressed to specialists—is Dr. Sidney A. Raemers' *America's Foremost Philosopher*. The title unluckily is calculated to put up the backs of specialists.[78] Brownson is *not* America's foremost philosopher, though perhaps he was potentially so. Had he not diffused his energies— they were enormous, but no man can diffuse himself with impunity —he would probably now have a higher reputation than is usually accorded him. On the other hand, it must be remembered that this busy journalist and lecturer dealt with whatever he touched— theology, politics, literature, sociology, or education—primarily as a philosopher. The coördination of his ideas is, under the circumstances, remarkable. But he never had quite sufficient time to round out his idea on any subject, with the exception of American constitutional theory. Some of his best things are dropped *obiter dicta,* as when in reply to the *Princeton Review's* review of *The Convert* he says: "Gioberti labors to prove that a man has a natural faculty, which he calls the faculty of the superintelligible; but the superintelligible and the supernatural are not the same. The superintelligible may be in the same order with the intelligible, and be superintelligible only in relation to us, through the impotency of our faculties; but the supernatural is of another order, and no natural faculty can naturally rise to its conception. The revelation of it must precede the conception, and therefore, in a certain sense, all our reasonings about it, for it, or even against it, must and do assume the fact of its revelation. Perhaps, this fact alone, since we all do reason more or less about it, is a conclusive proof that the supernatural exists, and that God has revealed it." [79] The passage shows the practical bearing he considered his metaphysical doctrine to have on all human life, and even its appeal to men who would be altogether incapable of formulating their ideas philosophically and who yet are capable at arriving at the essential knowledge which their nature, by its very constitution, needs.

Brownson once confessed: "Logic is the only part of philosophy we set much store by, and if we enter into the discussion of the higher metaphysical problems, it is chiefly for the sake of logic [a theory of knowledge?], because we cannot otherwise make sure of a logic which conforms to the real order of things." [80] If it be objected that he wrote this while still in Boston—though just on the eve of escaping Fitzpatrick's censorship—it is patent that his was always a logical process, so far as the clarification of truth was concerned. There is no real conflict between such a point of view and a typical "ontologistic" dictum of the kind for which he was so often blamed: "That of which we have immediate intuition in every process of reasoning and without which no such process would be possible or conceivable, is God the Creator." [81] Personally, I am willing to accept Father Raemer's thesis that "[Brownson's] critics have made the mistake of confounding intuition of God *by* the mind with the intuition of God *to* the mind, that is, with God creating, conserving, and pre-moving the mind and concurring with it in its action." [82] He thinks (and I incline to agree) that it is no more than fact that, while Brownson's language may sometimes have appeared to bear an ontologistic sense, he did not assert any immediate intuition of God. Though this is not to declare myself as agreeing with Brownson on all points on this or any other matter.

What must be stressed is that Brownson never materially altered his views on this question. He had been for some time gradually shifting his political ground, until during the Civil War, he at last reached a constitutional theory he was not again to change. He was on the point of going through a "liberal" phase, if he had not already begun it. He had adopted a new attitude towards apologetics, one that he afterwards gave up, though without returning fully to the methods he had used under Fitzpatrick in Boston. He shifted his ground on many points during his life, many times even after his conversion to Catholicism. But with regard to the metaphysical theories he first began to propound in 1850, he would never budge; all that he did was to give them greater clarity and coherence. It is true that he eventually came to speak more respectfully of scholasticism and of the Jesuits who were its exponents—yet without making any essential concessions. But as a philosopher, he stuck to his guns. If he was an ontologist in 1850, he was one when he died in 1876.

[1] *Latter Life,* p. 31.

[2] *Ibid.,* p. 33.

[3] *Ibid.,* p. 4.

[4] *Works,* Vol. XII, pp. 238–269.

[5] These racial explanations are always as fallacious as they are unCatholic. Mr. Belloc, for example, in his *Europe and the Faith* points out that the sole Roman province to revolt against the Church in the sixteenth century was England, and that the sole exception on the other side—a country that had never been in the Empire and yet remained Catholic—was Ireland. Though he does not pretend to say what inference should be drawn from the fact, he does present us with a formula to cover the general situation—a very unCatholic one. It is "Europe is the Faith, and the Faith is Europe." But the Faith is *not* Europe; the Faith is universal. Brownson's scheme, though avoiding Belloc's heresy, is nevertheless historically untenable.

[6] *Works,* Vol. XII, p. 251.

[7] *Works,* Vol. XI, p. 333. Again the argument is questionable, as the early history of the American Republic shows. Then Catholics of social standing and education had a far greater influence than they have ever enjoyed since. Some of the leading publishers were Catholics, and by no means confined themselves to issuing Catholic books. These Catholics of the older American stock found themselves segregated afterwards because of the influx of poor Catholics. Nativism was simply a fear of being swamped by the number of Catholics arriving. Had the number been smaller and the quality higher, Nativism would never have arisen. But there was of course a great advantage to the Church in having such numbers arrive, though it created problems and provoked antagonism. Brownson makes a much sounder point (*ibid.,* p. 337) in remarking that the building of the canals was providential for the evangelization of the country, even though this led to industrialism.

[8] *Works,* Vol. XX, pp. 89, 90.

[9] Catholics are especially prone to it because of their egalitarian spirit. But it is the vice of all democratic societies which, taking the average man as their standard, resent any man who rises above the common level.

[10] *Middle Life,* p. 168. The *Jesuit* to which Purcell refers was the Boston diocesan paper, founded in 1829. It had a truculent tone, and its title was itself an offence to most Protestants. It changed its name two years later but went back to it again, and when Bishop Fenwick, himself a Jesuit, withdrew his support, it ceased publication at the end of 1834.

[11] *Works,* Vol. III, p. 571.

[12] *Ibid.,* p. 566. Here, however, Brownson prejudged the matter. There was much in the *Rambler* to which legitimate exception could be taken, and Ullathorne was not the only one to raise objections. See Bishop Grant's letter in Gasquet's *Lord Acton and His Circle* (pp. 270–271 fn.) and Ward's *Life of Cardinal Newman* (Vol. I, pp. 506–508).

[13] *Latter Life,* p. 67.

[14] *Works,* Vol. XIV. In the issue of his *Review* for January, 1857, Brownson intimated that he was prepared, in the event of ecclesiastical interference, to carry his case to Rome. "If the bishop or archbishop who judges in the first instance does us wrong, our remedy is not in disobedience, resistance, or public discussion, but

in appeal to Rome, to the highest tribunal of the church." That fair warning having been given Hughes, Brownson could afford to make what seem excessively generous acknowledgments, saying that "the archbishop . . . has always treated us in this respect with the greatest possible delicacy." (*Works*, Vol. XX, 70, 71). As to just how far that delicacy extended, the reader must judge from what immediately follows.

15 *Latter Life*, p. 230.

16 *Ibid.*, pp. 71–72.

17 *Life of Hughes*, p. 383.

18 After a turbulent career in America, McGee migrated to Canada, where he completely changed his politics and became a great upholder of the concept of empire. It is largely due to him that Canada obtained dominion status. He was assassinated in 1868 at Ottawa by an Irishman who considered him a renegade. He wrote a valuable *History of the Irish Settlers in North America* in which he said (as of 1850) that "the torrent of immigration from Ireland must in a few years abate its force." It was a proposition Hughes disputed, and there Hughes was right; but McGee was right, as against Hughes, in maintaining that the policy (for which Hughes was largely responsible) of gathering the Irish into the large cities was against their best interests. On both scores Hughes and McGee were at odds.

19 *Latter Life*, pp. 67, 68.

20 *Latter Life*, p. 73.

21 *Works*, Vol. XI, p. 567. It was an opinion that Mr. Robert Wilberforce records his grand-uncle, Cardinal Manning, making to Mr. Wilberforce's mother: that the return of the English-speaking world to Catholic unity would be through America. (*Catholic World*, Vol. CLI, 1940, p. 66). Whether or not the judgment proves to be correct, it is surely harmless enough.

22 *Works*, Vol. XI, pp. 568, 569, 571, 576.

23 *Ibid.*, pp. 581, 584.

24 A. S. Will, *Life of Cardinal Gibbons*, Vol. I, p. 530.

25 *Latter Life*, p. 80. To do Hughes justice, he may have scented on the air something not unlike the "Americanism" which was condemned by Leo XIII in 1889 in his *Testem Benevolentiae*. Brownson never advocated anything like it, but its incipient tendencies already existed. Later, it should be added, Brownson veered away from Cummings's position, feeling that it implied a false emphasis. He then declared that there could be no objection to a foreign clergy—as the Church in America (as elsewhere) was not national but universal. (*Works*, Vol. XIV, p. 491).

26 *Latter Life*, p. 139. He continues with: "Father W. H. Hill [who was later very severely handled by Brownson] said to me a few years after his appointment to teach philosophy: 'I don't pretend to be a philosopher; I only try to repeat what I was taught as a student.' A little later, however, he took a very different view of his proficiency in philosophy." Though conditions have improved in this respect, they have not improved to such an extent that those acquainted with Catholic college education can say that the state of things described by Orestes Brownson and his son has quite ceased to exist.

27 *Works*, Vol. XX, pp. 50–73.

28 *Works*, Vol. XIV, p. 500.

29 *Ibid.*, p. 489. The differences really involved a good deal more than that, however. Brownson often had a way, after having stated his case in extreme terms, of restating it, under challenge, in far more moderate terms, and then saying that he had only *meant* the more moderate thing.

30 *Ibid.*, p. 495.

31 *Latter Life*, pp. 413, 414. Henry Brownson records that his father never complained of the conduct of the Jesuits on this occasion. But he suggests that there was some connection between this incident and the changed attitude of the Jesuits towards Brownson that was noticed later. He was certainly asked to leave Boston College not long afterwards, though he had only called to see Father Gresselin, who had been his confessor, and though Gresselin had written to say that the Rector "forbids you, most positively, when you come to Boston to take any other lodging than our house." (*Ibid.*, p. 249). Now it was the Rector who showed the visitor to the door, explaining that he was very sorry but that as Brownson had been announced to give a lecture attacking slavery, he could not afford to have him there, lest a wrong impression be given in the South as to the Jesuits' attitude towards that question. Henry Brownson says that they were afraid of having their holdings in the Southern States confiscated. His father's own account of the matter is in Volume XX of his *Works* (pp. 363–364). He regrets that "simple, worldly prudence or property considerations had more influence with the Jesuit body than we expected from a mendicant order," and that "the education of the Catholic youth of the nation should be entrusted to a society so destitute of loyalty that it could look on with indifference and see the nation rent asunder and destroyed by a rebellion which every principle of our religion, as we learned it, condemns." He draws the moral: the Jesuits suffer from foreign control. Therefore "they are not adapted to our age, and especially to our country." (*Ibid.*, pp. 365, 366).

Brownson's account of being asked to leave the Jesuit house in Boston appears to be contradicted by certain entries from the manuscript diaries kept for the years 1860–1863 by the Theologians and Philosophers studying at Boston College. These are now in the Archives at Woodstock. It seems that Dr. Brownson arrived on the afternoon of September 25, 1862, and visited the Philosophers at their recreation after supper on the 29th, and that October 1st was kept as a holiday in honor of his visit. There is of course the possibility of a second visit, when he was not so well received; another explanation is that, after having received him enthusiastically, the Rector became alarmed upon hearing why Brownson had come to Boston and then rid himself—though with tears—of one whose presence might prove embarrassing. However this may be, it is certain that it was Fordham that gave Brownson his degree of Doctors of Laws, the first doctorate conferred by that university. It is at Fordham that Kitson's heroic bust of Brownson now stands—placed on the very spot where the commencements used to be held, partly by way of reparation, so Father Robert I. Gannon, its President, writes to me.

32 *Brownson Papers*. There is a somewhat similar letter to Hecker dated August 29th among the *Hecker Papers*. And Henry Brownson gives on page 604 of *Middle Life* another draft of the letter to Huntington.

33 *Latter Life*, pp. 80–81. Dr. Manahan subsequently quarrelled with Brownson. (*Ibid.*, p. 252 fn.).

34 *Ibid.*, pp. 2, 3.

35 *Ibid.*, p. 128.

36 *Works*, Vol. X, p. 150.

37 *Ibid.*, p. 527.

38 *Ibid.*, pp. 547, 548.

39 Father Hecker believed in the usefulness of this idea to the end of his life, perhaps more than Brownson did in his last years. Father Joseph P. Donovan, the most learned of Brownsonians, in a letter to me calls it "a theory that some think

has big possibilities. It is a 1940 synthesis, not a 1840." How or why he does not explain.

40 P. 378. A typical instance of Brownson's habit of over-statement.

41 *Ibid.*, p. 379.

42 *Ibid.*, pp. 380, 381.

43 *Ibid.*, p. 382.

44 *Ibid.*, pp. 383, 384.

45 *Ibid.*, pp. 385, 386.

46 *Ibid.*, p. 387.

47 *Ibid.*, pp. 388, 390.

48 *Ibid.*, pp. 391, 392.

49 *Ibid.*, pp. 393, 394, 396.

50 *Ibid.*, p. 399.

51 *Ibid.*, p. 402.

52 *Ibid.*, p. 413.

53 *Ibid.*, pp. 417, 419.

54 *Works,* Vol. XX, pp. 252, 253.

55 The Paulists were not founded until 1858.

56 *Latter Life,* p. 60.

57 *Hecker Papers.*

58 *Works,* Vol. XIV, pp. 538, 539. This was in Brownson's review of Hecker's book, *Questions of the Soul.* Hecker wrote on December 2, 1853, to Brownson to tell him that Ripley was putting the volume through the press, and that the cost of its publication by Appleton was to be borne by George Hecker. (*Brownson Papers*).

59 *Works,* Vol. XIV, p. 540.

60 *Ibid.*, p. 541. Writing to Brownson on October 29, 1854, Hecker says that Thoreau "under his seeming trustfulness and frankness . . . conceals an immense amount of pride, pretention and infidelity." Yet he sees in Thoreau another indication that "the time is coming when our young, earnest, and enterprising American youth will find that it is the Church of God they seek." (*Brownson Papers*).

61 *Works,* Vol. XIV, pp. 542–543. Five years later Brownson even made some surprisingly friendly comments on Protestant revivalism. (*Works,* Vol. XX, pp. 100–101). The "Great Awakening" had occurred in 1858. It was at least on a higher plane than the earlier orgiastic camp-meetings.

62 *Ibid.*, p. 548.

63 *Ibid.*, XIV, p. 550.

64 *Ibid.*, pp. 557, 558.

65 *Ibid.*, pp. 565, 570. Hecker was naturally a little concerned over this review, especially as it was published just at the moment that he was in Rome. It was as a result of this visit that he was released by Pius IX from his vows as a Redemptorist and founded the Paulists. As the outcome was still in doubt, he wrote to Brownson on October 24, 1857: "The article will increase the unfounded suspicions of the General [of the Redemptorists] here and the Provincial in the U.S. and I fear that the latter will use it with terrible effect against the American Fathers." (*Latter Life,* p. 122). Another version of the same letter—apparently a first draft—is among the *Hecker Papers.*

66 *Works,* Vol. XIV, p. 575.

67 *Ibid.*, p. 563.

68 *Latter Life,* p. 189.

[69] *St. Thomas Aquinas and Medieval Philosophy*, p. 117.

[70] *Middle Life*, p. 624.

[71] *Works*, Vol. VIII, p. 25.

[72] Vol. LIV (1864), p. 62.

[73] *Latter Life*, p. 338.

[74] *Middle Life*, p. 633.

[75] *Works*, Vol. X, p. 190.

[76] *Works*, Vol. I, p. 407. Father Thomas T. McAvoy, C.S.C. prints in the *Catholic Historical Review*—Vol. XXVIII (1942), pp. 376–381—a letter of enquiry from a professor at Mount St. Mary's College to Brownson and Brownson's reply. Brownson says that on first glancing through the propositions of the ontologists condemned by the Sacred Congregation he thought that "some poor blunderhead had been trying to caricature & get prohibited the doctrine defended in my Review." He goes on to explain: "I have maintained that God is himself the light, that is, the objective light of the intellect, but never that the cognition of God was that light." Towards the end of his letter he adds: "I am no more an ontologist than I am a psychologist. My philosophy is synthetic, & starts from the original synthesis of things."

[77] *Latter Life*, p. 143. The assertion of Brownson's moderation might seem paradoxical, but is nevertheless sober truth. He was, however, often extremely immoderate in his language, and so conveyed an impression of something excessive and even eccentric.

[78] The Brownsonians often seem to have derived from their master a good deal of his truculence, and so defeat their own object, as he too often defeated his. But at least their passionate loyalty is a proof of the hold Brownson still has over many minds.

[79] *Works*, Vol. V, pp. 240–241.

[80] *Works*, Vol. I, p. 280.

[81] *Ibid.*, p. 270. A typical criticism of Brownson is that which appeared in the *Irish Ecclesiastical Record* (Vol. V, 1884, p. 15), written by Father John Healy: "The ontologism of Brownson is radically as untenable and as dangerous in its consequences as any of the systems which he reprehends."

[82] *America's Foremost Philosopher*, p. 109.

CHAPTER XIII

Lapse into Liberalism

On December 5, 1857, Richard Simpson said of Brownson in a letter to Father Hecker: "You know it is a law of nature. Every reformer in his old age becomes an obstructive. . . . He has turned Irishman." [1] This may have been good long-range prophecy on Simpson's part, but it was made at the very moment that Brownson was turning to liberalism. His recantation of it had to wait nearly ten years.

The word liberalism may be understood in several senses and in relation to several departments of life. In one sense—that of a broad spirit—all Catholics should be liberals, though of course their broadness cannot be indeterminate. In another sense—that of making a compromise with the world—no Catholic can be a liberal. As for theology, it is a little difficult to see why a man should be called a liberal because he rejects the greater part of historical Christianity. Yet both as a theologian and in his view of politics Brownson was accused of liberalism, or at least of liberal tendencies. After vigorously denying this at the time, he came at the end of his life to confess his guilt with almost excessive abasement.

Henry Brownson definitely places his father's liberal period as from 1860 to 1864. This is correct enough, if we regard those years as its culminating phase. But there are periods at both ends that might be included—one, while he was gradually approaching it, and the other while he was gradually edging away from it. His independence was gained in 1854, when Fitzpatrick went to Europe and Brownson was left to his own devices in regard to what went into his *Review*. But perhaps even 1850 may be taken as the date when he started on what ended as liberalism, for in that year he fell under the influence of Gioberti and began once more to air his doctrine of communion.[2] Nor can 1864 be said to have closed his liberal period. Part of it—certainly his so-called ontologism, if that is to be considered "liberal"—was never recanted. And he retained others of the leading ideas he advanced during the early 'sixties, however much modified they were, even when he made his subsequent *in globo* retractations. The fact is that it was a spirit rather than any specific doctrine that Brownson gave up. He was never involved in actual heresy, though he was twice delated to Rome (and acquitted); but he did show a harsh and bitter hyper-critical tone towards many Catholic personages and practices which he afterwards came to regret. Yet all this does not, properly speaking, constitute liberalism. As Henry Brownson wrote: "A liberal Catholic is a contradiction to himself; for so far as he is liberal he is uncatholic, and in so far as Catholic he is not liberal. Brownson, in this sense, was never a liberal Catholic." [3]

Nevertheless it is sufficiently accurate to speak of Brownson's lapse into liberalism, so long as due qualifications are made. So as to simplify the matter before elaborating it, we may regard Brownson's liberalism as all part of the new apologetic approach he was making by insisting on his Americanism in the face of what he considered reactionary elements in the Church both at home and abroad. He believed that he could thereby make Catholicism less objectionable to the mass of his fellow-countrymen, and at the same time bring the Catholic immigrants to a hearty and happy realization of their privileges as Americans. There certainly was a time when he thought that, by stating the "harder" doctrines of Catholicism softly, he might make them more acceptable to the general public. It was then that he aired speculative opinions which, though perhaps tenable by a Catholic, were such as to scandalize and pain most members of the Church, without in the least succeeding in presenting them in such a way that Catholicism became, as a whole, a whit more palatable to the non-Catholics he hoped to reach.

But before we come to that aspect of the matter, it would be as well to see what had happened to Brownson personally. This has some bearing on the case.

After two or three stormy years in New York, he left it for Elizabeth, New Jersey, where, after living first on Rahway Avenue, he found a pleasant home at 12 Pearl Street.[4] He had never cared for the social life of the great city; he wanted larger quarters and a garden where he could cultivate his roses. He felt the change would be good for his health, and he wanted to be outside of Archbishop Hughes's diocese. In James Roosevelt Bayley of Newark, who was himself a convert, he found a friend, though one who by no means accepted all his views. The future Archbishop of Baltimore called the big, gruff, hairy man *Ursa Major,*[5] and looked upon his eccentricities with good-humored tolerance.

Another reason why Brownson left New York was that he found it too expensive to live there. Henry Brownson merely indicates that his father needed to retrench because of the failure of his New York and London publishers.[6] Actually the situation seems to have been a good deal more serious than the statement would convey. For we hear several times of friends coming forward with gifts of money. Archbishop Kenrick gave him fifty dollars in May, 1857, and about the same time Hecker sent him another fifty dollars from an anonymous donor in the South.[7] After the second of his Fordham commencement addresses, and the second public attack made upon him by Archbishop Hughes, Brownson wrote to his wife that "in revenge my friends among the clergy in the City have made up a purse of $200."[8] And a little earlier a group of priests had presented him with over three hundred dollars. From all of which it is evident that Brownson was in dire straits. To rescue him a kind of "benefit performance" had been arranged in the Academy of Music in New York, when he gave a lecture, attended by 5,376 people and netting a profit of $1,018.65.[9] It was by far the largest lecture fee he ever obtained; usually he was glad to accept a hundred dollars. Without these lectures and the gifts he could hardly have

O.B. was at times in dire straits.

survived. The *Review* had suffered from the constant attacks to which he had been subjected, and many subscribers had dropped off.

In the years that followed it comes out that there were many times when the Brownson household was financially pinched. Several times money was reluctantly accepted from Henry, though Henry at other times was helped by his father. In the letter of July 17, 1860, Brownson told his wife that with the purse of two hundred dollars, and another couple of hundred which was in the bank, and the expectation of $140 for the Review and a similar sum from England, "I think we can get along till Lecture season commences." Perhaps he exaggerated when he told his daughter Sarah in 1865, "I came to Elizabeth a ruined man," [10] but it was not very far from the truth.

Worry had its effect upon even his iron nerves. And in addition to his worries he had pain that increased with every year. The gout spread from his eyes to his hands and feet, and neither Dr. Hewit nor the inspired Dr. Watson could do much to alleviate a disease which the patient provoked by the enormous quantities of meat he insisted on eating. He had always been irritable and explosive; now that he was in constant pain, he was all the more liable to make some outrageous statement. A man suffering as he was suffering cannot be expected to have the best of tempers. The *Review* was always at hand as a means for him to let off steam.

There were great mental sufferings that he also had to endure. Hardly ever did he express—at any rate in print—any sense that he was being shabbily treated by those whom he was trying to serve. Yet he must have felt their ingratitude. He could not fail to be conscious of his great powers—which he had put unreservedly, at some material loss to himself, at the service of the Catholic Church. To have nearly all the Catholic papers, and several of the most influential bishops, as enemies, must have hurt him. It is true that he seemed to go out of his way to antagonize people, and had to bear the consequences. But that did not alter the fact that he was rendering, or trying to render, every service in his power to American Catholics, and that they were often ungrateful.

On top of all this came private griefs. His son John died at the end of December, 1858. Another son, William, an officer in the Union army, was killed in an accident on July 11, 1864. And the following month his brother Edward, also an officer, was killed in battle. These happenings preyed upon Brownson's mind. How he struck his friends comes out in a letter that Acton wrote to Simpson on June 31, 1862: "[Brownson] is not sixty, and his decay is pitiful and premature; and his letter, to one who knew him, very melancholy." Acton added that it would be as well "to encourage him with fair promises, as it would be a comfort to him in deciding about giving up his review to know that he could write in another [the *Home and Foreign*] at his ease without the trouble of editing." [11] From which it is clear that in that year he was thinking of giving up what had already become a hopeless struggle. If Acton's judgment was itself premature—for Brownson was to continue working vigorously for another thirteen years—it reveals that he was already regarded as broken. A couple of years later his son noted that he looked ten years older than he was.[12] The tired old man was to gather his force again and to surprise the world; but that he was hitting harder and more wildly than ever must be accounted for on the ground of what he was going through.

But perhaps worst of all were the relations between Brownson and his daughter Sarah. This is so delicate a matter that I touch upon it at all with extreme reluctance and only because this is necessary to explain the situation. How bad that situation was is made evident by a letter which reveals that Sarah went off in August, 1865, to her brother Orestes, who was living in Dubuque, evidently intending never to return home.[13] It is this letter which Mr. Schlesinger uses to great dramatic effect on page 273 of his book, but as though the terrible words, "I am of low birth, poor, unrefined, coarse, brutal, wholly beneath my lady daughter," were spoken in a quarrel during 1873. They are, however, contained in this letter but are sand-

wiched between: "For your sake, my child, I regret that you had
not a more worthy father, one with more virtues and fewer infirmities of temper," and "God protect and help you . . . I shall love
you ever, but annoy you no more." [14]

Those last words, and others in the letter, would seem to indicate
that, when Sarah left Elizabeth, it was supposed that she might
consider herself making a final breach from her father. He therefore wrote to tell her that she must not feel that she had forfeited
all claim to his protection and support, should she ever need them
again, and that he had written no word to her brother Orestes to
prejudice him against her. "I am very glad," he added, "to have
you in my son's family where you will be loved and cherished. I
am glad that you are in a new home where you can commence
life anew with the advantages of your past experience." But it is
evident that at this same time Sarah also quarrelled with her
brother Henry, for Brownson wrote to him on November 11, 1865,
to say that Sarah had returned home, "and I believe has profited
much by her three months' stay in Dubuque. I hope when you come
that you will speak to the poor girl, without any allusions to the
past, do as I do, let bygones be bygones, and give me and your
mother the satisfaction of feeling that the few of our children that
remain to us, love one another, and embrace as brother and sister.
. . . I have said, and shall say, to Sarah nothing on the subject."
To make sure that he would come, Brownson wrote again to Henry
seventeen days later, begging him to come home for Thanksgiving,
which on that year was being kept on December 7th, "Come, if you
can, you know how my heart turns to you, and that in you are
my hopes. Do not let the fact that Sarah has returned keep you
away. Poor girl, the western Iowa has taught her some things, and
I think has cured her of some follies."

Just what the trouble was all about does not appear very clearly,
and possibly not even those concerned could have given an intelligible account of it, as is so often true in such cases. One gathers
merely that Sarah—the youngest of the family and the only girl—

was somewhat spoiled and that she had been cultivating society of which her parents disapproved. "Had you listened to your mother," her father told her, "instead of tyrannizing over her by your happy knack of falling sick when you could not have your own way, you would never have been annoyed with any surveillance of mine." Sarah's sickness, however, was very genuine, as was his own—and that neither father nor daughter recognized this would seem to be at the bottom of the unhappy state of affairs. How unhappy it was comes out in Brownson's cry, "You know not and never will know how you hindered me, and drove me to despair."

"Despair" is a strong expression, as are others in this letter. But despair can come from what seem to be trivial causes. What there can be no doubt about is that it filled Brownson's mind at this time, and that the tension had been increasing for several years. With Brownson it was an unendurable outrage upon his affection; in all likelihood he saw in this rebellion of his daughter something that was a repetition of the rebellion of the Southern States that so wrung his heart.

In this I am not seeking to fix blame on either party. How, indeed, can one blame the passionate and distraught old man, or his daughter for being so like her father? I mention it at all only because I think it casts light upon Brownson's general frame of mind, and also by way of preparing the reader for what happened when two such very Brownsonian people found themselves alone together after 1872. On July 9, 1863, Henry got an explanation which really does explain: "I am distracted with my anxieties, my health has gone. My country which I have loved so much is going and I am denounced by the Bishop of my Church. . . . It is hard, and you must not wonder if some times the gout gets into my temper, old, infirm, solitary, forsaken." [15]

Yet so as not to leave this unpleasant matter without presenting something on the other side, Sally Brownson's "savage but affectionate husband," as he signed himself, wrote to her on July 17, 1860, when she was visiting his mother: "I shall send money enough

. . . to bring you home, and so you & Sarah must on leaving empty your purses if they contain anything to Mother & Thorina." And this was during the lean summer, when there was little to spare. He concludes: "I am sure you find [Mother] a dear old lady, and Thorina is a dear good sister, my love to both of them, and to my own dear daughter." [16] Among the *Brownson Papers* there are several letters belonging to the 'seventies from Thorina (or Therina as she signed herself) and his other sister, his twin Daphne. These poor women, old and ill, wrote letters showing how strong was their love for the brother whom they could have very seldom seen since childhood—letters all the more touching because they are so badly written and so badly spelled. They also show that out of his poverty Brownson was frequently sending them substantial cheques. Daphne outlived him, but on October 27, 1875, his niece Sarah Bellamy, wrote to tell of Thorina's funeral:

"My deare uncle,
your kind letter it reached us in safty we thank you for the check their is enought all the expens we would have liked to have you. seen her we had everything nice to beary her, but; oh, shuch a change she did not look like Aunt therina . . . I Am so lonesome I donte no hardly what to do with myself, if she had lived till the first of next April it would have ben 5. years since she came to live with me . . . please write and tell me what you want don with Aunt therina things, please write for I am lonely now." [17]

Violent and perhaps overbearing as Brownson was, he nevertheless had a very warm and generous heart. It was his heart rather than his head that led him to make the mistakes that now have to be recounted.

In the matter of his new apologetic method he was, I believe, right upon the whole. But he had misjudged the situation in believing that, because his articles on questions of the day were being read by the general public he seemed to have permanently lost, he could win over that public to the Church. For instance, in 1863 he addressed an article to the Unitarians on "The Mysteries of Faith," in which he told them that "Unitarianism is not all false or all evil. Every system has its good side and its true side." The Unitarian, in his own mind, in rejecting the Trinity "was simply asserting the unity of God against tritheism, or an unintelligible form of words." [18] The too sweeping concession was made because Brownson's intention was to make a defence of the orthodox Christian position in such a way as to appeal to Unitarians. About the same time he wrote in "Faith and Theology": "Our own belief is that very few would reject our religion, if they did not confound the notions and practices of Catholics outside of the faith and the commands of the Church with her real faith and precepts." [19] It is evident that he had by now gone much further than he had intended to go in 1857; then he asserted no more than that the best mode of apologetics was to state the Catholic position, and allow it to do its own work, confident that it had the power to do so; now in 1863 he was saying, not merely that non-Catholics already had much of the truth and were seeking for its completion, which they would find nowhere but in the Church; he had begun to put Catholic doctrines in such very moderate terms as to be virtually whittling it down. It was all very well to say, as he did in 1860, that the difficulties to be overcome in converting the non-Catholic world are moral rather than intellectual and that Christ was working, even outside of His Church, to draw men to the Church and Himself; and that "at the bottom of the hearts of the most sceptical, indifferent, or worldly minded, there is a secret witness for God, for Christ, for the church. Conscience is still Catholic for most men." [20] It was something else again to attempt accommodation, as he certainly came to attempt it before he had run his liberal course to its close.

Henry Brownson—" 'Cub of the Old Bear' in cross and brightness," as Hecker once described him [21]—says that his father "yielded to an erroneous view of expediency, and encouraged a tendency which, had not divine grace restrained him from following it to its end, might have led him into error and schism." [22] The judgment

—which is aimed at Hecker—is unjust. Brownson may have taken a hint from Hecker, but in his headlong unsubtle way he had carried it much further than Hecker did. If anyone egged him on its was Dr. Cummings and Dr. Forbes. Even the apostacy of Dr. Forbes in 1859, and his reversion to the Episcopalian ministry, seemed to Brownson due to those—and he primarily meant Hughes —who "believe, or feel, or imagine that the Church is in her practical administration a spiritual despotism." He therefore regarded it as his special mission to take up an attitude that should demonstrate that "the Church is neither despotic nor leagued with despots; that neither her principles nor her interests oppose true liberalism, individual or social, and that in her teaching, faith and reason are reconcilable, and authority and private judgment, when rightly understood, are harmonious, and when they are not so, the fault is that of Catholics, not of Catholicity." [23] All of which is no doubt true, but is, at the same time, something that may easily be pushed to a point where it ceases to be true. A man of Brownson's temperament, and of his habit of overstatement, was quite unfitted to play the part of a liberal, for which he lacked the necessary finesse. For him the only alternatives were rigid conservatism, or blunt radicalism. When he found himself swept on to radicalism, he recoiled to his old position.

Henry Brownson's harsh words on Hecker were written in 1900, just after the scare that had fallen upon American Catholics because of Leo XIII's condemnation of "Americanism" the previous year—a condemnation which covered several points but which might be summed up in one—an absolute repudiation of the idea that there could be any such statement of Catholic doctrine as to accommodate it to the "modern" mind. What Henry Brownson wrote should therefore be read in the light of the *Testem Benevolentiae*. It is not quite accurate, however, to say that "after [Brownson's] removal to New York, some of his clerical friends there, with the Reverend Isaac Hecker at their head, urged that the best way to make converts in this country was to present only so much of Catholic doctrine to those not Catholic as was absolutely necessary for them to accept in order to enter the Church; and that they would be repelled rather than attracted by doctrines and practices too much opposed to their habits of belief and of conduct." [24] In other words, Catholicism was to be watered down for their consumption. But while Hecker cannot be fairly blamed, it must be admitted that the making of concessions—sometimes undue concessions—did for a while become Brownson's policy.

On Scripture he conveyed the impression that American Catholic theologians had a narrow view of its inspiration, and though he did not pronounce definitely, he raised the question whether in all cases the traditional interpretation and application must be followed.[25] At about the same time he pointed out that the doctrine of papal infallibility was not *de fide,* and that though he believed the doctrine himself as "the sounder theological opinion," a Catholic was not obliged to believe it.[26] Such views naturally caused a good deal of misgiving among Catholics, and many Protestants began to wonder how soon Brownson would find his way out of the Church. Certainly nobody was brought into it by these concessions and qualifications and speculations.

An example of Brownson's changed attitude may be found in what he wrote concerning the punishment of the lost. It is true that all that the Church positively teaches is that hell exists, that it is eternal, and that all who die out of a state of grace will go there, thus forever losing all possibility of union with God. But because the Church does not venture beyond this, it does not look with favor upon fanciful speculations on the subject, and still less upon the public airing of such speculations. Brownson now began to speculate very rashly in the pages of his *Review.*

Father John Banister Tabb, the poet, once preached at the children's Mass at Richmond, Virginia, and commenced the sermon by saying solemnly: "In all God's universe there is one, and only one, creature whom we know positively to be damned. And that creature is the Devil. But remember, my dear young friends, though the Devil is damned, he is no damn fool." [27] Upon which one may comment that one of the ways the Devil works most successfully is to make damned fools of people by getting them to believe that there is no hell: once they can be brought to that point, in most cases it is of very little practical consequence to the Devil whether or not they retain a theoretical belief in God. Which, however, is not to affirm that the kind of sermon James Joyce reports at such length in his *Portrait of the Artist as a Young Man* is the right line to take. The Church contents itself with a few statements; on these the Church is adamant.

Brownson made no positive affirmations; he merely raised some questions as to the nature and duration of the punishment of the lost. But as Henry Brownson admits, "Questions may be asked in such manner as to suggest and enforce their answers." [28] What emerged from Brownson's articles was that, though he did not doubt that hell was everlasting, its punishment might be gradually mitigated so as to allow a certain measure of what some theologians call "natural blessedness"—such as belongs to Limbo. He held that, strictly speaking, there could not be any "natural blessedness," as man was created for a supernatural end; but in so far as this natural blessedness could be said to exist, he seemed to think it might be eventually attained by the damned. [29] He protected himself by saying that they would be sufficiently wretched and added: "Our view of the case supposes as much misery for the damned as they are naturally capable of enduring." [30] What he was offering, therefore, by way of inducement for the acceptance of the Catholic doctrine of hell was nothing much.

His argument further was that, even in hell, the lost, being God's creatures, could not experience a complete and total severance from Him, without also suffering annihilation, for existence was possible only on condition that it was every instant sustained by God. It was what had been poetically expressed in the Psalm: "If I make my bed in hell, thou art there." And perhaps Brownson's expression of it was philosophically and even theologically sound. By living at all, although in an extreme of pain, the damned would retain some good. But the whole point was, after all, academic: the retention of such a good can only be a good in itself; it can hardly be conceived as a good in the eyes of those who possess it. This reminds us of the answer Dante put into the mouth of Virgil (who was quoting Aristotle) to the question whether, after the resurrection of the body, those in hell would suffer more or suffer less:

> Ritorna a tua scienza,
> che vuol, quanto la cosa è più perfetta,
> più senta il bene, e così la doglienza.[31]

But though, in the philosophical sense, those in hell will be more perfect when they obtain their bodies, if this means that they are going to suffer more than before, their perfection is assuredly not of a kind that they are going to enjoy. It is a good that God may be able to weigh, or a philosopher to acknowledge; it cannot be a good to the damned.

These purely academic opinions, being only academic, might have been allowed to pass. But Brownson asked the question: "May we not hope that the sins of this life may in some sense be expiated?"[32] And when charged in a letter to his *Review* with heresy, he would admit no more than that perhaps some inexact expressions might have escaped him, and pleaded that he had only discussed matters in which opinion is free. "It was far from our intention," he explained, "to imply, or in any manner to indicate, that the punishment of the wicked could ever absolutely end, or that they could ever fully attain to natural beatitude, in the sense that term is taken by theologians. . . . The most that can be made out of what we said is, that we thought it not contradictory to any definition of the church to concede that the sufferings of the damned may be eternally diminishing, without absolutely terminating."[33] He still stood firm for his main contention: "If we suppose hell to be a complete and absolute evil, we must suppose it to be a pure and absolute negation, therefore a simple nullity, nothing at all, and the damned in hell not to suffer, but to be annihilated. There must be, then, something good even in hell. . . . Hence, St. Augustine argues that simple existence is itself good, and says that it is better for the damned 'to exist than not to exist.' " [34]

Such speculations might be permissible but they pointed to dangerous ground, as did still more his contention: "We must be allowed to make those modifications in the human elements of the beliefs and doctrines of Catholics which the present state of non-Catholic thought and intelligence render necessary." [35] That, even if it did not mean all that was read into it, could certainly be taken as meaning that, at any rate to some extent, Catholic faith had to be suited to what non-Catholics wished it to be. Obviously Brownson had worked himself into a thoroughly bad position. He had started with the laudable hope of setting Catholic truth before the world in a new light; and he had ended, not by changing the light by which it was to be seen, but the object that was to be presented. Or so it seemed to his critics.

Yet what he was really trying to say was that "men embrace an erroneous system, and adhere to it, not for the sake of the error, but for the sake of the truth it contains." [36] He was sound when he maintained: "We do not refute false doctrines simply by pointing out their falsehood; we must do it by distinguishing between the true and the false, and showing that we accept the true, and integrate it into a higher unity. . . . In the earlier numbers of our *Review* we wrote not a few articles against Protestants and unbelievers in favor of Catholicity, which were perfectly satisfactory and conclusive to our Catholic friends, but which had little or no effect upon those who held the errors we labored to refute, except to puzzle and bewilder them. There was something not unjust in their reply: 'Your arguments are logical; they are well put; they silence, but do not convince.' " [37] He protested that he had not altered his views, but only his method of dealing with those outside the Church. Unfortunately he chose the same moment to advance a number of

opinions which, even when they might be admitted to be specula-
tively tenable, could only create a distrust of him in his Catholic
public. They could not but think that he had changed a good deal
more than his methods.

On the subject of the relation of faith and science Brownson kept
his head far better than many people of his own time. Darwin's
Origin of Species, which was published in 1859, shook the faith of
thousands. Those who managed to retain their faith, usually did
so by devising the comfortable formula that there could be no
conflict between faith and science. In effect, this too often meant
regarding all science as a waste of time, and clinging blindly to
faith. It was so in the case of the devout Plymouth Brother, Philip
Gosse, and his son describes how he dealt with his dilemma. The
patient scientific investigator, faced with new disturbing discoveries,
propounded a theory which (greatly to his annoyance) the press
represented as maintaining that God had hid the fossils in the rocks
in order to test the faith of geologists. "Geology certainly *seemed*
to be true, but the Bible, which was God's word, *was* true." [38]
Something not very dissimilar was the evasive attitude of many
Catholics.

It did not satisfy Brownson. The argument was one, he pointed
out, that can be used with as much practical effect against faith as
against science. On this basis the scientist was able to say, "There
can, if both are true, be no conflict between science and faith. We
know our science is true, and therefore that your faith, so far as it
conflicts with it, is a false faith, an impudent pretender." [39] As
against this Brownson distinguished between the opinions of scientific men (which are not always science) and the opinions of theologians, which are not always more than opinions. [40] It was therefore
not enough for Catholics to assert that there could be no conflict
between the two aspects of knowledge, but to prove there is none
by themselves entering the scientific field. "We must beat the
heterodox and unbelieving on their own ground, with their own

weapons. We must be more scientific than they, and more perfect masters of the sciences." [41] He went even further than that: "Of all people in the world . . . we Catholics are the most blameworthy, if we neglect science, or the sciences on which civilization more immediately depends. We have no excuse; the world can be saved only by the faith which we, and we alone, have in its unity and integrity, and God will demand a strict reckoning of us for the use we make of it." [42] The trouble with the scientific world, he pointed out, is that it had been content to regard science as "the simple observation of facts and inductions therefrom. . . . But the simple study and classification of phenomena is not science, for the excellent reason that nothing exists as pure phenomenon or appearance." Each science, to be successfully studied, has to be studied in its real relations. Unfortunately "we have separated the sciences from philosophy, that is, from science, and philosophy from theology, reason from revelation, and have therefore been compelled to attempt the construction of science and the sciences empirically, by the study and classification of particulars." [43] In this respect St. Thomas Aquinas was a better scientist than Sir Charles Lyell, or Professor Owen. "The recent work of Sir Charles on the *Antiquity of Man*," he said, "as well as that of Darwin on the *Origin of Species,* shows not the progress but the deterioration of science." Brownson sums up his argument with: "We are not asserting revelation as a foreign authority, or insisting that the naturalists, or physicists, are in their own department to bow to the *dicta* of the metaphysicians. We would impose no fetters on reason, no trammels on science; for the assertion of revelation as a trammel on reason, or philosophy as a restraint on science, would be to assert that very separation we complain of, that very divorce of religion and civilization which Bacon and Descartes so successfully inaugurated, and from which all modern society now suffers. What we assert is the synthesis of religion and civilization, of revelation and science, of faith and reason. . . . Faith does not restrain reason in matters of science; does not say to it, Thus far, but no further; but bids us use all the light it has, and aids it to go further than by its own light it could go." [44] Here, as elsewhere, Brownson was insisting on the integration of all knowledge. It was such an integration that he had in mind in his excursion into liberalism. If it led him into some excess, it also saved him in the end.

There is, properly speaking, no liberalism in Catholic theology. What does exist, even among the most orthodox of theologians, is a certain amount of difference of opinion, of a minor character. There are strict and less strict statements of the same doctrines. The point to remember, however, is that they are always the same doctrines. To be a Catholic at all a man must be orthodox. The term "liberal" as applied to theology by Protestants, though already freely used in Brownson's day, has no meaning in Catholicism. When Brownson was thought of as a "liberal" people had something else in mind.

It did not have precisely a political connotation, either. Brownson, though once regarded as a very wild radical, had actually been basically rather conservative in political theory long before he became a Catholic—more conservative, in fact, in his general political theory than were the bulk of his fellow Catholics in America. What was meant was that he showed a tendency towards the kind of liberalism which was condemned by Piux IX at the close of 1864 in his *Syllabus of Errors*. As that condemnation has often been misunderstood, a word or two of explanation should be offered now.

A number of specific points were singled out for the Pope's disapproval. This led to the supposition that he was making a headlong and wholesale onslaught on modern progress and civilization. What was really at issue was the frame of mind that regarded progress only under its material aspect, and placed in such progress the crown of man's being on earth. Actually there was no objection to the paraphernalia of modern life. There was, and could be, no objection to man's free use of the admirable ingenuity of man. But there was a serious objection to man's measuring the value of his life by such standards. And by now it should be obvious to everybody that, while ingenious devices may contribute to human comfort, they can also be used to increase human misery. No denial was attempted—or even implied—that scientific discoveries, or an improved machinery of living, are good things in themselves; all that the Church denied was that they constitute the *summum bonum*. When they are taken as such, they can only do great harm.

All the cant terms, "progress," "improvement," "civilization," "reaction," and so forth, have little meaning. As Gilbert Chesterton sensibly said, the word, "progress," is nothing but a metaphor of a man's walking down a road—which may very likely be the wrong road—and that so far from things tending of themselves to get better, "the only real reason for being a progressive [here for want of a better term he falls back on the one he regards as misleading] is that things naturally tend to grow worse. . . . The conservative theory would really be quite sweeping and unanswerable if it were not for this one fact." [45] So also with the other terms: a man may be a "reactionary" in the sense of trying to return to the spirit of St. Francis, or a reactionary in the sense of trying to return to the absolutism of Louis XIV; civilization may mean what Aldous Huxley has horrifyingly depicted in *Brave New World,* or what it meant in the time of Pericles, or Confucius. How shall anyone decide what is "improvement" unless he has an ideal standard towards which he is working? Hitler would consider it a decided improvement if he could kill every Jew; similarly there are other people who think that improvement would be better attained if a Jew killed Hitler.

The goal and ultimate vision are what matter. And the goal that leaves out of account the one thing important to man, his eternal destiny, cannot be good, even though it incidentally seeks to effect many things that all men would admit to be desirable objects. Brownson of course always stoutly affirmed that man's health and happiness and prosperity on earth, however legitimately they are to be sought for, are not the purpose of man's being on earth; that man, in short, does not have merely a natural but a supernatural destiny. But he did for a time come to a partial acceptance of what he had previously denounced (and was to denounce again) as "gentilism"—the effort to conform the Church to the world.

It will not be disputed that liberalism, considered even in this sense, had got hold of a truth, and a very important one. To reject the material outright would be very unCatholic. For the Church has insisted, against the recurrent heresies, that all material things are in themselves good and that some material things are capable of being transformed to the spiritual, or at least point to a spiritual significance. Especially is this true of the relation between the sexes, which may be taken as a kind of test case. It was Patmore, the Catholic poet—one not yet indeed a Catholic but one who was already on his way to the Church because of his insight into the nature of human love—who sang:

> Though love is all of earth that's dear,
> Its home, my Children, is not here;
> The pathos of eternity
> Does in its fullest pleasure sigh.

There we have an instance of the supernatural hint that the natural always gives to those ready to accept it. The sin of gentilism is not that it sets too much value on the natural but that it fails to reach beyond it. Brownson, being a political philosopher and not at all a poet, came to the problem from the political angle, though always with an eye open to its apologetic possibilities. "We gain nothing for religion," he wrote in his *Review* for July, 1861, "by standing aloof from modern civilization and denouncing it as low, earthly and unchristian, for it is not in our power to arrest its tendency." [46] But his argument almost reduces itself to the proposition that the Church must compromise with what it cannot resist, in the hope that, by doing so, it may somehow Christianize it. "If we would redeem [civilization] . . . the church must accept it, take it to herself, and breathe into it her own pure and divine spirit.

There is no intrinsic and invincible incompatibility between modern civilization and our holy religion," [47]—any more than there was between the Church and medieval society.

The antagonism that has come about is, as he sees it, mainly accidental. "The republican movements of the day have generally assumed a character of hostility to the church, we grant; but not because there was any inherent hostility between them." [48] Too often the adherents of the Church have relied on political absolutism, and this has forced reform movements into anti-clericalism. But we must not mistake what is accidental as being necessary and permanent. "Unhappily," he writes, "the friends of religion and the friends of progress fall into precisely the same error, each hold that liberty and religion are mutually repugnant one to the other." The complaint he brings against the reactionary Catholics is not that they resist reform in their capacity as citizens, but that they "attempt to bind the church to the order they defend and to render her interests inseparable from its preservation." "We may be wrong," he concludes, "but we regard the conservative cause in Europe as a lost cause." Those who tried to bind Catholicism to it, were only defeating the Catholic purpose. [49]

Brownson may have been, as he usually was, stating his case with too much force, but even Newman remarked of the times that they were those when "a man who was not extravagant was thought treacherous." [50] Brownson throughout stood as one ready to throw his weight to the side most needing his help to redress the balance. In his somewhat unsatisfactory *Conversations at Our Club,* which appeared during 1859–60, he wrote: "In 1848 the tendency was to identify Catholicity with democracy; the tendency since the *coup d'état* of December, 1851, has been to identify it with caesarism." [51] Precisely because he had opposed the extravagances of democracy, he was now opposing the extravagances of absolutism. By way of counteracting what he considered the baleful influence of Louis Veuillot over Catholics, Brownson took up his liberal attitude. It was the duty of the conservative to assume the rôle, not so much that of the radical, as of the prophet of inevitable reform. Catholics, he believed, had to recognize the signs of the times and make the necessary conformity.[52]

In the matter of his liberalism, as in that of his ontologism, Brownson was to a considerable extent under the influence of Gioberti.[53] But in both respects he went less far than the Abbate, though in the matter of attempting accommodation in apologetics he went a good deal further than Hecker, from whom, at this point, he had derived his hint. Gioberti was of course right to the extent of holding that the material things of the world were to be thankfully accepted as God's good gifts; to regard them as evil was to fall into the old error of Manicheism, or the newer errors of Calvinism and Jansenism which thought nature tainted along with a depraved humanity. He saw—and Brownson saw with him—a dialectical harmony between the material and the spiritual, body and soul, nature and grace; and to that extent both men were soundly Catholic. But they displayed at least a tendency to the opposite error —that of placing man's good here below. In the case of the average sensual man this became a search for comfort and a disinclination to accept long-suffering, patience, meekness and chastity. Pleasure was preferred to joy. In the case of men of a more spiritual and intellectual type, it became indeed an altruistic dream of human good, but in terms of earthly felicity, and a forgetfulness of St. Paul's warning about not being conformed to the world. When such liberals talked about the *Weltgeist* they imagined that, because they had a high-sounding (and foreign) word, the spirit of the world must be admirable instead of being, as it was, opposed to the spirit of Christianity.

Yet a moment's reflection should have shown them that, however admirable their ideals for human society might be, very different ideals had prevailed in the past—the *Weltgeist* of those times; and a little knowledge of human nature added to history should have informed them that the *Weltgeist* might again become a dreadful thing, as has happened among the very people who coined the expression. Unfortunately all that they could recognize was their own good intentions—which may be admitted to be good, so far as they went; what the Church saw, with its sense of history and its knowledge of man was that, when the *Weltgeist* was worshipped, what was really enthroned was things as they are. They might be positively and nakedly evil; at best they would necessarily fall short of the best. In effect, therefore, liberalism, in this sense, meant either a denial of the spiritual or its subordination to material ends and technical improvements.

This attitude towards humanity was not by any means invariably confined to those who regarded themselves as "progressives." The most ruthless absolutism, the narrowest conservatism could also have as their essential objects the same ends that the progressive postulated. The reactionary would, it goes without saying, have a different means than that of the progressive for attaining his goal, but it did not follow that the goal itself would be essentially different. If it comes to that, the progressive or radical is much more likely to retain (by virtue of his altruism) larger elements of Christianity than the reactionary commonly retains. But both are all too likely to claim that their program is religious in aspect: the reactionary identifying social stability with religion, and the radical identifying social progress with religion. Both are alike in showing a disposition to label Christ as a good party member; both are alike in rejecting the gospel of Christ. Neither perceives that Christ's kingdom is not of this world.

It must be admitted, however, that only too often the Church— or at least the Church as a local organization—has been willing to transform a proper coöperation with established government—even of an absolutist kind—into a virtual alliance with established government. This naturally seemed to the liberal an alliance with absolutism—and sometimes it actually was just that. Such an alliance invariably worked at long range to the detriment of the Church, both by alienating the mass of the oppressed and by putting the Church under the domination of the civil power as the price to be paid for protection. And since the upheaval of the French Revolution there had been a great fear of any liberal movement, with the result that large numbers of Catholics had stiffened into a support of absolutism. It was a situation that need never have occurred, and for which the Church was not the party mainly at fault. Only because the Revolution had fallen upon the Church, making of it an enemy, had the Church been forced to seek a support in the monarchical principle. Never had the Church said that the monarchical was the best, or even the preferred, form of government. It had merely taken refuge—and then only locally—in such a form of government because it had been virtually obliged to seek that refuge. Meanwhile the issue was further clouded by the fact that such Catholic protests as were made in favor of democracy—by Félicité de Lamennais, for example—were often cast in so extreme a form as almost to deify democracy and therefore to result in a condemnation that appeared to be a condemnation of democracy itself.

Brownson during his Unitarian days had read Lamennais with sympathetic interest. Now he was reading the writings of Lacordaire with equal sympathy, and he had struck up a close friendship by correspondence with the Comte de Montalembert who, like the Dominican Lacordaire, had been a disciple of Lamennais, though both of them submitted to the decision of Rome when Lamennais was condemned. They stopped far short of his extravagance, but they continued to stand in France for a Catholicism which their reactionary enemies described as "liberal" and which was certainly democratic.

Brownson did not like the word "democratic"; he said he was not a democrat but a republican, and that the United States was not a democracy but a republic.[54] Yet the objection was mainly to a word; he always insisted that he believed in democracy as the end of government and did no more than reject it as the means to that end. Strongly as he disapproved of what he called the Jacobinical spirit prevalent among extreme democrats, he agreed with them in a disapproval of absolutism. He could only feel alarm

at the way so many leading European Catholics had thrown themselves into the protecting but stifling arms of monarchy.

When Louis Napoleon's *coup d'état* occurred at the end of
December, 1851, he was one of the very few American Catholics
who did not lustily cheer the "new St. Louis," as he was absurdly
styled by his clerical flatterers. In an article on "Lacordaire and
Catholic Progress" he contrived to link his view of European politics
—especially regarding the new Emperor—with his own shift in
apologetic method. Of his former method he wrote: "It was a mistake, the commission of which separated us much further than was
necessary from our own age and country." He therefore announced
that he intended "to resume the work we should never have abandoned." [55] Then after claiming "we had true catholic principles,
true catholic thoughts, catholic aspirations and tendencies, long
before we had the happiness of being received into the church" [56]—
the reference is of course to his "doctrine of communion"—he said
that he considered that he had "carried the work of combatting
liberalism far enough." "For seven years," he continues, "we stood
alone in this country, almost in the world, among Catholic publicists
in warning Catholics against any entangling alliance with the new-
fangled caesarism of Napoleon III." [57]

It is true that he sometimes qualified his opposition to the Imperial regime in France. In August, 1856, he wrote to Montalembert
saying that, much as he disliked Napoleon's policy, he believed that
he should be sustained on the French throne. "I am a republican,"
he explained, "growing every day more so, but I see no chance for
a republic in France for a long time to come. Nothing remains but
Bonapartism. I don't like it, but I believe it the best thing practicable
within your reach." [58] The two men continued to agree, however,
in opposition to Louis Veuillot, who took the lead in whipping up
Catholic support for the Emperor; and when Veuillot wrote to
Brownson on August 28, 1856, he got a reply telling him that his
virtual identification of Catholicism with the cause of absolutism
was "very embarrassing to us who live under republican and con-

stitutional governments, and are daily and hourly called on to defend the church against the charge of being hostile to civil and political liberty." [59]

In later articles Brownson sometimes echoed the phrases found in Montalembert's letters to himself. Veuillot he considered worse than Napoleon, for the Emperor was merely doing what might be expected in serving his own interests, whereas Veuillot was doing his utmost "to enlist Catholicism on the side of Caesarism," [60] and left "no alternative between Caesarism and red republicanism." But Veuillot had largely won over French Catholics. "As far as the bishops and clergy of a single nation can," Brownson said indignantly, "those of France confirmed the standing charge of the enemies of the Church that her existence in a state is incompatible with its political and civil liberty." [61]

In this particular case Brownson not only shows a much keener insight than most of his Catholic contemporaries, but expresses views that have a striking modern parallel. The pretence of the Emperor that his absolutist methods were necessary as a safeguard against socialism, Brownson brushed aside as unfounded, pointing out that the French republic had already defeated the socialists. Almost the same argument has been used in our own time—especially in America—in favor of fascism. It still seems to be forgotten that whatever support individual Catholics give to any form of absolutism can only work to the undeserved discredit of the Church.

Brownson's attitude towards Napoleon III gave grave offence to many American Catholics, though afterwards it was rather generally admitted that he had been right all along and that they had been wrong. On top of all this and the philosophical and theological ideas he threw out, and that were often regarded as dubious if not subversive, came what seemed an unaccountable reversal of his position towards the temporal power.

He had got himself into hot water in the 'fifties by defending, as a corollary to the primacy of the spiritual, the indirect (or judicial deposing power of the Pope. It was logical enough but admittedly only academic, as even Brownson did not claim that that power could be effectively used in the world constituted as it was. Now he seemed to swing to the opposite extreme by attacking the temporal power of the Pope.

Actually he did not attack it at all. Writing in 1859 on "The Roman Question," he fully acknowledged that "the Roman states are the patrimony or possessions of the Holy See." [62] But he went on to say, what was obvious, that "the special assistance of the Holy Ghost . . . is not granted [the Pope] as temporal ruler" of the papal states, and that "the pope . . . as temporal sovereign, can no more be Caesar than Caesar can be pope." [63] His rights, Brownson pointed out, "though originating in the fact of his being pope, do not derive from his spiritual sovereignty." Therefore, "if the interests of religion in his judgment imperatively demand it, the pope can alienate his temporal sovereignty." [64] Yet two years later Brownson had advanced his position, so that he could write: "[The possession of the papal states] may have been necessary, or, at least, useful, in times past; . . . but we are not certain that it is either the one or the other in the present changed circumstances of the political world." [65] While he still recognized the Pope's right of sovereignty, and regarded his dispossession as unjust, he considered the assertion of the temporal power as impracticable.[66] In his view the subjects of the papal states had precisely the same rights against the Pope, as secular ruler, as any other people had against their prince.[67] He felt, as Henry Brownson remarks, it very awkward to try to defend the Church against the common accusation of hostility to free political institutions, "if obliged to defend the Pope's temporal government as essential to the Pontiff's freedom and independence." [68]

The shortest summary of what he held on this matter is the one he gave in a letter, dated April 15, 1862, to the Philadelphia *Herald and Visitor:* "I have never opposed the temporal sovereignty of the Pope in the Ecclesiastical States, nor urged its surrender, save on

the hypothesis that it is already virtually gone and cannot be effec
tively sustained. . . . Assuming this, I suggested, argued, if you will
that the voluntary surrender by the Holy Father of his tempora
principality . . . would contribute more to the political and socia
interests of the Peninsula, and to the interests of Catholicity, both
in Italy and elsewhere, than a prolonged and unavailing struggle t
maintain it against the almost universal popular sentiment. I may o
may not have been wrong in this opinion but you will not preten
that it is not an opinion which a good Catholic may hold." He wind
up his letter by declaring: "Neither you nor your *confrères* will eve
drive me into heresy or schism. . . . Never was I more worthy o
the confidence and support of Catholics than I am now; never wa
my Catholic faith firmer, or my filial devotion more unreserved."

What must be admitted is that some of the expressions he use
regarding the Pope were lacking in respect. His explanation wa
that he was not so much expressing his own feelings as those of th
Italian patriots,[70] something he by no means made clear in h
articles. Moreover, in some of his theological discussions, he ha
a tendency to show off his virtuosity as a walker on the tight-rop
Time after time he boasted that he knew the precise line th
divides orthodoxy from heresy; "though we may at times find
necessary to come plump up to it, we have, and have had, no di
position to pass beyond it."[71] People should understand that h
"bold assertions and free strictures" were the marks not of a wea
but a strong faith. Possibly so, but it was hardly to be wondered
that Catholics of the more timid sort were not so sure about h
safety, especially as he selected this particular moment to make wh
many took as disedifying comments on certain popular Catho
devotional practices. The devotion to the Sacred Heart—at any ra
in some of the forms it took—had never appealed to him, and
said so.[72] He pointed out that the wearing of Our Lady's scapular
actually he always wore one himself—was, if taken as a guarant
against eternal punishment, "mere superstition, and not a harml

superstition either." [73] And what had once been an unbounded reverence for the clergy and the bishops of the Church he confessed had become considerably diminished as a consequence of his own experience of them. [74] Though he never failed to draw a due distinction between the man and his office, those who heard him talk or read him, sometimes supposed him anti-clerical. Like his friend Montalembert, he had discovered that "*good* Catholics or so-called people are not always *honest,* and care very little for honesty, still less for *honor,* which is the flower and fragrance of honesty"; [75] and he indiscreetly proclaimed his discovery. Sometimes the cases he cited were trivial. [76] What was not trivial was that Brownson was getting a reputation, not merely for truculence and eccentricity, but for a hypercritical attitude towards much that Catholics treated with reverence. As Father Hewit said of him after his death: "He remained . . . as many of the old, heroic Christians who were converted from heathenism did, more or less, the lion of the forest, with many of the idiosyncracies and other characteristics, the product of his past history, but partially subdued and modified." [77]

Yet he was, in his own way, very pious. He said the rosary every day and meditated constantly upon the mysteries of the faith. Cardinal Manning, when writing to him, remarked that their devotion to the Holy Ghost was a bond they had in common. [78] And Brownson let it out, in a letter to the future Bishop McMullen that, while writing one of the most offensive of his articles—the one on "The Rights of the Temporal" he had been to communion four times. [79] His was a piety of a practical and unobtrusive sort which, if it was untouched with mysticism, was also free of the sentimentality which some people suppose to be spirituality. What he need not have done was to have gone out of his way to vent opinions which struck many people as temerarious if not actually heretical. These inevitably caused scandal and gave his enemies weapons to use against him. People had not forgotten his past. Even those who put nothing into words, arched their eyebrows to imply that Brownson was on his way back to Protestantism.

Some of his friends did what they could to advise him. Fathe Gresselin, the Jesuit, who had been his confessor, wrote on Decembe 30, 1860, to warn him, "You strike too hard." [80] And Bishop Lue of Fort Wayne wrote to say: "You seem to me to carry even delicat questions to their *extreme logical consequences* without paying a tention to their *practical bearings or results. . . .* For the last s months or more, I have spoken with several bishops, priests, an others, *your real friends and well-wishers,* and they all desire an are extremely anxious to see you drop, for the present, all tho irritating questions which have been the source of so much calumn and personal abuse against you." [81] When William Elder, the Bishc of Natchez, admonished him in the same vein, Brownson replie "I do not complain that Catholics oppose me. I complain that I a unfairly opposed, on some collateral point, or for some accident reason, never on the real issue, or on the merits of the questic itself." [82] He explained that his was an unusual method—that using a language, which, though it might have a non-Catholic sour in Catholic ears, conveyed a Catholic sense to non-Catholics. U fortunately this was not the case; to both parties it sometim sounded unCatholic. But so far from taking Elder's letter as it w meant, Brownson raged against the way the bishops had of putti up their diocesan organs to attack him instead of telling him direct what was amiss. "All I say is," he declared hotly, "you may kill n Review, but you cannot manage me through newspapers." [83]

Elder sent him another and still longer letter—a model of kindn —on July 26, 1861, mildly remarking that Brownson could n reasonably expect the bishops to write him private letters abo everything they disapproved of in his *Review.* "I must simp inform you that you are mistaken totally with regard to our spi . . . A great portion of the censure which has been put on you I been owing to your not expressing your meaning until after [yo own] censure has been given." He continued: "The great outc against your articles on the Temporal Power of the Pope, so years ago, arose in great measure from your not explaining in t beginning what you did explain at last after prejudices had been pretty solidly formed . . . that the power was not *temporal*, but *spiritual*, affecting indeed temporal things, but only in their spiritual relations." [84] The Bishop believed Brownson might say nearly all that he did say, providing it was attempted in the proper spirit. "But there is where you fail. You do it in a spirit of grumbling, of general censure of the most odious kind on the Catholic clergy— of holding us all up as wilfully guilty of the obnoxious charge made against us by the most bigoted Protestants." [85] As Brownson had pleaded that he had had his confessor's approbation for what he had written, Elder told him that, in that case, "he is not a safe man for you to intrust your conscience to. He may be a profound theologian, and an acute reasoner, but he is not a *discreet practical* guide for one in your position." [86] A less friendly critic than Elder, Bishop Wood of Philadelphia, a year later announced in his paper that *Brownson's Quarterly Review* was no longer to be regarded as a Catholic periodical "or a reliable exponent of Catholic doctrines and principles." [87] Though Brownson had some right to object that much of the opposition to him was disingenuous, there can be no doubt that he laid himself wide open to the shafts of his enemies.

Edward Gibbon once said that a man should be careful to avoid attacking institutions. To attack an individual was to attack someone who would eventually die. The institution lived on and neither forgot nor forgave. Henry Brownson—who had himself been a Jesuit novice—said truly that his father committed "a mistake, a grave mistake, to butt his head against the Society of Jesus." [88] Brownson charged them with being the leaders of the obscurantists, with a philosophical system to some extent outmoded, and believed that, because they were a military order under a foreign general, they were out of sympathy with American democracy.[89] For these reasons they had exhausted their usefulness. "All that is the work of man's hands grows old and changes, though the men are moved by the Holy Ghost, as, no doubt, was St. Ignatius; and though they are the greatest and best men that ever lived. Decay and death are written on the face of every thing human, and they who would follow their Lord must leave 'the dead to bury their dead.'" [90]

That was written because Brownson considered that the Jesuits had shown themselves insufficiently devoted to the Union cause during the Civil War. It was, however, remembered against him long after the Civil War. So also was what he said about the Jesuit school of theology: "We regard their system as the weakest and least philosophical of all the systems of Catholic theology that have been emitted. . . . The Jesuit may differ from me, refute me by natural reason, or by what is called the *ratio theologica,* if he can; but he must not denounce me, or pretend that I am unsound in the faith, for my opinion is as free in the church as his; nor is it permitted me to denounce or defame him, for his opinion is as free as mine." But as he immediately added, "Under the influence of the society, as we believe, theology has become a dead science," [91] the Jesuits cannot reasonably be blamed for feeling that he had defamed them. Nor is it any wonder that they questioned Brownson's orthodoxy, by way of retort to a man who had bluntly asserted that what they held might be a permissible opinion but was not Catholic doctrine.[92] That Gioberti had been openly their antagonist, and that Brownson had borrowed some of his ideas from Gioberti, was an additional reason for regarding him with suspicion.

To attack the Jesuits' philosophical orthodoxy, and even their theological orthodoxy, was of course a deadly offence. To make matters worse, if possible, Brownson wrote slightingly of *The Spiritual Exercises,* the occasion being a new exposition of that famous work. He gave, it is true, praise to St. Ignatius and a kind of commendation to the *Exercises,* saying that if a uniform mode of meditation had to be adopted, he did not doubt that this method would prove the best for general purposes. "But," he added rather loftily, "we have for ourselves always found it impossible to meditate after any prescribed method or formula." [93] His review was mild enough, and might have been written without his having read the book supposedly under consideration—as may have been the case. But when he commented: "We are disposed sometimes to think that piety is weakened, and spiritual growth stunted by the very multiplicity of appliances for their nurture and progress. We have too many helps, and are the weaker Christians for it," [94] he touched the Jesuits again on a very sort spot. And he was the last man in the world who could afford to do so.

Reviewing Montalembert's *L'Église libre dans l'État libre,* he again went out of his way to criticize the Jesuits, who were by now almost an obsession with him. Their magazine, the *Civiltà Cattolica,* he described as "the organ of a society which has outlived its day and generation, and which is now not inaptly symbolized by the barren fig-tree of the Gospel." [95] "The world went on, and as [the Society of Jesus] neither would or [*sic*] could go on with it, the world went on without it. . . . [The Jesuits] are good men, learned men, excellent scholars, earnest, devoted, and self-sacrificing priests, none more so in the church; but they understand not the work of this age." [96] But when he wrote that at the Council of Trent "there were no dogmatic questions that could not have been adjusted [to the satisfaction of Germany, England and Scandinavia] without serious difficulty," he raised some doubts as to whether he understood the past. And when he further asserted: "There were bishops at the Council of Trent who differed, before the decisions were arrived at, from the doctrine finally declared at the Council, as widely as did Luther or Calvin," [97] the inference is that a different doctrine—supposing *per impossibile* that a different doctrine could have been accepted—would have been equally Catholic. It was not precisely what he meant, but it was the sense that his words could be made to bear.

As might have been expected, Brownson was delated to the Congregation *de Propaganda Fide*. Who brought the charges we do not positively know, though Henry Brownson hints at Hughes, while his father believed it was Purcell. [98] In any event the charges

Brownson and Rome

failed. Propaganda was somewhat puzzled by Brownson's position on the Temporal Power, but could find no heresy in it and expressed itself as satisfied with his explanations and the assurance: "If my *Review* 'has gone astray,' I am anxious that it should at the earliest moment return to the true path, and I assure his eminence [Cardinal Barnabò] that I have no pride of opinion to gratify, and that the Holy See will always find me a docile and obedient subject."

William George McCloskey, who was at the time Rector of the North American College at Rome, wrote in 1900, when he was Bishop of Louisville, to Henry Brownson, giving an account of how Cardinal Barnabò strongly deprecated the attacks that had been made on Brownson. Had not the Cardinal been a very small man and the Reviewer of the build of Daniel Webster, only several inches taller, McCloskey would have thought he had the fiery, shaggy old Doctor before him.[100] It was one more instance of how much more level-headed the Roman authorities so often are than the men locally in charge.

This, however, was not precisely a certificate of approbation from the Pope; all that was conveyed was that no ground for condemnation had been discovered. Rome had been displeased by the articles on the Temporal Power. But the failure of his enemies enabled Brownson to announce: "Heretofore on theological questions our articles have, for the most part, been submitted to theological revision and censorship before publication; hereafter they will not be so submitted. . . . [But] each number as it appears will be sent to Rome, and any corrections of any sort the Holy See may require or suggest will be most cheerfully made."[101] He proceeded to explain that this is not what it has been taken to be, "a bold defiance of episcopal authority, and the proud declaration that the editor of the *Review* will recognize no court, but the court of last resort." Yet the very title he used, "The Church Not a Despotism," managed to imply that despots were sometimes to be met with in particular bishops. He rubbed in his triumph with: "We hope this explanation will prove satisfactory to all who are willing to be satisfied, and convince those who secretly try to get condemned at Rome a man who is wearing his life out in the cause they profess to have at heart, that Rome only acts with deliberation, and with a sense of justice." [102] Having said which, he reaffirmed the essence of his "liberalism" by declaring: "reform . . . touching the relations between religion and civilization, understanding by *civilization* all that can be included under the terms of human organization and human culture, is needed by the church, and in the church now. For such a reform, on and by Catholic principles, we confess, we look and labor as the means of bringing back the world to Catholic unity, and advancing the cause both of religion and civilization, the church and society." [103]

After that bit of truculence, he put in another word, equally characteristic of the man: "Err we may, inaccurate in our expression we sometimes may be, but we hope we know enough not to follow our errors so far as to get out of the orthodox communion, and we have humility enough—though, we confess, we have no humility to boast of—to correct our errors when we see them, and to recoil from the abyss when we behold it yawning before us." [104]

[1] *Hecker Papers.* Curiously enough Brownson wrote much the same thing to Hecker himself, but not until March 18, 1868: "The truth is I am beginning to be once more an *oscurantisti.* . . . I never had a spice of real radicalism in my composition . . . I think I am turning Paddy." (*Ibid.*).

[2] In *The Spirit-Rapper,* however, which was published in 1854, he gave an imaginary account of a meeting with Gioberti, even contriving the episode of a European tour for his hero for that very purpose. There he chiefly condemns Gioberti for his "gentilism" while following him to some extent in his ontologistic theories.

[3] *Latter Life,* p. 307.

[4] The house is still standing, reconditioned, but is now 115 Pearl St.

[5] Lathrop, *Atlantic Monthly,* Vol. LXXVII (1896), p. 779.

[6] *Latter Life,* p. 197.

[7] *Ibid.,* pp. 88, 91.

[8] Letter in possession of Mrs. Odiorne. It is dated July 17, 1860.

[9] *Latter Life,* pp. 128–128 fn.

[10] This is from a letter in the *Brownson Papers,* undated but written in August, 1865.

[11] Gasquet, *Lord Acton and His Circle,* p. 289.

[12] *Latter Life,* p. 438.

[13] This letter is among the *Brownson Papers* at Notre Dame. Though the first

page is missing (and with it the date) I am able to assign it definitely to August, 1865, on the strength of internal evidence.

[14] Quite possibly this letter was never sent. Sarah did not keep the one that preceded it (to which it makes reference), so we may suppose she would have destroyed this one also had she received it. Brownson had a way of keeping back his angrier letters, or of considerably softening what he had written in first draft. These and other letters drawn upon for the first time by Mr. Schlesinger were in Henry Brownson's possession, but were not used by him when he was writing his father's biography. After Henry's death, his widow sent all the papers he had— apparently without looking to see what they contained—to Notre Dame University, where they are now carefully preserved. I shall have occasion to refer to them again in my concluding chapter.

[15] *Brownson Papers.* The previous year he had written to his son: "I am perplexed and half distracted with troubles of all sorts." (*Latter Life,* p. 422).

[16] Letter in possession of Mrs. Odiorne.

[17] *Brownson Papers.*

[18] *Works,* Vol. VIII, p. 29.

[19] *Ibid.,* p. 21.

[20] *Works,* Vol. XX, p. 103.

[21] In a letter scrawled at the foot of one written to him by Father W. Lockhart of London, dated Good Friday, 1887, and answered by Hecker on May 16, 1887. (*Brownson Papers*).

[22] *Latter Life,* pp. 262, 305.

[23] *Latter Life,* p. 194, 195–196. Dr. Cummings' death in January, 1866, may have had something to do with Brownson's reversion to conservatism.

[24] *Latter Life,* p. 262. This was a serious misstatement of Hecker's purpose. But it was the easiest way to exculpate his father by blaming his father's friend.

[25] *Works,* Vol. XX, pp. 124–125.

[26] *Works,* Vol. VIII, p. 13.

[27] Francis A. Litz, *Father Tabb,* p. 38.

[28] *Latter Life,* p. 266.

[29] For this view he was severely taken to task by William George Ward in the *Dublin Review.* Brownson's claims to be a theologian were rather loftily dismissed (Vol. LIV, 1864, p. 59), and Brownson's views were identified with those that were advanced by Baius and taken over by the Jansenists, "affirming that God could not have created man in a merely natural state, but must have destined him for a supernatural end; and consequently must have endowed him with supernatural means (called by Baius, in accordance with his system, natural) for the attainment of that end." (P. 71. See also pp. 72–76).

[30] *Works,* Vol. XX, p. 196.

[31] Return to thy science, which has it, that the more a thing is perfect, the more it feels pleasure and likewise pain.

—*Inferno,* VI, 106–108. John Aitken Carlyle's translation.

[32] *Works,* Vol. XX, p. 124.

[33] *Ibid.,* pp. 147, 148.

[34] *Ibid.,* p. 151. Here of course Brownson seems to be using the word "good" in two different senses—the technical one and the ordinary one—which is a little confusing.

[35] *Ibid.*, p. 127.

[36] *Ibid.*, p. 140.

[37] *Ibid.*, pp. 140, 141.

[38] Sir Edmund Gosse, *Father and Son* (popular edition, 1916), pp. 108, 121.

[39] *Works*, Vol. IX, p. 255.

[40] *Ibid.*, p. 256.

[41] *Ibid.*, p. 260.

[42] *Ibid.*, p. 261.

[43] *Ibid.*, pp. 262, 264.

[44] *Ibid.*, pp. 265, 266.

[45] *Orthodoxy* (English ed.), p. 210.

[46] *Works*, Vol. XVIII, p. 439.

[47] *Ibid.*, p. 440.

[48] *Ibid.*, p. 440.

[49] *Ibid.*, pp. 441, 442, 443.

[50] Ward, *Newman*, Vol. I, p. 10.

[51] *Works*, Vol. XI, p. 291.

[52] *Works*, Vol. XX, p. 238.

[53] *Latter Life*, p. 338.

[54] In this he was like his friend Calhoun, who said it was a pity that his party had given up the old name of *Republican*—leaving the Whigs free to adopt it—and had taken instead the misleading name of *Democratic*.

[55] *Works*, Vol. XX, p. 251.

[56] *Ibid.*, p. 253.

[57] *Ibid.*, p. 254.

[58] *Latter Life*, p. 47. This was in reply to a long letter from Montalembert in which the Count showed his disapproval of one of Brownson's articles by writing to him in French instead of English. This coolness did not last long.

[59] *Ibid.*, p. 54.

[60] *Ibid.*, p. 175.

[61] *Ibid.*, p. 176.

[62] *Works*, Vol. XVIII, p. 418.

[63] *Ibid.*, pp. 418, 427–428.

[64] *Ibid.*, p. 428.

[65] *Ibid.*, p. 432.

[66] *Ibid.*, pp. 433, 434.

[67] *Works*, Vol. XII, p. 387.

[68] *Latter Life*, p. 187.

[69] *Ibid.*, pp. 285, 286.

[70] *Ibid.*, p. 225.

[71] *Works*, Vol. XX, p. 303.

[72] For that matter, he maintained his position to the end. In the July, 1874, issue of his *Review*, he was still saying "there are fashions in devotion as well as in dress" and making it clear that he was not attracted by this "fashion," as he regarded it. (Pp. 422–423). And when a Jesuit wrote a letter of protest to the *Review* (pp. 532–536), Brownson defended himself, saying that he always gathered that the adoration of the Sacred Heart was to be in a "material sense," and not simply as "a special form of adoring God in his humanity, a form far less attractive to us than adoration of him in the Blessed Sacrament." (P. 547). The fact that his critic sent

a hundred dollars with his letter, may be taken as conclusive proof that he did not regard Brownson as too outrageous.

[73] *Works,* Vol. XII, p. 378.

[74] *Latter Life,* p. 278.

[75] *Ibid.,* p. 432.

[76] For instance, writing in 1857, he made a great fuss over the fact that Hughes had let him know that he disapproved of "several paragraphs" in the *Review,* and that afterwards, when writing an article, the Archbishop had enlarged this into "many articles." (*Works,* Vol. XX, p. 69). It was hardly more than a form of words: there is no doubt that Hughes disapproved of a great deal that Brownson was writing at that time.

[77] *Catholic World,* Vol. XXIII (1876), p. 371. Ward in the *Dublin Review* put it a good deal more severely: "From having been the ardent and uncompromising champion of authority, he has come to assume towards it a tone often captious and disrespectful, sometimes even bordering on the defiant and disloyal. He has, moreover, exhibited a decided partiality for doctrines and modes of speech that, to use the very mildest terms, have in them a sound that is both novel and harsh." (Vol. LIV, 1864, pp. 58–59).

[78] *Latter Life,* pp. 273, 274.

[79] *Ibid.,* p. 210. See also his letter to Bishop Elder (*Ibid.,* p. 229).

[80] *Ibid.,* p. 205. See also p. 261. This second letter was printed in the *Review* for October, 1861, and may be found quoted in the *Works,* (Vol. XX, 130–132). Gresselin wrote about this time to Mother Hardey, the Vicar of the Society of the Sacred Heart in America: "Do not give up your subscription to the *Review.* . . . Let us not forget the eminent services that Brownson has rendered to religion, and which he is yet to render. If he is wrong on many points, those who pursue and abandon him are still more guilty." (Margaret Williams, *Second Sowing,* p. 341).

[81] *Latter Life,* pp. 219, 220. This was on November 29, 1860. He suggested as better topics, hell and the Catholic view of the slavery question—topics on which Brownson did write, only to provoke further criticism.

[82] *Ibid.,* p. 227.

[83] *Ibid.,* pp. 228–229.

[84] *Ibid.,* pp. 233, 235.

[85] *Ibid.,* p. 236, 237.

[86] *Ibid.,* p. 240.

[87] *Ibid.,* p. 287.

[88] *Latter Life,* p. 420.

[89] *Works,* Vol. XX, p. 365.

[90] *Ibid.,* p. 366.

[91] *Ibid.,* p. 283.

[92] *Ibid.,* p. 282.

[93] *Works,* Vol. XIV, p. 579.

[94] *Ibid.,* p. 580. The Jesuits have had their system severely criticized by some of the older orders; but what they could accept with a good grace when it came from Benedictines or Dominicans, they were not at all disposed to accept from a layman who was notoriously not very sympathetic to asceticism.

[95] *Works,* Vol. XX, pp. 309–310.

[96] *Ibid.,* pp. 310–311.

[97] *Ibid.,* p. 315.

[98] *Works,* Vol. VIII, p. 26. Of Hughes he wrote: "He was not one of those who preferred charges against us to the Holy See; but in the very height of the opposition wrote us that he had written to Rome, giving the Holy See assurances of his full confidence in our personal orthodoxy." (*Works,* Vol. XIV, p. 496). The letter in question, as published in *Latter Life* (pp. 257–258) hardly bears this out, and Henry Brownson acidly comments, "Almost every sentence . . . is contradictory of what we have seen to be the facts." (*Ibid.,* p. 257).

[99] *Latter Life,* pp. 254, 255.

[100] *Latter Life,* p. 260. Father Hewit says that Cardinal Franzelin, who was then professor at the Roman College, was deputed to examine Brownson's writings. (*Catholic World,* Vol. XXIII, 1876, p. 373).

[101] *Works,* Vol. XX, p. 215.

[102] *Ibid.,* pp. 220–221.

[103] *Ibid.,* p. 223.

[104] *Ibid.,* p. 223.

CHAPTER XIV

The Patriot

Though Henry Brownson sets his father's "liberal" period between 1860 and 1864, he admits in his introduction to the eleventh volume of the *Works* that a gradual change was noticeable after 1855.[1] I should say that it really began with the 1854 articles about the Nativists and the Irish, for though there was nothing specially "liberal" about them, it was by stressing his Americanism that Brownson was forced along the liberal path. The attacks made upon him by those who misinterpreted what he said about the Irish, and who showed their animosity on this ground, could be borne with a reasonable degree of equanimity; so also could the disapproval of those who felt that his insistence on the indirect deposing power of the Pope was embarrassing. As for the metaphysical doctrines Brownson began to air as early as 1850, they remained matters of abstract discussion—which may also be said of some of his peculiar theological ideas. But everything else had a close relationship to his strongly American feelings, as had his new apologetic mode of approach to his non-Catholic fellow-countrymen. Probably, however, none of these factors would have led him to take his extreme stand had the Civil War not broken out. Then his patriotism burned fiercely, and because he saw (or thought he saw) American Catholics to be often deficient in loyalty, he took up an attitude more and more antagonistic towards them. It was not in the least antagonistic towards the officials of the Church, though it was often taken as such. He was so anxious to vindicate, as an American Catholic, his American patriotism, that he accentuated whatever there was of excess in his liberalism.

318

He now found that he had a new opportunity for regaining the ear of the general public. Only with languid interest had they listened to him since his conversion, except for those who searched the pages of his *Review* for passages that might be garbled and used against the Church. Now he was being listened to by an audience he thought lost forever; it was because he was speaking as a patriot. But while most of his articles and lectures were on public affairs, he was also glad to use this opportunity to induce the more fair-minded non-Catholics to hear or read something about religion.[2] Especially by his speeches he did much to increase the loyalty of the Northern states, where many people at the beginning of the war were still confused as to its issues. It was heartening to him to find that he was not so completely forgotten as he had supposed among those who had been his friends. He was greatly in demand as a speaker, and never had he shown such power on the platform.[3] We hear of President Lincoln himself attending one of Brownson's lectures in Washington; and his acquaintance at Brook Farm, Horace Greeley, suddenly woke up to his existence and called him the "ablest of all the Catholic writers who use the English language."[4]

The lecturing saved the family fortunes—but only just barely saved them. The *Review* had lost two-thirds of its subscribers, including all those who had taken it in the South and many of those in the North, for Brownson's stand against slavery was not popular among Catholics.[5] If he refused to let his *Quarterly* die, this was out of a sense of duty, for he felt that he had an obligation to keep Catholics informed. Yet his lectures, though many, were not particularly profitable. Two out of many family letters indicate how empty the coffers were. On January 25, 1863, he wrote to his wife from the Middle West to say that his trip promised "fair." "Send Mother ten or twenty dollars, & pay such bills as you have money for. . . . I trust to be able to continue the Review. Tell dear Sarah to keep up her spirits, and give her my love & blessing, I shall one of these days have something for her."[6] The following July 9th he thanks his son Henry for forty dollars. He says he badly needed the money, but "it seemed to me as though I was taking your blood."[7]

Though there were many matters on which Brownson's judgment was bad—in thinking, for example, that "the South threatens terribly, but will submit," [8] and in his too high estimate of second-rate men like Frémont and his contempt for Lincoln—he was nearly always worth listening to. On the central question of slavery he was one of the few Catholics who had something of importance to say. He agreed with the majority among them only in not being an abolitionist. But what with the Irish was a dislike of the Yankee and a fear that the freeing of the Negroes would work to their own economic disadvantage,[9] was with Brownson something very different. When it became a question of saving the Union, he was one of the first to demand emancipation of the slaves.

As against the South he maintained, with the bulk of Northerners, that not secession but rebellion was involved. And he pointed out that though "we may, as Catholics, lawfully resist tyranny or usurpation, . . . we cannot conspire to overthrow a legitimate government, which has not transcended its constitutional powers, or resist its authority without failing not only in our civil, but in our Catholic duty." [10] The principle he proclaims himself to be defending here, he says, is the same that he had defended for years against the revolutionists of Europe. On this ground he had repelled with indignation the charge that Catholics could not be loyal Americans. Now he was obliged to admit, "The assertion . . . has not been entirely justified. The conduct of our Catholic population, especially that of their leaders, has not wholly answered our expectations." [11] Of the twelve Catholic journals published in English, he noted that only two of them, the one at Pittsburgh and the *Tablet* of New York could be called "decidedly loyal." A couple of others were occasionally loyal, and the *Metropolitan* was, "when last we read it, striving hard to be both sides. All the rest are really secession sheets." As for the clergy, the majority everywhere had Southern sympathies and a portion of them, "a small minority, we hope, are decidedly disloyal." He made some allowances for the *Te Deums* rumored to have been sung by the Bishops of Charleston and Richmond after the fall of Fort Sumter, but declared that, if the fact were as reported, they were "doing all in their power to justify the Know-nothings in their grave charges against the loyalty of Catholics." [12]

On the other hand, he pointed to the fact that Catholics had volunteered for the armed forces out of all proportion to their numbers in the general population; [13] and when the draft riots broke out in 1863 he denied that they gave any "confirmation to the standing charge against the Catholic Church. . . . [They] may prove that all Catholics are not what they should be, and even that our clergy may have been remiss in their duty to instruct and look after the morals of their people . . . but not that the church is disloyal, or incompatible with republican freedom, or national unity and independence." [14] He had often to distinguish between the Church and those who belong to it. He could do so while emphatically asserting: "It is undeniable that no religious body in the country stands so generally committed to slavery and the rebellion, or as a body have shown so little sympathy with the effort of the government to save the unity and life of the nation, as the Catholic. This fact is known, and we need not be surprised to find it some day made use of to our prejudice." [15] Though his assertions were much too sweeping, we may at least draw a little comfort when we set Brownson's accusations against American Catholics at the time of the Civil War with the situation today. Those who have thought that the isolationism of Catholics and the tendency of a few individuals among them towards fascism will recoil upon the Church may discount their fears. The alleged Catholic disloyalty in the early 'sixties, in so far as it existed at all, was soon forgotten. Instead of the Know-nothings being able to make capital out of it, the War destroyed them utterly. Catholics, whatever may have been their lack of enthusiasm at the first clash of arms, soon came to do their share, and more than their share, in fighting for the preservation of the Union.

Moreover, much of what looked to Brownson like disloyalty was not really disloyalty at all; it was merely a different means of reaching the same end that he was striving for. For instance, Archbishop Hughes, with whom Brownson had a controversy on the relation of slavery to the war, was anxious only to prevent American Catholics from getting it into their heads that the war was being fought for the emancipation of the Negroes; otherwise he knew that their loyalty would suffer. He put his position in a letter to Simon Cameron, the Secretary of War: "There is being insinuated in this part of the country an idea to the effect that the purpose of the war is the abolition of slavery in the South. If that idea should prevail among a certain class, it would make the business of recruiting slack indeed. The Catholics, so far as I know, whether of native or foreign birth, are willing to fight to the death for the support of the constitution, the Government, and the laws of the country. But if it should be understood that, with or without knowing it, they are to fight for the abolition of slavery then, indeed, they will turn away in disgust from the discharge of what would otherwise be a patriotic duty." [16] To suggest that Brownson was "insinuating" this was itself a masterpiece of insinuation. For Brownson was already advocating the abolition of slavery by presidential proclamation as a means of winning the war. What he did not say was that the ending of slavery was the object of the war.

Hughes, however, showed a good deal of disingenuousness in this matter. He denied that he had written the article on slavery that appeared in the *Metropolitan,* or rather he told a French interviewer that he had not "signed" the article. Brownson was not to be deceived by this equivocation. To Montalembert he wrote: "The Archbishop wrote, that is, dictated the article in question. . . . It was written for the express purpose of checking the anti-slavery sentiment of the country, and to bring the pro-slavery prejudices almost universal among the Irish Catholics of this country to bear in crushing me and my Review. The Archbishop is a man whose word cannot be relied on, and he remembers to speak the truth only when truth best serves his purpose." [17] Later, finding all subterfuges unavailing, Hughes made no further pretense that the denunciation of Brownson did not come from him. To Seward he confided, "If I had not corrected the reviewer's position, he would have done vast mischief, without, I think, intending it, to the struggle in which the country is now engaged." [18] Good as the Archbishop's intentions no doubt were—and tactless as Brownson may have been in insisting on the fact that slavery was at the bottom of the war—it was Hughes who came to grief in the controversy that followed.

Brownson opened his reply in the January, 1862, issue of his *Review* by apologizing to his readers for taking any notice of such a miserable rag as the *Metropolitan*. He does so only, he explains, because an article in it "was actually written, dictated, or inspired by the most reverend archbishop." [19] Though he admitted that of this he had "no positive proof," he insisted that the article must be by Hughes because "it has the stamp of his peculiar genius, the well-known characteristics of his somewhat original mind." [20] He even managed to get in a telling blow by meeting the argument that the article could not have possibly come from the pen of Hughes because it was so full of "slang and billingsgate." With grave charity he accounted for this: of course he can see the literary style to be "deficient in that dignity and classic purity always to be presumed in the writings of an archbishop," but the style had, in this instance, been lowered to the comprehension of the audience the writer hoped to influence. [21]

Loftily Brownson conceded: "He does not fully approve every judgment of ours, any more than we approve every judgment of his." [22] But at least the Archbishop might try to be logical, for while denying that slavery is the cause of the war, he attributes the war to the Northern abolitionists, and so virtually makes slavery the cause. [23] On this point Brownson quoted his previous article: "The liberation of the slave is *not* the purpose and end of the war. . . . The war is a war against rebellion." Even though the destruction of slavery should become necessary, it would not change the character of the war. [24]

By way of placating the Irish, Brownson went on to say truly of them that no people love liberty more, but (less truly) that no people have a deeper horror of slavery. He then proceeded to undo his concession by commenting that no doubt Hughes "treats the rebels with tenderness, [because] he comes of a nation in which rebellion, or what England treats as rebellion, has been chronic for nearly eight centuries." [25] He also had his first good word for the abolitionists, as they are now his allies: "Perhaps, if we who have so long sneered at them as fanatics, had studied less to be wise and politic, and been more truly living men . . . more truly heroic in our devotion to the right and the just instead of the merely prudent and expedient, their fanaticism would have revolted us less." [26] In a later article, he even decided that those whom he had formerly accused of being ready to wreck the Constitution in order to aid their cause, were now on the side of the Union, and that "the conditional loyalism [of the abolitionists], as things stand, is practically unconditional loyalism." [27]

So far Brownson had not dealt Hughes the killing stroke. He did so at last by pointing out that, by defending the slave-trade, the Archbishop had incurred excommunication, for the Church, by the Letter of Gregory XVI written in 1839, "absolutely prohibits and interdicts all ecclesiastics and laymen from maintaining that this traffic in blacks is permitted, under any pretext or color whatsoever; or to preach, or teach in public or private, in any way whatever, anything in its favor or extenuation." [28] Though Hughes had not really defended the slave-trade (or even the institution of slavery as it existed in the South), he had been so unwary in his *Metropolitan* article as to cite a somewhat improbable case to show that, under certain circumstances—the buying of captives taken in war by an African king who was about to slaughter them [29]— the slave-trade might be permissible and even laudable.

To have convicted Hughes of heresy was a sweet revenge for a man whom Hughes had so recently delated to Rome. But as Brownson knew very well that he was only scoring a debating point against the Archbishop, he came to the rescue of the man

whom he had put in such a predicament. He therefore said that
he believed a defence of the slave-trade was not the intention of
the writer and restates his case for him: "Understood in this way,
we are under no necessity of so interpreting his language as to
make it a defence of a traffic which the church has condemned." [30]
Little wonder that, the next time they met, Hughes said to Brownson, "I will never write anything against you again." [31]

Brownson was a dangerous foe for any man to challenge. About
this time Bishop Spalding of Louisville took offence at the article
on his book on the Reformation that appeared in the *Review*.
When he replied to it in his own paper, Brownson, "out of our
profound respect to him as a prelate, our high appreciation of his
merits as an author"—and so forth—reprinted the entire letter.
But as the Bishop had suggested that, because Brownson was a
convert, he could hardly be expected to have "the docile spirit of
a true child of the Church," Brownson appended a single sentence:
"We do not recollect that the elder brother, in the parable of the
Prodigal Son, was commended for being angry at the reception the
returning prodigal received from his father." [32]
Spalding, however, was merely an author whose feelings had
been ruffled. He was supposed to have secessionist leanings, but
did not attack Brownson for his stand on the war. But if he did
not, other bishops did, though usually covertly. Bishop Whelan of
Wheeling, for example, cancelled his subscription to the *Review*
on the ground that some of its articles "would better suit a publication under Republican direction; indeed [they] would not
misfit a Marat or a Robespierre." [33] It was not that these prelates
considered loyalty to the Union as equivalent to revolution, or
those opposed to slavery as subversive of the whole social order,
but that they feared, as did many people, that such arguments as
Brownson was using would bring about the horrors of a slave
insurrection. We now know them to have been mistaken; we
should in justice remember the genuineness of their dread.
The final judgment to be passed upon American Catholics during

the Civil War is that, upon the whole, both sides kept their heads fairly well, considering the violent passions the war raised. Bishops and priests and lay people, North and South, had their private opinions, which they expressed vigorously and sometimes even with absurd exaggeration; but there was nothing approaching the bitterness which brought about a schism in most of the Protestant denominations. After due allowances have been made for Brownson's patriotic fervor, and for the rather too violent things he (like other people) said during the excitement of those days, his articles on slavery—if taken as a series—are as good an exposition of the Catholic position regarding this matter as was produced in America.

It is interesting to observe how Brownson's political philosophy was largely conditioned by political realities. His road to the Church had itself been to a great extent political. His road to his so-called theological liberalism had similarly led through his patriotism. Now it was his patriotism, at the hour when his country was in its extreme peril, that caused him to refashion his political ideas. He had not yet come quite to the end of this particular road, but we can watch him advancing upon it until he at last arrived at the full and rounded principles of his finest book, *The American Republic*.

In taking his articles upon the crisis of his country for examination, it would not be difficult to find apparent flaws in his reasoning; his gradual shift of position, culminating in a very wide shift, offers anybody an opportunity for confuting him out of his own mouth. That, however, may be left to people who think they have caught a man out because they find he is honest enough to admit that he has changed his mind. The main thing to seize is Brownson's clearness of thought and the warmth of his heart.

Writing in 1851 upon the abolitionists' "Higher Law," he appears almost to be defending slavery. While he "does not doubt" that slavery, as it exists in the Southern states is an evil *per se,* he thinks also that "to the slave it is always good or evil according as he wills it to be one or the other, or according to the spirit with which he bears it. If he regards it as a penance, and submits to it in a true penitential spirit, it is a blessing to him,—as are on the same conditions to every one of us all the sufferings and afflictions of this life." [34] The only real evils Brownson admits seeing in slavery at this time are not the "physical and sentimental evils, or pretended evils, about which abolitionists and philanthropists keep up such a clamor" but moral and spiritual ones. If only he could be sure that the slave-owners would bring up their slaves as Christians, "there would be no evil in negro slavery to disturb us." He supplements this with, "We place not the slightest value on what the men of this world call liberty." [35] All of which strikes one as special pleading and even as cant. Or it would did we not see that he was determined to put the burden of proof on the abolitionists whom he detested.

He is on slightly firmer ground when he gets to his central argument. William H. Seward, against whom he is addressing his remarks, has no right to make his appeal to "the higher law" because that is to appeal against the Constitution under which he holds his seat in the Senate. [36] "Who," Brownson asks, "is to decide whether a special civil enactment be or be not repugnant to the law of God?" Obviously it can only be done on the Protestant principle of private judgment. "Here is a sad dilemma for our uncatholic countrymen, which admirably demonstrates the unsuitableness of Protestant principles for practical life." He summarily disregards the individual conscience as having any authority in such a case. "There is no principle," he concludes, "on which the abolitionists and free-soilers can justify their resistance to the fugitive slave-law." [37]

Even then, though standing for state-sovereignty, he declares: "We regard the Union as we do marriage, that is, as legally indissoluble." Yet he has no sympathy whatever for Sumner's party, and uses what was a common Southern argument—that the slaves are really better off than white laborers. [38] It may all have been logical, but it was the kind of reasoning that left most people cold and that probably did not quite convince Brownson himself. One gets the impression of a man speaking from a brief. He was to unsay most of this in due time.

In 1857 the Supreme Court had decided that slavery was merely a local institution. Upon this, Brownson pleaded that slavery could have no validity in a territory not a state, and therefore disagreed with the Dred Scott decision of his fellow-Catholic, Chief Justice Taney.[39] The closer he saw Civil War to be, the closer he came towards an unequivocal position. The fact is that the "peculiar institution" which his friend Calhoun (dead since 1850) believed in with passionate conviction, Brownson believed in (if at all) only in an academic fashion and because of his hope that the agrarian and aristocratic system of the South would check the industrialism he so hated in the North. Having backed Calhoun, in this matter, he was obliged to accept slavery, though with reluctance.

By 1861 he was sure of himself, so far as the support of the Union was concerned, but still not quite sure of his theory. Reminding his readers that he had been associated with Calhoun, and had always been against the abolitionists, "he owes it to himself to say that he has always been attached to the Union of these states." [40] True, he had defended nullification, up to 1847, and had held that the several states were each sovereign, and that the federal government possessed only delegated powers, and that the Union was "formed by sovereign states by mutual compact"; he nevertheless had never admitted the right of any state to secede.[41] Even if the Union is only a compact—he now believes it to be considerably more—it is a compact that can be dissolved only by the unanimous consent of all the contracting parties. Yet on the very next page he says that the South was wrong in its action, because what should have been done was to have called a convention, which no doubt would have dissolved the Union amicably.[42] Here he shows himself either out of touch with political realities or (more probably) is merely trying to score a debating point. What has become of his contention that the Union is indissoluble except by "unanimous" consent? Not until July, 1862, did he complete his theory. Then he declared, "Secession itself is another illustration of the importance of theory. Secession is only a logical deduction from the theory of state sovereignty."[43] He had been one of the chief exponents of that theory. Now he holds, not that secession is impossible in the sense that Lincoln held it to be so, but that a state by seceding from the Union simply ceased to be.

By now there was no fiercer anti-slavery man than Brownson. Yet his attack on the institution was only a means to an end; it had to be destroyed or it would destroy the Union. Formerly Brownson had contended that Congress had no power to exclude new states that permitted slavery, adding that in any event such exclusion would prove ineffective, for the obvious reason that slavery could be introduced as soon as statehood had been obtained. But from the beginning of the war he pressed Lincoln—seeing the President several times—to issue an Emancipation Proclamation, something Lincoln did not want to do. Brownson defended the Proclamation on the one ground upon which it could be defended —that of its military advantages.

This of course was nothing but an appeal to expediency: most American Catholics recoiled before the immorality of such a proposal. The mild terms Lincoln used—advising the slaves to remain where they were and holding out vague hopes of compensation to their owners—Brownson considered wishy-washy. The plea that the loyal border states would suffer was brushed aside: they ought to be glad to suffer in the noble cause; otherwise their loyalty was questionable.[44] When Brownson urged the President in August, 1862, to issue orders to the generals in command in the South to proclaim emancipation, each in his own department, Lincoln told him that it would only lose him fifty thousand bayonets. Not until the intervention of England and France threatened—so Lincoln also told him—could he be driven to do what Brownson had demanded from the first.[45] If here the Catholic publicist was, for once, politically sagacious (in a narrow sense), it is hard to see upon what moral principle the confiscation of property guaranteed under the Constitution could be defended. For in this case the confiscation would have to be absolute and without compensation. And there is a vast difference between seizing ordinary property as a war measure and setting the slaves (even of enemies) against their masters.

Except for what is in my opinion a moral lapse in this matter of the Emancipation Proclamation, Brownson was usually sound in his defence of principles—much sounder than he often showed himself to be in his judgment of men and affairs. Of Lincoln—though he had voted for him in 1860—he retained a low opinion to the day of his own death. On December 26, 1862, he wrote to Sumner: "[The President] is thick-headed; he is ignorant; he is tricky, somewhat astute in a small way, and obstinate as a mule." [46] A few months later he told Sumner again: "The President is no statesman, is no constitutional lawyer, and has no conception of our real system of government. . . . I give all credit to his good intentions; but he is weak, ignorant, and wrongheaded, precisely the sort of man to ruin in times of crisis the liberties of a nation." [47] Nor did he confine his comments to private letters or conversation. In October, 1864, he asked in his *Review:* "When such a man as Abraham Lincoln can become president, who may not hope one day also to be president?" [48]

On the other hand, he approved of men whose reputation in history does not stand high. He thought either Benjamin Butler or General Frémont would make a good president, and in fact he supported Frémont in the 1864 election, until Frémont had the good sense to withdraw of his own accord. In this case it would seem that about all he had to go on was the fact that his son Edward, who was on the General's staff, had conceived a boyish admiration for his commander; that and the fascinations of Mrs. Frémont.[49] Rosecrans he unjustly attacked, but afterwards made a handsome apology.[50] And he seems to have esteemed the incompetent Burnside, who is remembered today more for his whiskers than his

warlike qualities. That General even got the news of his appointment to command the Army of the Potomac from Henry Brownson, to whom his father had just written.[51] "My God," he cried,
"I hope not! I am not fit for it." Brownson called Stanton "his
man" and looked upon Seward as a "malign influence." [52] His
great political crony now was Charles Sumner.

The handsome, polished, smug and vindictive Senator was a man
whom Brownson had known in Boston. His younger brother had
been at Brook Farm and had become a Catholic. It was Charles
Sumner who, after his interview with Cousin at Paris, had tried
to get Brownson appointed professor of philosophy at Harvard.
Since 1844 Brownson had been out of touch with him, as with the
rest of his former friends, except to attack him for his abolitionist
views. Now all was forgiven; the Civil War made them political
bed-fellows, though Brownson sometimes feared that Sumner was
weakening the national cause by his obsession with slavery. For
the Senator abolition was something to be demanded for the sake
of the slave; for Brownson it was no more than a means of striking
at the Southern enemy.[53]

On one very important matter, however, they saw eye to eye. It
was one upon which I believe both men to have been wrong—
Sumner even more so than Brownson: the theory of "state suicide"
as applied to the seceding states of the South. Because of Brownson's
powerful support, Sumner backed him when he ran in 1862 for
Congress. Yet Brownson had not wanted to go to Washington and
consented to try his political luck mainly, he said, to please his
children, especially Edward and Sarah.[54] He was nominated because it was thought that he could draw a sufficiently large number of Catholic Democrats to vote for him in a district normally
Democratic. The manoeuvre failed: instead many Republicans refused to vote for a Catholic.

After the returns were in the defeated candidate met a prominent
politician on a train and happened to mention that he had once
been a Mason. "Had we only known that, we should have elected

you," was the comment. "But that was more than thirty years ago." "Makes no difference; if we had known it, you would have been elected." [55] It was, however, just as well that Brownson did not go to Congress. That he ran at all as a Republican damaged him in the eyes of many Catholics who regarded it as almost a sign of theological orthodoxy that a man should belong to the right political party. In 1864 he told the readers of his *Review* that when he was nominated, "he was interiorly alarmed, and began a self-examination to ascertain what political folly or iniquity he had committed; and he became reconciled to himself, and his conscience was at ease, only when he found his election defeated by an overwhelming majority." [56] Possibly no candidate for Congress has ever taken a trouncing in just this way; but then, philosophers very seldom engage in politics.

By being defeated Brownson was spared being embroiled in one of the most disgraceful of legislative assemblies. As it was, his advocacy of the thesis of state suicide—though he steered clear of some of Sumner's excesses—did him little credit. Here was a logical argument that led to grave inhumanity during the period of reconstruction. To the extent that Brownson helped to propagate the theory, Brownson must be blamed. Yet it must be admitted to have considerable bearing upon the general constitutional theory he was evolving at this time, and to have both interest and consistency. It was this theory which he was to develop in 1866 in *The American Republic*.

In the *Review* for October, 1863, he wrote: "The mistake of the secessionists was in supposing that in seceding from the Union the states became independent. Precisely the reverse is the legal effect of secession." [57] He rejected the doctrine advanced by the administration, that it was impossible for the states, as such, to secede, and that it was a case only of rebellion on the part of a certain number of the citizens of the states in question. For this reason he deplored the admission to Congress of loyalists from Virginia, Tennessee and Louisiana as creating an unfortunate precedent, which had no validity. And when Lincoln issued at the end of 1863 a proclamation of amnesty, Brownson asserted that he had exceeded his powers; Congress could override him. His own position was plain: "We have no vindictive feelings to gratify, and we ask not for vengeance. . . . But we would offer no terms at all to rebels till they have submitted." [58] According to him, though slavery had been perfectly legal in the states where it had prevailed, once those states had seceded all local laws ceased to have any effect, and the states themselves were reduced automatically to territories, in which the only prevalent law was that of the United States.[59] "Undoubtedly there is something severe in treating the rebellion of a state as state suicide; but we have yet to learn that the way of rebellion ought to be graded, macadamized, and made easy." [60] All of which is patently no proof of his theory, but merely a justification—as was also true of the Emancipation Proclamation—of severity as a means of waging war.

He tried to support his argument by citing a conversation he had had with Calhoun in 1841. Then Calhoun, defending nullification, had told him: "You cannot coerce a state, because you can never get power enough to do it." He explained that too many other states would make common cause with that state to make coercion possible, but "Mr. Calhoun did not deny . . . the *right,* but simply the *ability* of the federal government to coerce a state." [61] As it had now been conclusively shown that the federal government did possess that power, "the population and territory remain within the jurisdiction of the United States, but the entity called the *state* is out of the Union, as completely so, as though it had never been in it, and therefore is no longer a state at all." [62]

In all this Brownson was trying, with whatever errors of fact or theory, to serve the Church as well as his country. Catholics, he said, very unjustly regard the abolitionists as the real authors of the rebellion. The reason for this is that Catholics, especially Irish Catholics, "are strong, not unfrequently intolerant partizans." He adds, "We often find Irish Catholics who regard apostacy from the Democratic party as little less criminal than apostasy from the church." [63] He suspects that Archbishop Hughes's article against him had been inspired by Seward and Thurlow Weed, whose policy he describes as that of conciliating the rebels "by convincing them that we are determined to suppress the rebellion without disturbing the existing relation of master and slave—a policy which we should expect from such men as Weed and Seward." [64] Calhoun himself had admitted to him that slavery was indefensible, as such: he regarded it as a kind of "wardship"; notwithstanding which "fine theory" Brownson asserted slavery in the South to be simply chattel slavery. [65] The real question he saw to be, "not slavery or abolition, but are the United States a nation, one political people possessing national sovereignty in its plenitude, or are they a mere aggregation of sovereign states?" [66]

Catholics, he thinks, do not understand the war, which they look upon as one between two political parties. They would not object to the secession of the South, even though they perhaps prefer to have the Union remain undivided. "Not having the feelings and associations of our old American-born population, whose fathers shed their blood to gain us a country and to make us a nation . . . to them it is much the same whether they live under the stars and bars or under the stars and stripes, since they were born under neither." [67] No Know-nothing could have said much more.

Nor could anybody have been much less ceremonious than was Brownson towards a letter the Pope had written to Archbishop Hughes. Brownson pointed out that it had been published in the early fall of 1862, while dated nearly a year earlier. He declared himself certain "that the letter . . . either has been forged in his name, or has been solicited and obtained on a gross misrepresentation of the actual state of American affairs." And as though the accusation of forgery were not enough, he did not hesitate to strike indirectly at the Pope himself. American Catholics since 1848, according to Brownson, had decided to link their cause with caesarism; the only exceptions being a small group of liberals among them. The content of the Pope's letter was not in consonance with Catholicism: "It is no Catholic doctrine that the magistrate bears not the sword, or that a sovereign nation has not the right to defend itself, to maintain its unity and the integrity of its territory, so far as able, against any and every foe, foreign or domestic." [68] And as though even that were not enough, Brownson went on, "The Holy Father himself, if the letter ascribed to him is authentic, has been induced to lend the conspiracy his powerful aid." [69]

Here, as throughout his liberal period, Brownson implied that the policy of the Holy See was working against true Catholic interests by accepting the protection of absolutist governments which had no concern for Catholicism except as a political force that might be used to further their own advantage. That there was something in the idea need not be denied—though in so far as it was true, it was true locally and not of the universal Church. There was more in his thesis that "the ruin of the American republic would be the most serious calamity that could befall the Catholic Church, not only here, but throughout the world." "Catholics, therefore, in warring against our republic, and laboring to extinguish republican liberty, are really warring against the interests alike of their church and of humanity. One is practically a traitor to the church in taking sides with the rebellion, no less than to his country." [70]

This strong expression of patriotic feeling, which enforced all that Brownson had been saying for several years about the necessity for Catholics becoming fully American in their outlook, accounts for the attitude he took on the theory of "state suicide." A mind like his had to have some sort of a theory to justify his emotions. The theory to hand was that of the sovereignty residing, not in the states severally—as he had maintained when it was a question of opposing the growth of the industrialism of the North—but of sovereignty residing in the states only when they were in the Union. With that quasi-mystical idea possessing him, it was inevitable that he should take the position that a state literally ceased to exist the moment it withdrew from the Union, within which alone it could be said to have any life.

On the subject of the Negro he offers a curious mixture of good sense and misjudgment. He would leave the whole question of Negro suffrage to the states (when they were reorganized), feeling confident as to how the South would deal with the matter. Fore-seeing the horrors of Negro rule under reconstruction, he said: "Free them, give them votes, and put them on the footing of political equality with their former masters, and [their] amiable qualities . . . will disappear, and your beloved negroes will become vain, proud, insolent, overbearing, and exhibit the usual vices and manners of freedmen." [71] Even emancipation he thought should have been brought about by means of an intervening period of serfdom, and he believed that the liberation of the Negroes from slavery would be the first step toward their extinction. In this time has shown him to be very wide of the mark, and one's blood runs cold to read: "We had, and have no wish to preserve, here or else-where, the negro race. Do not be shocked, my dear madam, you know I am no philanthropist, and you must expect me to speak as a reasonable man, who respects things, not fine phrases." Oh no, he would not do any harm to the Negro; he merely hoped that the Negro and the Indian would disappear from American soil. Only "let the disappearance be by a law of Providence, not by human wrong or oppression." "Could we have had our way, and had we wished to preserve the negro race in the United States, we would never have emancipated the slaves." [72] By the time the war was over he was sick of the subject. The Union had been preserved, and that was all that mattered. In 1867 he wrote to one of his sons, "I am tired of the eternal negro." [73]

To his credit he parted company with Sumner over reconstruction, though here too he was plagued by his constitutional theories. He did not approve of the persecution of the defeated rebels of the South; they were, after all, the only people with whom these states could be reconstructed. "Besides," he wrote to John Sherman of Ohio, "we need the Southern individualism to temper the New England socialism. You and I are both New England men, but I do not want the South completely new-englandized." [74] To General Sherman he said, "The insisting that the state shall adopt a constitution prohibiting slavery before being allowed its representation in Congress, is repugnant to the first principles of the Constitution of the United States." [75] He believed that now that the Southern states acknowledged themselves defeated, no more warm friends to the Union could be found there if only confidence were placed in them and their humiliation were permitted to end. When Greeley told him that he was proposing "abstractions" because he wished to be fair, Brownson retorted that it was a common device for a man who cannot meet an argument to dismiss it as an abstraction. Nevertheless in the New York *Times* he wrote in defence of the amendment abolishing slavery, saying that, as the Southern states had ceased to be states by their rebellion, the amendment could be passed by three-fourths of the states remaining in the Union—those most concerned being ruled out of the discussion. "It matters nothing in a constitutional point of view," he contended, "whether any or all of the ex-states ratify it or not." [76] Yet he opposed giving Congress any right to determine the question of Negro suffrage, as under the Constitution it was one to be handled by the individual states. Writing to his son Henry in 1866 he snorted, "I have lost all sympathy with Sumner, who has the nigger on the brain worse than ever." [77]

Though he regarded President Johnson as "violent, wrong-headed, arbitrary," he saw that he was upholding the Constitution against Congress, and when his impeachment was attempted, Brownson took his side. At least he was "a far less dangerous President than was Mr. Lincoln." [78] The whole frame of things depressed him and he was glad that he was too old and infirm to be an active politician. In 1870 he wrote to his son: "For my part, I have come to old Judge Parsons's conclusion, 'The young man that is not a Democrat is a knave; the old man that is a Democrat is a fool.' I have ceased to believe in Democracy at all." [79] By this time Grant was President, and Brownson, who considered him "absolutely destitute of moral sense, a low vulgar mind," quoted Dr. Hewit, who was Grant's personal friend, as saying that he was "at ease only when surrounded by blackguards." [80] His opinion on the situation was given with a Jeffersonian ring: "The true policy of the country is light taxation and free trade. The great fault of our statesmen has been to make what should be a great agricultural and commercial people prematurely a great manufacturing people. . . . But the great industrial corporations have got the control, and the government is simply their factor." [81]

When he looked at the world in general, the sight depressed him still further. "The Church is now, if Catholics could see it, a missionary church in an infidel world, and is now compelled to begin anew and reconvert the people." And the Pope was a prisoner. "I think he would have done better to have followed my advice in 1860." The worst feature was that "the Holy Father holds on to the civil powers for protection, when they spurn him, and seek only to enslave the Church, and secures for religion all the odium in the minds of the people attached to the governments they detest and seek to overthrow. . . . Christendom will be reëstablished on a republican, not a feudal or monarchical basis. The Church should let go the arm of flesh, and trust to her resources as the spiritual kingdom of God on earth." His only consolation was that "Satan is never more signally defeated than when he has won his victory." [82]

He had reason to be depressed. At the end of 1864 he decided to cease publication of his *Review*. The opposition was too strong; health was failing; and he was overwhelmed by private griefs. One of the articles of the last issue was written with the body of one of his sons lying in an adjoining room.[83] He considered that his own active life was over.

In 1863 he had decided to withdraw from the field of theological and philosophical discussion, as he was meeting with so much obloquy, and to confine himself to questions of the day. With that he began what he called the "National Series." In the first issue for 1864 he told his readers: "We are what we have been, what we always shall be,—a bold, rough, independent man, but a sincere, earnest, and devoted Catholic, who believes that he can save his soul only in the Church, and has no wish to lose it. The Church is our mother, and never knowingly will we grieve her maternal heart, or, knowingly, have we done so. We have not sought our personal glory. We have remained poor when we could easily have made ourselves rich, and received censure when we could with more ease have gained applause. We have labored, in thought, word, and deed, for what we regarded as the true interests of Catholicity in our age and country. We may have erred in judgment: when we are shown or are convinced that we have, we shall confess, and make reparation. The best thing is never to err, and the next best thing is to own and correct the error. We claim not the former, but we shall never shrink from the latter." [84]

Unfortunately he at once made the disastrous mistake of backing John C. Frémont for the presidency, and though the General took a thousand subscriptions for campaign purposes, they perhaps did no more than balance the cancellations. Frémont soon threw in his sponge, and the following year Brownson wrote to Sumner, "My Review died of Fremont. Had I not supported the Pathfinder, or had he not withdrawn and left me in the lurch, I should have continued it, and I hope to be able yet to resume it. I stopped it because I had sacrificed my position, and had no party to fall back upon." [85]

That, however, does not tell the whole story. He was too tired and sick at heart to go on. And he was ill. He often had to call upon others—sometimes one of his children—to correct his proofs for him. Yet at the beginning of 1863 he had told his readers (half in jest and half in earnest) that he had thoughts of applying for a commission of major-general in the army, and that he would do so except for having grown too stout to sit on a horse. "We think we could make a better major-general than some in the army, for there is, after all, a good deal of fight in us." [86] Now, winding up his *Review* at the end of 1864, he struck blows all around him in his "Explanations to Catholics." [87] It was a general reaffirmation of his views. He ended with: "We have not attempted to soften or explain away any thing we have ever really meant or supposed we were maintaining. We wished to present our views such as they honestly were. Wrong they may be, uncatholic in intention we know they are not. . . . From our youth up we have loved truth, and wooed her as a bride, and we wish to die in her embrace. . . . We submit all our writings to the judgment of the church; and any doctrine or proposition in them that the Holy See will point out as contrary to faith, to sound doctrine, or to the spirit of obedience which should animate every Catholic, we will modify, alter, or retract, in such way and manner as she shall prescribe. More we cannot say, and less no Catholic ought to say." [88]

To the period of retirement that followed we owe the best of Brownson's books, *The American Republic.* Having more leisure now, he wrote it more carefully than was usual with him, for as he told Sumner, he wished it to be his political testament. [89] Even so, his journalistic habits got the better of him, as he confessed in the preface. But while drawing freely upon his old political articles— going as far back as to those he wrote in 1843 for the *Democratic Review,* he reshaped them so as to accord with his modified opinions. The consequence is that the book is somewhat repetitious and has "very little artistic merit." [90] It has, nevertheless, more than he credits himself with, and quite sufficient for a work of exposition. As such it is clear, forceful and immensely provocative of thought. Nobody perhaps will agree with all that Brownson has to say, but nobody can deny that what he has to say is striking and profound.

Though Brownson believed that his book would not be neglected merely because it was written by a Catholic and brought out by a Catholic publisher, [91] it has been neglected—as usually happens to anything a Catholic writes. Even his old friend George Ripley saw in it hardly more than a psychological curiosity and remarked that Brownson's readers would "admire his skill in combination and his fertility of resource with the same wonder with which they watch the movements of an adroit chess player." [92] Elsewhere Brownson was generally damned by the reputation he possessed as a logician.

The writing of the book, however, brought him into contact with another friend of former days—George Bancroft, to whom he dedicated the work as "a sort of public atonement" for the strictures he had made on the earlier volumes of his *History of the United States*.[93] Bancroft had sent him the ninth volume of that great work, and Brownson wrote to tell him: "I find in [it] expressions I should not as a Catholic use, but nothing which seriously conflicts with my Catholic faith, and far more that accords with it than in any other non-Catholic, and even most professedly Catholic historians I am acquainted with." [94] He is glad to find that they agree on the Constitution, especially on the "territorial doctrine," but he takes Bancroft mildly to task for giving "undue praise to the Society of Jesus. . . . The Jesuits are generally admirable as men, but as a society, I think, since it was remodelled by Aquaviva, their fifth general, they have been equally hurtful to the church and to society. They are in our day the real *obscurantists*." [95] He had said the same thing when winding up his *Review* in 1864.

Henry Brownson considers *The American Republic* one of the strongest arguments his father ever advanced for Catholicism, and claims for it, as its greatest originality, "the assertion of the American Democracy as territorial . . . and in placing the sovereignty in the states, against the consolidationists, and in the states united, not severally, against the secessionists. The states are collectively, not individually, sovereign. The people, he maintained after Suarez, are, under God, collectively sovereign. These two points are new, and had been made, so far as his knowledge extended, by no writer before him." [96]

An absolute originality of course cannot be claimed here—if an absolute originality can ever be said to exist anywhere. As Brownson wrote in his letters to Bancroft, he found the "territorial doctrine" in his *History,* though that was not from where he had derived it. In the preface to his book he acknowledges his indebtedness to John C. Hurd's *Law of Freedom and Bondage in the United States,* saying, "I could not have written my work without the aid derived from its suggestions, any more than I could without Plato, Aristotle, St. Augustine, St. Thomas, Suarez, Pierre Leroux, and the Abbate Gioberti." [97] In a letter to Hurd, dated December 28, 1865, he tells him: "I think for myself, but I do not claim to have any inventive genius, and wish to give every man his due. Every man who helps me to a truth I knew not is my friend and benefactor, and whether you like it or not, I shall always rank you among my friends and benefactors." [98] It was often Brownson's way after reading a book with which he agreed to claim that he had held its doctrine before reading it. But to some extent, that is everybody's way. It was so with his reading of Saint-Simon, Cousin, Leroux, and Gioberti. Brownson's originality lay in applying what he found in a new way. In Hurd he had discovered a whetstone rather than an authority. Brownson was no man's disciple, even if he remained to the end a bit of an eclectic. In that sense his son does not make any too excessive an assertion.

Taking Henry Brownson's summary of *The American Republic* as the basis of discussion at this point, I must remind the reader that Orestes Brownson had once argued, against John Quincy Adams, in favor of individual state sovereignty, instancing as historical proof that the colonies were independent of one another, each being directly dependent on the Crown; therefore their federation gave no more to the central administration than a certain amount of delegated authority. I must confess that I cannot see how it is possible to get around that historical fact. In 1787 a compact was effected between the states that declared their independence of the Mother Country, but it was neither explicitly nor implicitly affirmed that none of them could secede from their Union, and secession was several times threatened (once by Massachusetts) long before the Civil War. What may be reasonably maintained is that, after the Civil War, a new compact was virtually made, though at the point of the sword, and that this compact has since been willingly ratified by all the states. Even so, such a freely made compact cannot be said to have existed at the time Brownson wrote his book, and it is at best only a theory, though probably no better one can be found to cover the situation as it at present exists.

What Brownson attempted to do was to restate what he had always held regarding state sovereignty, but now in such a way as to vest that sovereignty, not in the states separately considered, but in the states only as within the federal Union. Even this was rather more than the ordinary "states' rights" doctrine, if for practical purposes it is not easy to distinguish between the two. Long before he wrote *The American Republic* Brownson had come to despair of the idea he and Calhoun had advanced, that the Congress and President could be held in check only by balancing one section of the country against another on the basis of their diverse interests. He did not cease hating industrialism, but he saw no hope of eradicating it; in any event anything was preferable to a constitutional theory which would give the individual state the right of nullification and even of secession. Nothing but the threat of Civil War could have brought him to this conclusion. Now, with circumstances changed, he had to remodel his theory so as to make it fit actual realities. As to how well it does fit must remain a matter of opinion.

The whole case really turns on historical fact. And here Brownson was a bit weak, though there are people who consider him a notable philosopher of history. What may be conceded is that his "Essays on the Reformation" [99]—which Henry Brownson thinks were unsurpassed by anything his father ever wrote—represent a considerable advance upon the nonsense he perpetrated at times in *The Spirit-Rapper*. The occasion for his writing on the Reformation was that Bishop Spalding of Louisville had written on the same subject, in order to confute d'Aubigné, and that the only difference between the Bishop and the Swiss Protestant was that the one regarded the Reformation as satanic and that the other regarded the Catholic Church as satanic.[100] Brownson protested against such an over-simplification of a complicated question. His main thesis was one that he had already touched upon several times: that there was in the relations of the Church and the Empire something like the transference of personalities that had occurred between the two thieves in Dante's *Inferno:* [101] the Papacy took on the free character of the barbarians who had conquered the old empire, while the new Germanic empire took on the despotic character of ancient Rome, after which the Papacy allied itself with feudalism against the absolutism of monarchy. The theory has the merit of ingenuity and is at least arguable, though I for one cannot think very highly of Brownson's philosophy of history—even supposing a satisfactory philosophy of history to be possible. He knew a good deal more about American history, but even there he was too prone to arrange his facts to support an *a priori* argument.

Brownson had always made altogether too much of the idea that democracy means that the "voice of the people" must be regarded in an absolute and unqualified sense as the "voice of God." With an air of producing a startling discovery, he informs us that mob-rule is dangerous, that the representative system does not always represent the people, that the real control is usually not in their hands at all but in those of the "interests," that politicians have been known to care more about getting votes than the good of their country, and that democratically elected governments have been as corrupt as any others. To which one may mildly protest that the most convinced democrat is able to admit all the defects of the machinery of democracy and yet believe in the democratic ideal, and that it would be hard to come across a democrat who does not believe that above the people there is a standard of justice to which appeal may be made. The Christian (and for that matter, a man of any religious conviction, except perhaps in a state in which the

Defects of the democratic ideal.

ruler is deified) will call that higher tribunal "God," and the Catholic believes that the representative of God on earth is the Church. Brownson, in his incessant girding against democracy as what he called the means of government instead of the end that it should be, was largely wasting his energy, for he was destroying an enemy who was hardly more than a figment of his own imagination. A large part of his book—especially the part of it that had appeared as articles in the Democratic Review in 1843—is devoted to this thesis. Once again he triumphantly disproves what no sensible man had ever doubted. The remarkable thing is that when writing the articles upon which the earlier chapters are based, he had not as yet read St. Thomas or Suarez or Bellarmine, but followed their principles without knowing it.[102]

The core of Brownson's book is the striking constitutional theory already indicated; it is this that gives him his claim to be remembered as a political philosopher. For whatever he may have derived from John C. Hurd and others, he is highly original in his presentation of his case. It is a pity that it has been so neglected. As he himself wrote in a belated review in 1873: "The work, of which a new Edition has just been published, was not received, except by a very few, with much favor. It was condemned at the North as southern, at the South as northern; it was abused both North and South because it was dedicated to my old friend George Bancroft, by Protestants because written by a Catholic, and by Catholics because it did not favor their political prejudices. As nobody took up its defence, its success was not flattering." [103] What seems to have escaped him is that perhaps the reason the book did not meet with more success was that it had the air of a brilliant *tour de force* and was not quite convincing. Woodrow Wilson, however, called it the most masterly work on the American Constitution,[104] and whether or not it is precisely that, it is surely among the most interesting of all such studies. A few passages should be given here as an indication of its method and power.

Excellent passing points are made, as when the old radical writes: "The men of wealth . . . are the men who exert the worst influence on government in every country, for they always strive to use it as an instrument for advancing their private interests. They act on the beautiful maxim, 'Let the government take care of the rich, and the rich will take care of the poor,' instead of the far safer maxim, 'Let government take care of the weak, the strong can take care of themselves.' Universal suffrage is better than restricted suffrage, but even universal suffrage is too weak to prevent private property from having an undue political influence." [105] No wonder that by now Brownson was disgusted with the Republican party with which, because of the Civil War, he had thrown in his lot.

He defends his theory against other expounders of the Constitution—all of them more or less wrong, except himself. "Mr. Jefferson maintains that before the convention of 1787 [the States] existed as several independent sovereign states, but that since that convention . . . they exist as one political people in regard to foreign nations, and several sovereign states in regard to their internal and domestic affairs. Mr. Webster concedes that originally the States existed as severally sovereign states, but contends that by ratifying the constitution they have been made one sovereign political people, state, or nation, and that the General government is a supreme national government, though with a reservation in favor of State rights. But both are wrong. If the several States of the Union were severally sovereign states when they met in the convention, they are so now; and the constitution is only an agreement or compact between sovereigns, and the United States are, as Mr. Calhoun maintained, only a confederation of sovereign states, and not a single state or one political community. But if the sovereignty persists in the States severally, any State, saving its faith, may, whenever it chooses to do so, withdraw from the Union, absolve its subjects from all obligation to the Federal authorities, and make it treason in them to adhere to the Federal government. Secession is, then, an incontestable right." [106]

Brownson's own view is that "there is no sovereign people or existence of the United States distinguishable from the people or existence of the particular States united. . . . The solidarity of the members constitutes the unity of the body. The difference between this view and Mr. Madison's is, that while his view supposes the solidarity to be conventional, originating and existing in compact . . . this supposes it to be real, living, and prior to the convention." [107] On this ground he again advances his "state suicide" theory.[108]

He does not flinch from any of the implications of his central doctrine. He had admitted that, if Calhoun was correct in his interpretation of the Constitution, secession was an inalienable right. He applies this to what had just happened with: "The citizens in [any of the States] that made war on the United States . . . acted by its authority. The only men, on this supposition, in them, who have been traitors or rebels, are precisely the Union men who have refused to go with their respective States, and have resisted, even with armed force, the secession ordinances." [109] On this supposition the Confederate States would have been perfectly justified in hanging all its citizens who remained faithful to the Union, and the Federal government would have had no right to interfere. Neither could the Federal government of course justly punish any rebels, because they were, on Brownson's showing, not rebels at all. Only the state itself could suffer, by extinguishing itself by withdrawing from the Union.

Of further interest was Brownson's prophecy that the United States would have to become a first-class military and naval power. It is to her that the hegemony of the New World will henceforth belong, and "she will have a potent voice in adjusting the balance of power even in Europe." [110] He even thinks that the whole of Central and South America, and Canada, would have eventually to be absorbed, for "they represent no idea, and the work of civilization could go on without them as well as with them." [111] It is but just to him, however, to add that he did not propose conquest;

he saw the United States as America—a single entity—drawing the whole Western hemisphere into its orbit by virtue of its own superior political principles.[112]

He applied his concept of the universal validity of the American idea to American Catholics, thereby rounding out his book but also arousing criticism from people who might have been sympathetic had he not said, "Catholics are better fitted by their religion to comprehend the real character of the American constitution than any other class of Americans, the moment they study it in the light of their own theology." [113] That needed to be said, though perhaps the concluding chapters of *The American Republic* might with better advantage have been worked up into a separate book. I cite other of the "Catholic" passages: "In the United States, false religions are legally as free as the true religion; but all false religions being one-sided, sophistical, and uncatholic, are opposed to the principles of the state, which tend, by their silent but effective workings, to eliminate them. The American state recognizes only the catholic religion." He explains that, "the church being free, and the state harmonizing with her, catholicity has, in the freedom of both, all the protection it needs, all the security it can ask, and all the support it can, in the nature of the case, receive from external institutions, or from social and political organizations." [114]

This then, as he had said before, is the shining destiny of America. "The religious mission of the United States is not . . . to establish the church by external law, or to protect her by legal disabilities, pains, and penalties against the sects, however uncatholic they may be; but to maintain catholic freedom, neither absorbing the state in the church nor the church in the state, but leaving each to move freely, according to its own nature, in the sphere assigned it in the internal order of things. . . . The effect of this mission of our country fully realized, would be to harmonize church and state, religion and politics, not by absorbing either in the other, or by obliterating the natural distinction between them, but by conforming both to the real or Divine order, which is supreme and immutable." [115]

Relation between Church and State.

The main value—a very great value—of *The American Republic* seems to me to reside in these last chapters. It is a pity that they were lost by being tacked on to an interpretation of the Constitution which many will find dubious, however brilliant it may be. So far from there being much organic connection between the two theses, Brownson's attempt to squeeze them together into a logical whole tends to have the effect of making a reader who questions one question both. That is very unfortunate, for no man ever exhibited more clearly the truth of the essentially Catholic mission of America than did Orestes Brownson. It was the heart of all that he tried to say since his conversion to Catholicism.

[1] P. v.

[2] *Latter Life,* p. 339.

[3] *Ibid.,* pp. 411, 412, 413.

[4] New York *Tribune* for October 9, 1861. We need not take the judgment too seriously. Greeley praised Brownson in these terms because he recognized in him a powerful political ally.

[5] *Latter Life,* p. 339.

[6] Letter in the possession of Mrs. Odiorne. The "something" for Sarah seems to have been the painting that George P. Healy made of him.

[7] *Brownson Papers.*

[8] *Latter Life,* p. 348.

[9] On this point the Irish had been deaf even to Daniel O'Connell.

[10] *Works,* Vol. XVII, p. 156. This was written for the October, 1861, issue of the *Review.* Later it became necessary for Brownson to revise his theory, so as to deny rebellion (properly so called) and to assert the theory of state suicide.

[11] *Works,* Vol. XVII, p. 156.

[12] *Ibid.,* pp. 156, 157.

[13] *Ibid.,* p. 158. Elsewhere he denied this. See *Latter Life,* pp. 377–378.

[14] *Ibid.,* p. 414.

[15] *Latter Life,* p. 378. Again Brownson exaggerates, but unfortunately he had some basis for his assertions, because of the wild statements of some individual Catholics. (See *A. C. Cole's Irrepressible Conflict,* p. 257 fn.)

[16] Hassard, *Hughes,* p. 437. He wrote in October, 1861, following an article in *Brownson's Quarterly Review* (reprinted in *Works,* Vol. XVII, pp. 144–178). Brownson had declared roundly: "Everybody knows that slavery is at the bottom of the whole controversy" (p. 174). Everybody did, but Hughes considered it politic to minimize that issue.

[17] *Latter Life,* p. 367.

[18] Hassard, *op. cit.,* p. 437. Dr. Hewit wrote to Brownson on October 16th: "The Archbishop is *wroth*—in fact savage; and if times had not changed, you and the Review would probably have the pleasure of contributing to the brilliancy of a wood-pile in full blaze." (*Latter Life,* p. 360 fn.)

[19] *Works,* Vol. XVII, p. 179.

[20] *Ibid.*, p. 179.
[21] *Ibid.*, p. 180.
[22] *Ibid.*, p. 181.
[23] *Ibid.*, pp. 181, 182.
[24] *Ibid.*, p. 183.
[25] *Ibid.*, p. 187.
[26] *Ibid.*, p. 196.
[27] *Ibid.*, p. 322.
[28] *Ibid.*, p. 204.
[29] *Ibid.*, p. 203.
[30] *Ibid.*, p. 205.
[31] *Latter Life*, p. 363.
[32] *Ibid.*, pp. 313, 314.
[33] *Ibid.*, p. 368.
[34] *Works,* Vol. XVII, p. 2.
[35] *Ibid.*, pp. 2, 3.
[36] *Ibid.*, pp. 6, 7.
[37] *Ibid.*, pp. 8, 12.
[38] *Ibid.*, pp. 23, 39, 42.
[39] *Ibid.*, pp. 80, 81, 84.
[40] *Ibid.*, p. 123.
[41] *Ibid.*, p. 124.
[42] *Ibid.*, pp. 132, 133.
[43] *Ibid.*, p. 276.
[44] *Ibid.*, pp. 310, 390, 403.
[45] *Latter Life*, p. 395.
[46] *Sumner Papers,* Harvard Library.
[47] *Latter Life*, pp. 391–392.
[48] *Works,* Vol. XX, p. 357. See also p. 338.
[49] *Latter Life*, pp. 402, 404.
[50] *Ibid.*, pp. 404–409.
[51] *Ibid.*, p. 389 fn.
[52] *Ibid.*, p. 425.
[53] An instance of Brownson's moderation, despite his fierce talk, was his appealing to Lincoln to spare Appleton Oaksmith. Sumner wrote to Brownson to say that, though he was in general opposed to capital punishment, this man, who was accused of slave-trading, should be hanged, and that he had told the President so. Brownson thought otherwise, and managed to get him spared. (*Latter Life*, p. 387).
[54] *Latter Life*, p. 426.
[55] *Latter Life*, p. 381.
[56] *Works,* Vol. XX, p. 355.
[57] *Works,* Vol. XVII, p. 453.
[58] *Ibid.*, pp. 512, 513.
[59] *Ibid.*, p. 235.
[60] *Ibid.*, p. 236.
[61] *Ibid.*, p. 243.
[62] *Ibid.*, p. 245.
[63] *Ibid.*, p. 318.
[64] *Ibid.*, p. 324. That Seward and Weed had something to do with Archbishop

Hughes's article is likely enough but hardly substantiates Doran Whalen's picture of Seward and Weed as enemies of Brownson who were determined to "down" him on account of his "horrible doctrines" article of 1840. Hughes had his weak side and was flattered by politicians. When he went on his diplomatic mission to Europe he took Weed along, paying his expenses. It has been suggested that Weed was the real ambassador and that Hughes accompanied him as a matter of form. If so, Hughes was completely taken in. Weed's own account of the matter is in Barnes's *Memoir of Thurlow Weed,* Vol. I, pp. 634–637. There is, however, nothing to show that the cause of the animosity of Weed and Seward was Brownson's old radicalism. They had reason enough to object to him on account of his stand in the Civil War, and Hughes had his own reasons for objecting to Brownson. The study of Seward in Piatt's *Memories of the Men Who Saved the Union* (pp. 132–171) is apparently Doran Whalen's only authority—and a poor one at that. All that Piatt indicates is what everyone knows, that Weed was a wily politician. Yet Horace Greeley, writing to George E. Baker on February 8, 1855, says: "Weed is a giant . . . [He] can be swindled by men who are fair to his face . . . It is hard for him to realize that men can 'smile and smile and be a villain.' . . . but he is, after all, the greatest man we have left, Seward *not* excepted." (Barnes, *Memoir of Thurlow Weed,* Vol. II, p. 232). Weed's artfulness seemingly was so consummate as to have an air of naïveté, and Seward used him accordingly. Even so, we need not make him what Doran Whalen represents him as being. Neither he nor Seward loom very large in Brownson's true story.

65 *Works,* Vol. XVII, p. 333.

66 *Ibid.,* p. 329.

67 *Ibid.,* pp. 435, 436.

68 *Ibid.,* pp. 436, 437, 438. The letter was of course perfectly authentic. But it was only a paternal plea for peace. In any event Brownson's interpretation of the Constitution in the Unionist sense cannot be described as the sole possible Catholic doctrine. He had one theory as to state sovereignty, the seceding states had another. However, assuming the correctness of his theory, Brownson might reasonably maintain that the only peace possible was one that followed the defeat of the South.

69 *Ibid.,* p. 444.

70 *Ibid.,* pp. 445, 446. The flaw in the argument is that the South did not consider itself as warring against republican liberty at all. Had it triumphed, the American idea would not have perished. It would merely have developed somewhat differently.

71 *Ibid.,* pp. 551, 555.

72 *Ibid.,* p. 558.

73 *Latter Life,* p. 490.

74 *Ibid.,* p. 465.

75 *Ibid.,* p. 471.

76 *Ibid.,* p. 476.

77 *Ibid.,* p. 481.

78 *Ibid.,* pp. 481, 485.

79 *Ibid.,* p. 493.

80 *Ibid.,* p. 497.

81 *Ibid.,* pp. 495–496.

82 *Ibid.,* pp. 494, 495, 496.

83 *Latter Life,* p. 437. *Works,* Vol. XX, p. 362.

[84] *Brownson's Quarterly Review,* Third New York Series, Vol. IV (1863), p. 128.

[85] *Latter Life,* p. 450.

[86] *Brownson's Quarterly Review,* Third New York Series, Vol. IV (1863), p. 127.

[87] *Works,* Vol. XX, pp. 361–381.

[88] *Ibid.,* pp. 380–381.

[89] *Latter Life,* pp. 449, 451.

[90] *The American Republic,* pp. vii, viii.

[91] *Ibid.,* p. xiv.

[92] New York *Tribune,* December 28, 1865.

[93] *Latter Life,* p. 456. Brownson has a number of references to Bancroft, but his chief article on him is in the *Works,* Vol. XIX, pp. 382–418. It was written in 1852.

[94] *Latter Life,* p. 456. On October 14 of the following year we find Brownson writing to Bancroft saying that he hopes he will send him volumes VII and VIII, as he cannot afford to buy them. He has all the earlier volumes. (Letter in the Massachusetts Historical Society.)

[95] *Latter Life,* p. 459.

[96] *Ibid.,* pp. 449–450.

[97] *American Republic,* p. x. In the *Review* for October, 1864, he also said: "We have, since secession took place, rejected state sovereignty, but not state rights, and we have done it for the reasons we have given, and for which we are chiefly indebted to Mr. Hurd. . . . We do not know whether Mr. Hurd intended to teach the doctrine as to the federal constitution we have defended, but we do know that we have been led to it by reading his work." (*Works,* Vol. XVII, 583–584. See also p. 567). Hurd, writing on December 27, 1865, thanks Brownson for "so flattering a distinction, one I can hardly believe to be deserved." (*Latter Life,* p. 477.)

[98] *Latter Life,* p. 478.

[99] *Works,* Vol. XII, pp. 514–607.

[100] *Ibid.,* p. 518.

[101] Canto XXV, 100–133.

[102] But as he pointed out in 1875, the Founding Fathers had also followed the scholastic political philosophers without knowing it. I might add that they derived their ideas from Locke, who had derived from Hooker, who had derived from St. Thomas Aquinas. It can be shown that Jefferson had read Filmer—whom Locke wrote to refute—and Filmer had been an honest enough controversialist to represent fairly the doctrine of Bellarmine, whom it had been his intention to refute. Jefferson's copy of Filmer's *Patriarcha* is in the Congressional Library. But for that matter, education in eighteenth century America was largely scholastic in form. Perry Miller in *The New England Mind* has shown how steeped were the Puritan divines in their Aquinas. Too much of course may be made of all this, but too little is usually made. Brownson, by going to the Founding Fathers and the American Constitution, obtained, while still a Protestant, a good deal more Catholic thought than he was conscious of at the time.

[103] *Brownson's Quarterly Review,* Last Series, Vol. I (1873), p. 420.

[104] I cannot find it proved that Wilson ever said this. But he is reported to have delivered this judgment while teaching at a summer school at Johns Hopkins University in the days when he was still a college professor. (See Sister M. Felicia Corrigan's *Some Social Principles of Orestes A. Brownson,* p. 15 fn.)

[105] *American Republic,* p. 383.

106 *Ibid.*, pp. 195–196.

107 *Ibid.*, p. 246.

108 *Ibid.*, pp. 290, 291.

109 *Ibid.*, p. 304.

110 *Ibid.*, pp. 390–391.

111 *Ibid.*, p. 392. See also p. 436, where he says that Mexico will eventually add some fifteen or twenty new States to the American Union.

112 It is evident from this that Brownson was the reverse of an isolationist, though he might appear a totalitarian, even if of a different stripe from any that has so far appeared. From this possible accusation Professors Thomas I. Cook of Washington University and Arnaud B. Leavelle of Swarthmore College have defended him in the most careful and scholarly study written of *The American Republic*. They conclude, however, that "in his analysis . . . Brownson's passion for logic is sometimes more apparent than his sense of political realism," but that "his organismic conception of the state, based upon the Providential constitution, was an attempt to avoid atomism, and does not make him a genuine precursor of totalitarianism. His idea of territorial democracy was designed so to divide political power as to prevent the excesses which would lead to absolutism." Sandwiched between these passages from their articles is another: "It is precisely this balance between a moderate conservatism and a constructive liberalism that gives Brownson's thought its significance and appositeness today. By avoiding a static conservatism, on the one hand, and a radicalism unrelated to social and moral realities on the other, he demonstrated that true conservatism and true liberalism are not necessarily opposed, but simply two sides of the same shield." (*The Review of Politics*, Vol. IV, 1942, pp. 183, 191).

113 *American Republic*, p. 378.

114 *Ibid.*, pp. 418, 419.

115 *Ibid.*, pp. 428–429.

CHAPTER XV

Under a Cloud

BROWNSON WAS EXTREMELY LUCKY to have ceased publishing his
Review with the issue for October, 1864, because the following
December Pope Pius IX issued his *Syllabus of Errors* which condemned, among other things, the doctrine of liberalism. Had the
Review still been in existence, Brownson's enemies would have done
their best to prove that the condemnation applied to him. It invariably happens on such occasions that a witch-hunt begins: a thing
like this is a heaven-sent opportunity, so that anybody who happens
to be the least bit out of the ordinary—especially if his superiority
has made him an object of envy—is sure to be accused by somebody
who does not like him.

As it was, there were those who said that Brownson was one of
those at whom the *Syllabus* was aimed, though he took what occasion served to contradict this.[1] In 1865 he wrote: "Some honest
people have supposed that I am myself among those who have
incurred the censures of the encyclical, and I have wished to show
them that in my own opinion I am not." [2] And in *The American
Republic,* which was issued the following year, he took pains again
to demonstrate that the condemnation of the proposition that Church
and State should be separated did not apply to him, or to the United
States; "for nowhere else is the state organized on catholic principles
or capable of acting, when acting from its own constitution, in
harmony with a really catholic church. . . . What is not practicable
in the Old World is perfectly practicable in the New. The state here
being organized in accordance with catholic principles, there can
be no antagonism between it and the church." [3] By 1873 he even
354

ventured to claim that the *Syllabus* and the definitions of the Vatican
Council had completely justified him in the fight he had made in
days when "it was hardly safe for a poor layman like ourselves
to assert the supremacy of the spiritual order, and the subordination
of the temporal to the eternal, unless in some vague and indeterminate sense." [4] The fact is, however, that Brownson was by then
telescoping the various phases of his life, and had come to believe
that his views had a greater consistency than was the case. It can
hardly be questioned that at least during 1860 to 1864, with a period
stretching at both ends, he had come perilously close to some of
the condemned propositions. That he would have retracted under
rebuke there can be no doubt; but he was fortunate in being saved
the necessity of having to retract.

He was fortunate also in other ways. He had warm friends as well
as bitter enemies, and the friends raised enough to purchase an
annuity of a thousand dollars a year, with its reversion to Sally
Brownson in the event of his dying before she did. Such a sum was
in those days almost enough for a man and his wife living in their
modest style. Their two surviving sons were married and self-sup-
porting; only Sarah, their one daughter, was at home. On his annuity
Brownson could be independent and write the books he projected.

At least that was the expectation. It was supposed that Brownson,
having given up his *Review,* would be free from the necessity of
turning out copy on a dead-line for magazines; indeed, his friends
did not see how a man in his precarious health could keep up his
journalism. Still less did they suppose that he would be capable
of the lecturing which had for so many years been his main means
of support. It was indeed well that he could now count upon that
half-yearly five hundred dollars. Yet the old journalist was still
driven to ply his pen, held though it now was with pain and difficulty
by his gouty hand and directed by nearly blind eyes. And he accepted
a position on the faculty at Seton Hall at South Orange, lecturing
there each week until he found the journey to and from Elizabeth

too much for him. When that happened the future Bishop Corrigan tried to get him to move to South Orange.[5] It was perhaps this work at Seton Hall that prevented him from going back to live at Chelsea again. For on January 2, 1866, Henry Brownson was commissioned to look for a house there—one of at least six rooms and a rent not over $200 a year.[6]

Moreover, in spite of the fact that Brownson could hardly drag himself about his own house, he undertook a certain amount of other lecturing, though not nearly so much as in the past. Even as late as the end of January, 1870, he ventured as far as Chicago for a lecture, but then fell ill and had to send hurriedly for Henry to take his place.[7] In September of the same year he appeared at Brooklyn before an audience of two thousand people, and the following December went to Boston for a lecture, getting on that occasion, in addition to his fee, a Christmas present of a hundred and twenty-five dollars.[8]

The explanation of this unexpected activity would seem to be that he was obliged to supplement his income so as to be able to send money to his sisters who were in need, and now and then even to Orestes Junior and Henry. Though he could write of Thorina in January, 1875, only a few months before her death from consumption, describing her as "a Methodist saint, . . . [who] has not committed a sin for forty years. She is superstitious as all Methodists are, sees visions, has wonderful dreams, and is always, by *sortes biblianae* and other modes of divination, trying to divine the future," [9] his purse was always open to her and to his twin, Daphne. These demands upon him could only be met by lecturing. His journalism may be sufficiently accounted for on the ground that nothing is more irksome to a man used to activity than to be idle.

When he was presented with his annuity in 1865, to buy which even some Protestants had joined, Dr. Cummings made a speech in which he said that though Dr. Brownson had sometimes said or written things of which his best friends could not approve, they all admired his perfect honesty and the valiant defence of what he believed to be true. Brownson in reply admitted that, looking back over his career, "he was satisfied that he might have effected his purpose just as well without giving any offence" and that "the difficulties that he had encountered were in a great measure created by him. . . . More prudence, mildness, and dexterity would have been better; and often after mature reflection he thought some views he had expressed should be so modified as to sever his connection with a tendency to which he was wrong in yielding." [10] After the speech-making on that August day in 1865 he went home happy with the insurance policy in his pocket.

Already he had made large plans for the future. Writing to Senator Sumner on January 17, 1865, he told him that the book on which he was engaged (that on the American Constitution) would be, "if Providence spares my life and health and reason . . . followed by a work on Philosophy, another on Theology, another on the Church, and another on the Catholic and Protestant controversy. Under the head of philosophy I propose to treat of Metaphysics, Ethics, and Aesthetics, and under that of theology, the Christian Revelation, and the Greek and Roman, Hindo and Egyptian Mythologies. Is this not pretty well for a man to propose to himself in the 62nd year of his age? But the materials are all collected, the greater part already written, and nothing remains to be done but to throw the whole into shape, and give it the finishing hand. So you see, I do not mean, old man as I am, to be idle, and that I have lost neither heart nor hope." [11]

It is evident from this grandiose scheme that what Brownson had in mind was to work up the articles he had already written, so as to make books of them. This is what he did in writing *The American Republic,* and one may easily discover in his collected *Works* the materials he intended to draw upon for his other projected books. Actually he completed none of these things, though perhaps he might have attempted them had his *American Republic* met with a better reception. As events developed, he turned instead to the more immediately remunerative journalism, which was also the kind of writing that best suited his temperament. Lord Acton was premature in writing in 1862 of Brownson's premature decay.[12] Though his health was undoubtedly gone, the vigor of his mind remained undiminished. Some of the best work he ever did was that done by the broken old man during the last ten years of his life. One stands amazed at the quality as well as the quantity of work he was to do for the *Ave Maria,* the *Catholic World,* and the New York *Tablet.* At rates which worked out at about a cent a word he earned several hundred dollars a month.[13] And it is clear that he needed all that he could make by his pen as well as what he made on the platform.

In 1842 Father Sorin had started in the wilderness of northern Indiana a college which is now the great University of Notre Dame. Begun with hardly five hundred dollars and a handful of men, by 1865 it had prospered so much that a second building was put up, with the first dome surmounted by the statue of Our Lady. In that same year, too, the *Ave Maria* was founded and Brownson was asked to write for it.

Sorin had the happy inspiration of getting Brownson to break what was for him virtually new ground by producing a series of articles on devotion to the saints, and in particular to the Queen of the Saints. When Brownson felt a little shy about what he thought of as "piety"—and he had come to regard what usually passed for piety as being sentimental—he was encouraged to deal with the philosophical principle underlying popular Catholic practices. It was in this way that he was induced to write his articles on Saint Worship.

Nobody could have been better fitted for such a task. People had often thought there was a lack of spirituality in him, and undoubtedly his nature was not what is generally described as poetic or mystical. But he had at bottom a very genuine piety, and a special devotion to the Blessed Virgin. If he used the word "mystical" with some contempt, this was because he remembered the haziness of Transcendentalism. Mysticism had come to have for him the further connotation of a muddle-headed sort of German metaphysics, born of lager-beer and clouds of sleepy tobacco smoke. This sometimes made him unable to do justice to the religious sentiments of those whose formal theology happened to be defective. He was concerned that men should have right ideas about God; that they should love God he regarded as something outside his province. He knew from personal experience that in everything except orthodoxy and the means of grace at their disposal many Protestants are superior to many Catholics; yet he insisted upon the most rigorous sense of the principle that there is no salvation outside of the Church—so much so that his theological rigidity made him appear arid and forbidding. Now a new Brownson was to manifest himself.

To a great extent his so-called liberalism had been no more than a hyper-critical tone. His harshness was due to the treatment he had received; that he was attacked only made him the more combative and extreme. It might now be said that it was Our Lady herself who led him back to peace, and that with his regained peace he found spiritual security. Certainly he came to a balance that was not again to be disturbed. He remained of course himself; not even the Blessed Virgin could make him anyone except Orestes Brownson, argumentative, aggressive, self-assured, belligerent. But one cannot fail to notice that his carping spirit disappeared. He did not become more orthodox; he did become more Christian.

His best theological articles were written from 1865 on. Some of his admirers will tell you that he knew the whole Greek and Latin Patrology almost by heart. He himself—and he was not given to claiming too little—said merely that he had read some of the Fathers. But it is never so much the amount of a man's reading that counts; rather it is his capacity to digest and apply what he has read, and here Brownson had a phenomenal capacity. Quite unparalleled among laymen of his time, he had few equals even among priests, at least for grasp and force, though of course many had more theological learning than he could boast. When he first started out as a Catholic controversialist he had to learn while he wrote, and many an article that looked formidably erudite contained the whole of what Brownson knew on the subject—got up specially for the purpose. But since then he had been steadily reading and thinking. Now out of the fulness of his mind he was able to write with mastery.

Two passages may be quoted to show how he conceived his purpose. "In this whole series of articles on saint-worship, if I have written indeed as a believer, I have aimed to write with all the sobriety and reason of the philosopher. I have rarely given way to any devotional impulses of my own, or appealed to the devotional sentiments of my readers. I have no doubt seemed to most readers cold and insensible, a bold speculator to some, and a soulless logic-grinder to all. My aim has been to state and defend the naked truth to the unsympathizing understanding, and to show to the coolest and most exacting reason that the whole system and practice of saint-worship among Catholics is defensible on the most rigid theological reason, and must be accepted or Christianity itself rejected as a delusion." [14] The other passage is: "If my articles have been profitable to no others, their preparation has been profitable to me, and has given me much peace and serenity of mind, quickened my love to Mary and the saints of our Lord, and rendered dearer both the Catholic faith and the Catholic worship." [15]

In 1853 he had written on "The Worship of Mary," a single article —and this was probably what suggested to Father Sorin that others might be drawn from the same pen. For that article was theological, stressing the point that devotion to Our Lady is due to her peculiar relation to the mystery of the Incarnation, and therefore to our salvation. "There is and can be," he had said, "no truer test of one's active, living faith . . . than a firm attachment to the worship of Mary. . . . This is, probably, why devotion to Mary is commonly regarded by the saints as a sign of election." [16] Thirteen years later he said in the *Ave Maria*: "It is not easy to love our Lady too much; and I have found it always easy to distinguish those who really love her, and are really devoted to her, by their purity of thought and expression, their gentleness and sweetness of temper, and their amiable and obliging disposition, from all others." [17] Here in the piety of Brownson appears Brownson's orthodoxy. If his own hot temper may seem to exclude him from the Christians he described, it should at least be remembered that he bore no malice and that he endured malice patiently. We may safely surmise that to nobody was his own natural disposition more of a burden than to himself. The arrogance of the man was all on the surface; underneath there lay a genuine and touching humility. And he carried his Catholic heart on his sleeve.

In 1871 Brownson wrote on "The Religious Orders" for the *Ave Maria*. The significance of this article is that Brownson had hitherto shown no great sympathy for asceticism and had tended to disparage the monastic life. Now he dealt with the Orders, not historically or philosophically so much as in a practical fashion, by indicating the bearing of the ideal of monasticism upon the needs of the day. He took this occasion to make a new recantation of his liberalism. "My faith was firm," he declared, "and my confidence in the church unshaken, but I yielded to what seemed at the moment a wise and desirable policy. All I gained was the distrust of a large portion of the Catholic public, and a suspicion among non-Catholics that I was losing my confidence in Catholicity, and was on the point of turning back to some form of Protestantism or infidelity. But I was not long, through the grace of God, in discovering that the tendency I was encouraging would, if followed to the end, lead me out of the church." [18] Now more explicitly—for the passage just quoted is a repudiation of his apologetic method rather than of any specific propositions—he goes on to express his dissent from Gioberti and those liberal, "that is, worldly-minded Catholics," who doubt the necessity of a warfare between the Church and the world. "Undoubtedly," Brownson explains, "all the works of the Creator are dialectic, and considered physically, as the works of the Creator, there is no antagonism between earth and heaven. Both are parts of one stupendous and harmonious whole. But it does not follow from this that there is no moral antagonism between a life lived for the world and a life lived for God. The antagonism is moral, not physical, and is removable only by the renunciation of the world, detachment from it, and placing our affections on the unseen and the eternal." [19]

In this article he makes the *amende honorable* to the Jesuits, though hardly by beslavering them with sickening praise and still in such a way as to keep himself free to regard their philosophical and theological system a bit critically. But he acknowledges their zeal and efficiency and affirms that "nothing is less applicable to the Jesuit than the epithet *jesuitical* in its popular sense." "Prudence is a virtue, but what the world calls prudence oftener leads to death than to life. . . . If [the Jesuits] are as prudent as serpents, they add to it the simplicity of the dove." In short, "it will always be found that the Jesuit heart is open to every one whose spirit is truly Catholic." [20] Such a testimonial, coming from Brownson, meant a good deal.

He takes the three monastic vows as exemplifying not only the highest forms of Christian renunciation but the ideal of Christian virtue. Perhaps he is most interesting in what he has to say about poverty. Here, as often before, he declares that the American is not covetous. But this is only in the sense of the American not being miserly; if more free-handed than the European, the American may nevertheless love wealth quite as much. The European has had it impressed upon him that he must save; the American spends because he believes that there is plenty more where the rest came from. He has, to an even greater degree than men of other nations, a disdain for poverty in the sense of looking upon success as a sign of virtue. "Making good," according to his ethos, is in danger of being confused with being good. Just as much as other people, Americans need to preserve the ideal of poverty.

Yet Brownson's own view of poverty is somewhat narrow, though it should always be remembered that he had always had it in his power to become affluent and that he had remained poor for the sake of the cause he served. Poverty, he says truly, is a good, but one that is such only to those who make it a good. His own practice is beyond praise. What causes some uneasiness is the disillusionment of the old social reformer when faced with the unlovely poverty created by industrialism. The problem being to him insoluble, he had fallen back on the reflection, "The poor you have always with you,"—the reflection that has been so comforting to callous men. Christ, however, never said that the poor *must* always be with us. He was merely pointing to existing conditions, not to a law of nature. Recent papal encyclicals amply recognize that for masses of men their poverty makes it virtually impossible for them to live a Christian life. Brownson's excuse is that the papal social program had not appeared in his day. That poverty will never be completely eliminated is probably true, but certainly something more than the alleviation of distress must be the Christian goal. Justice comes before charity, and charity (in the material sense) can be at best only a temporary expedient. Its scope should, in the physical sphere, be progressively reduced. There is therefore something a little unsatisfactory in Brownson's advice to the poor to be content with their lot, as it cannot be remedied and is so beautiful in itself.

His general argument, however, is entirely sound. "The remedy is to be found only in the old Christian principle of self-denial and sacrifice." Chastity, poverty and obedience are not merely for monks—they are the ideal to which all Christians are called, to be practiced according to their state in life. And if Americans seemed to him of all people the least disposed "to self-denial and sacrifice, [the most] averse to the ascetic or monastic virtues," he pointed out that this is not more true of our country than of those in which these very virtues came signally to flourish. What America needed most was a great increase of monasticism, to set a social standard.[21]

As was so often the case with Brownson, an article on any subject was likely to contain a good deal of personal matter. He had begun by repudiating his liberalism; he ended even more emphatically. Though he had produced a vast quantity of journalism since the cessation of his *Review,* most of it had been printed unsigned. Because of this the Catholic public had got the impression, he said, that "I have been doing nothing, and what is worse, that I have virtually ceased to be a Catholic, or at least an orthodox Catholic, and have become indifferent, if not hostile, to Catholic interests." [22] Accordingly he indicates what he had been doing during this period of obscurity, and adds: "I hope the readers of the *Ave Maria* will pardon me this personal explanation, as they are the only public I at present address under my own name. . . . In writing to them I merely think aloud, for I regard them as true, warm-hearted friends. . . . All my hopes for my country as for my own salvation are centred in the church, the living body of Christ, who only hath the words of eternal life." [23]

Even his articles in the *Ave Maria* did not spare him a new charge of formal heresy. The diocesan organ of an archbishop picked out the phrase, "as God is, in His essence, triune" for disapprobation. Father Sorin was alarmed and therefore submitted the whole article to Cardinal Barnabò, the Prefect of Propaganda, who in turn submitted it to some theologians in Rome. They reported that they did not particularly like the expression—"because probably," as Henry Brownson suggests, "it was not in the text-books they had studied," [24] —but they had to admit that there was nothing in it that was not orthodox. To avoid further criticism, Brownson agreed not to use it again. On which Henry Brownson, who had a rather waspish temper, commented: "God, in his providence, has not thought best to make archbishops infallible." [25]

Meanwhile Brownson had been contributing a large number of articles to the *Catholic World,* which Isaac Hecker founded in 1865, backed by his brother George, whose flour-mills had prospered marvellously.[26] He also meant to establish a daily paper, for which half the necessary funds had been collected when he became incapacitated for active work. When this happened the editorship of the *Catholic World* was taken over by Father Hewit.

Here we come to a period in Brownson's life that has been grossly misunderstood and misrepresented by Doran Whalen in her *Granite for God's House*. The excuse that she followed Henry Brownson is hardly sufficient, for in the first place she goes far beyond her authority, and in the second, she could have availed herself of the archival materials in the possession of the Paulists and at the University of Notre Dame. Perhaps the simplest way of indicating the extent of her unreliability is to quote a single sentence from her book, which manages to contain four distinct and serious errors of fact. It is: "Even Father Hecker, whose child-letters Brownson preserved to the end, quarrelled with Brownson; and finally, on a false charge, denied him space in the *Catholic World*." [27]

The first letter Hecker wrote to Brownson was in 1841, when he was in his twenty-second year. To call it a "child-letter" is a little absurd, but otherwise does not matter. What does matter is to say that Hecker and Brownson quarrelled, for they remained firm friends to the end, and that Brownson was "denied space" in the *Catholic World* on a "false charge." There was no charge of any kind, and when Brownson ceased to write for the *Catholic World* it was because he himself decided on this for a number of reasons. Finally Doran Whalen says that "the fact of the matter seems to be that the *Catholic World* had met ecclesiastical censure. Then, since no article had been signed by any author, Brownson was cited for blame. The law of self-preservation is strong in humanity, whether in matter of physical safety or of reputation. Father Hewit was not the first drowning man to strangle the swimmer next to him." [28] This is sheer invention, as is the case with so much else in Doran Whalen's book. There was no ecclesiastical censure of the *Catholic World*, nor did Hewit try to shift any blame on Brownson. The only thing true in all this is that no articles in the magazine were signed.

That is what caused the trouble. It would have been better had the contributions not been published anonymously. But when Brownson suggested this, Hecker told him that it would involve a change in editorial policy which did not seem to him advisable.[29] The result was not the making of any "false charges," but an amount of editing on the part of Father Hewit which struck the testy and touchy Brownson as excessive. He may be pardoned for feeling as he did; Hewit must also be pardoned—as he had to accept a personal responsibility for everything that appeared in his columns. That is about all the affair amounts to.

Henry Brownson was never quite fair to Hecker, whom he several times accused of having led his father into liberalism. He actually talks about "the new Catholic Church which Hecker and his associates [meaning especially Hewit] were trying to build up."[30] But at least he, being a man, understood what Doran Whalen, being a woman, cannot be expected to understand, that men can pound the table and roar at one another in argument and yet remain on the most affectionate terms with one another. That there were several points on which Brownson and the Paulists strongly disagreed is true. And such disagreement made it difficult for Brownson to produce work that always satisfied his editors. There was, however, no breach of friendship between them and their star contributor. So far from that, Father Elliott gives a charming account of Brownson's monthly visits to the Paulists' house on 59th Street. Then of course there were loud theological arguments late into the night; but the last thing of all was that Brownson sought out Father Deshon, the novice-master, to make his confession. In the morning, at the end of the row of rosy-cheeked novices, knelt the shaggy old philosopher at the Communion rail.[31]

As there were certain theological and philosophical differences between Hecker and his associate Hewit, on the one side, and Brownson, on the other, it had better be indicated what these were. The whole thing can be put in a single sentence: Brownson accused the Paulists of being too sanguine about human nature; the Paulists accused Brownson of being too despondent about human nature. Put in theological language, Brownson considered the Paulists to be semi-Pelagians, because of not emphasizing original sin strongly

enough; the Paulists considered Brownson to have retained some
of the Calvinist virus and to be over-emphasizing it. This was an
old disagreement between them. Even when reviewing Hecker's
Aspirations of Nature at the time when he was most under Hecker's
influence, Brownson did not hesitate to criticize him on this score.[32]
But such criticism did not disturb their friendly relations.

By the time Brownson came to write for the *Catholic World,* he
had swung so far away from the liberalism he had so recently advanced, that he was critical of Hecker on other scores. He was to
tell his son, in a letter dated November 12, 1870, that democracy
was "simply the logical political development of Protestantism."
This was pointed at Hecker, for later in the same letter he remarked: "Father Hecker's notion that Democracy is favorable to
Catholicity is worse than foolish. Democracy rests on popular
opinion, and never looks beyond, and no people that makes popular
opinion its criterion of right or wrong is or can be Catholic." [33]
Brownson, in short, had by now completely abandoned his effort
to find a new apologetic mode of approach and had reverted to
his first rigid and uncompromising position. Hecker's method, according to the Abbé Xavier Dufresne, was to draw "his hearers to
discover the truth in their own minds instead of receiving it by force
of argument." [34] It is the method of the poet, who creates recognition for what he has to impart but who ruins everything once he
begins to argue. Brownson, though he had confessed that his own
method—that of logic—was the worst of all, returned to a remorseless
logic as the only method he could use. This of course somewhat
hampered him when writing for a magazine whose policy was in
some respects different from his own, but it did not prevent him
from writing for that magazine, nor did it cause any quarrel between Brownson and the Paulists.

Finally, there was a disagreement between Brownson and Hewit
—this was a matter from which Hecker prescinded as much as
possible—over ontologism. Each man accused the other of being an
ontologist; or rather Brownson accused Hewit of having formerly

Brownson's return to the old approach

been one and of now reading into the Brownsonian metaphysical system the errors Hewit himself had once held. But again, the debate was academic. It did not result in any hard feelings on either side. Nor did anybody mind when Brownson grumbled that the *Catholic World* had too many feminine writers, "whether they wear skirts or breeches." They understood what he meant when he said that he felt "only half a man" when he had to repress the "rough vigor of thought and expression" natural to him.[35]

All these matters added up, however, to a state of tension, especially as Brownson's health made him more than ordinarily explosive. He had been accustomed to being his own editor, and it was not easy for such a man to submit to the editing of others. Writing to Hewit, on February 25, 1870, he informs him: "Father Hecker restrains me, and my mind does not, and will not work freely under his eye. He patronizes me, but treats me as an inferior. I can face to face converse more at my ease with him than with you, but I can work far more freely under you than under him. You do not disarrange my working gear, nor wound my amour-propre."[36] Which was a way of saying that, as Hewit had never been his disciple, Brownson could more easily bear from him what he could not bear from Hecker. And yet it is clear that this complaint was no more than a passing characteristic snort, not to be taken too seriously.

Brownson sometimes objected to Hewit's editorial changes,—a little more often than Father Parsons is disposed to admit in his article "Brownson, Hecker and Hewit,"[37] though far less strenuously and persistently than Doran Whalen asserts. An undated letter among the *Hecker Papers* is his strongest protest: "I can bear the rejection of an article, but I find I cannot bear its mutilation by any hand but my own. I am too old a writer and too old an editor to be treated as a schoolboy writing his theme for his master." Yet he understood that, as the *Catholic World* articles were unsigned, the editors had to accept a degree of direct responsibility greater than if the articles appeared under the contributors' names. His letters

n this subject have to be balanced one against the other. On
february 4, 1869, he wrote to Hecker: "If you tone me down too
much, you will make me weak & insipid, deprive me of my masculin-
ty. I must be allowed to work a little in my own way, or I cannot
work at all. Pegasus could never be made to draw in harness." The
ollowing August 24th he wrote to say that he found it impossible
o treat adequately the subjects with which he deals when he was
onfined to a short article. He feels that his articles are therefore
omewhat tame, because of being toned down by himself. "If I
venture into a higher key and give fuller play to my natural
endencies, and study to make them more animated and interesting,
 should most likely say something that would jar on the mild and
onciliatory tone of the magazine." He suggests signing his articles,
r even using a pen name.[38] In the same letter he tells Hecker:
You have forty or fifty better magazine writers than I, who have
 grace, a vivacity, a finish of style I cannot aspire to, and who can
ell their whole thought on a subject in a single article, in other
vords, who can restrict their purpose to what they are able to effect
n a single article. Alas, for me, the writing of a single article sug-
ests matter for a dozen articles, & it is only the least part of my
hought that I am able to get into a single article. It is a deplorable
efect in a magazine writer." Similar complaints were made to
Iewit, when he acted as editor, during Hecker's absence in
turope. But it is clear that the main difficulty was that Brownson
vas writing for a magazine in which the articles had to be shorter
han those he used to write for his own *Review*.

On the other side of the question we have Brownson writing to
Iecker on January 24, 1868, telling him, "Cut out, cut down, alter,
mend, or reject altogether at your own sovereign pleasure." At
he same time he explains that if any of his articles are rejected
ecause of their doctrine, this not only worries him so much as to
ring on an attack of the gout, but that the rejection "would . . . so
perate on my crochety and sensitive nature, as to render me unable
vith all my endeavors to write on anything else." Five days later

he tells Hecker that his worry has in fact brought on an attack of the gout, but adds, "What you did and said was perfectly right. An editor is and always should be, an autocrat. The whole responsibility is on you and your power should be absolute. Yet having been myself an autocrat for thirty years, I have some difficulty in making my mind work freely, if while I am writing, I am in doubt whether what I write will be accepted or not."

On February 12th of the same year he wrote again to Hecker, "My gout never made me more amiable, or better able to appreciate the virtues of others. I am one of those who never profit by suffering. I never murmur against Providence, for I know that I deserve all I suffer, and more, too, but I get mad at myself, for my folly, and when mad at myself, I am in good humor with nobody. The gout did not make me feel more kindly to you, but your letter did, while it pained me to hear that you had been suffering." [39]

So far from Hecker's having given "minute direction as though to an incompetent mind," [40] he rarely did more than indicate the subjects he would like Brownson to write about. Both he and Hewit were well aware of the resplendent gifts of their contributor, being also aware of his idiosyncrasies, they did their best to humor him. But a certain amount of editing was unavoidable under the circumstances. Very meekly Hewit wrote to him on March 3, 1870, "It is undoubtedly a great humiliation for you to be in any respect subject to one so much inferior to yourself in intellect and most departments of knowledge." He suggests that Brownson make this an opportunity for gaining spiritual merit, and expresses the hope that "Dr. Brownson may become as great a Saint as he is a Philosopher." Mrs. Brownson had better pray for them both; the "who knows but we might even at the eleventh hour get the grace of conversion and become like two little lambs." But as for the editing, "The powers which I must necessarily have and exercise I always use with scrupulous respect toward every author who is master in his art, and to you especially, and never meddle with a word unless conscience or an evident reason of propriety requires it." [41] All of which is not only fair, but kindly, and not only kindly but affectionate. Doran Whalen has misunderstood the whole relationship. A little humor should be applied to such expressions as Brownson's comment—in a letter to Henry—on Hecker in 1867, "We will, I trust, be able to jog on together without too much mutual snarling and growling," or his letter of the following year in which he says, "Fr. Hecker and I have had a fight, but it is over now. . . . Father Hewit might contradict the Council of Trent, but nobody on the *Catholic World* must contradict Father Hewit, whose orthodoxy on more than one point is suspect." [42] He wrote to Hecker on January 24, 1868, regarding their different views on the subject of original sin: "I pray you and F. H[ewit] to forgive me the freedom of these strictures. It is never without much misgiving that I differ from you or from him. It may be he is right and I am wrong, but I have given what appears to me a just criticism." [43] Such amenities are common enough when men start wrangling over theology.

Another bone of contention was the interpretation of the doctrine *Extra ecclesiam nulla salus*. Brownson wrote to his son in horror in 1871 to tell him: "Father Hewit . . . does not believe that it is necessary to be in communion with the Church in order to be saved. He holds that Protestants may be saved by invincible ignorance." [44] Writing in the *Ave Maria* in 1867 Brownson had admitted that "men may err against faith, not indeed, without heresy, but without incurring the *guilt* of heresy, and it is as well for us that it is so, for we are all liable to err. One may be, as the theologians say, a *material* heretic without being a *formal* heretic, and it is not impossible that there are some such in the several sects." [45] But he came to resume his old position—one from which he was never again to recede—that to make the slightest admission that anyone not a Catholic, in the sense of being a member of the visible Church, might be saved, would be to destroy all possibility of getting anyone to join the Church. It was, in effect, to declare that men care nothing for the truth but only for their own skins—a very strange attitude for a man whose whole life was a ceaseless quest for the truth. The con tradition runs throughout Brownson: an absolute confidence i reason, and a seeming lack of confidence in the reasonableness o men. Optimistic by disposition, he was pessimistic because of th hangover of his puritan mood. Having rejected Hecker's mode o apologetics, as part and parcel of the repudiated liberalism (whic it was not), Brownson became more adamantine than ever.

He did, however, cling to the metaphysical theories that hav brought upon him the charge of ontologism. As to just what wer his views, even Hecker did not pretend to be able to pronounce, and the controversy on this point was not with him but with Hewi But legitimate controversy is one thing, and the accusation of doubl dealing made by Doran Whalen against Hewit is something els again. Here apparently she is misled by a couple of paragraphs i Henry Brownson, the point of which I, too, find it a little hard t grasp: "It was hardly right in the *Catholic World* to repudiat ontologism without acknowledging the fact, and still less withou distinguishing the ontologism which it very justly repudiated an which has been improbated by the Holy See, from the syntheti philosophy which it previously defended but now rejected. Th *Catholic World* was before and for some time afterwards im personal and . . . it could not shift the responsibility of its forme philosophical essays from itself to the writer, let him be who h may. . . . Not a few persons knew, however, that its leadin philosophical articles were written by Brownson, and that throug misapprehension or misrepresentation the public confounded th philosophy advocated in them with the ontologism which he re pudiated, from which it widely differs. It was due to itself, to th public, and to Brownson personally that it should have recognize this difference and corrected this false impression." [47] Just how th magazine could "repudiate" ontologism "without acknowledging th fact," I am at a loss to understand. But I gather that Henry Brownso meant that the *Catholic World,* after having itself advocated (as he al leges) something like ontologism, kept silence and allowed the blam

fall on Brownson when it should have accepted the blame (if there
were any) itself. This meaning, as we have seen, Doran Whalen
extends to a crafty shifting of the blame to Brownson. Quite
definitely she writes: "Since no article had been signed by any
author, Brownson was cited for blame." [48] It was on this account,
she tells us, that a breach occurred between the editor and his contributor.

What actually happened was rather different. On February 25,
1870, Brownson wrote to Hewit: "My articles are of course subject,
even when accepted, to your editorial revision and correction; but
I am rather particular in my choice of terms, and a little sensitive
to verbal changes. . . . I think I am more nice and exact in the
use of terms than you are yourself. . . . I would more willingly
submit to your doctrinal corrections than to your verbal changes,
unless in cases where I have been careless and have obviously used
an incorrect term." [49] The editorial principle therefore was not con-
tested, and was indeed freely admitted in several other letters to
Hewit and Hecker; the only complaint Brownson ever made was
on the score of particular instances of editorial revision. But Doran
Whalen bases nearly her whole contention on the instance of a footnote that Hewit omitted as "unnecessary and inadvisable" from
one of his articles in the issue for October, 1871. When Brownson
received the proofs in August, he at once wrote to Hewit: "I am
not quite sure that I like the omission of my note. . . . I have no
doubt that in omitting [it] you have done what was best for yourself,
for you really had maintained a proposition which the Holy See
had censured,—immediate intuition of God." He added, "If you
strike out the note, it strikes me that you should strike out all allusion
to Gioberti and me in the text." [50] And when Hewit rejected an
article on Ontologism, saying in a letter to Brownson dated January
7, 1872, that he considered that one of his expressions could be interpreted in a wrong sense, "and that the prevalence of errors on this
subject makes it necessary to exclude all possibility of such interpretation," [51] Brownson replied four days later, signing himself

"very truly and affectionately yours,": "I understand the Holy See
to have improbated what you call *immediateness,* or that we have
immediate cognition of God, and this cognition is the very light
of the intellect, in fact, the intellect itself. . . . [But] I have fallen
into neither of the errors of ontologism improbated by the Holy See
for I hold that the human intellect is a created light, and that we
have neither immediate cognition nor immediate intuition of God
and attain to a knowledge that God is, only mediately." [52]

On January 10th Brownson wrote to Hecker, "You are the judge
not I, of what is suitable for your pages, and I regret that my
philosophy and theology are under the ban of the *Catholic World.*"
Two days later he wrote again: "As there is a manifest difference
between me and the *Catholic World* on the important subjects of
philosophy and theology, the best thing will be for me, and probably
for it, to discontinue my articles for its pages, and with a friendly
mutual understanding. I am not willing, indeed it would greatly
grieve me, to have our long continued friendship interrupted or
grow cool, and I trust it will not. . . . Understand, dear Father, that
I do not withdraw in a pet, or with the slightest unkind feeling."
On the 24th it was: "I am an old man, & probably approaching my
second childhood, & very likely I am oversensitive, as well as silly.
But it goes hard with me not to be trusted, & to be regarded by my
dearest friend as the world has always regarded [me] as a man
without judgment." On the 31st he explained a little further: "The
rejection of my two articles may have been the occasion of my
withdrawal from the *Catholic World,* but not the cause or the
reason. I was a little vexed I admit, but I could and should have
soon got over that. But I found that neither my head, nor my eyes,
nor even my hand would allow me to write as much as I was
writing." [53] Meanwhile he had written to Henry: "I find I had
undertaken more work than I could accomplish, that I could not
write for the *Catholic World* and the *Tablet,* and have any time left
to prepare the series of works I have, as you know, in contempla-
tion. Consequently I have broken off my connection with the C. W.

. . . I shall hereafter devote my time to the *Tablet* and the preparation of my contemplated works. The Refutation of Atheism, I have more than half done." [54] That was the end of Brownson's association with the *Catholic World*. It is clear that it did not come about as the result of any quarrel.

Brownson was quite serious about wishing to complete the books he had planned. On May 23, 1872, he wrote to Henry to say: "I intend going to the city tomorrow for a few days to make arrangements for bringing out one or other of my books." [55] Actually, however, none of them was ever completed. Not even the *Essays in Refutation of Atheism* ever got into book form, though what he had done of them appeared later as a series of articles. The fact seems to be that he was now too old for the labor that a book entails. And perhaps publishers were not particularly enthusiastic about undertakings that did not promise much success. In 1870 he had brought out a little volume of 183 pages entitled *Conversations on Liberalism and the Church*. He told his son that he did so "as a feeler," [56] and apparently as such it did not altogether serve its purpose. At all events, it was the last of his books, though he continued to write until almost the end.

Henry had been told in a letter written to him on March 12, 1866: "I wish to do something for my age similar to what St. Augustine did in his *Civitate Dei* for his age and St. Thomas in his *Contra Gentiles* for his age." [57] But not even a projected text-book of philosophy was ever rounded out. Brownson found it impossible to attain the concision such a works demands. He doubted moreover whether his book would be adopted by colleges, as the Jesuits had a controlling influence over Catholic education "and it is against their conscience to go out of their society for a text-book of philosophy. Besides, I am a layman, and under a cloud. No work I could write would be received and used in our higher schools generally." [58] He found similar reasons for not completing any of his half-finished books.

Conversations on Liberalism and the Church illustrates Brownson's weakness for easily-turned-out productions in which, instead of casting his arguments into a formal mould, he used the device of having a couple of men or a group of men argue about a subject —of course always taking care, like Dr. Johnson, that the Whig dogs got the worst of it. His two novels, *Charles Elwood* and *The Spirit-Rapper* are hardly more than this, though they have a slight framework of plot. In the rest of the many "Conversations" that fill up so much space in the collected *Works,* it is conversation alone that we get. If in "Conversations of Our Club" Brownson attempted a little characterization,[59] *Liberalism and the Church* is bald "argufying" from start to finish.

The protagonists are not so much as named: they are merely a successful young newspaper editor and an elderly priest of foreign birth. We are told that the debates took place at a spa, and now and then we suppose there is a listening circle. But we are conscious of nothing except a loud aggressive voice, and a quiet reasonable one. The whole of what takes place is reported by another man in the hotel, one who is not a Catholic and who occasionally writes his own comments at the end of the reports he makes. He is not convinced by anything that the priest says, except to the extent of remarking, on the last page, that he intends to look into the Catholic claims. Brownson must have believed that by this method he made arid argument more interesting and comprehensible. To my mind, however, by trying to reduce hard thought to simplicity, he succeeds only in thinning it out. One is even left with a suspicion that he wrote in this way because it caused him less mental exertion than the presentation of a formally elaborated case.

Effective points, it need hardly be said, are made. Thus the priest tells the editor: "The Church, if herself movable or progressive, could not aid either social or individual progress; she would simply change with the changes going on around her, and could neither aid nor control them." If there were not this immovable

rock for the fulcrum, "We should . . . deny progress in the very
act of asserting it." [60] The stock objections to the Church's suppositious obscurantism are easily disposed of, one by one. And when
the editor brings the charge that the Church denies liberty of
opinion, the thrust comes: "According to her doctrine, as I have
learned it, opinions are free, and she in no degree restricts them in
anything which is a matter of opinion, or on which truth is not
revealed or known." [61] After which of course the priest makes the
demonstration that the mind is not free to disbelieve what is known
to be true—either in mathematics or theology; opinions are a
different story. Yet at the end one is left wondering how such a
fool as the priest's antagonist could have become the editor of a
metropolitan daily. The book might have been better entitled,
*Conversations About the More Muddled Notions of a So-Called
Progressive*. The priest's central argument, "I defend progress, but
by preserving the principles and institutions by which it is effected," [62] makes good sense. But the debate is too much watered
down for the less vigorous sort of intelligence to be particularly
stimulating to a mind that wants something a little stiffer.

Brownson published his book to test how anything brought out
under his name would be received. Whether it was because he was
still a celebrated man—even if a much abused one—or because
people who could not bring themselves to work their way through
long knotty metaphysical articles were more at home with apologetics made easy, the book went into a second edition; and Brownson once again began to think of reviving his *Review* or of having
his son do so. He suggested that this might be a very nice little
property for him to inherit. [63] It was an idea that he frequently
turned over in his mind. Just after he had closed the "National
Series" in 1864, some of his friends, sorry to see *Brownson's
Quarterly Review* disappear, cast about for means of reëstablishing
it under the same name but under a different editor. [64] Though
that project fell through, he wrote in 1866 to his son Henry, who

was then still a Major in the Army, asking him whether there was "anything in the rules of the service that would directly or indirectly be interfered with were an officer to become an editor, providing he discharged faithfully his military duties." [65] As there certainly was, the project had to be dropped. But on June 2, 1868, he wrote to Henry again, saying that the *Review* would probably be revived under the firm of Sadlier [66]—another project that came to nothing. But the idea persisted in Brownson's mind and in 1870 Henry heard once more from his father: "I believe the public would now support it. The amount of writing would cost me less labor than I now bestow on the Catholic World." [67] It is clear that he had never reconciled himself to being without a magazine of his own.

If he had some friction with the *Catholic World,* he was not without his annoyances on the *Tablet,* which was to him a means of livelihood rather than a medium of expression. An indication of this peeps out every now and then, especially in a letter that his wife wrote him on May 7, 1871, while he was on a visit to their son in Detroit. The usually gentle Mrs. Brownson said, "Perhaps Sadlier will, by-and-bye, see it not best to exclude your articles and put in Mrs. Sadlier's. No doubt it is gratifying to the Priests and their friends, to know who was deacon and sub-deacon at every great celebration, but it is not quite so interesting to those outside." [68] He wanted to have his *Review* again. Only because this seemed to be impossible did he decide to devote what life remained to him in the writing of books.

In a mood of despondency he had written on March 8, 1870, to Father Hewit: "I say unaffectedly that to me it seems I have done nothing, and that my life has been frittered away. I have not fulfilled my early promise, nor used the opportunities I have had given me. . . . Of all my mighty plans not one has been executed, and I cannot persuade myself that I have done or can do anything worth remembering. This is said as sincerely as if in the confessional." To which Hewit made the conventional reply that

probably everybody felt like that when looking back over his life.[69]
It was in the hope that he would be able to write some books that he dropped his connection with the *Catholic World* in 1872. Yet he must have known in his heart that he would not be able to write any of them. At any rate nothing was done during the months that followed. The collected *Works* stand before us, twenty closely printed and formidable volumes—the editing of which, together with the Life he wrote, is Henry Brownson's monument to his father. But the *Works* contain for the most part articles which are only the raw materials for the series of great books of which he dreamed. He came to see that he would never produce them. There was, however, one thing more that remained for him—something that he owed not only to himself but to his children and his grand-children: he would somehow emerge from the cloud that had hung over him so long; he would prove beyond all doubt his orthodoxy, his papistry, even (if you like) his intolerance. He would reëstablish *Brownson's Quarterly Review.*

[1] The idea still seems to persist. Thus John J. Shea in *The Two Archbishop Kenricks* (p. 204) even says that *Brownson's Quarterly Review* was suppressed because of the *Syllabus.* He had failed to check his dates sufficiently carefully.

[2] *Works,* Vol. VIII, p. 146.

[3] Pp. 416–417.

[4] *Brownson's Quarterly Review,* Last Series, Vol. I (1873), pp. 325, 362.

[5] *Latter Life,* pp. 548–549.

[6] *Brownson Papers.*

[7] Brownson to Henry Brownson, January 24, and February 7, 1870, *Brownson Papers.*

[8] Mrs. Brownson to Henry Brownson, September 6 and December 21, 1870, *Brownson Papers.*

[9] *Brownson's Quarterly Review,* Last Series, Vol. III (1875), p. 64.

[10] *Latter Life,* pp. 444, 445–446.

[11] *Ibid.,* pp. 451–452.

[12] Gasquet, *Lord Acton and His Circle,* p. 289.

[13] Among the *Brownson Papers* are a number of financial statements from Lawrence Kehoe, the publisher of the *Catholic World,* which show that Brownson usually made a couple of hundred dollars a month by his work for that magazine—not counting of course what he earned elsewhere. The household in Elizabeth seems to have cost more than one might expect—owing to Brownson's demand for a lavish table and the amount of domestic help he needed because of his infirmities. These expenses—and what he gave away—kept him sufficiently poor and industrious.

[14] *Works,* Vol. VIII, p. 174.

[15] *Ibid.,* p. 185.

[16] *Ibid.,* pp. 66, 67.

[17] *Ibid.,* p. 102.

[18] *Ibid.,* p. 221. To this his editor (Henry Brownson) adds a footnote: "Although nothing contrary to faith could be found in those writings . . . yet their tone is uncongenial with. true Catholic feeling."

[19] *Ibid.,* pp. 224–225.

[20] *Ibid.,* p. 256.

[21] *Ibid.,* pp. 236, 237.

[22] *Ibid.,* p. 237. Henry Brownson says, "In many circles he was distrusted as a Catholic, and the common talk was that he had returned, or soon would return to some form of Protestantism. It was said that he was disgusted with Catholicity, and was turning against it." (*Latter Life,* p. 582.)

[23] *Works,* Vol. VIII, p. 238.

[24] *Latter Life,* pp. 501, 506. And also perhaps because it was liable to be misunderstood.

[25] *Ibid.,* p. 502.

[26] *Ibid.,* pp. 506–507. Their elder brother John had become an Episcopalian.

[27] *Granite for God's House,* p. 349.

[28] *Ibid.,* p. 355.

[29] *Latter Life,* p. 521.

[30] *Ibid.,* p. 448.

[31] *Catholic World,* Vol. CI (1911), p. 54. Mrs. Burton has drawn upon Father Elliott's article in her *Celestial Homespun* (p. 321).

[32] *Works,* Vol. XIV, pp. 557–558.

[33] *Latter Life,* pp. 493, 494.

[34] Elliott, *Hecker,* p. 424.

[35] *Latter Life,* p. 532.

[36] *Ibid.,* p. 532.

[37] *Catholic World,* Vol. CLIII (1941), pp. 396–408.

[38] Both of these letters are among the *Hecker Papers.*

[39] *Hecker Papers.*

[40] *Granite for God's House,* p. 351. A letter that Doran Whalen might have used is one that Brownson wrote to his son Henry on February 1, 1869: "The excellent man [Father Hecker] is utterly unconscious of the despotism he would exercise, but n'importe. I am sorry his prudence is so excessive but I shall write as I please or not at all." He did write as he pleased. (*Brownson Papers*).

[41] *Latter Life,* pp. 533, 534.

[42] *Brownson Papers.*

[43] *Hecker Papers.*

[44] *Latter Life,* p. 565.

[45] *Works,* Vol. VIII, p. 187.

[46] "I answer, Yes and No. Yes, if you mean by intuitive perception of God that God's existence is a primary apprehension of the human mind. No, if you mean the peculiar ontological views of Dr. Brownson. What these were I have never been able to fully satisfy myself." (*Catholic World,* Vol. XLV, 1887, p. 5).

[47] *Latter Life,* pp. 578–579.

[48] *Granite for God's House,* p. 355.

[49] *Latter Life,* pp. 531, 532.

[50] *Ibid.,* p. 567. It should be said, however, that Hewit wrote to Brownson "I have preserved the Note, in case you may want to use it elsewhere." (*Latter Life,* p. 567), and that Henry Brownson did not incorporate it in the article when reprinting it in his father's collected *Works* (Vol. II, pp. 428–447). This probably means that he decided that the note was not so very important after all. But if it was because he did not have a copy of the erased footnote, he could at least have told us that there was a footnote that could not be found. Letters from Mrs. Brownson (who was away during September of this year) indicate that Father Hecker had called to see her husband at Elizabeth. "I am very glad," she said in one of these letters, "Father Hecker likes your articles, although it would be hard to persuade myself that they were not good without his approbation—Still it is gratifying to have him say so." These letters are dated September 11 and 18, 1871, and are among the *Brownson Papers.*

[51] *Hecker Papers.* The expression objected to was: "Identification in the sense in which that which exists in God eminenter, and causaliter, may be said to be identified with that which He creates after the limitation of His essence." Hewit did not think it incorrect but merely open to misunderstanding.

[52] *Latter Life,* p. 574.

[53] All these letters are among the *Hecker Papers.*

[54] *Latter Life,* p. 576. He sketches out his projected books and concludes: "This is my design, and if I should not live to complete it, you will be able to complete it substantially from what I have already written and published."

[55] *Brownson Papers.* The books in question were on the Papal Supremacy and the unfinished *Refutation of Atheism.*

[56] *Latter Life,* p. 523.

[57] *Brownson Papers.*

[58] *Latter Life,* pp. 558, 561.

[59] Concerning a life of Lacordaire Brownson wrote to Hecker on March 30, 1868: "It is beautifully written, with a loving and really filial tenderness towards the author's spiritual father. But somehow or other I have no special interest for tracing the interior life of individuals, any more than I have for the psychological analysis of one's own feelings." (*Hecker Papers*). This may explain the absence of characterization in Brownson's novels and "Conversations" and also his frequent poor judgment of men.

[60] *Conversations on Liberalism and the Church,* pp. 12, 15.

[61] *Ibid.,* p. 151.

[62] *Ibid.,* p. 171.

[63] *Latter Life,* p. 523.

[64] *Ibid.,* p. 443.

[65] *Ibid.,* p. 562. "You are on good terms with the Jesuits," Brownson wrote to his son, "and by publishing in the first No. an article favorable to them you would at once secure their support, which would insure your success."

[66] *Brownson Papers.*

[67] *Latter Life,* p. 523.

[68] *Brownson Papers.*

[69] *Latter Life,* pp. 535–536, 537.

CHAPTER XVI

The Revived Review

ON MARCH 25, 1872, Brownson wrote to his son Henry, now a lawyer in Detroit: "I have finally resolved to revive my Review, Brownson's Quarterly Review, Last Series, Vol. I, No. 1, beginning the year 1873. . . . I want . . . to place myself rectus in curia before I die, for the sake of the cause, for the sake of my children and grandchildren, which I could not do in the C. W., and cannot do in the Tablet. Do not try to discourage me, but speak encouragingly." [1] Even so, he had not quite given up the idea of completing his books, as we know from the letter he wrote to Henry to which reference has already been made. What must be suspected, however, is that this was an idea he now held on to only for form's sake. It was pleasant to toy with the notion of another *De Civitate Dei* and *Contra Gentiles;* it was more practical to revive the *Review.* But if writing for the *Catholic World* made other tasks difficult, he most have understood that *Brownson's Quarterly Review* would make them almost impossible.

What decided him in the wavering state of his mind, was what his wife said to him on her death-bed—what she may be surmised to have said because she saw clearly that there would be no books but that there might be another way for him to rehabilitate himself. Though she had kept herself in the background and her influence over her husband was not always obvious, he often admitted it was great and that he considered her his superior in intelligence. She was not that, but she had better judgment than he commonly displayed, and she understood that he was fundamentally a journalist. In January the frail little woman, who kept

382

up her practice of attending Mass daily, though it involved a long walk to St. Mary's Church [2] in Elizabeth (which the Brownsons now attended instead of St. Michael's since it was nearer the Pearl St. house), got caught in a snow-storm on her way home. The cold she contracted developed into pneumonia, and in April she died. Almost her last words to her husband were that he was to reissue *Brownson's Quarterly Review*. After that there was no doubt in his mind. In any event her advice accorded with his secret convictions. On February 20th she wrote to Henry: "I am sick with cough and weakness and spend most of time in Father's big chair, he has been the best of nurses and no doctor could do better. Sarah has been sick with chills and fever, nurse for her. . . . Father to start his Review." [3] One suspects that all the time—despite what he told Hecker—the *Review* rather than the books had been in his mind.

To Father Sorin, who had written a letter of sympathy, telling that he was saying a Mass for the repose of Mrs. Brownson's soul and offering to give the widower a home at Notre Dame University, should he feel inclined to retire there, Brownson replied on May 23, 1872: "My wife was a true and Christian woman, a devout Catholic, and I do not believe she ever committed a mortal sin in her life. . . . Her loss to me is irreparable, but I trust that the loss to me is her gain." [4] But he declined the kind offer of a home among the Fathers of the Holy Cross, as he also declined a similar offer from Father Thébaud of Fordham.[5] He could not conduct his *Review* from either place. Being too busy and ill to do so much work served as a convenient excuse to give Hecker; and there were no doubt times when Brownson felt himself overwhelmed by his writing for the *Catholic World* and the *Tablet* and his increasing ailments. In spite of which, on February 22, 1870, he told Hewit: "You wonder at the amount of work I do, yet I am idle half my time, and do not a quarter of the work you do, for I work only on my past work." [6] After making all allowances for the contradictions and exaggerations that sprang from his constantly changing moods, to revive his *Review* was a tremendous undertaking for a man who was now half blind, crippled with gout, and seventy years old.

On November 22, 1872, he wrote to Henry saying that he expected to obtain a thousand subscribers, and that the cost of getting out a thousand copies would be $280—"which is very reasonable." [7] It was, indeed. To us it seems an editor's heaven—that world where a magazine could maintain itself with a circulation of a thousand and no advertisements. On the basis of a five-dollar subscription, he expected to clear twenty-five hundred dollars a year.[8]

When the first issue appeared in January, 1873, it had a better reception than Brownson had anticipated. By now even those who had been opposed to him or who disliked him realized that the disappearance of his *Quarterly* had left a gap in American Catholic life, one that only Brownson could fill. Besides, though the general public had lost sight of him since 1864, the leaders of Catholic thought were aware that he had given up his dangerous ideas. They had read, or had heard of, his articles in the *Ave Maria,* and they knew he had been writing for the *Catholic World*. His *Conversations on Liberalism and the Church* had also helped to effect his rehabilitation, and even those who were unable to accept the interpretation he offered of the Constitution in *The American Republic* at least perceived that in its Catholic sections, Brownson was unimpeachably orthodox. A good many people had by now begun to regret their attacks on him, especially as their consciences told them that the accusations of heresy were at least partly inspired by personal prejudice or political disagreement. Even Bishop Whelan of Wheeling, who had said that his anti-slavery arguments showed him another Robespierre, became a subscriber. And Archbishop McCloskey of New York took no offence that he had not been asked to give his consent to the establishment of the *Review* in his diocese, while Brownson's own bishop at Newark,

Michael Corrigan, who was similarly ignored, took it in good part.[9] After all, Brownson's was a special case. He was reviving a review, not starting a new one. They understood that if he was to do his work, it had to be in his own way. They were prepared for him to be still stormy and truculent. They knew that he still had his enemies. They also knew that his vigorous honesty was needed. Brownson found what was, upon the whole, a friendlier atmosphere than that of the past.

At the house at Elizabeth, however, there were difficulties. The old man was alone there with Sarah, and Sarah did not find him easy to live with. It was for this reason that he thought of retiring to South Bend or Fordham, or to Seton Hall College.[10] In a letter to Henry, dated April 18, 1872, Sarah grumbled to her brother of the way their father went around in old clothes: "I don't know anything more demoralizing than rags and shabbiness," harping particularly upon the thread-bare dressing-gown he wore. On July 21st she wrote again, saying, "I do all I can for him, but he complains of being always neglected. Fortunately he has a great deal of company, and so gets along." On August 11th her letter says: "He is quite well and amiable now, but for six weeks was so hard to get along with that I was almost desperate. I think Dr. Hewit is very much to blame for letting him take so many medicines of all sorts and kinds one right after another. . . . I do not feel much like talking when anyone comes here, life seems so very dreary and desolate."[11] Life had indeed pressed hard upon her since her mother's death.

A large part of the tension that began at this time must surely be set down to the fact that she had not been in good health for many years, as many anxious references to this matter in the family letters show. This probably accounted for her angry flight to her brother Orestes in Dubuque in 1865. And certainly her father was, as he often admitted in his letters, sometimes in a bad mood, aggravated by the intense pain he was suffering.

Sarah's nerves were also on edge because of the book she was writing on the famous and eccentric Prince Gallitzin. It was not her first book, for she had previously written a couple of novels;[12] but this was the book which cost her the most trouble. It involved several journeys to Loretto in Pennsylvania, where Gallitzin had worked as a priest under the name of "Mr. Smith," and Sarah got at loggerheads with Father Henry Lemcke,[13] who had been Gallitzin's assistant and whose church of St. Michael's the Brownsons attended at Elizabeth. As he had published a life of Gallitzin in German in 1861, he was furious with Sarah Brownson for poaching on his preserves and did all he could to prevent her gathering information at Loretto.[14] The strain of all this, and of getting her book through the press, told upon nerves already sufficiently frayed. At the same time she was apparently doing some secretarial work for her father. It is no wonder that she was in an upset condition.[15]

The fact that she was very much of a Brownson, as may be seen from her photographs, did not help matters. She naturally wanted to be in charge of the household and also in charge of her father —whom she did what she could to spruce up—and this irritated him. What the old man would accept from a gentle wife he was by no means disposed to accept from a daughter, whom he considered domineering. His own complaints went off to Henry in a letter dated May 23, 1872. Sarah, he thinks, will become a very able housekeeper, but she is "as imperious as any old maid in the land. Her great point is that she will let no one into her confidence or suffer me to make a suggestion to her or ask a question; so far as I can gather from a few hints she has thrown out she looks upon me as having made your mother lead a life of martyrdom, crossing her in every possible way and that she must revenge her mother on me. . . . So you see that while she keeps my house for me and secures a home for herself, I am to have no companionship with her and am to remain in solitude. No young wife could be more jealous of her husband's speaking to a servant maid than she is of her old father. Yet she is high principled, honest but old maidish; she is uncommonly gifted and firmly attached to her religion, but with many impractical notions. With all her faults I dearly love her and though my life with her must be in about complete solitude it would well nigh break my heart to be separated from her. Happily I have nearly finished my course and it matters not much if for a few days I am a victim to a daughter's tyranny. Perhaps it is only what I deserve." Though we need not take such letters too seriously—for men as well as women are given to writing this sort of thing in black moments, forgetting the larger stretches of placidity—the only definite quarrel we hear of at this time occurred when Brownson insisted on taking the painting of his wife from where it hung downstairs and putting it in her room. Sarah had come to regard it as belonging to herself.

Brownson was, in truth, somewhat disappointed in his children. Henry and Sarah were too like himself to be comfortable companions.[16] Yet he preferred their waspishness to the too easy-going and shiftless disposition of his eldest son, Orestes. The rest of the eight children he and Sally had had were all dead.

Orestes had shown himself, even when at Brook Farm, indifferent to study, much to the annoyance of Charles Dana, and had gone to sea. But it was only for a single voyage. On returning home, he flaunted his independence by refusing at first to join the rest of the family, who had all become Catholics during his absence. However, he too submitted before long, while getting his education with the Jesuits in Cincinnati.[17] Since then he had tried his hand at several things, at farming and at teaching school and finally —to his father's disgust—at writing what he described as "comic draminas."[18] At no occupation did he succeed. The only Brownsonian trait discoverable in him was his expert knowledge of chess, the game his father had taught him in childhood. The long hours when the gaunt Vermont preacher took a little relaxation from Cousin and Saint-Simon, playing relentlessly against his small son, bore some fruit when Orestes Junior edited a chess-magazine in later life.[19]

What was more distressing to his father even than the burlesque dramas was that in 1873, when he was forty-five, he seemed to be giving up his religion.[20] For he wrote on November 7th of that year to say: "in temporals we are making a comfortable living, in spirituals receding ever further and further from the Catholic Church. . . . There seems absolutely no other way for me to support my large family than by pursuing my present avocation, which in spite of all I can do, leads us every day further from the Church. Have you any counsel or advice to give me? What do you recommend? . . . Is it better to attend some Protestant Church, rather than none at all & if so what one? I suppose I have no faith, certainly I have none in the clerical management of things in Dubuque, which seems devoid of everything except sordid money-making." This to the man whom he calls in his letter so eloquent an advocate of Catholicism! Fortunately his father did not adopt the high tone of the Dubuque priest but instead sent him money to help him set up a little farm when he found himself in straits again. The upshot was that he wrote a few months later to say: "I shall do my best to get myself back and for all the others to practice their religion. I can not be a Protestant and there is no warmth or comfort in infidelity."[21] One gets from all this a shadowy picture of an amiable but not very reliable man.

It was troubled by such domestic happenings and worn down by ill health and sufferings that Brownson roused himself like an old lion for his final spring.

Brownson had often enough recanted his liberalism. Indeed, he managed to combine repentance for his liberalism with a denial that he had ever been a liberal, meaning that he was more sorry for the impression he had given people than for anything he had actually said—which in fact had been sufficiently orthodox even if the tone of his writings had for a time been bad. In June, 1872, he had written again: "Whatever else I may be, I am not a liberal Catholic, but heartily accept the Syllabus and the decrees of the Vatican. I am content with the church as she is. I came to the church in 1844 in order to be liberated from my bondage to Satan, and to save my soul. It was not so much my intellectual wants as the need of moral helps, of the spiritual assistance of supernatural grace, in recovering moral purity and integrity of life, that led me to her door to beg admission into her communion. I came not to reform her, but that she might reform me. If I have even for a moment seemed to forget this, it has been unconsciously, and I ask pardon of God and man." [22] Now this revived *Review* was to show on nearly every page that the Brownson of 1860 to 1864 was repentant.

In an introduction he intended for the "Last Series," and then suppressed, he said of his dead wife that she "was what the Scriptures call a valiant woman, and under God, I am principally indebted to her meek and unobtrusive virtues in all the relations of her heroic life that my mind was turned to the study of the truth, and by her generous encouragements led to embrace it, although she was not at the time within the pale of the Church. Her instincts were always pure, and her judgment was rarely, if ever, at fault, and her wish so clearly expressed in the last days of her earthly career became sacred, and I dare not resist it." [23] Then, perhaps as that might read too much like a belated obituary notice, he printed instead: "It was almost the last wish expressed to me by my late wife, whose judgment I never found at fault, that I should revive my Review, if only for a single year, and prove to the world that my faith has never wavered; that I am still an humble but devoted son of the church; and that I am, as I always professed to be, a thorough-going Papist." He was not willing, he said, that his name should go down to posterity with the slightest suspicion resting on it of disloyalty to the Church— "not, indeed, that I care much for it on my own personal account, but for the sake of the Catholic cause, . . . and also for the sake of my surviving children, to whom I can leave no inheritance, but that of an untarnished name." He continues: "I willingly admit that I made many mistakes; but I regard as the greatest of all the mistakes into which I fell during the last three or four years that I published my Review, that of holding back the stronger points of the Catholic faith, on which I had previously insisted; of laboring to present Catholicity in a form as little repulsive to my non-Catholic countrymen as possible; and of insisting only on the minimum [24] of Catholicity, or what had been expressly defined by the Holy See or a General Council. I am not likely to fall into that mistake again. . . . A *liberal* Catholic I am not, never was, save in appearance for a brief moment, and never can be. . . . The times, if I read them aright, demand Catholicity in its strength, not in its weakness." All of which means that he is going to assert more strongly than ever the doctrine *Extra ecclesiam nulla salus*.[25]

In this matter, as all others, any talk about maximum and minimum Catholicism is somewhat meaningless. No Catholic can deny that there is no salvation outside of the Church. To the extent that this is something to be kept always clearly in mind, Brownson was right. But he was wrong in relying upon it as the fulcrum for his apologetics. The Church has never said positively that those dying outside her communion will be saved if they have good will but "invincible ignorance"; but neither has the Church positively said the opposite. It is, however, generally held by Catholic theologians that factors of which we know little will operate, and they sometimes suggest that we had better hold ourselves prepared to be surprised at some of the people we shall meet in heaven (if we get there) and equally surprised at some of the people we shall meet in hell, if that is where we go. But Brownson seems to have considered that he had made a weak and shameful concession by writing in 1864, "we by no means hold that we are to consign to perdition all who are not in [the Church's] visible communion."[26] Therefore in 1874 he reprinted a large part of one of his 1847 articles, adding what was intended to reaffirm his old rigor and to concede nothing, but instead to express his contempt for "the theologians, who by their explanations open wide the door of salvation." They only labor, he said, "to prove that those who apparently die outside of the Church, and whose salvation, they tell us, is not to be despaired of, do not really die out of her communion, but, in fact, in it, and as Catholics." [27] He could not see that these theologians, quite as much as himself, affirm *Extra ecclesiam nulla salus,* so he scornfuly dismissed them as latitudinarians, trimmers, waterers-down of orthodoxy. He had exchanged liberalism for a very un-Catholic illiberality.

Very few contemporary Catholics, if it comes to that, were orthodox enough to suit Brownson. Thus he regarded Newman as wishy-washy in his famous *Letter to the Duke of Norfolk* upon Gladstone and the Vatican decrees. Newman he declares to be still half an Anglican, or at least "to retain an affection for Anglicanism which we do not share." With him conversion has been merely "a putting on, not a putting off"—but perhaps this is due to "his English dread of overdoing, and appearing too demonstrative." [28] He strikes Brownson as "somewhat stingy" in his avowals of obedience to the Holy See. "It may be good policy, so far as those who are prejudiced against the papacy, but we think the effect is bad, so far as regards the faithful themselves." As for himself, *"Papist* is a title of honor, and we glory in it." [29]

Later he makes a boast of his obedience: "The hardest thing, we apprehend, for converts from Protestantism to acquire, is the virtue of obedience: a virtue which we have never acquired, for it came natural to us; and our unreserved obedience to lawful authority has never had any merit. To obey where obedience is due and formally demanded, has never cost us a moment's effort; and we have never experienced any of that interior struggle between authority and our own will or private conviction, which we have remarked in others: and hence we conclude that we were born to follow, not to lead; to obey, not to command." [30] One gets a little irritated by Brownson's claim to possess so naturally all the Catholic virtues. That he logically also disclaims any merit for possessing them hardly lessens the irritation. For always the assumption is that he is right and that those who disagree with him, in the slightest particular, must be rather dubious Catholics.

Yet if we remember the times in which he lived and conditions in America, he must be admitted to have done an immense service. He did it even when he seemed to many people excessive or wrong-headed, or to be raising dangerous questions, or displaying a carping and cantankerous spirit. It was a way of sharpening the intelligence of Catholics by discussion. Now that he had discarded his "liberal" past he had a still better effect upon them, for he was less inclined to confuse them with eccentric opinions. His mind was as powerful as ever, but it did not fly off any more into tangents, or not often. Hewing to a straight line, he could be accepted not only as a champion of orthodoxy but of an orthodoxy stimulatingly presented. If the effect on Protestants was not good, he was no longer bothering with them. They had their choice: the Church or hell. His work was now exclusively for Catholics.

American Catholics were then (as to some extent they still are) somewhat timid people, who asked for little more than to be left alone. The problem that engrossed the ecclesiastical authorities was one of taking care of the flood of Catholic immigrants; it was impossible to make any general apostolic effort, though this was the work to which the Paulists specially addressed themselves. Whatever controversy was engaged in reduced itself to attempts to refute anti-Catholic calumny. Otherwise it was best for Catholics not to make themselves too conspicuous among a people with whom Nativism had not ceased to be endemic. They wanted to give no offence, and they sometimes came to regard their intellectual and spiritual sloth as humility. For that fatal spirit Brownson was the best possible corrective. He did not win Protestants; on the contrary, he antagonized them. But he did succeed in stiffening the Catholic backbone.

When in 1874 he wrote an article on Archbishop Spalding, who had died two years previously, and praised him for his work, the *Catholic Advocate* of Louisville, where Spalding had been bishop before being transferred to Baltimore, commented: "In lifting the countenances of Catholics from their time-out-of-mind cringingness to brute force, we are disposed to assign, as the chief instrument in

God's hands, not his Grace of Baltimore, but Dr. Brownson him-self. . . . At his feet, more than at those of any other man that taught in America, have the Catholic Bishops sat. . . . Brownson's vocation has been to teach the teachers. . . . Brownson has been an eminently providential man." [31] Of himself he could say with perfect truth: "Born and reared in the bosom of the persecuting class, we did not and could not make a proper allowance for the effect of ages of persecution or oppression on its victims. We came into the church with a bold, determined spirit, which had never been crushed by persecution, and very naturally gained among Catholics the reputation of being haughty, proud, arrogant, harsh, and overbearing, especially of being shockingly imprudent, while we thought we only exercised the firm and independent spirit that became the freeman, and the defender of the rights and dignity of the truth he loves and knows he possesses." [32] He increased Catholic morale even when he was a disturbing force among Catholics.

We know, however, from war propaganda, that not all methods of raising morale are equally good. The easiest way to raise it may be by fomenting hatred of the enemy; it is also the surest way of coarsening (and eventually weakening) the character of those who are stiffened by it. So also with Brownson's onslaughts upon Protestants. Granted, that he did not hate them; but it is to be feared that they came to hate Catholics all the more because of the aggressive tone he used in order "to put Protestantism on the de-fensive" as he called it. [33] While he made Catholics cheer, he hardly put the truth exactly—and what but an exact statement of truth can be Catholic?—when he asserted without qualification that Prot-estantism is anti-Christian. "Infidels they are," he declared, "and it is of no little importance to let it be seen that no man can be a Protestant and be at the same time a Christian or follower of our Lord and Saviour Jesus Christ." "If Catholicity is Christian, if reason is authoritative in its own province, nothing is more certain than that Protestantism is in no sense Christian, and that persons living and dying Protestants cannot be saved." [34] It is all very well to describe Brownson in his own terms as an "uncompromising Catholic"; the fact is that he was a bigot, and every bigot plumes himself upon his refusal to temporize or compromise. The narrow driving force can accomplish wonders; the only trouble is that it often loses as much as it gains. The man who had set out with such high hopes of converting his fellow countrymen, or large numbers of them, had long ago despairingly concluded that controversy with Protestants was quite useless—except as it instructs Catholics and perhaps a few individual Protestants "who retain some sense of religion and confidence in reason." [35] But if there were even a few such, they were to that extent Christian, on Brownson's own showing; so his whole argument breaks down. The truth is that he had discovered the syllogism not to be so overpowering a weapon as he had expected. He therefore threw the blame on Protestants instead of on his method. It was so even in face-to-face arguments with his Catholic friends: if they did not admit the force of his reasoning, he would get angry and bellow at them for being so thick-headed. That did not work at all when he was arguing with non-Catholics. Except for zeal, his, alas, was a temperament almost the reverse of what an apostle's should be.

His importance is that he always had magnificent things to say, especially when he could be induced to treat religion in the less narrowly controversial fashion. Nobody ever put this point better: "Revelation brings its own solution with it, and we doubt, if men had never had a supernatural revelation, that they would ever have felt either its necessity, or seen its possibility. It is the fact of revelation that stimulates thought, quickens the faculties, and directs the mind to the facts which prove its necessity and possibility." [36] But he still asserted his independence from the prevailing school of Catholic philosophy. Heading a review in 1874 with the titles of four books by Jesuits, he blandly announced: "We have no intention of reviewing them. We have introduced their titles only as a fitting text for some comments on the admonitions addressed to us and others from various quarters, not to depart from the traditional and generally received philosophy taught in our Catholic schools—an admonition that we are quite prepared to heed the moment it is made to appear that there is such a philosophy, and we are told precisely what it is." [37] Having turned his review into a defence of his own metaphysical system, he reopened his old quarrel with the Jesuits. Oh yes, he has the "profoundest veneration for the illustrious Society of Jesus," but their official philosophy is incapable of "solving satisfactorily the great problems pressing on us on every hand for solution. . . . It may be true that their colleges are the best we have, but judging them by the intellectual inefficiency of their graduates, we risk little in expressing the opinion that they are but imperfectly performing the work of higher education demanded here and now." [38]

The occasion of all this was a review in the *Catholic World* of Father Louange's *Course in Philosophy,* in which not only Louange was accused of ontologism, but Brownson himself was struck at through him. "That Dr. Brownson, in his *Review,*" wrote the anonymous writer (who probably was the editor himself), "should try to show that *his own* ontologism can be philosophically defended and does not fall under ecclesiastical condemnation, we do not wonder. He is not a priest; he does not write for school-boys, but addresses himself to educated men, who can sift his arguments, and dismiss with a benign smile what they think to be unsound; and, after all, he takes great care to screen himself behind a newly invented distinction between ideal intuition, and perception or cognition." After which the reviewer infuriated Brownson still further by recommending the manual by the Jesuit Father Hill which Brownson considered that he had torn to shreds. [39] Brownson roared back that this was written because the *Catholic World* had been so frightened by the Papal improbation of the ontologism it had once favored that it had swung to the other extreme of psychologism. There was all the difference in the world, he insisted, between his system and that of the Louvain Professors. "That Dr. Brownson is not a priest, is very true, but we do not know that he has any right on that account to defend a philosophy improbated by the Holy See, or that his errors can be smiled at any more benignly than if the errors of a priest; nor are we aware that the fact that he is a layman gives even a priest the right to miscall or misrepresent his philosophy. The 'benign smile' is very charming on the editor's lips, no doubt, but men have been known to smile benignly, not from superior knowledge." [40]

He steadily maintained that, in the sense in which ontologism had been condemned by the Holy See, he was not an ontologist at all. What he had taken from Gioberti was no more than a formula, but this he had applied in his own way, so as not merely to avoid pantheism but to provide the only philosophy capable of resisting pantheism. As his son says, the fashion has been to set forth the doctrines he refuted, and then to refute these over again, while claiming to refute him. [41] In a letter to Henry written in 1867 Brownson goes into his indebtedness to Gioberti, at the same time indicating to what a limited degree he had ever sat at any man's feet. "I never master any one till I have made myself his disciple, and allowed him to master me. . . . We . . . never master an author till we have seen his doctrine under an aspect which is not false, or till we see what has led him to believe it true." By that process he had mastered all the philosophers to whom, at various periods of his life, he owed so much. "The world has never known, and never will know, the steadiness with which I have adhered to my principles, any more than it will know the loving heart and generous sympathy with which I have always studied. The loving heart is the true auxiliary of the comprehensive mind, —the truth Plato had in view when he made love and intelligence the two wings of the soul, on which it soars into the Empyrean." The drawback in his case, he admitted, is that the circumstances of his life had compelled him to write and publish while the process of digestion was still going on. "Hence the charge of fickleness and frequent changes of opinion." [42] To a priest who had written an article on him in 1870 he explained, "What I owe to Gioberti is simply a more exact technology. He led me into no error, but enabled me to guard myself against pantheism." [43]

In his *Essays in Refutation of Atheism,* which he had intended to issue as a book,[44] and which was (in part) the excuse upon which he withdrew from the *Catholic World,* Brownson again defends his ontologism. The very title would indicate that he was less concerned with the purely speculative issue than the practical application. Here as always—and perhaps in this "Last Series" more than ever—he had an apologetic purpose; he was writing to be of service to his fellow-Catholics. He had no longer any hope that anyone else would listen to him.

It is so also when he treats what was with him a favorite subject —that of education, in which he was all the more interested because he had had so little formal education himself. Asserting in his introductory paragraphs that "the perfectibility of man is a Christian doctrine and [one that] can be effected only by supernatural means," [45] he goes on to devastate the Godwinian delusion that perfectibility can be naturally attained. "It is singular," he says, "that men who deny the supernatural, God, and Providence, and assert only the natural, should hold the sufficiency of nature, and ascribe all the evils they war against to unnatural or extra-natural causes. If there is only nature, these evils must have originated in nature, therefore from within, not as they pretend, from without. Religion, we are told at one time, is an invention of the priests; but how could there be priests before there was a religion? The priest presupposes religion. Another time we are told that tyrannical rulers invented religion as a means of enslaving the people and of tyrannizing over them"—and so on until the whole absurd hypothesis is destroyed.[46] But when he reaches his main theme and asks what Catholics are doing to produce men trained to meet the needs of the time, he is not very hopeful. Catholic colleges fail to teach philosophy properly, and their graduates go forth "without the philosophical principles that either enable them to grasp religion in its unity and Catholicity, or to defend it logically against the heterodox philosophy of the day." [47] "The weakest, the most milk-and-water, and least zealous and efficient Catholics one meets are precisely those who have graduated with high honors from our Catholic colleges." Catholic higher education was even yielding to "the present infidel movement to abolish the study of the Greek and Roman classics. . . . The study of the classics in non-Catholic schools can have only a Catholic tendency. The classics contain the highest religion that is to be found in non-Catholic society. Abolish them, and non-Catholic education would be thoroughly utilitarian, materialistic, and atheistic." [48]

In any event, he thinks, what many besides him have suspected, that too many people go to college and so are taken out of the class to which they properly belong. He speaks out of his own experience: "We ourselves sprung [sic] from them by our own personal efforts; yet never have we known in the life of letters the peace and contentment, the joy and happiness we experienced as a day-laborer." On the other hand, "the most wretched class of all, and the most barren of good works in all ages and nations, is the so-called middle class, who are the chief worshippers of Mammon, engrossed in money-making or the accumulation of wealth. They are the chief supporters of heresy, and the bitterest enemies of the religion of Christ. Their conversion is, in modern society at least, wellnigh hopeless. . . . They are inborn Protestants." [49]

To a Jesuit who wrote protesting against this attack on Jesuit colleges and accusing Brownson of an "inveterate hatred" [50] of the Society, he replied that he referred to the Jesuits only because "they are our most approved educators." But he reaffirms his views. "In our times every educated man needs to be in some measure a theologian." It is just here that Catholic education fails, and "Catholic colleges . . . by no means merit the extravagant laudations they are in the habit of receiving from the Catholic press."

He had pointed out their defects only in the hope that his criticisms would help to bring about an improvement. As for the Jesuits themselves: "We think them too intolerant to those who differ from them, not in faith, but in opinion, and they are more ready to denounce or decry than to refute those from whom they differ. We think them too prone to parade the services of their own order, and to forget those of other orders, perhaps not less dear to our Lord than themselves." [51] It is evident that the wasp has not lost its sting.

Perhaps the Jesuits may have considered that in denouncing intolerance Brownson was assuming the attitude of Satan rebuking sin. We must understand all this to rest, however, not upon a mere personal prejudice, but on a reasoned preference for a philosophical system other than theirs, and one to which, after all, he had a perfect right. Sometimes he called himself a follower of St. Thomas, though with the reservation "but we try to understand him"; more commonly he said he was an Augustinian rather than a Thomist, and when he rated Aristotle above Plato this was on account of his method, not for the point of view or even the result achieved. [52] He had a hearty dislike of the kind of text-book philosophizing that was (and is) so frequently encountered in Catholic circles. This was the root of his objection to Father Walter H. Hill, whom he refused to consider a real philosopher. "He lacks the true philosophical instinct; and we should doubt if he has ever engaged in any original investigations, or made his loans from others his own by digesting and assimilating them to his own mind." It was necessary, he maintained, if we are to understand St. Thomas's solution of a problem, that we first solve it ourselves. People merely able to quote St. Thomas are not Thomists. [53]

Father Hill did not relish this onslaught on his text-book. But instead of replying, he got one of his friends to accuse Brownson of not knowing Latin well enough to understand the technical philosophical terms that had been employed. This kind of oblique rejoinder was unfortunate for Father Hill. Brownson saw his opening and took it. "Is it necessary to charge us with ignorance of Latin in order to prove that we misunderstand or cannot understand Fr. Hill's English? This would only confirm the criticism made in our first notice of his work, that his English is unintelligible to a reader who is ignorant of the scholastic philosophy and of the Latin. Indeed it is a grave objection to the work, as an English work, that it is not intelligible to a simple English reader who knows no language but his own. The attempt to make out that our criticisms must be unfounded because we are ignorant of Latin, only justifies our criticism." [54] Eight pages further on, he fastens on this point again: "Though we find no difficulty in understanding the author when he explains his meaning in Latin, which we are said to be ignorant of, we have no little difficulty in getting at his meaning when he expresses it in English. . . . Fr. Hill's English is far less intelligible to us than any scholastic Latin we have ever encountered."

Brownson was justly proud of his ability to make himself perfectly clear. And one of his favorite devices against an opponent was to profess mystification over his meaning. [55] Thus he said of William George Ward, with whom he had several brushes: "He writes good English, we suppose, but he is often well-nigh unintelligible to us. We are frequently at a loss to make out what he is driving at." Yet the sentences immediately preceding that— those describing Ward—might seem to some people to describe Brownson himself: "We acknowledge his ability and his learning, we love and honor the man; but, somehow or other, we can hardly read a page of his writings, no matter on what subject, without having our patience tried, or our irascibility excited, and we want to fight him, metaphorically, not literally." [56]

The irritation that Brownson caused, unlike Ward, was not due to his haziness but to his being almost insufferably clear and, with that, positive. No doubt even more may occasionally be derived from writers of the opposite type, those who open up vague and vast vistas, who are poets rather than philosophers—the Thomas Brownes and Emersons. But for most purposes lucidity is preferable. Brownson's lucidity was all part of the practicality governing him. He studied only to use his learning. He concocted metaphysical theories, not for his own delectation, or even for that of professional metaphysicians, but to use for the refutation of error. Outside of what he needed for his purpose, he was content to be ignorant, though it should be added that almost anything was useful to him. Thus he knew scholastic Latin well enough but read little in the Latin classics; and if he had learned to "read and understand six or seven" languages, as he explained to a correspondent, in several instances this was only when he was "hard pressed"; he talked and wrote no other language but English. He disclaimed having been what is called a hard student, and acknowledged that he had always shrunk "from long-continued, close application." He added, "The only subjects I have really studied are English style, philosophy, the philosophy of history and of religion, or theology. Under the head of philosophy I include politics, or the moral law applied to the state." [57]

If the "National Series" of 1864 had been almost exclusively devoted to public affairs—theology and philosophy being barred— now that he went back to his old themes, he by no means dropped politics, since there could be no effective application of abstract speculations to life except through the visible organizations of Church and State. In a fine passage on Gallicanism, he says that it is "based on the assumption of an original dualism, that the natural law and the revealed law are two distinct, coördinate, and mutually independent orders. It assumes that the state holds from the natural law, and is supreme in the natural order, therefore in all questions touching natural society and natural morality; and that the church holds from the revealed law, and is supreme only in matters appertaining to the revealed order, or the mysteries and dogmas of faith, and the sacraments and their administration.

. . . The law of nature being understood to be independent of the revealed law, it required very little refinement to assert, first in practice and then in theory, that the state, holding under it, is independent of the spiritual order, then not subject to the dominion of Christ, and therefore not subject to the dominion of God: which is downright political atheism." [58] Though Brownson was in this, as in other matters, perhaps disposed to allow too little to the natural, at least he was a valuable corrective of the opposite error. If he did nothing else, he deserves to be remembered for the valiant battle he fought in an age during which—prior to the Vatican Council—Gallicanism in various forms was rampant.

His political discussions were not all theory; some of his *obiter dicta* at this time throw a good deal of light upon his personal history. He tells us again that it was "Tippecanoe and Tyler too" that upset his faith in democracy, "by showing how easily the people can be humbugged and carried away by a song. Till then I had believed in democracy, though I believed little else." "I ceased henceforth to believe in democracy." [59] But while rejecting the principle that founds government in convention and sees it as deriving its powers from the consent of the governed, he is far from wishing to see any change in the American Constitution "It is the spirit and opinions of the American people, or the majority of them, that I want changed"—in particular in respect to regarding as authority for government "the arbitrary will of the people, or practically, the unrestricted rule of the majority for the time." [60] The day was now so evil in his eyes that he had come to consider the Martin Van Buren he once so despised as "the last first-class man that sat, or probably that ever will sit in the presidential chair of the United States." [61]

He girds against the press as propagating the popular or democratic errors, and denounces Thomas Paine for his perfectionism. What Brownson leaves out of account is the kind of democracy which holds that, though the people are always liable to err, they may, over a period, be counted upon to act with justice, reason and moderation. It never seemed to occur to him that democracy may actually beget a just habit of mind, or that the majority in a democracy is virtually constrained to grant due liberty to the wishes of a minority, if for no other reason than that the minority may in its turn become the majority. Nevertheless, as a protest against an absolute or caesarist democracy, a democracy which deifies the people (or a chance majority of them)—if such really existed outside of his imagination—Brownson's political writings undoubtedly did real service. He did vast good by his insistence that God was paramount in all human affairs, and that human interests could be truly served only by obedience to God.

Yet the old radical tended to carry his conservatism a little too far. He coldly remarks: "It is to the honor of the church that she has always had a special regard and tenderness for the poor; and it is no less to her honor that she has never attempted to remove poverty. She . . . treats poverty as a blessing, not as a misfortune." [62] This, too, is part of his pessimism. As Mr. Schlesinger comments, "No one in America surpassed Brownson in his hatred of capitalism, but probably few surpassed him in the hatred of the only forces likely to restrain the capitalists." [63] Even if there are other forces (and possibly more potent ones) than those Mr. Schlesinger has in mind, the only force that Brownson could see was that of red revolution, against which he set his face; he did not know that Catholicism, in the persons of the Popes—though unfortunately not to any notable extent in the persons of our prosperous Catholics— was going to hold out a hope to the poor other than a supine acceptance of the lot of poverty. The Church does and must attempt to remove poverty. Anything meekly accepted by the Christian gives him merit—cancer and defamation of character and injustice directed against himself, as well as poverty—but this is no reason why the Christian should shirk his responsibility for doing his utmost to remove these ills, as well as to preserve his soul from sin. Brownson had, in fact, swung too far in the direction of otherworldliness by way of recoil from the world. He had all but given up hope of the harmony of nature and grace, the material and the spiritual, although still formally asserting it. The kingdom of God was indeed to come, but for him there was no prospect whatever of its coming on earth as it is in heaven.

He still had a way of irritating Catholics as well as Protestants. Even in giving a kind of apology to the Jesuits—saying that he had wished more than once to recall what he had written about them—he contrived in the same breath to repeat his old charges.[64] And he gave pain and scandal by saying again, what he might well have left unsaid, that he had never felt attracted to the devotion to the Sacred Heart. No wonder that a correspondent accused him of an "anti-Catholic" spirit.[65] He need not have written: "It is just now the fashionable devotion: all the Bishops in the Union, and for aught we know in the whole world, have consecrated each his own diocese to the Sacred Heart, but we have yet to see that love and fidelity to Jesus keep pace with the spread of the Devotion. There are fashions in devotion as well as in dress." [66] But he would not have been Brownson had he not—on at least some minor points asserted his independence, let Catholics like it or not. As for the Giobertian formula, *ens creat existentias,* he continued to stand by it stoutly: "It may, for aught we know, have been censured by the general of the Jesuits, but not, so far as known to us, by the Successor of Peter and Vicar of Christ." [67] If he often repeated himself, this was partly because he knew the pedagogical value of repetition, and partly also because he wished to approach an old idea from a new angle. He was, for that matter, a man of relatively few ideas, though he saw many aspects in them. But this, after all, is the mark of a really fruitful mind. The teeming fancy dissipates itself.

So it went on to the end, the same sturdy, stormy, individualistic Brownson. He had modified many of his opinions, and yet in the essence of his beliefs he never changed, any more than he changed in character. Precisely because he was an opinionative man with no pride of opinion, but instead an undeviating determination to

seek out and follow truth, he kept his reputation for being unaccountable. Without giving any indication of his intentions, on the
approach of Autumn, 1875, he decided to close the "Last Series"
of his *Review*. He had come to the end of his tether. Obese and
gouty and deaf and blind—his infirmities were too much for him.
On his good days he might hobble down to his rose-garden; except
for this he now never went out of the house, not even to go to
Mass, as the nearest church was too far away. Communion was
sometimes brought to him. Most of the time he spent in his study,
and there he was often in a wheel-chair.

The winding-up of the *Review* came suddenly. In the last issue
for 1874 he had said that one of his aims was that of "forming
able and well-trained reviewers among our younger clergy and
educated young laymen." As he was not publishing his magazine
for gain, "the profits, if any, will go to those who may assist us in
conducting it." [68] He wrote to Henry on May 25, 1874, asking
for an article, for which he told him he could afford to pay fifty
dollars. In this letter, and another written on August 18th of the
same year, [69] he lets it out that the circulation has dropped from
seventeen to twelve hundred. The Irish papers, he says, are beginning to snap at him, but he will try to carry on another year,
though with "diminishing courage and some disgust. The Review
is too Papal for the majority of our bishops and clergy. It goes
against the public opinion of the Catholic population of the country and will meet with little success as long as Fr. Tom Burke,
O.P. furnishes their reading. It is only a wind bag that can be
popular with Paddy." Yet it was some months later that Henry,
realizing that he must act, arrived in Elizabeth and persuaded his
father to retire and to go with him to Detroit. Brownson had achieved
his purpose in reviving the *Review*. His wife had urged him to
bring it to life again, if only for a year. He had kept it going, all
but single-handed, for three years. Surely that was enough. With
pain he scrawled out his "Valedictory" to his readers, addressing
them as his personal friends.

The *Review,* he told them, originated with him and must die with him. "Others may publish a Quarterly Review far more valuable than mine has ever been, but no other man can produce BROWNSON'S QUARTERLY REVIEW." It is now to be discontinued not for lack of support but solely on account of the failure of his eyes. He has not found it possible to employ an amanuensis or secretary, and for this reason has been sometimes obliged to reprint articles from earlier issues. There have been occasions when he was too ill to produce new matter. In fact, "much of the time for the present year I have been unable to hold a pen in my hand." No man willingly, he went on, gives up his life's vocation, and he has loved his vocation as a reviewer; but it was now time to retire. There is a hint that not only his eyes and hearing and hands are failing him but that his marvellous memory is not all that it used to be.[70] Father Hewit, writing his obituary the following year, spoke of "the desolation and loneliness which is usually the cloud in which the setting sun of genius goes down." [71]

"That there has been more or less of antagonism between the *Review* and a portion of the Irish Catholic press . . . it were idle to deny," Brownson wrote; but that had nothing to do with its ceasing publication. He could also say: "The warmest and most esteemed friends of its editor, and its firmest and most generous supporters, have been Catholics of Irish birth or Irish descent." Though he has never been able to realize in it his ideal of what a Catholic Review should be, he has at least done his best. "None will be found more sincerely Catholic, or more earnestly devoted to Catholic interests, though, no doubt, men will be found with more prudence, and with a far better understanding of those interests, as well as ability to advance them." [72]

He cannot refrain from one boast: he has recently been approached by the "Old Catholics," and they have assured him that, if he would go over to their party, he would become immensely popular and obtain an almost unlimited circulation for the *Review;* but the letter might have added, "belie all my convictions and the whole Catholic faith, and damn my own soul." "I did not seek admission into the Church for the sake of wealth, honors or popularity! If I am, as I know I am, measureably unpopular even with Catholics, I can truly say that I have never sought popularity, but have rather despised it, . . . and have been even more popular with Catholics than I ever expected to be." Besides, what is wealth to him! He has his annuity; "she, who, for nearly half a century, was my faithful companion and my devoted wife, is, I devoutly trust, safe with the saints"; his surviving children are able to take care of themselves. What does he want of wealth? What could he do with it, if he had it? "What do I care for the popularity which I never sought, and on which I turned my back, when not yet of age?" It is his last snort of scorn—one that nobody will begrudge him.

Only one word remained to be spoken—his blessing on all his Catholic brethren, whom he has tried to serve. In return he asks them to pray for the repose of his soul. "I have, and I desire to have, no home out of the Catholic Church. . . . My only ambition is to live and die in her communion."

[1] *Latter Life,* pp. 579–580.

[2] In case anybody would like to have the detail preserved: their pew was number 12. It is amusing also to record that Sarah, who had been annoyed by hearing the pastor, Father Kane, talk Sunday after Sunday about money, made her protest by going outside while this was going on. She in turn annoyed the priest, and he ordered the doors locked so that she could not get back. Henry Brownson had a similar way of showing his independence. He could never be induced to stay after the Last Gospel, as the prayers that followed, he argued, did not belong to Mass. Very ostentatiously, therefore, he used to get up and leave. This last bit of information was supplied by one of his Detroit nieces.

[3] *Brownson Papers.*

[4] In this connection might be quoted a letter from Brownson to his wife which is in the possession of Mrs. Odiorne. It was written to her on July 17, 1860, during her absence from home: "We are quite well & get along well xcept myself, I am about as fidgetty when you are gone as they say you are when I am gone, & though my health is well enough, I shall not be worth much till you return. I really did not know before, how necessary you are to me, & that I really am nothing without you."

[5] Letters to Sorin and Henry Brownson, both dated May 23, 1872, among the *Brownson Papers.* See also Sarah Brownson to Henry Brownson, April 18, 1872.

[6] *Latter Life,* p. 529.

[7] *Brownson Papers.* A large item of expense was the cost of maintaining sub-

scription agents in various parts of the country. These were often inefficient, and sometimes not very honest. Time after time Brownson lost heavily on their account.

8 Letter of March 25, 1872 from Orestes Brownson to Henry. (*Brownson Papers*).

9 *Latter Life*, pp. 584, 585.

10 Sarah to Henry Brownson, April 18, 1872. *Brownson Papers*.

11 These and other family letters that will be quoted, with exceptions indicated, are all to be found among the *Brownson Papers* at the University of Notre Dame.

12 Of her novels I have read only her *Marian Elwood; or, How Girls Live.* The most remarkable thing about it is its name, as this suggests that it might have been intended as the other side of the shield of her father's *Charles Elwood.* There is, however, no connection between the two books. Sarah's novel attempts a fashionable tone, with amusingly "aristocratic" names for the characters; but it has a Catholic theme loosely tied to its naïve pictures of "high life." If it is a rather poor performance, it should be remembered that she wrote it when she was about twenty. Sarah may have had her mother in mind in her description of Mr. Weston's housekeeper as "neat, orderly, systematic, and most rigidly pious, but her most laudable virtue was her never-failing, all-enduring patience with Mr. Weston." (P. 55). Even if this be so, Brownson clearly did not "sit for the portrait of Mr. Weston."

13 He became a Benedictine in 1852 and in 1860 was appointed pastor of St. Michael's, the German church at Elizabeth, from Christmas, 1870, serving also as pastor of St. Henry's Church until, owing to the dissatisfaction of his parishioners at St. Michael's, he confined himself to St. Henry's. This new church was started at first in the academy of the Benedictine Sisters, and was afterwards known as the Church of the Sacred Heart. A good deal has been written about Lemcke, but some of the details I supply here were taken for me by Father Matthew Hoehn, O.S.B., from the hand-written history of St. Henry's parish. The Very Rev. Bonaventure Schwinn, O.S.B. has also gone to some pains to gather information for me. An interesting detail is that Henry Street at Elizabeth was named after Father Henry.

14 Letter from Sarah to Henry Brownson, April 18, 1872. (*Brownson Papers*).

15 Sarah to Henry, December 4, 1872, and April 17, 1876. (*Brownson Papers*).

16 Mrs. Odiorne has shown me a letter containing an account of Mrs. Henry Brownson's asking her mother-in-law how she came to have so strange a son as Henry, who was such a contrast to the other Brownson boys. Sally Brownson could explain it only on the ground that she was worrying so much about her husband's loss of faith in the 'thirties that this must have had a pre-natal influence on the son she was to bear.

17 Purcell at that time was friendly towards Brownson and arranged with the Jesuits to take young Orestes at half the ordinary amount charged. (*Middle Life,* pp. 163, 165).

18 Judging from *Caroline* and *Coriolanus,* they must all have been about as bad as can be imagined. *Coriolanus* at least does not pretend to be funny, but *Caroline* has a comic German and a still worse comic Irishman who reach the limits of dull drollery.

19 Orestes Brownson, Jr. to his brother Henry, February 22, 1887. *Brownson Papers.*

20 He helped to found the public school at Dubuque, Iowa, getting associated with this work in 1869. (Mrs. Orestes Brownson to her son Henry, September 26, 1869—*Brownson Papers*). When he sent his own children to the public school he was denounced from the altar, which only served to antagonize him against the local clergy and (as he imagined for a time) against the Church.

21 Letters to his father dated February 23, 1874, and March 1, 1875. Father Hewit

in his obituary article on Orestes Brownson describes the younger Orestes as a teacher and a farmer, "living the life of a good Catholic with the spirit of a recluse, altogether uninterested in the great affairs of the world." (*Catholic World,* Vol. XXIII, 1876, p. 368).

22 *Works,* Vol. XI, p. vii.

23 *Latter Life,* pp. 580–581.

24 Is "minimum" just the right word? The definition of a doctrine does not of course bring it into existence but merely pronounces as to precisely what the doctrine is and always had been. Yet to advocate an undefined "maximum" doctrine before it was defined might be rather temerarious.

25 *Brownson's Quarterly Review,* Last Series, Vol. I (1873), pp. 1, 2.

26 *Works,* Vol. XX, p. 333.

27 *Brownson's Quarterly Review,* Last Series, Vol. II (1874), p. 226.

28 *Works,* Vol. XIII, p. 500.

29 *Ibid.,* pp. 508, 509, 510.

30 *Brownson's Quarterly Review,* Last Series, Vol. III (1875), pp. 66–67.

31 Quoted in *Latter Life,* pp. 587–589.

32 *Works,* Vol. XIV, p. 507.

33 *Ibid.,* p. 507.

34 *Brownson's Quarterly Review,* Last Series, Vol. I (1873), pp. 481, 482.

35 *Ibid.,* p. 484. See also pp. 486, 487.

36 *Brownson's Quarterly Review,* Last Series, Vol. I (1873), p. 155.

37 *Brownson's Quarterly Review,* Last Series, Vol. II (1874), p. 357.

38 *Ibid.,* p. 375.

39 *Catholic World,* Vol. XIX (1874), pp. 243, 244.

40 *Brownson's Quarterly Review,* Last Series, Vol. II (1874), pp. 360–361.

41 *Latter Life,* p. 559.

42 *Latter Life,* pp. 525, 526.

43 *Ibid.,* p. 556.

44 That he was perfectly serious about his intention of completing these as a book is evident from the fact that he did not use the *Essays*—which are reprinted in his *Works* (Vol. II, pp. 1–100)—until he was sure that the book would never be completed. Then he printed in the last number of his *Review* for 1873 what had been written, carrying the series on through the first two numbers for 1874.

45 *Brownson's Quarterly Review,* Last Series, Vol. II (1874), p. 38.

46 *Ibid.,* p. 39.

47 *Ibid.,* pp. 47–48.

48 *Ibid.,* pp. 46–47.

49 *Ibid.,* pp. 50, 51.

50 *Ibid.,* p. 536.

51 *Ibid.,* pp. 539–540.

52 *Brownson's Quarterly Review,* National Series, Vol. IV (1864), p. 69.

53 *Brownson's Quarterly Review,* Last Series, Vol. III (1875), p. 261. Upon this passage Dr. Siegfried commented twenty years after Brownson's death: "May it not have been that Dr. Brownson had first made up his mind that the primary principle of thought and things, of the logical and of the ontological order, is *ens creat existentias* and that, therefore, he found a warrant for it in his study of St. Thomas?" The writer went on to say he doubted whether Brownson *could* study St. Thomas, as his intellect was first and last synthetic and his genius too impatient. "He saw too much at a glance to examine detail. . . . Moreover, he took up the study of St. Thomas too late in life, at a time when his philosophical opinions and convic-

tions had already been formed and settled." *American Ecclesiastical Review*, Vol. XIV (1896), p. 67.

[54] *Brownson's Quarterly Review*, Last Series, Vol. III (1875), pp. 490–491.

[55] At times, however, he failed, when dealing with especially abstruse matters: then he would groan, "Well, it is at least clear to me, even if it is not clear to others."

[56] *Works*, Vol. XIX, p. 591. It is a pity that he was too ill to answer Ward's last article on his philosophy. In it Ward repaid the compliment: "Try how we may to get a precise notion of Dr. Brownson's meaning, we fail. His words resolve themselves into Ontologism, but he solemnly asseverates that he is no Ontologist. We can only affirm that he is oracular and sibylline, and that we have no gift of interpreting the gods." (*Dublin Review*, Vol. LXXVIII (1876), p. 52.) Ward does, however, hold Brownson up as a shining example of the power of Catholicism over minds that have ranged freely and also of showing "that humility is the guide and safeguard of wisdom." (Pp. 54, 55).

[57] *Latter Life*, pp. 554–555.

[58] *Brownson's Quarterly Review*, Last Series, Vol. I (1873), p. 363.

[59] *Brownson's Quarterly Review*, Last Series, Vol. I (1873), pp. 235, 237. As a matter of fact he had said repeatedly before the 1840 election that the people could not be sovereign in the absolute sense of having nothing superior to them, whether one called that ultimate sovereignty God or justice. The 1840 election merely sharpened his conviction and illustrated it.

[60] Ibid., p. 241.

[61] *Ibid.*, p. 237.

[62] *Ibid.*, p. 248.

[63] *Op. cit.*, p. 268.

[64] *Brownson's Quarterly Review*, Last Series, Vol. II (1874), pp. 537, 539.

[65] *Ibid.*, p. 460.

[66] *Ibid.*, p. 422.

[67] *Brownson's Quarterly Review*, Last Series, Vol. III (1875), p. 508.

[68] *Brownson's Quarterly Review*, Last Series, Vol. II (1874), pp. 571, 572.

[69] *Brownson Papers*.

[70] In the issue for October, 1874 (p. 455), he apologized for his mistake in calling "the dear St. Elizabeth" *Queen* of Hungary. It was because the failure of his eyes had obliged him to rely on his memory.

[71] *Catholic World*, Vol. XXIII (1876), p. 369.

[72] A general reference for all this will suffice. The Valedictory occupies pages 578–580 of the last number of *Brownson's Quarterly Review* and is reprinted in the Collected *Works*, Vol. XX, pp. 436–438.

CHAPTER XVII

The Death of the Lion

A LITTLE GIRL who was visiting the house at Elizabeth during these last years gazed, astonished, at the huge shaggy old man she saw there and then whispered to her mother, "Is he not just like a great lion!" Father Hewit, who tells the story, adds that the description hit Brownson off perfectly; perhaps it hit him off even better than Bishop Bayley's *Ursa Major*. But Hewit continues: "The marks of infirmity which time had imprinted upon him, with the expression of loneliness and childlike longing for sympathy, added a touch of the pathetic to the picture, fitted to awaken a sentiment of compassion, tempering to a more gentle mood the awe and admiration excited by his venerable appearance." [1]

Brownson's had always been a lonely life, one spent mainly in the study, and perhaps he was never more lonely than when he appeared on the lecture platform. His real friendships were with the readers of his *Review*: to them he spoke always in a personal tone, regarding them as his friends even when he was furiously fighting them. It was for this reason that he had to depend, perhaps even more than most men, upon the understanding and sympathy his wife gave. After her death he was desolate.

Two very revealing personal passages appeared in the April number of his *Review*, just after it was revived. One was: "I myself am even more of an exile in my present residence, than my Irish or German neighbor; for he has near him those whom he was brought up with, knew him in his youth, while I have not one,—not one with whom I can talk over old times, or who knew me before I had reached middle age." The other is: "Men are but half

411

men, unless inspired and sustained in whatever is good and noble by woman's sympathy and coöperation." [2]

He had an enormous correspondence, but it was to a great extent with strangers, and even when it was not, there is little that is personal in it. He did not do much to keep his friendships in repair. His letters more often than not were discussions of political or philosophical questions, even when he was writing to his sons. Only now and then do we get purely the intimate detail, as when he told his wife in a letter dated January 3, 1854, that he had had a cold and had been drinking quantities of eggnog to cure it. We might not have heard of that had not the cold been caused by an accident on a Mississippi river boat, when all the passengers were in great danger for twenty hours before they were taken off. [3] Most of his letters are minor dissertations or deal with business matters.

He did, however, during these last years have a correspondence with William Seton, [4] the grandson of Mother Seton. Brownson's own letters have been lost, and we can infer their nature only from Seton's own letters as they exist among the *Brownson Papers*. They show him as ebullient, charmingly guileless but not very hard-headed. Possibly Brownson found him a relief from the rigors of metaphysics, and he tolerated from him many blasts against ecclesiastical machinery. On February 28, 1872, Seton told the old man: "Do not imagine that I am flying at a tangent, & giving up my religion. *I am not going* to let any old fogy doctrines drive me out of the Church. I express my opinions here in Munich quite openly—if this were the 15th century, I would already have been burnt at the stake." After which he proceeded to quote a passage from the *Mirari Vos* of Gregory XVI, pronouncing it "unChristian." But his admiration of the philosopher was welcome—especially when he wrote, as he did on the following March 9th, "You still will be remembered—you will—and long years hence when people go wandering through Elizabeth they will point their fingers to a house and say 'There is where Brownson lived.' Perhaps when

the Jesuits will have their Head Quarters in America instead of
Rome, some future Father Beckx will say, 'Well, there was something in Brownson after all—but as we did not understand English
we did not find it out.'" In his loneliness and despondency it was
pleasant hearing such things from a friend in Munich.

What is to follow was far from being so pleasant. It must be
dealt with because Mr. Schlesinger has taken some bones of a skele-
ton out of the cupboard [5]—for that, if for no other reasons. It is now
necessary to produce all the facts. Henry Brownson could hardly be
expected to do otherwise than draw a discreet veil over these happenings,[6] though he had in his possession all the letters upon which our
knowledge must be based. I confess that when I went to the
University of Notre Dame, to examine the *Brownson Papers,* I
hoped I would find that the account had been highly colored in
the style of Stracheyian biography.[7] It must be candidly said that
such is not the case.

Candor also demands that the matter be treated here, though it
is impossible to do more than quote excerpts from this painful
correspondence. But surely a biographer of Brownson should try
to emulate him in honesty. What must be borne in mind are the
circumstances: Brownson was a giant in decay; he had been for
about ten years a sick man, and prematurely old; and Sarah herself,
who in 1873 was only thirty-four, had been subject to attacks of
intermittent fever since at least 1864.[8] They were alone now, with
no discerning wife and mother to stand between the clash of their
temperaments.

Brownson's own touchiness and truculence have already been
sufficiently displayed. They tended to increase, the older and sicker
he became. And Sarah's over-wrought condition comes out in the
extraordinary letter she wrote to Father Hewit—spelling his name
"Hewet"—on New Year's Day, 1873. She told him she was sending
him a copy of her life of Gallitzin, and she demanded that, if it
was to be reviewed in the *Catholic World,* he review it himself;

"for I felt convinced that whatever might be your judgment of it, *you* would not make it the occasion of an insulting notice . . . nor use it to gratify private enmity to my father by a supercilious and contemptuous notice of his daughter's hard labor." That she could write in this strain shows a somewhat hysterical state.[9] Though if she gave way to it, she had sufficient excuse in the crushing burden of work she now was carrying. Brownson wrote to his son on May 23, 1872, "I could not call upon Sarah, hardly able to be about the house, to wait on me." On the previous April 18th she had told Henry, that she constantly wonders how she could do what has to be done and live. On December 4th of the same year she says she has "hardly strength to crawl about." She adds: "I feel at night that I cannot get up again . . . but the morning comes, and I have to go through it all just the same." By pitying, one also pardons. A large part of the trouble lay in the fact that neither of these suffering souls realized how sick was the other; each could see nothing but its own woe.

Now letters are of course very important evidence. But even letters are to be taken cautiously. Many people have a habit of writing them only when they are in an "upset" condition. The placid days are taken as normal and receive no comment, while hours, or even moments, of tension are given a prominent place that does not really belong to them. Mrs. Odiorne, Sarah's daughter, has suggested that when Sarah wrote as she did to her brother Henry, in the letters that follow, it was in order to force him to shoulder his responsibility to their father, and that therefore she represented matters as being darker than they actually were.[10] Clearly if a subjective element ever entered into letters, it is here. They have to be accepted—but accepted with reasonable reservations.

Though Sarah believed that her father was writing to Henry, giving his version of events, he very seldom wrote at all.[11] But when he did, he of course used that sledge-hammer style of his which he had developed in controversy but which is hardly the best of instruments for conveying the delicate complexities of

domestic relationships. His complaints against her boil down to
charges that she was an old maid—a condition soon to be remedied
—and that she was domineering and jealous. He also considered
that she neglected him, which means that he was making many
querulous demands upon her which, in the state of her own health,
she could not be expected to fulfill. Her complaints against him were
that he was exacting and capricious and untidy and smelling of
tobacco, and that he took too many medicines and drank whiskey
and flirted with the servants. On neither side was there anything
very serious, though of course little things like these—especially
in accumulation—can exasperate to the breaking-point.

There is no reason to doubt that the accusations father and
daughter brought against one another were true; the only question
is as to just *how* true they were. To say, as Sarah did, that his
"whiskey flowed like water" is obviously only a fashion of speaking. In any case Sarah told Henry that this was "by report," and
the basis for the gossip was that "the policeman on the beat told
somebody that the Doctor kept good whiskey" and that one night
a young man saw one of the servants give the policeman a glass of
it.[12] She probably did not know that whiskey is one of the most
effective of pain-killers and she could never be brought to believe that
her father was often in great pain. But not even Sarah charges
him with any excess, and one may fancy that it would have taken
about a gallon of it to have put Brownson under the table, even
though he describes himself as having now dwindled to 228 pounds.
To the teetotaller Hecker he had written on September 1, 1871, "My
heart is a bit muddy, & I have to wet it."[13] The thing does not
sound very bad, and most of us know how easily a harmless glass
or two can be magnified by the censorious imagination.

So also with regard to Brownson's medicines, about which we
hear a great deal. Quite likely they *were* used too freely, and for
this Sarah blames Dr. Hewit.[14] She attributed her father's irritability
to his taking twenty drops of colchicum a day, though I am informed that this is not at all an excessive dose, and that it would

not have induced an excited state of mind. Yet Sarah told Henry
that "he cut up so just after Mammy died, from the effects of it,
that I told him I would never give it to him. . . . I wish he might
once get such a fright that he would leave off doctoring himself." [15]
One can only conclude that if Brownson did "cut up" at any time,
it could not have been on account of the colchicum. More likely
the amateur doctoring induced the air of listlessness she noted in
her letter of January 5, 1874.

The charge of flirtation is a little more serious, and more difficult
to estimate properly. But again one knows how such matters can
be grossly exaggerated, and one gathers from Sarah's own letters
that she was often making a mountain out of a molehill. Perhaps
the explanation is that, as she said to Henry, "You know I am of
a doleful nature." [16] It was enough for Brownson to be heard
laughing with the servant who looked after his room for Sarah
to be annoyed. [17] She resented it that he seemed to be so jovial with
his visitors, as he was not very jolly in her society. Time after time
she tells Henry that "notre Père" cannot be so ill as he pretends
because he is so evidently enjoying life. [18] "I am perfectly certain,"
she wrote, "that he puts on that infirm air to excite pity, for I have
been told by those I cannot doubt that as soon as he gets out of
sight from me, it is all dropped." [19] Brownson's own side of that
story was: "The day was passed in unbroken silence and in great
suffering for I was very ill. I was thankful, however, that I was
alone and no virago entered my room to scold and abuse me." [20]

There was one person in particular to whom Sarah strongly
objected—a comely Irish girl named Agnes who had a little education and whom Brownson sometimes called his secretary because
she may now and then have written to his dictation. [21] Both father
and daughter described her as "terribly pious," and Sarah admitted
that she was pretty. She and Dolly, the colored girl who worked
as cook for the household, used to say the rosary with the old man
at nine every evening—which also annoyed Sarah. [22] This in her eyes
added the offence of hypocrisy to the "dear creature," whose char-

acter, she told her father, was thoroughly bad, though the only badness specified to Henry was that Agnes had once given a policeman a drink and received what used to be called "followers" in the parlor.[23]

It is of course quite possible that the aged Brownson allowed Agnes more liberties than are usually accorded a girl in her position. At all events Sarah began to think that her father intended to marry her, and one suspects that he deliberately encouraged the daughter with whom he was so irritated to think so, extracting some entertainment from her delusion. To his son he wrote: "Sarah keeps a close watch over me lest I marry again and disgrace the family. This is very kind in her. Do not be uneasy, if her vigilance should sleep for no woman will ever take the place of your mother." [24] Sarah was certainly incensed that her father let Agnes have her meals with him and was polite to her. It seemed to her that the hussy "nearly monopolised the conversation and talked with a freedom which not one of us ever used at his table." If Agnes did marry him, Sarah wrote to Henry, "she will not make his fire for him and be chambermaid any longer. I am thinking her but such a tyrant as only a low born Irish woman can be when set in a comfortable position." [25] But Agnes, whom her father regarded as "an angel, or at least a saint," had "beaux of her own age, as thick as flies about molasses." It was on this account also that Sarah thought "her character would never be patched together this side of the grave." [26]

The most distressing thing about these letters of Sarah's is not so much what they accuse her father of doing or saying as the spiteful remarks she hands around gratuitously. Thus when Henry had a son and named him Orestes she wrote: "Of course nothing could please the great doctor more than to have a namesake at last. I hope the Orestes of the future will have all the splendors of the name, and none of its disadvantages." [27] In a later letter she added: "I pity him for the name he has to carry through life! If I think of him as Orestes I cannot look at [his photograph]." [28]

These things merely show irritation over nothing in particular. Even when she makes definite complaints, one is often left with a feeling that much has been made out of little. On one occasion, after having said that her father always broke the promises he had given the day before, she checked herself and added: "That is a little too strong, please consider it a little modified." [29] No doubt Henry took a good deal of all this with at least a grain of salt.

Sarah was even scornful because the New York *Tribune* had gathered some of the more personal remarks that had been scattered through the April, 1873, issue of the *Review* and had published them under the heading "Dr. Brownson's Confessions." Two of these have already been quoted in this chapter and are surely sufficiently harmless. But Sarah commented: "The last paragraph on the last page is enough to frighten anybody from subscribing, but I assure you it is all a pleasant fiction." She said she "shivered" at the prospect of other references to his age and infirmities; yet when we turn to the words as printed, all we can find that could possibly have annoyed Sarah is "A man in the seventieth year of his age can hardly have the elasticity and vigor of a man in his forty-second, and I am no exception to the general rule, suffering as I am from bodily infirmities still more than from age." [30] Sarah admitted of these confessions, "Probably they do not strike other people as they do me." [31]

She was on more solid ground when she said that her father ate too much. Perhaps there was a family joke in the "As long as he keeps within ten pounds of meat a day [he] is very well," though she makes too many such remarks for us to be able to dismiss them lightly, in the same letter saying: "When I see him eat three fearful meals, each enough for a large family every day without flagging and that he lives through it, I rather laugh at the feeble tone he seems to delight in assuming." When she came across his butcher's bills she was horrified to discover that he was spending over forty dollars a month for meat alone. Yet she was not exactly surprised, "because I had heard that in beer saloons

and kindred places it was said, 'If you want a good square meal
old Brownson's is the place to go for it!' " [32] No doubt it was highly
injudicious of the gouty old man to indulge his appetite, but he had
always been a famous trencherman, even if in his own opinion
he was abstemious. Such quantities of meat aggravated his gout,
and of course the gout did not improve his temper.

The owner of the more modern house on First Avenue and
Fourth Street,[33] to which Sarah and her father had moved since
Mrs. Brownson's death, was William J. Tenney, at one time a
judge and a holder of a minor political office, but now a reader
at the publishing house of Appleton's.[34] He was the son of a
minister, a grave, taciturn and even somewhat puritanical person
who, though he had become a Catholic, used to reprove children
for playing on Sunday. Brownson had known him for some years
and liked him. When Mrs. Tenney died, the Judge proceeded to
fall in love with Sarah, much to Brownson's disgust. In the letter
in which he told Henry about the engagement, the old man's hand
shook so much—whether from agitation or gout is not certain—that
his script is more than usually illegible. It is, however, clear enough
to convey that he was greatly displeased. "Between them," he said,
"they had arranged for him, his daughter, & wife to live with me,
or I with them, & of course bear the chief xpense of their support." [35] Though he succeeded in preventing that arrangement, he
had to reconcile himself to the marriage, which was solemnized by
Bishop Corrigan on November 26, 1873.

Just before this Sarah in an undated letter to her brother said
that their father had given her carte blanche for the wedding
breakfast. But she complained that he was capricious, changing
his arrangements every day and "the least allusion to any of these
matters raises a storm at once, showing that under all the feeling
is intensely bitter." She added in a postscript that he was not giving
her any trouble just then because "he is too much under fear of me
to say much in his old angry way." That her own feelings were

bitter comes out in another undated letter she wrote her father, also just before the wedding. In it she thanked him for what he had done but said that she knew he was only thinking of his own comfort and ease and that "for the future I hope to be no expense whatever to you. . . . We all three [herself, the Judge, and the Judge's daughter Jessie] appreciate that Better is a dry morsel where love is than a house full of victims with strife." There can be little wonder that she was glad to be married and have a house of her own.

Her marriage to the elderly widower was very happy. "The days go by so fast," she wrote to Henry, "that I feel sometimes that my life will run away from me. I want to linger over it—it is so delightful, but there are so many things to think of, so many pleasant things to do, that there is no possibility of lingering." [36] All her anticipations were fulfilled. Just before the wedding she wrote to her brother: "I have suffered so much that any one younger and less gentle than the Judge would not do. . . . A world of perfect love, peace, and protection it is sure to be to me." [37] Afterwards she told him: "No woman ever had more to be grateful for than I have now." [38] In the same letter she wrote that she had never seen anything like her husband's patience towards her father. Brownson's own comment on his son-in-law was merely: "He is much spruced up. He is to me inscrutable." [39]

At first the married couple lived at Judge Tenney's former house, 85—now 1086—Elizabeth Avenue. But Sarah could not bear the thought of his *ménage* with Agnes and Dolly. Seizing upon a remark of her father's to the effect that he wished he could be spared the necessity of supplementing his annuity and could end the *Review,* Sarah sent him a long complicated memorandum showing just how much it would cost him to live with her if he would give up his establishment. The figures all pointed in one direction: he must let Agnes and Dolly go and allow her to engage the servants.[40] To this he would not agree; but on March 31, 1874, Sarah wrote to Henry that the health of "the Government" had not been very good that winter and confided, "I believe he has had about as much of his Irish girl as he could stand." In the end it was her father who himself, much to her surprise, suggested the setting up of the double household where he was living. Then she was able to tell Henry, "I have two darkies, so he can't flirt with them." [41]

It must be remembered that Sarah had started out with the conviction that he would marry one of the servants, and this long before Agnes had arrived on the scene.[42] But when Agnes had come into his house, Sarah fastened the suspicion upon her. And not until Agnes was safely out of the way did she say: "Nothing would please me better than to see him married." [43] A few lines later in the same letter she exulted: "As he has another young woman sewing for him I presume Agnes' day is over." To get a "rise" out of Sarah—one must presume it was that—the old man continued to make jokes about marrying again, jokes which Sarah said she pretended to enjoy, "though every word was a sword cut." [44] He even told visitors, according to Sarah, that she had prevented him from marrying. "They condoled with him, they said, while they nearly died laughing at his absurdity." [45] It was all a queer kind of humor which she naturally did not relish.

The double household, as might have been expected, did not prove at all a success, even though Agnes had been disposed of. Sarah was still worried on this account, as her father still saw her every now and then when on his afternoon drives, and Henry was warned to be "prepared for any catastrophe." "If she were to marry him (which she might now to save herself) he could not bring her here, for he has made the arrangement in writing that we were to take the house and furniture and board him." [46] Sarah could at least breathe a little more easily and hope for the best. At the worst she would be able to keep the detested Agnes out.

Sarah described the new situation. Her father talked to her very little, except when they happened to meet in the hall or when they had guests. This, however, she seems to contradict by saying that meal-times were torture: "He is quite hard of hearing, and to talk

with him at every meal at the top of my voice is martyrdom." [47]
Yet she thought he was well looked after. His fire was made at six
every morning, after which he came down to a huge breakfast
and to give the Judge various commissions for him. Then he went
back to his room, where he had a woman within call to make him
comfortable. There he would sit with his ice-water and whiskey
until lunch—again a huge meal—and the climactic dinner. "At
meals he does all the talking, never allowing a remark to be made
between other persons at the table, and as he is very deaf you can
imagine how disagreeable he can make it." Except for meals together, she added, "We live our life as independently of him as
we can, and it is wonderfully happy." [48]

It could not have been wonderfully happy for her father. He wrote
to Henry: "She means, I presume, to treat her old father well and
does so as far as [this is] in her nature." He believed that she took
good care to carry on the conversation with others in such a low
tone of voice that he could neither take part in it nor catch a word
that was said.[49] It is to be feared that he was exacting and wearing.

One event, however, delighted him. In February, 1875, Sarah bore
her first child, Ruth. The Judge wrote to Henry describing how the
grandfather put on his spectacles and subjected the eleven-pound
infant to a rheumy, myopic scrutiny. Then he pronounced its head
"to be truly a Brownson one." Every morning, as long as Brownson
was in Elizabeth, the baby was taken in to him at his request. He
would walk up and down with her in his arms.[50] Brownson wrote
to Henry on May 25, 1875: "Poor Sarah finds her hands full in
taking care of her. I want her to get a nurse and offer to pay the
expense, but she is afraid a nurse will spoil her temper . . . [but]
is well nigh worn out taking care of her. The nurse must come."
He added in another key: "The Judge and her majesty, the Queen,
are grown quite complaisant since they find that I am doing more
for them than they are for me." But still neither of them ever entered
his room, "except the Judge when I send for him."

After February there are no complaining letters on either side,[51] perhaps because Henry came to investigate the whole situation. However this may be, Brownson wrote to his son on August 30, 1875, to say that he had made up his mind and would move to Detroit. "The prospect of getting away from the Tenneys and finding a home and at least somebody to converse with has already put new life into me and my health seems much better than when you were here." The move simply had to be made; Sarah's health was failing fast, and she died in October of the following year, after bearing a second daughter. The sick and harassed woman could no longer be saddled with the responsibility of looking after a sick crochety old man. It was a relief all round.

I should like to be able to relate how this life ended in a blaze of glory—the setting sun and music at the close. As that cannot be, it would be infinitely better, from the artistic point of view, to round things off with a tragedy instead of having to tell what is a dismal story, even though it is not more dismal than the story of many other people in a similar situation. Through it all, however, there gleamed occasional rays. Complain as they might against one another, affection every now and then glints out. And even while father and daughter quarrelled, they united in exercising their love at long-range upon the children of the Detroit household.[52] Their grandfather was always sending them kindly messages, and Sarah wrote that "if their venerable aunt ever gets into decent spirits again she will come and play South American forests—bears and wolves thrown in—with them." [53] It is the all too common case of a couple of otherwise excellent people who had a "temperament" and who inevitably got on one another's nerves. Contemplating it, we might in charity remember that we, in our turn, may come to something not unlike it.

> Should no disease thy torpid veins invade,
> Nor Melancholy's phantoms haunt thy shade;
> Yet hope not life from grief or danger free,
> Nor think the doom of man reversed for thee.[54]

We have before us a misfortune we should pity and try to understand; it is not for us to condemn anybody concerned.

The father at parting left for his daughter a note headed "Thursday" which read: "I am very sorry, my dear Sarah, that I showed so much reluctance to the arrangement you & Henry thought the best. I am now perfectly satisfied that you were right, and I want you to feel that I am perfectly convinced of it, and am perfectly reconciled to the arrangement. You need & must have a change of scene, and a change of air, and the sooner the better. . . . I am anxious only for you; I shall do well enough, and shall not be unhappy. You need feel no uneasiness on my account. Your loving Father." [55]

Brownson's books and papers and some furniture followed, and at Henry's house he settled down to work in his rooms on the second floor. But he got only one article done, that on "The Philosophy of the Supernatural," which he intended as the first of a series to be contributed to the newly-founded *American Catholic Quarterly Review*.[56] In it he made an attempt to show the nexus between the natural and the supernatural—not, as commonly viewed, as two orders existing in parallels, but as closely inter-related. When Sarah heard that he had been approached by the *Catholic World* for an article, she wrote off with characteristic indignation to her brother on January 30th: "How can you let him so demean himself as even to think of writing for the Catholic World? I would not mail the article for him if he were to write it here. After all F. Hecker's insults—to think the government should have so little self-respect as to receive such a proposition with anything but scorn." [57] But she need not have been alarmed: Brownson was not equal even to answering the article by William George Ward—Tennyson's "Most generous of all Ultramontanes, Ward"—in the *Dublin Review;* [58] and this though it revived the old accusation of ontologism, upon which he had always been ready to fight at the drop of a hat. Even for his second article for the

American Catholic Quarterly Review he got no further than the title. By January he felt a strong disinclination to work, and every day the desire for rest grew stronger, so that only by an effort could he rouse himself even to talk [59]—which for him meant to argue.

It was pleasant basking in that kindly household. Fifine, his daughter-in-law, had always been a special favorite of his. Being accustomed to manage a difficult husband, she understood the Brownson temperament; and he was charmed by his small grand-children. One day five-year-old Sally [60] happened to mention that she would like to have a statue of the Blessed Virgin she had seen in a store, but that her mother had told her it cost too much. At once the old man's hand went into his pocket and he pulled out a few crumpled dollar bills. This child too showed herself a true Brownson by telling him, "Oh, but you can't afford it."

"Why not, young lady?" he wanted to know.

"Because you don't go to an office or do any work or earn any money. If my father can't afford to buy it——"

The huge paw took the tiny hand and pressed the bills into it. "Never mind about that. Go and buy your statue." If she had wanted a doll he might have given it to her; as it was a statue of Mary she wanted, he simply could not refuse it.

The mood of Sarah in Elizabeth mellowed, too. One has always the feeling that, beneath the exasperation that had existed during those last years, affection never ceased to flow strongly under-ground. But the situation had been too hard for them both. Only in separation could they be at peace with one another. For what was to be her father's last Christmas—and her own as well—she wrote to him a letter it is a solace to print here. "My dear Father," it read: "We were all taken by surprise night before last by a box from Detroit. We were equally delighted. Ruthie had one of the quails yesterday, and smacked her lips over the first taste, and cried for more. She evidently knows good things. We expect to celebrate the big turkey in fine style when I have no doubt its principal sauce will be regrets at your absence. Frs. Hennessey and Thebeau [61] were here the other day, and expressed the greatest regret that you should have left. Fr. Hennessey told me to tell you that, in the language of an Irish poet, 'The nights were long until you returned' and that if you did return they would come to see you much oftener. They both sent kind regards and good wishes, as do all whom we see." She went on to say that a visitor who saw Ruth exclaimed, "Why, Sarah, she is the very image of your father," and added on her own account, "She certainly does look Brownsonian, and sometimes so much so that the judge calls her Dr. Brownson." To the resemblance between Brownson and this grand-daughter, as she is today, anyone who knows her can give his testimony. Perhaps there could be no more complete proof of her Brownsonian propensities than her eating quail at the age of ten months.

Soon after Christmas it began to be noticed that the old man was definitely beginning to fail. It was no longer merely a question of ailments, but of a lethargy nobody had ever observed in him before. He read a little but wrote nothing and was less and less inclined for a philosophical or theological wrangle. They hoped his energy would come back, but he gave no sign of that happening.

At lunch on Good Friday he and Henry got into an argument on the question of the unforgiveable sin. [62] It proved to be too much of an effort for the aged philosopher, especially as his son could not be brought to see the force of his logic. Suddenly he felt that he had had enough. Henry was stupid, and his father angrily dragged his huge bulk up the stairs to his room. When Fifine came up with his supper tray and knocked on his door, he called out, "If that's you, Francis, I'm too tired to make it any plainer tonight." [63] All he would take from Fifine was a cup of tea. Now she and Henry were really alarmed. Never before had the old lion been known to refuse his meat.

By midnight he was seriously ill. On Holy Saturday his friend, Father Hennaert, came and heard his confession, and on Easter

Sunday Orestes Brownson received the Last Sacraments. At dawn the next morning April 17th, while the prayers for the departing soul were being said by his bedside, he died. They buried him from St. Anne's Church, which was the first Catholic church he had ever seen—fifty-three years earlier, but that was a different edifice. Ten years later his body was transferred to the crypt of the University church at Notre Dame. There it lies in the middle aisle, and over it hundreds of young men pass every morning as they go to the altar-rail to receive Holy Communion. In no more fitting place could Orestes Brownson rest.

---

[1] *Catholic World*, Vol. XXIII (1876), p. 366.

[2] *Brownson's Quarterly Review*, Last Series, Vol. I (1873), pp. 251, 258.

[3] Letter in the possession of Mrs. Odiorne.

[4] William Seton graduated from Mount St. Mary's College in 1855. (Meline and McSweeny, *The Story of the Mountain*, Vol. II, p. 78). Brownson had presumably first met him there when lecturing in 1853. He was a man of artistic tastes and wrote several historical romances, and apparently he had private means that enabled him to travel a good deal. (*Ibid.*, Vol. I, p. 470).

[5] *Orestes A. Brownson*, pp. 272–274.

[6] *Latter Life*, pp. 611–612.

[7] At first, too, I could not find all the letters, and this seemed to confirm my suspicion that a great deal had been made out of a little. It is, however, only due to Mr. Schlesinger to say that, though for these last letters he gave no dates, he utilized their very phrases and invented nothing. The only fault I can find was his quoting a paragraph from one of Brownson's letters to Sarah as though it was spoken in a quarrel and at this time. Actually it belongs to 1865, not to 1873. There is some reason to believe (as I have indicated in a previous chapter) that the letter was never sent.

[8] This is amply borne out by many family letters, especially those from Brownson to Henry, dated June 9, 1867, and Mrs. Brownson to Henry, dated May 12th of the same year. In 1871 when Sarah and her mother were staying at Loretto, Pa., Mrs. Brownson wrote to her husband saying that Sarah seemed to be better but was still far from well. "If anything disturbs her she looks very pale." (Letters dated September 11th and 18th). All of which would indicate "nerves" as well as fever.

[9] The fact, however, that this letter is among the *Brownson Papers* at Notre Dame and not in the Paulist Archives suggests that, on second thoughts, Sarah did not mail it. Her book was an excellent one. Indeed Hewit pronounced it "the best religious biography which has been written by one of our American Catholic authors." (*Catholic World*, Vol. XVI, 1873, p. 712). Her father, who wrote an introduction to it, called it, "a model biography, a work of sterling merit, which is a valuable contribution to our rising Catholic literature." (*Brownson's Quarterly Review*, Last Series, 1873, p. 130). What is instructive to note is that in her letter to Hewit (as elsewhere) Sarah was up in arms at once when it was a question of defending her

father against outsiders. As for her relations with Hewit, it is sufficient to say that he acted as god-father for her second daughter.

[10] This is in a letter dated July 27, 1939, now among the *Brownson Papers*. Mrs. Odiorne has said and written as much to me.

[11] See her letter to Henry dated December 4, 1872.

[12] July 9, 1874.

[13] *Hecker Papers*.

[14] Sarah to Henry, August 11, 1872. See also her letter of December 30 [1874].

[15] January 30, 1876.

[16] December 4, 1872.

[17] Sarah to Henry, December 30 [1874].

[18] For instance, her letter of November 10, 1874.

[19] Sarah to Henry, October 1 [1874].

[20] Orestes Brownson to Henry, September 25, 1874.

[21] On February 6, 1874, he told Henry that she served as "secretary, chambermaid, nurse and seamstress." To Sarah she was simply a chambermaid.

[22] Sarah to Henry, July 9, 1874.

[23] Sarah to Henry, January 5, 1874.

[24] January 9, 1875.

[25] January 5, 1874. It is rather amusing to note Sarah's anti-Irish animus. She did not forget the many brushes her father had had with members of that race and perhaps was taking out her resentment on Agnes. Quarrel with him as she might, she was still his violent partisan against the world.

[26] Sarah to Henry, July 9, 1874.

[27] To Henry, July 21, 1872.

[28] To Henry, December 30 [1874]. It is possible, however, that these remarks were digs at her brother Orestes, for she dealt with him rather severely in a letter to Henry dated April 27, 1876—one about the division of the little property their father had left. One infers that her stay with Orestes in 1865 had not worked out well. As for the naming of the child, Brownson says in a letter to Henry on August 18, 1874, that he hoped the third Orestes in the family, "will be like his noble uncle after whom he is named." So it is clear that the child's grandfather did not consider himself as being honored by the name.

[29] Sarah to Henry, October 1 [1874].

[30] *Brownson's Quarterly Review,* Last Series, Vol. I (1873), p. 288.

[31] Sarah to Henry, April 13, 1873.

[32] Sarah to Henry, July 9, 1874.

[33] It is still standing.

[34] He also helped Jefferson Davis to write his Memoirs.

[35] Letter to Henry Brownson, November 7, 1872.

[36] November 10, 1874.

[37] Undated.

[38] December 30 [1874].

[39] To Henry, January 9, 1875.

[40] Undated, except for the heading "Friday," but belonging to the early part of 1874.

[41] July 9, 1874.

[42] Undated letter of 1873.

[43] November 10, 1874.

44 October 1 [1874].

45 Sarah to Henry, November 10, 1874.

46 Sarah to Henry, July 9, 1874.

47 Sarah to Henry, October 1 [1874].

48 Sarah to Henry, November 10, 1874.

49 August 18, 1874.

50 W. J. Tenney to Henry, February 11, 1875.

51 Or none that I have been able to find.

52 As instances see Sarah's letter to Henry, dated January 5, 1874, and her father's to Henry, dated February 6, 1874, and January 9, 1875.

53 Sarah to Henry, April 18, 1872.

54 Dr. Johnson, *The Vanity of Human Wishes.*

55 Letter in the possession of Mrs. Odiorne.

56 *Works,* Vol. II, pp. 271–283.

57 It is a woman's judgment upon a situation she had never understood. Brownson never felt that Father Hecker had ever "insulted" him, though in all likelihood his roars of rage during 1867–1872 had often made his wife and daughter feel that he had been badly treated. Again we have an instance of Sarah's partisanship, when it was a question of her father against the world.

58 Vol. LXXVIII (1876), pp. 36–55.

59 *Latter Life,* p. 615.

60 She is now Mother Brownson, a religious of the Sacred Heart.

61 This was the Breton Jesuit, Augustus J. Thébaud (Sarah never could spell his name correctly) whose *Irish Race in the Past and Present* Brownson reviewed at length in his *Quarterly,* thereby making some amends to the Irish. The article is in the collected *Works,* Vol. XIII, pp. 547–566. Father Thébaud's highly entertaining and instructive *Forty Years in the United States* was not published until 1904.

62 Mrs. Odiorne tells me that this was the subject of the debate.

63 He and he alone called his son by his second name of Francis. Doran Whalen tells us that he did so even in his prayers. One wonders how she knows.

Appendix

RECORDS FROM THE FAMILY BIBLE

(This Bible is in the possession of Mrs. Thomas H. Odiorne. Most of the entries it contains were made in Brownson's own script, though sometimes, it would seem, a good while after the events recorded. Thus, William, who was named for Dr. William Ellery Channing, is given also the name of Ignatius he received at Confirmation. Sarah dropped the name of Nicolena which appears here, and signed herself in later life by her Confirmation name of Mary. The spelling of the name of the wife of Brownson's eldest son is given in both the ways it appears.)

PARENTS' REGISTER

Father Orestes Augustus Brownson, born September 16, 1803, at Stockbridge Vt.
Died at Detroit, Mich., April 17, 1876.
Mother Sally Healy, January 17, 1804, Camillus (Elbridge) New York.
Married at Elbridge, June 19, 1827.
Died at Elizabeth, N. J. April 9, 1872.

MARRIAGES

Orestes A., June 21, 1849, at Evansville, Ga. to Madamoiselle Pauline Capett.
Orestes A. March 18, 1856 at Sweet Springs, Va. to Miss Margaret Baker.
John H. August 26, 1856 at Brighton, Mass. to Miss Anna Isabella Rogers.
Henry F. Jan. 8, 1868, at Detroit, Mich. and Miss Josephine Van Dyke.
Sarah M. Nov. 26, 1873 to Wm. J. Tenney at Elizabeth, N. J. by Rt. Rev. M. Corrigan.
(On the next page which was blank)
Sarah M. to Wm. J. Tenney.

431

Births

Mary Elizabeth Ruth Channing, born at Elizabeth, New Jersey, Feb. 7, 1875. Baptized at home Feb. 20, 1875 by Rev. A. V. Schilgen, pastor of St. Micheals [sic]. Sponsors: Right Rev. R. Seton, D.D. Protonothary Apostolic, and Jessaline Rose Tenney.

Mary Brownson Tenney, born at Elizabeth, N. J., May 12th, 1876. Baptized at home May 18th, 1876 by Rev. A. V. Schilgen, pastor of St. Michael's. Sponsors: Rev. A. Hewit, C.S.P. and Jessaline R. B. Tenney.

Births

Orestes Augustus Brownson, jr., born Ithaca, New York, April 18, 1828.

John Healy Brownson, Auburn, N. Y., April 14, 1829.

William Ignatius, Walpole, N. H., Jan. 4, 1834.

Henry Francis, Canton, Mass., August 7, 1835.

Sarah Nicolena, Chelsea, Mass., June 7, 1839.

George, Chelsea, Mass., November 20, 1840.

Edward Patrick, October 16, 1843.

Charles Joseph Maria, Nov. 15, 1845.

Deaths

George, March 26, 1849.

Charles Joseph Maria, Sept. 7, 1851.

Pauline Cassett, Wife of O. A. Brownson, jr., July 18, 1855.

John H. at St. Paul, Minnesota, Dec. 4, 1858, aged 29 years, 7 months, 20 days.

William I. near Virginia City, Nevada Territory, July 11, 1864, aged 30 years, 6 months, 7 days.

Edward P. Killed in battle at Reams' Station, Virginia, August 25, 1864, aged 20 years, 10 m. 9 days. (Rank—Captain and A.A.D.C. U.S.A., Commissary of Musters, 2nd Corps, Army of the Potomac).

Sarah B. Tenney, at Elizabeth, N. J., October 30th, 1876, aged 37 years, 4 mo. & 23 days.

William J. Tenney at Newark, N. J. September 20th, 1883.

Bibliography

THE CHIEF COLLECTION of Brownson documents—one very rich and excellently arranged—is that at the University of Notre Dame. This contains also photostats of important letters to be found elsewhere and a number of letters addressed to Henry Brownson by members of his family. These have been of great service. Though I have usually found it convenient to give my references to the documents as printed by Henry Brownson in his three-volume *Life* of his father (which will also be a convenience for the reader), it must be remembered that Henry Brownson was often able to use only the first-drafts of letters and that the letter as sent was not always quite the same. Sometimes, too, there is a question as to whether it was sent at all. When letters are quoted that Henry Brownson did not print, they are given under the reference of *Brownson Papers*. In addition the *Hecker Papers* at the Paulist Archives in New York City proved invaluable, as did the family letters in the possession of Mrs. Thomas H. Odiorne, one of Brownson's grand-daughters.

These letters, together with the twenty volumes of Brownson's collected *Works* and some items not included there but which may be found in *Brownson's Quarterly Review,* form the basis of this biography. In cases in which Brownson published his books separately, I have used them rather than the same books as included in the *Works,* for the simple reason that their printing makes them easier to read. The only exceptions are *Charles Elwood* and the collection of *Essays and Reviews* published in 1852. Sometimes I have also cited *Brownson's Quarterly Review* even when the article in question appeared in the *Works.*

Acton, Lord. "Lord Acton's American Diaries." The *Fortnightly Review,* Vol. CX, New Series (1921), pp. 727–742, 917–934, and Vol. CXI (1922), pp. 63–83.

Adams, John Quincy. *Memoirs* (ed. by Charles Francis Adams), 12 vols. Philadelphia, 1874–1877.

Alcott, Amos Bronson. *Journals* (ed. by Odell Shepard). Boston, 1938.

Allen, Cuthbert Edward, O.S.B. "The Slavery Question in Catholic Newspapers." *Historical Records and Studies,* Vol. XXVI (1936), pp. 99–169.

Allen, Joseph Henry. *Our Liberal Movement in Theology.* Boston, 1882.

American Catholic Quarterly Review. "In Memoriam Orestes A. Brownson." Vol. I (1876), pp. 560–566.

American Quarterly Church Review. "Orestes A. Brownson as a Philosopher." Vol. XIX (1868), pp. 532–547.

Arvin, Newton. *Hawthorne.* Boston, 1928.

Ballou, Adin. *Autobiography.* Lowell, Mass., 1896.

Bancroft, Frederic. *The Life of William H. Seward,* 2 vols. New York and London, 1900.

Barnes, Thurlow Weed. *Memoir of Thurlow Weed,* 2 vols. Boston, 1883–1884.

Baumgartner, A. W. *Catholic Journalism: a Study of Its Development in the United States, 1789–1930.* New York, 1931.

Beard, Charles A., and Mary. *The American Spirit.* New York, 1943.

Beer, Max. *A History of British Socialism,* Vol. I. London, 1920.

Bell, Margaret. *Margaret Fuller.* New York, 1930.

Billington, Ray Allen. *The Protestant Crusade, 1800–1860.* New York, 1939.

Bowers, Claude G. *The Tragic Era.* Cambridge, Mass., 1929.

Bradford, George P. "Reminiscences of Brook Farm." *Century Magazine,* Vol. XLV (1892), pp. 141–148.

——————. See also under *Ripley, George.*

Brailsford, H. N. *Shelley, Godwin, and Their Circle* (Home University Library Series). London and New York.

Brooks, Van Wyck. *The Flowering of New England.* New York, 1936.

——————. *The Life of Emerson.* New York, 1932.

Brownson, Henry F. *Orestes A. Brownson's Early Life: from 1803 to 1844.* Detroit, 1898.

——————. *Orestes A. Brownson's Middle Life: from 1845 to 1855.* Detroit, 1899.

——————. *Orestes A. Brownson's Latter Life: from 1855 to 1876.* Detroit, 1900.

—————— (ed). *Brownson's Works.* 20 vols. Detroit, 1882–1887.

Brownson, Henry F. (ed.). *Literary, Scientific and Political Views of Orestes A. Brownson.* New York, 1893.

Brownson, Orestes A. *New Views of Chritianity, Society, and the Church,* Boston, 1836.

————. *Charles Elwood, or The Infidel Converted.* Boston, 1840.

————. *Essays and Reviews, chiefly on Theology, Politics, and Socialism.* New York, 1852.

Brownson, Orestes A. *The Spirit-Rapper, an Autobiography.* Cambridge, Mass., 1854.

————. *The Convert: or, Leaves from My Experience.* New York, 1857.

————. *The American Republic: Its Constitution, Tendencies, and Destiny.* New York, 1866.

————. *Conversations on Liberalism and the Church,* New York, 1870.

————. *Brownson's Works* (collected and arranged by Henry F. Brownson), 20 vols. Detroit, 1882–1887.

————. *An Address on the Fifty-Fifth Anniversary of American Independence Delivered at Ovid, Ithaca Co., New York, July 4, 1831.* Ithaca, 1831.

————. *Address on Intemperance.* Keene, N. H., 1833.

————. *An Address Delivered at Dedham on the Fifty-Eighth Independence.* Dedham, 1834.

————. *Babylon Is Falling.* Boston, 1837.

————. *Address on Social Reform.* Boston, 1844.

————. *Boston Quarterly Review.* Boston, 1838–1842.

————. *Brownson's Quarterly Review.* 1844–1855, Boston; 1856–1864, 1873–1875. New York.

Brownson's Review Reviewed: Being a Mild and Vigorous Vindication of the Rights and Privileges of Adopted Citizens against the Assaults and Aspersions of Dr. O. A. Brownson by the Catholic Press of the United States (pamphlet). Boston, 1854.

Burton, Katherine. *Paradise Planters: The Story of Brook Farm.* New York, 1939.

————. *Celestial Homespun: The Life of Isaac Thomas Hecker.* New York, 1943.

Cabot, James Elliott. *A Memoir of Ralph Waldo Emerson,* 2 vols. Boston and New York, 1888.

Canby, Henry Seidel. *Thoreau.* New York, 1939.

Carleton, T. F. "The Working-Men's Party of New York City, 1829–1831." *Political Science Quarterly,* Vol. XXII (1907), pp. 401–415.

Catholic World. "F. Louange's Philosophy." Vol. XIX (1874), pp. 231–245.

Channing, William Ellery. *Thoreau, the Poet Naturalist,* rev. ed. Boston, 1902.

Channing, William Henry. *Memoir of William Ellery Channing,* 8th ed., 3 vols. Boston, 1860.

Christian Examiner. "New Views of Christianity, Society, and the Church." Vol. XXII (1837), pp. 127–130.

————. "A Review of Brownson's Charles Elwood." Vol. XXVIII (1840), pp. 180–198.

————. "Orestes A. Brownson's Argument for the Roman Church." Vol. XLVIII (1850), pp. 227–247. This was signed J[ames] F[reeman] C[larke].

Christian Review. "Charles Elwood." Vol. V (1840), pp. 419–442.

Clarke, James Freeman. See *Christian Examiner.*

Code, Joseph Bernard. *Dictionary of the American Hierarchy.* New York, 1940.

Codman, John Thomas. *Brook Farm: Historic and Personal Memoirs.* Boston, 1894.

Cole, Arthur C. *The Irrepressible Conflict, 1850–1865.* New York, 1934.

Commager, Henry Steele. *Theodore Parker.* Boston, 1936.

Commons, John R., and Associates. *History of Labour in the United States,* Vol. I. New York, 1940.

Cook, Thomas I., and Leavelle, Arnaud B. "Orestes A. Brownson's *The American Republic.*" *Review of Politics,* Vol. IV (1942), pp. 77–90, 173–193.

Cooke, George Willis. *Unitarianism in America.* Boston, 1902.

Corrigan, Sister M. Felicia. *Some Social Principles of Orestes A. Brownson.* Washington, 1939.

Curtis, George William. *Early Letters of George Wm. Curtis to John S. Dwight* (ed. by George Willis Cooke). New York and London, 1898.

D'Arusmont, Frances Wright. *Biography, Notes and Political Letters.* New York, 1844.

Democratic Review. "Mr. Brownson's Recent Articles in the Democratic Review." Vol. XIII (1843), pp. 653–660.

Donovan, Joseph P., C.M. "Why a Brownson Revival?" *Acolyte,*
March 12, 1927, pp. 6–7.

——————. "Brownson, the Philosophical Expounder of the Constitution." *American Catholic Philosophical Association: Proceedings
of the Seventh Annual Meeting (1931),* pp. 148–165.

Dublin Review. "Orestes A. Brownson's Early Life." Vol. CXXIII
(1898), pp. 460–462.

——————. "Orestes A. Brownson's Middle Life." Vol. CXXVII
(1900), pp. 196–198.

——————. "Orestes A. Brownson's Latter Life." Vol. CXXIX (1901),
pp. 189–190.

Elliott, Walter. *The Life of Father Hecker,* 2nd ed. New York, 1894.

——————. "Personal Reminiscences." *Catholic World,* Vol. CI (1915),
pp. 50–55.

Emerson, Ralph Waldo. *Journals,* Vols. IV, V, and VI. Boston and
New York, 1911.

——————. *Letters* (ed. by Ralph L. Lusk), Vols. II, III, and IV. New
York, 1939.

Fish, Carl R. *The Rise of the Common Man, 1830–1850.* New York,
1927.

Foik, Paul J., C.S.C. *Pioneer Catholic Journalism.* New York, 1930.

Frese, Joseph R., S.J. "Brownson on Know Nothingism." *Historical
Records and Studies,* Vol. XXVII (1937), pp. 52–74.

——————. "The Hierarchy and Peace in the War of Secession,"
Thought, Vol. XVIII (1943), pp. 293–305.

Frothingham, Octavius Brooks. *Transcendentalism in New England:
a History.* New York, 1886.

——————. *Theodore Parker.* Boston, 1874.

——————. *George Ripley.* Boston, 1882.

——————. *Memoir of William H. Channing.* New York, 1886.

Gasquet, Abbot, O.S.B. (ed.). *Lord Acton and His Circle.* New York,
1906.

Gildea, William L. "An English View of Brownson's Conversion."
Catholic World, Vol. LXIX (1899), pp. 24–31.

Gillis, James M., C.S.P. *The Paulists.* New York, 1932.

Goddard, Harold Clarke. *Studies in New England Transcendentalism.*
New York, 1908.

[Godwin, Parke]. "Mr. Brownson on Association." *Harbinger,* Vol.
VI (1848), p. 84.

Godwin, William. *An Enquiry Concerning Political Justice and Its Influence on General Virtue and Happiness* (ed. and ab. by Raymond A. Preston), 2 vols. New York, 1926.

Gohdes, Clarence L. F. *The Periodicals of American Transcendentalism.* Durham, N. C., 1931.

Guilday, Peter. "Gaetano Bedini." *Historical Records and Studies,* Vol. XXIV (1933), pp. 87–131.

Hall, Basil. *Travels in North America in the Years 1827 and 1828,* 2 vols. Philadelphia, 1828.

Haraszti, Zoltán. *The Idyll of Brook Farm.* Boston, 1937.

Harson, M. J. "Orestes A. Brownson, LL.D., 'A Man of Courage and a Great American.'" *Catholic World,* Vol. LXXIX (1904), pp. 1–21.

Hassard, John R. G. *The Life of the Most Reverend John Hughes, D.D.* New York, 1866.

Healy, John. "Brownson's Works." *Irish Ecclesiastical Record,* Vol. V (1884), pp. 13–22.

[Hecker, Isaac T.] "The Transcendental Movement in New England." *Catholic World,* Vol. XXIII (1876), pp. 528–537.

——————. "Dr. Brownson and Bishop Fitzpatrick." *Catholic World,* Vol. XLV (1887), pp. 1–7.

——————. "Dr. Brownson and the Workingman's Party Fifty Years Ago." *Catholic World,* Vol. XLV (1887), pp. 200–208.

——————. "Dr. Brownson in Boston." *Catholic World,* Vol. XLVI (1887), pp. 466–472.

——————. "Dr. Brownson's Road to the Church." *Catholic World,* Vol. XLVI (1887), pp. 1–11.

——————. "Dr. Brownson and Catholicity." *Catholic World,* Vol. XLVI (1887), pp. 222–235.

[Hewit, Augustine F.] "Dr. Brownson." *Catholic World,* Vol. XXIII (1876), pp. 366–377.

Higginson, Thomas Wentworth. *Margaret Fuller Ossoli.* Boston, 1892.

Hildreth, Richard. *A Joint Letter to Orestes A. Brownson and the Editor of the North American Review in Which the Editor of the North American Review Is Proved to Be No Christian and Little Better than an Atheist* (pamphlet). Boston, 1844.

Hoagland, Henry E. "Humanitarianism (1840–1860)." *Commons' History of Labour in the United States,* Vol. I, pp. 478–620. New York, 1940.

Holden, Vincent F. *The Early Years of Isaac Thomas Hecker (1819–1844).* Washington, 1939.

Hurd, John C. *The Law of Freedom and Bondage in the United States,* 2 vols. New York, 1858–1862.

Kirby, Georgiana Bruce. *Years of Experience.* New York, 1887.

Ladu, Arthur I. "Political Ideas of Orestes A. Brownson, Transcendentalist." *Philological Quarterly,* Vol. XII (1933), pp. 280–289.

Lathrop, George Parsons. "Orestes A. Brownson." *Atlantic Monthly,* Vol. LXXVII (1896), pp. 770–780.

Levealle, Arnaud B. See *Cook, Thomas I.*

Martineau, Harriet. *Society in America,* 3 vols. London, 1837.

————. *Retrospect of Western Travel,* 2 vols. London, 1838.

Maynard, Theodore. *The Story of American Catholicism.* New York, 1941.

————. "Orestes Brownson, Journalist." *Commonweal,* Vol. XXXVII (1943), pp. 390–393.

McAvoy, Thomas T., C.S.C. "Brownson's Ontologism." *Catholic Historical Review,* Vol. XXVIII (1942), pp. 376–381.

McCarthy, Charles. *The Antimasonic Party.* Washington, 1903.

McLoughlin, J. Fairfax. "A Study of Dr. Brownson." *Catholic World,* Vol. LXXVII (1903), pp. 310–319.

Meline, Mary, and McSweeny, E. F. X. *The Story of the Mountain,* 2 vols. Emmitsburg, Md., 1911.

Mercersburg Review (later absorbed by the *Reformed Church Review*). "Brownson's Quarterly Review." Vol. II (1850), pp. 33–80.

————. "Brownson's Review Again." Vol. II (1850), pp. 307–324.

[McMaster, James A.] "Brownson's Review." *Freeman's Journal,* July 14, 1853, p. 40.

————. "Brownson's Review—Its Value and Appreciation." *Freeman's Journal,* November 10, 1855, p. 5.

————. "Brownson's Review." *Freeman's Journal,* January 5, 1856, p. 4.

————. "The Rambler on Brownson." *Freeman's Journal,* November 15, 1856, p. 4.

Methodist Quarterly. "The Rich Against the Poor. The Laboring Classes. By O. A. Brownson." Vol. XXIII (1841), pp. 92–122.

————. "Brownson's Quarterly Review." Vol. XXVII (1845), pp. 454–478.

Michel, Virgil, O.S.B. *The Critical Principles of Orestes A. Brownson.* Washington, 1918.

————. "Brownson's Political Philosophy and Today." *American Catholic Quarterly Review,* Vol. XLIV (1919), pp. 193–202.

Michel, Virgil, O.S.B. "Orestes A. Brownson." *Catholic World,* Vol. CXXV (1927), pp. 499–505.

—————. "Brownson: a Man of Men." *Catholic World,* Vol. CXXV (1927), pp. 754–762.

Month. "Brownson's Works." Vol. XLVII (1883), pp. 429–431.

—————. "The Works of Orestes A. Brownson." Vol. XLVIII (1883), pp. 439–442.

—————. "Brownson's Works." Vol. LIII (1885), pp. 444–448.

—————. "Brownson's Political and Literary Essays." Vol. LV (1885), pp. 439–443.

Mott, Frank Luther. *History of American Magazines,* 3 vols. New York, 1938.

Nation. "Orestes A. Brownson's Early Life." Vol. LXVII (1898), pp. 205–206.

—————. "Orestes A. Brownson's Middle Life." Vol. LXXI (1900), p. 77.

—————. "Orestes A. Brownson's Latter Life." Vol. LXXIII (1901), pp. 16–17.

Nevin, J. W. See *Mercersburg Review.*

Nevins, Allen. *The Emergence of Modern America, 1865–1878.* New York, 1927.

Newman, John Henry. *An Essay on the Development of Christian Doctrine.* London, 1909.

—————. *My Campaign in Ireland* (printed for private circulation only), 1898.

New Quarterly. "Essays and Reviews, Chiefly on Theology, Politics, and Socialism, by O. A. Brownson, LL.D." Vol. II (1853), pp. 109–110.

Norton, A. B. *The Great Revolution of 1840.* Mt. Vernon, Ohio, 1888.

Orvis, Marianne Dwight. *Letters from Brook Farm, 1844–1847* (ed. by Amy L. Reed), Poughkeepsie, N. Y., 1928.

O'Sullivan, John L. See *Democratic Review.*

Owen, Robert Dale. *Twenty-Seven Years of Autobiography: Threading My Way.* New York, 1874.

Parrington, Vernon Louis. *Main Currents of American Thought,* Vol. II (*The Romantic Revolution in America*). New York, 1938.

Parsons, Wilfred, S.J. "Brownson, Hecker, and Hewit." *Catholic World,* Vol. CLIII (1941), pp. 396–408.

Peabody, Elizabeth Palmer. *Reminiscences of Rev. Wm. Ellery Channing, D.D.* Boston, 1880.

Perkins, Alice J. G., and Wolfson, Theresa. *Frances Wright: Free Enquirer. The Study of a Temperament.* New York and London, 1939.

Piatt, Donn. *Memories of the Men Who Saved the Union.* New York and Chicago, 1887.

Pierce, Edward L. *Memoir and Letters of Charles Sumner,* 4 vols. Boston, 1877–1893.

Post, Albert. *Popular Freethought in America, 1825–1830.* New York, 1943.

Princeton Review. "Brownson's Exposition of Himself." Vol. XXX (1858), pp. 117–150.

—————. "Brownson's Development of Himself" (a letter from Reuben Smith). Vol. XXX (1858), pp. 390–392.

Raemers, Sidney A. *America's Foremost Philosopher.* Washington, 1931.

Rambler. "Brownson's Quarterly Review." Vol. XVIII (1856), pp. 315–317.

[Ripley, George]. "Brownson's Writings." *Dial,* Vol. I (1840), pp. 22–46.

Ripley, George, and Bradford, George P. "Philosophic Thought in Boston." In Vol. IV of Justin Winsor's *Memorial History of Boston.* Boston, 1881.

Rowland, James P. "Brownson and the American Republic Today." *Catholic World,* Vol. CLII (1941), pp. 537–541.

Russell, Amelia A. *Home Life of the Brook Farm Association.* Boston, 1900.

Ryan, Edwin. "Brownson and Newman." *American Ecclesiastical Review,* Vol. LII (1915), pp. 406–413.

—————. "Orestes Augustine [*sic*] Brownson." *Downside Review,* Vol. XLIV (1926), pp. 115–124.

Ryan, Thomas, C.PP.S. "Why Continue to Smear Brownson?" *Acolyte,* Vol. XVII (1941), pp. 11–14.

—————. "Brownson Speaks of England." *Catholic World,* Vol. CLIV (1942), pp. 426–429.

Sanborn, F. B., and Harris, W. T. *A. Bronson Alcott: His Life and Philosophy,* 2 vols. Boston, 1893.

Sargent, Daniel. *Four Independents.* New York, 1935.

Schlesinger, Arthur M., Jr. *Orestes A. Brownson: A Pilgrim's Progress.* Boston, 1939.

Sedgwick, Ora Gannett. "A Girl of Sixteen at Brook Farm." *Atlantic Monthly,* Vol. LXXXV (1900), pp. 394–404.

Seldes, Gilbert. *The Stammering Century*. New York, 1928.

Siegfried, Francis P. "A Recent Work on Faith and Science." *American Ecclesiastical Review*, Vol. VIX (1896), pp. 61–73.

Shea, John Gilmary. *History of the Catholic Church in the United States*, Vols. III and IV. New York, 1892.

Shepard, Odell. *Pedlar's Progress: the Life of Bronson Alcott*. Boston, 1937.

Stern, Madeleine B. *The Life of Margaret Fuller*. New York, 1942.

Sturzo, Luigi. *Church and State*. New York, 1939.

Sumner, Helen L. "Citizenship (1827–1833)." Commons' *History of Labour in the United States*, Vol. I, pp. 169–332. New York, 1940.

Swift, Lindsay. *Brook Farm: Its Members, Scholars, and Visitors*. New York, 1900.

Thomas, Abel C. *Civilization and Roman Catholicism. A Review of O. A. Brownson's Four Lectures* (pamphlet). Philadelphia, 1851.

Thomas, Charles Grandison. *Hereditary Property Justified. Reply to Brownson's Article on the Laboring Classes. By One Whose Personal Experience Should Enable Him to Feel the Wants and Sympathize with the Condition of the Laborer* (pamphlet). Cambridge, Mass., 1841.

Thomas, P. Félix. *Pierre Leroux: sa Vie, son Oeuvre, sa Doctrine*. Paris, 1904.

Thurston, Herbert, S.J. *The Church and Spiritualism*. Milwaukee, 1933.

Trollope, Frances. *Domestic Manners of the Americans*, 2 vols. London, 1832.

United States Catholic Magazine and Monthly Review. "Brownson's Quarterly Review." Vol. IV (1845), pp. 152–164.

United States Democratic Review. See *Democratic Review*.

Wade, Mason. *Margaret Fuller: Whetstone of Genius*. New York, 1940.

Walsh, Augustine, O.S.B. "Orestes Augustus Brownson." *Placidian*, Vol. IV (1927), pp. 37–43.

——————. "Brownson on War." *Placidian*, Vol. IV (1927), pp. 240–246.

——————. "Glossary of Brownson on War." *Placidian*, Vol. IV (1927), pp. 377–381.

This glossary was written merely by way of explaining to English readers the meaning of some of Brownson's terms. Many of these would be immediately intelligible to Americans. Others, however, define some of the philosophical terms used by Brownson. A com-

plete glossary would be useful, as much of the criticism he received
was due to his use of technicalities in a sense of his own.

Ward, Wilfred. *The Life and Times of Cardinal Wiseman*. London,
1887.

————. *William George Ward and the Oxford Movement*. London,
1890.

————. *William George Ward and the Catholic Revival*. London,
1893.

————. *The Life of John Henry Cardinal Newman*, 2 vols.
London, 1912.

[Ward, William George]. "Brownson's Quarterly Review." *Dublin
Review*. Vol. XIX (1845), pp. 390–400.

————. "Mr. Brownson on Developments." *Dublin Review*, Vol.
XXIII (1847), pp. 373–405.

————. "Thelogical Errors of the Day—Brownson's Review."
Dublin Review, Vol. LIV (1864), pp. 58–95.

————. "A Few Words on Dr. Brownson's Philosophy." *Dublin
Review*, Vol. LXXVIII (1876), pp. 36–55.

Waterman, William Randall. *Frances Wright*. New York, 1924.

Weed, Thurlow. *The Facts Stated. Hon. Thurlow Weed on the Morgan
Abduction*. Chicago, 1882.

————. See also *Barnes, Thurlow Weed*.

Weiss, John. *Life and Correspondence of Theodore Parker*, 2 vols.
New York, 1864.

Whalen, Doran (Sister Rose Gertrude Whalen, C.S.C.). *Some Aspects
of the Influence of Orestes A. Brownson on his Contemporaries*.
Notre Dame, Indiana, 1933.

————. *Granite for God's House*. New York, 1941.

Wolfson, Theresa. See *Perkins, Alice J. G.*

Wright, Frances. See *D'Arusmont, Frances Wright*.

Index

A

Abolitionism, 39, 53, 65, 183–4, 320 ff., 331 ff., 337
Acton, Lord, 189, n.28, 358; quoted 206–7, 284
Adams, John Q., 92, 99, n.39, 184, 342
Alcott, Bronson, 40, n.3, 58, 60, n.45, 75, 82, 83, 87, 88, 113 ff., 122, n.48, n.54, 176, 224
Alcott, Louisa M., 87
Alcott, Mrs., 122, n.48
Allen, Ethan, 16
Allen, Joseph Henry, 148; quoted 171
Allen, Samuel C., 56–7
Ambrose, St., quoted, 163
American Catholic Quarterly Review, 424–5
American Celt, 249–50
America's Foremost Philosopher, 273
Ancient Mariner, 216
Anglicanism, 391–2
Antiquity of Man, 295
Anti-Masonic Party, 39–40
Apologia, quoted, 209
Appleton's, 278, n.58, 419
Aristotle, 268, 292, 342, 399
Aspirations of Nature, 264, 367
Atlantic Monthly, quoted 24, n.12
d'Aubigne, Agrippa, 344
Augustine, St., 128, 268, 342, 375, 399; quoted, 293
Austen, Jane, 218
Ave Maria, 133, 358, 361, 364, 384; quoted 360–1, 361–2, 371
Awful Disclosures, 189, n.34

B

Bacon, Francis, 295
Ballou, Adin, 53

Ballou, Hosea, 15, 16
Bancroft, George, 60, n.25, 68, 69, 82, 91, 96, 104, 114, 119, 183, 217, 341–2, 345, 352, nn.93–4
Barnabò, Cardinal, 312, 364
Bayley, Archbishop, 282, 411
Beckx, S. J., Rev. Peter, 413
Bede, Venerable, 12, n.14
Bedini, Archbishop, 227
Beecher, Henry W., 5
Beecher, Lyman, 176
Beer, Max, 41, n.7
Bellamy, Sarah, 287
Bellarmine, St. Robert, 102, 345, 352
Belloc, Hilaire, 275, n.5
Bentham, Jeremy, 41, n.13
Billington, Ray Allen, 237
Blake, William, quoted, 28
"Blodgett, Levi," 90
Bonaparte, Louis Napoleon, 227–8, 303–4
Bonapartism, 303
Boston College, 277, n.31
Boston Reformer, 67
Boston Quarterly Review, 69, 71, 73, 79, 82 ff., 90, 91, 94, 102, 105, 106, 107, 127
Bowditch's *Practical Navigator,* 115
Boyce, Rev. John, 245–6
Bradford, George, 61, 116, 119, 121, n.33, 137, 141
Brailsford, H. N., 41, n.7
Branchereau, Abbé L., 267
Brave New World, 297
Bray, John Francis, 99, n.42
Brisbane, Albert, 112
Brontë, Charlotte, 218
Brook Farm, 59, 108 ff., 121, n.40, 141, 157, 162, 188, n.7, 189, n.14, 331, 387
Brooks, Charles, 104
Brooks, Van Wyck, 193, 210, n.2; quoted, 152

445